Syntactic Categories and Grammatical Relations

Syntactic Categories and Grammatical Relations

The Cognitive Organization of Information

William Croft

The University of Chicago Press

Chicago and London

William Croft is assistant professor of linguistics at the University of Michigan at Ann Arbor.

The University of Chicago Press, Chicago 60637
The University of Chicago Press, Ltd., London

Printed in the United States of America
00 99 98 97 96 95 94 93 92 91   5 4 3 2 1

Library of Congress Cataloging-in-Publication Data

Croft, William.
Syntactic categories and grammatical relations : the cognitive organization of information / William Croft.
p. cm.
Revision of the author's thesis (Ph.D.)—Stanford University, 1986.
Includes bibliographical references and index.
ISBN 0-226-12089-9 (cl. : acid-free paper). — ISBN 0-226-12090-2 (pbk. : acid-free paper)
1. Grammar, Comparative and general—Grammatical categories.
2. Grammar, Comparative and general—Syntax. I. Title.
P240.5.C76 1991
415—dc20   90-38349

∞ The paper used in this publication meets the minimum requirements of the American National Standard for Information Sciences—Permanence of Paper for Printed Library Materials, ANSI Z39.48-1984.

To the memory of my father,
Donald Judson Croft
1924–1984

"We are here like a flower—to bloom and die."
Jacques Cousteau

CONTENTS

④

⑤

ACKNOWLEDGMENTS

This book is based on my doctoral dissertation at Stanford University (Croft 1986); it has been considerably rethought and almost completely rewritten, with a substantial amount of new data added. My first thanks go to my dissertation committee: the chair and one of the great linguists of our time, Joseph H. Greenberg; Tom Wasow; Jerry Hobbs; and Terry Winograd. Elizabeth Traugott was a de facto member of the committee and has continued to provide encouragement and advice. Tom Wasow brought the manuscript to the attention of the University of Chicago Press and continued to support my efforts in revising the manuscript for publication. Not least to be thanked are my fellow students at Stanford, who did much to make it an intellectually exciting place when I was there: Kathie Carpenter, Richard Dasher, Keith Denning, Suzanne Kemmer, Kurt Queller, and Nancy Wiegand. I must also thank SRI International for financially (and computationally) supporting the initial research.

Three anonymous reviewers for the Press provided substantial comments, both general and specific, which proved helpful, if not essential, in improving the manuscript. I also wish to thank Kluwer Academic Publishers for permission to reproduce most of my article (1990a) in *Semantics and the Lexicon,* edited by James Pustejovsky as section 5.5.1 and Trisha Svaib for help in the preparation of the penultimate manuscript.

Tom Toon, director of the Program in Linguistics at the University of Michigan, provided sage advice to my unending queries and requests, not to mention a semester leave in winter 1989 that allowed me to complete the long-delayed revisions to the manuscript. My colleagues at Michigan have continued to provide a stimulating intellectual environment for me as well as personal support: Pam Beddor, Susan Gelman, Steve Lytinen, John Myhill, and (again) Nancy Wiegand. Dwight Bolinger provided some last-minute comments, in his usual conscientious and thoughtful way.

Last but not at all least, I must pay my respects to others, some of whom have passed from this earth forever. The powerful beauty and spirituality of the redwood and sequoia forests of California, the canyonlands of Utah, and other fast-disappearing places have long given me joy and solace, as have the same features in the music of the medieval church, the baroque lutenists, the villages of Bulgaria, and many other lost and soon-to-be-lost cultures. Above all, I owe my deepest thanks to my wife, Carol Toffaleti, whose patience, support, and faith have kept me going; and to my parents, Irene and Donald Croft, who instilled the love of knowledge and beauty in me and had the love, generosity, and commitment to allow me to pursue them.

LIST OF ABBREVIATIONS

1,2,3	1st, 2d, 3d person
A	transitive subject
Aff	affective causal arc
ABL	ablative
ABS	absolutive
ACC	accusative
ACT	actor
ADV	adverb
AOR	aorist
APP	applicative
ASP	aspectual marker
ASSOC	associative
AUX	auxiliary
CAUS	causative
CLASS	classifier
COMP	complementizer
COP	copula
CRS	currently relevant state
DAT	dative
DEF	definite
DEP	dependent verb form
DET	determiner
DS	different subject
ERG	ergative
EXP	expectation
FOC	focus
FUT	future
GEN	genitive
HABIT	habitual
IMPER	imperative
IMPF	imperfective
INC	incorporated noun
INCH	inchoative
INCOMP	incompletive
INDIC	indicative
INDIR	indirect object, applicative
IN	infinitive
INST	instrumental
INTERR	interrogative
LOC	locative
MOD	modification marker
NCL	numeral classifier
NEG	negative
NFEM	nonfeminine
NMNL	nominalization
NOM	nominative
NONVOL	nonvolitional
OBJ	object
OBL	oblique
OBLIG	obligation
P	transitive object
PASS	passive
PAT	patient
PCL	possessive classifier
PERF	perfective
Phys	physical causal arc
PL	plural
POSS	possessor
PREP	preposition
PRES	present
PRT	particle
PSTPRT	past participle
REFL	reflexive
REL	relative clause marker
S	intransitive subject
SBJ	subject
SEQ	sequenced action
SG	singular
STAT	stative
SUFF	suffix
TOP	topic
TRANS	transitive
UND	undergoer
Vol	volitional causal arc

1

Syntactic Methodology and Universal Grammar

1.1 Approaches to Universal Grammar

The foundations of any theory of universal grammar are the structures that it assigns to utterances and the motivation (or EXPLANATION) for those structures. We may illustrate this by providing a thumbnail sketch of the two major approaches to universal grammar found today. In the current Chomskyan theory, universal grammar consists of a set of "theories," such as the binding theory, case theory, X′ theory, and so on, each of which specifies certain elements and constraints on the structure of sentences and each of which is generally manifested in any given sentence of the language in question. The motivation for the theory is ultimately a biological one: the hypothesis that these theories are entities that exist innately in the mind of every human being and are brought to bear on the linguistic input presented to the child (in a fashion I will describe below).

This approach can be contrasted with the "functionalist" approach to universal grammar, which has not been unified under the impact of a single person but is manifested in different versions by linguists such as Talmy Givón, Paul Hopper and Sandra Thompson, and a number of others. For these linguists, universal grammar consists of a variety of functions that language is intended to serve.[1] These functions specify certain elements of sentence structure and constraints on sentence structure. The motivation for the functionalist approach to universal grammar is also ultimately biological, but it focuses on another aspect of biology, namely, the evolutionary concept of adaptation: language is part of man's adaptation to his environment, and the structure of language is determined by the functions that it is intended to perform.

These, then, are the bare outlines of the two best-known current approaches to universal grammar. The term "approach" has come to be used to characterize these views of universal grammar because both views encompass a number of more or less well-defined linguistic theories. The Chomskyan or generative approach, now often called the "formal" approach,[2] embraces such contemporary linguistic theories as Government and Binding Theory (Chomsky 1981), Lexical Functional Grammar (Bresnan 1982a), Relational Grammar (Perlmutter 1983), Generalized Phrase Structure Grammar (Gazdar et al. 1985), and Head-driven Phrase Structure Grammar (Pollard and Sag 1987). The functionalist approaches include Role and Reference Grammar (Foley and Van Valin 1984), Cognitive Grammar (Langacker 1987a), Grammatical Construction Theory (Lakoff 1987:462–585; Fillmore, Kay, and O'Connor 1988), and the discourse-based theories of Hopper and Thompson (1980, 1984) and Givón (1979, 1984b). It should be pointed out that there are many very real conceptual differences between all these linguistic theories. Nevertheless, we may reasonably safely assign the theories to the two approaches to universal grammar in the way that I have suggested here. This is not to say that some theories do not attempt to bridge the gap in one way or another—for example, Lexical Functional Grammar has recently incorporated elements of discourse structure in its syntactic analyses (Bresnan and Kanerva 1988); and Kuno's "functional syntax" (Kuno 1987) is built on a chiefly generative rule base.

The central question for any version of universal grammar is, or ought to be, the status of the basic distinctions recognized by traditional grammar. The reason for this is, of course, that they are the building blocks of the larger syntactic units, and this is the major focus of modern syntactic theory. For example, any characterization of the passive construction must refer to the concepts "verb" and "subject NP"; in turn, a definition of NP must refer to the concepts "noun" and "head." Among the most important of these fundamental concepts are the distinctions defining the major lexical categories, "noun," "verb," and "adjective," and the grammatical relations that hold within the clause, "subject," "object," and "oblique." These are not the only distinctions recognized by traditional grammar, of course, or even the only ones of current interest in contemporary linguistic theory.[3] However, the centrality of the classification of words and the structure of clauses to the understanding of the grammar of human languages means that a proper analysis of these distinctions is almost certainly necessary in order to address other important grammatical problems.

There is also widespread but by no means universal agreement among linguists that the aforementioned basic distinctions are probably universal in one form or another: that is, they are found in all human languages and would be found in any new human language that is discovered or comes to exist. This statement may appear to some linguists to be too strong, and perhaps it should be qualified. Although almost all agree on the universality of "noun" and "verb," many linguists question the universality of the syntactic category "adjective." Also, many linguists question the existence of subjects in at least some languages, preferring a designation "topic" or else restricting the concept of "subject" in various ways. The reason for some of these difficulties will be discussed shortly, but for the time being let us say that we will take as putatively universal the distinction between some nominal argument of the verb that has distinctive grammatical properties, be it called "subject" or "topic," and other nominal arguments (and, a less-discussed issue, that the remaining arguments can again be divided into "objects" and "obliques").

The difficulty in coming up with a universal characterization of "subject" that would satisfy most linguists reveals a fundamental methodological issue involved in determining the universality of these distinctions. Is there a universal method for identifying the fundamental grammatical concepts such as "adjective" or "subject" in any given language—or determining whether the language has "adjectives" or "subjects" at all? Any linguistic theory that claims to have universal validity must have an answer to this question in order to do syntax at all (e.g., to study universal properties of passive constructions or any other syntactic structure).[4] In fact, the answer to this question is the central topic of this book.

Surprisingly, the answer to this question is often taken for granted by most linguists:

> Every linguist relies on these concepts ["noun," "verb," "subject," etc.], but few if any are prepared to define them in an adequate, explicit, and revealing way. . . . The linguistic community has not yet achieved generable, workable, deeply revelatory characterizations of these constructs in terms of more fundamental notions in the context of a coherent overall conceptual framework. [Langacker 1987a: 2]

There are several reasons for this state of affairs, three of which stand out. The first is that there is no simple answer to this question. The grammatical distinctions on which concepts such as "noun" or "subject" are built are not directly visible in the way that, for example, word order is. One cannot always look at a sentence and directly "read off" what is a noun or a verb and what is the subject or the object in the same way that one can directly read off the word order. This is true in general for all the central structural concepts in grammar: syntactic categories of all types, constituent structures, and dependencies that hold between words or constituents in a sentence. All we can observe (at the grammatical level) is a string of words, or at most a string of morphemes.[5] In this sense, all these basic structural concepts are abstract or covert. In fact, the covert character of even the basic grammatical distinctions is what makes linguistics a complex and interesting endeavor, meriting its establishment as an independent scientific discipline. But the first complex issue that must be raised in this regard is the method by which the categories "noun" and "verb" and the relations "subject" and "object" are determined. That method goes under the name of SYNTACTIC ARGUMENTATION.

The second reason is that languages vary enough, at least superficially, to make problematic the establishment of universal criteria for the fundamental concepts of grammatical theory. This too makes linguistics an interesting endeavor, but it also provides the explanation for the indeterminacy at its roots, as I will argue below.

The third reason for lack of general agreement on the fundamentals of grammar is that, despite the lack of explicit discussion of the question, there are two general answers currently on offer, corresponding to the two approaches to universal grammar described above. In fact, the different answers constitute one of the primary differences, if not *the* primary difference, between the two approaches. The aim of this chapter is to describe how the methods of syntactic argumentation of the formalist and the functionalist approaches are fundamentally different because of two different strategies of extracting universal concepts from covert and variable evidence.

The contrast in methods of argumentation can be observed directly simply by inspecting papers written in the two approaches. The significant differences that I will focus on are the following. A typical formalist analysis of a linguistic phenomenon in a particular language will depend on the recognition of certain grammatical distinctions, for example, recognizing that a particular NP "really is" or "really is not" a direct object. The justification for the status of the element in question will be examining the grammatical behavior of the linguistic element in question under various systematic structural alterations (usually called "tests," e.g., tests for direct object–hood). The universality of the grammatical distinction in question is demonstrated by discovering its relevance to the analysis of linguistic phenomena in other languages. On the other hand, a typical functionalist analysis of a linguistic phenomenon in a particular language will examine the semantic and pragmatic function of the linguistic construction in question and explain the presence of the phenomenon in terms of the linguistic feature in question being appropriate in light of the function of the construction in which it occurs. An argument for the universality of the analysis is based on comparing equivalent phenomena in other languages and looking for a pattern in the variation found, a pattern that usually takes the form of a hierarchy or prototype structure.

These two methods of analysis and argumentation appear to have very little in common, and, not surprisingly, they yield different results. The more important point, however, is that the different methods reflect a difference between the two approaches' conceptualizations of universal grammar. This is an important point to make because it reflects a general characteristic of scientific approaches in which there are significant differences in method and argumentation. Differences in method, not just differences in empirical coverage or even differences in assumptions about what merits a suitable explanation, distinguish scientific paradigms such as the formalist and the functionalist approaches to universal grammar.[6] And differences in method are so fundamental to scientific endeavor that it is easy for misunderstanding (and, hence, polemic) to arise between paradigms. For example, the functionalist critique of formalist approaches to grammar is generally cast in terms of insufficient observation of the facts and insufficiency in explanation. It is argued that formalist approaches to language do not examine enough data from enough languages and that it is easy to provide counterexamples to formalist theories of language. It is also argued that formalist approaches do not provide legitimate explanations of linguistic phenomena, that instead they merely provide abstract descriptions of language structure without external explanations. On the other side, the formalists accuse the functionalists of being merely descriptive as well, providing superficial descriptions of linguistic structures. They also accuse functionalists of being concerned exclusively with "peripheral" aspects of grammar, such as subtle lexical, semantic, pragmatic, and discourse-functional effects rather than facts about language structure that the formalists consider more important.

Each approach claims that the other is ignoring data that it thinks important and providing only descriptions, not explanations of the data—both clues that methodological issues, and hence paradigm differences, are involved in the debate. The reasons for this can be found in the role that method, or argumentation, plays in a theory. A method is a way to make sense of the facts; that is, it is a way to relate data to explanatory concepts. One can even think of argumentation as a function that maps data into explanatory concepts. Using this analogy, we can see that both the domain and the range of two different functions may be different. That is, it is not surprising that two different methods will consider somewhat different kinds of data to be worth explaining—more precisely, two different methods generally look at different aspects of the same data. Nor is it surprising that two different methods will also result in different kinds of concepts used in explanation. Therefore, proponents of one method will see proponents of another method as examining the "wrong" kind of data or as coming up with "nonexplanations," or as doing both.

This is not to advocate complete scientific relativism. I am not arguing that what formalists and functionalists are doing in linguistic analysis is completely different and thus equally acceptable (or unacceptable). In fact, there are some basic commonalities to the two approaches, in particular, the common search for universal grammar or, more generally, universally valid constraints on what is a possible human language. One can examine the methods of argumentation more closely in order to uncover just what the differences are in their view of universal grammar and then ask the question, Which method gets us further? Which method produces the most interesting results? The rest of this book will present a number of interesting results regarding the basic distinctions of word classes and clause structure, using a variant of the functionalist method. In order to put these results in some theoretical perspective, however, this chapter will briefly outline the relevant differences in syntactic argumentation and the significance of those differences.

1.2 Syntactic Tests and Domains of Application

The main methodological issue that any approach to universal grammar faces is, How does a linguist determine what the language-specific manifestation of a universal grammatical distinction such as noun/verb or subject/object is? It would be safe to say that all linguists would require the linguistic unit in question to display some grammatical behavior that would indicate that it was indeed a noun or a verb, a subject or an object, etc. I will call this behavior a morphosyntactic "test."

This term was first used widely in transformational grammar. In transformational grammar, a syntactic "test" was generally a transformational rule that required a certain sort of input to yield a certain output. For example, the transformational rule of passive required a direct object in the input structure to yield a well-formed output structure. Thus, it could be used as a "test" for the direct object–hood of the underlying NP (which in turn was manifested in the corresponding active sentence). Although the transformational analysis of passive has changed, and has even been abandoned by some, the concept of a test for determining a category like "noun," a constituent like "verb phrase," or a grammatical relation like "direct object" remains. We may more neutrally describe a morphosyntactic test as a grammatical construction, one or more features of which define or require a specific type of linguistic unit to satisfy it or fill it. The unit can be a lexical class, a higher-level constituent, a dependency relation—in sum, any element of linguistic structure. The class of linguistic units of the appropriate type will be called the DOMAIN OF APPLICATION—another term that dates back to transformational grammar since the presence of the linguistic unit in question controls whether the transformational rule can apply.

A few examples will illustrate the concept. Let us consider a potential test for subjecthood in Spanish, the agreement of the verb with the candidate NP. In this case, the test construction is any finite clause containing one or more NPs in Spanish, and the relevant features of the construction are the relation between the person and number inflection of the verb and the person or number of one of the NPs. If the verb inflection covaries with the filler of the relevant NP slot, then we may say that the NP is the subject of the clause and that any other NPs present are not the subject of the clause:

(1)	*El*	*soldado*	*quebr*	*-ó*	*la*	*-s*	*ventana*	*-s*
	the.SG	soldier	break	-3SG.PAST	the	-PL	window	-PL

'The soldier broke the windows.'

(2)	*Los*	*soldados*	*quebr*	*-aron*	*la*	*-s*	*ventana*	*-s*
	the.PL	soldier	break	-3PL.PAST	the	-PL	window	-PL

'The soldiers broke the windows.'

By examining the linguistic element inflected for person, number, and tense, the same construction in Spanish can also be used as a test for whether a lexical root is a verb. Using this test, if a lexical root can fit in that position in the construction and take the person-number-tense inflections, then it is a verb; if it cannot, then it is not a verb:

(3)	**Los*	*soldados*	*libr*	*-aron*	*la*	*-s*	*ventana*	*-s*
	the.PL	soldier	book	-3PL.PAST	the	-PL	window	-PL

Another example is the English syntactic construction that contains an active voice verb immediately followed by an NP that is not governed by a preposition. This could be a test for direct objects in English (in the view of some, not a very good test). If an NP can fit in that position, then it is a direct object; if it cannot, then it is not. Another test for direct object status is the passive construction. This is a more complex test since what is really being tested is a property of the counterpart active voice construction (however that counterpart relation is defined in the theory), not the passive construction. The ability of an NP to be the subject of a passive construction is taken to be a test for that NP being the direct object of the counterpart active construction:

(4) *Tim ate my custard.*

(5) *My custard was eaten by Tim.*

(6) *Tim weighs 250 pounds.*

(7) **250 pounds is weighed by Tim.*

Such indirect tests presuppose some sort of a structural derivational relation between the passive verb construction and the active verb construction, though not necessarily a transformational one. We will take this for granted now and return to it in the next section.

The essential concept behind a test is that some grammatical characteristic of some structurally defined class of sentences (what we have called "constructions") is sensitive to the grammatical distinction at hand—subject/nonsubject etc. The grammatical distinction defines the domain of application of the test. The important question is, Which tests are appropriate for determining the putatively universal grammatical distinctions? That is, Which tests have domains of application that are supposed to be defined by the universal distinctions?

The simplest hypothesis of universality would be that the grammars of all languages made reference to the same grammatical distinctions and did so in the same way and for the same purposes. I will call this the UNIVERSALIST IDEAL. This hypothesis can be divided into two parts. First, within a single language the various tests for a distinction like subject/object will consistently produce the same domain of application (the same category). Second, across languages the equivalent syntactic tests will yield the equivalent domains of application. In other words, we would have complete uniformity of grammatical behavior within a language and across languages. If this were the case, then the establishment of the universal categories would not be a problem, and linguists of any persuasion could move immediately to the problem of motivating the existence and distribution of these distinctions.

However, this simple hypothesis simply fails in both its parts in the face of even the most elementary linguistic facts. First, different syntactic tests that putatively refer to the same grammatical distinction yield different results in some cases. For example, consider the two definitions of direct objects in English offered above. The first test we will call the positional test: the prepositionless NP occupying the immediate postverbal position in a sentence. The second test we will call the passive test: the subject NP in the passive sentence that is taken to be the counterpart to the active sentence whose object we are trying to determine.[7] In the simple universalist hypothesis, these two tests should always yield the same results; that is, the same NPs should be judged to be direct objects. However, that is not the case, as can be seen from examples (4)–(7) given above: *my custard* is a direct object by both tests, but *250 pounds* fails the passive test. Thus, the two tests do not always yield the same results—in fact, careful examination demonstrates that the behavior of almost any two tests will be different (see Gross 1979).

Nor is it true that the equivalent test yields equivalent results across languages. One possible test for subjecthood is the ability of the verb to agree with the NP in question. In Spanish, this yields more or less straightforward results, though certainly not quite the same results as English (cf. *John likes these shirts* and its translation, *Le gustan a Juan estas camisas*, where the verb agrees with *las camisas* 'the shirts,' not *Juan*). However, comparing English to Quiché and Lakhota, the results are very different:

Quiché:

(8) *š- at- w- iloh*
PAST- 2SG.B- 1SG.A- see
'I saw you.'

(9) *š- im- petik*
PAST- 1SG.B- come
'I came.'

Lakhota:

(10) *ó- ma- ya- kiye*
LOC- 1.UND- 2.ACT- help
'You help/helped me.'

(11) *wa- ʔu*
1.ACT- come
'I am coming.'

(12) *ma- khuže*
1.UND- sick
'I am sick.'

As can be seen from the examples, Quiché and Lakhota verbs agree with not one but two NPs (in Quiché, the two agreement prefixes are glossed "A" and "B," following standard Mayanist practice; in Lakhota, they are glossed "Act" and "Und," for "actor" and "undergoer"). This raises the question of which of the two agreement affixes should be equated to the single set of Spanish subject agreement suffixes. It turns out that no choice will yield comparable categories. In Spanish, the agreement test produces a subject category including all transitive subjects and all intransitive subjects. In Quiché, identification of the set A agreement prefix with "subject" produces a category including only transitive subjects (the "ergative"), but using the set B prefix produces a category including intransitive subjects and transitive objects (the "absolutive"). In Lakhota, identification of the actor prefixes with "subject" produces a category including transitive subjects but only some intransitive subjects (the "actor" or "active"). Thus, this test produces highly variable results cross-linguistically.

In the face of this data, which can be easily generated and multiplied for any major grammatical distinction, the method of determining the presence and applicability of putatively universal distinctions such as noun/verb and subject/object must be refined in one way or another. This is the point at which formalist and functionalist method, and therefore styles of argumentation, diverge. I will begin by describing the formalist method, which actually dates back considerably further than generative grammar. Then I will present a series of objections to the method and show how these are really objections to the formalist's view of universal grammar, which reflects a compromise between the universalist ideal and its empirical shortcomings. I will present the functionalist alternative, which rejects the formalist's compromise view of universal grammar in favor of a different compromise between the universalist ideal and the facts. Finally, I will discuss how one can evaluate the alternative approaches.

The first problem with the universalist ideal is a within-language problem: different tests for the same putative universal distinction yield different results. The solution to this problem that the formalist method provides is the concept of a CRITERIAL test or tests: only certain aspects of grammatical behavior should be taken as indicative of a universal category. The other aspects of grammatical behavior simply are not good tests; that is, they are not indicative of the universal category. An example of this is the discrepancy between the positional test and the passive test for direct objecthood in English seen in examples (4)–(7): the positional test is simply not a good test for direct objecthood because prepositionless NPs that one would not want to call direct objects, such as the measure expression *160 lb.*, can occur postnominally. The passive test is a "better" test (though still not a perfect one, as will be seen below).

The concept of a criterial syntactic test also allows a way around the problem of cross-linguistic variation of equivalent tests. In each language, one must search for a suitable criterial test for the universal distinction in question. However, one need not use the same test across languages—indeed, sometimes one cannot, if the equivalent to the criterial test does not exist (e.g., the language does not have a passive). For example, in determining the category "verb" in various languages, the ability to take certain inflections is commonly used for criterial tests. But the tests must necessarily be different in Japanese, in which verbs inflect for tense but not person, Lakhota, in which verbs inflect for person but not tense, and Yoruba, in which verbs do not inflect for either person or tense.

One of the best-known examples of this method of argumentation applied to problems of universal grammar is the analysis of ergativity and subjecthood in Anderson (1976), a paper notable for its attention to data from a large number of languages and its continuing importance. Anderson addressed the question of the status of subject in languages such as Quiché and Lakhota in which (as we have seen) the traditional tests for subjecthood yield a great deal of cross-linguistic variation; that variation in turn questioned the universality of subjects. Anderson produced evidence for a category that was basically equivalent to the category of subject found by traditional means in European languages.

The traditional tests for subjecthood included case marking of and agreement of the verb with the transitive subject, transitive object, and intransitive subject (following Comrie [1978], I will employ the abbreviations "A," "S," and "P" for transitive subject, intransitive subject, and transitive object, respectively). In an "ergative" system, case marking and/or agreement conflates S and P ("absolutive") as opposed to the transitive subject A ("ergative"), as in the Quiché examples (8)–(9) given above. In the European "accusative" system, case marking and/or agreement conflates A and S ("nominative") as opposed to the transitive object P ("accusative"). The latter system corresponds to the intuitive notion of a universal subject/nonsubject distinction. A third system, the "active" system, combines some Ss with A ("actor") and some Ss with P ("undergoer"), as in the Lakhota examples (10)–(12).

Anderson argues that almost all the "ergative" languages contain constructions that manifest the standard subject/nonsubject distinction. This is generally true of the following constructions: the control patterns still known as "equi" and "raising"; "conjunction formation," that is, the absence of a shared argument from one of two conjuncts; and reflexivization. These constructions are illustrated below:

(13) *John told Fred to leave.* ('Fred' = S of complement)

(14) *John told Fred to sell the house.* ('Fred' = A of complement)

(15) *Rhonda seems to be sleeping.* ('Rhonda' = S of complement)

(16) *Rhonda seems to have eaten all the brownies.* ('Rhonda' = A of complement)

(17) *Tina went to the bedroom and fell asleep.* ('Tina' = S of second conjunct)

(18) *Tina went to the bedroom and turned off the light.* ('Tina' = A of second conjunct)

(19) *Max shaved himself.* (Reflexive pronoun = P, not A, or S either)

In the English examples given above, S patterns with A and not P with respect to those rules. That is, these rules follow an "accusative" pattern; hence, the subject/nonsubject distinction is manifested in English. More strikingly, in almost all the languages that Anderson examined, including the "ergative" and "active" ones, the same facts hold. Thus, Anderson was able to argue that the subject/nonsubject distinction was basically the same for almost all the languages that have been called "ergative" or "active." As a consequence, Anderson argues that case marking and agreement are "superficial" (he also describes them as "morphological") or peripheral characteristics of the grammar, at least with respect to the subject category in those languages.

However, even allowing this sort of flexibility in determining basic grammatical distinctions will not yield perfectly unequivocal results across languages. For example, Anderson observed that, in the Australian language Dyirbal (Dixon 1972), it appears that no syntactic test of the usual sort for the subject/nonsubject distinction yielded results comparable to those for the other languages that he examined; instead, the intransitive subject is paired off with the transitive object (the "absolutive" pattern). In these cases, one may "let the grammar decide": that is, accept the category specified by the relevant test. In his paper, Anderson concludes that Dyirbal has a subject but that it is simply very different from the subject category in other languages. The crucial element here is that Anderson did decide that Dyirbal has a subject—he is not denying the universality of the subject/nonsubject distinction. Less drastic examples are more common. For example, given certain criteria for determining nouns, verbs, and adjectives in a language, one usually accommodates the fact that not every translation equivalent of, say, an English adjective will be an adjective in other languages. Although these phenomena are problematic for the formalist methodology, they are generally considered to be relatively peripheral and less important to the theory than the overall universal patterns that the method reveals.

Thus, the formalist method allows a linguist to discover the universal categories that appear to be denied to the follower of the universalist ideal. The concept that some aspects of grammatical behavior, that is, some tests, are more important or crucial than others has permitted the firming up of distinctions such as the subject/nonsubject distinction (and also the object/oblique distinction) that appear to be problematic within individual languages. Adding flexibility to the choice of criterial grammatical behavior across languages has permitted the reestablishment of the universality of the basic grammatical distinctions even in languages that are quite different in structure from the standard European ones. Nevertheless, such successes have been acquired for a theoretical price, and one may legitimately ask whether the price was worth it, that is, whether something essential has been lost from universal grammar.

The first set of questions that can be asked pertain to the problem of the variability of languages with respect to certain grammatical tests, the "peripheral" ones. Why should equivalent syntactic tests vary so much across languages? Why should we not take that variation seriously? In fact, comparing the "peripheral" tests to the critical ones, we could also ask, Why do the criterial tests vary less?

A more serious question is raised when the possibility of "letting the grammar decide" is allowed. When do we let the grammar decide, and when can we turn to another syntactic test? In fact, there was some disagreement about the analysis of ergative languages before Anderson's paper: some linguists had suggested that the absolutive NP is indeed the "subject" NP in those languages. Returning to Dyirbal, one could still ask, How can one decide if Dyirbal has a "subject," albeit a very different subject from the one that is found in almost all other languages, or if the Dyirbal category is so different that one cannot call it a "subject" anymore? At what point do we say that the category "subject" does not exist, as opposed to saying that it exists but that it is very different from the English category? Anderson chose the latter course presumably because maintaining the universality of subject was a central tenet to his theory and because he considered smaller cross-linguistic variations acceptable. But one could still say, Why ignore case marking and agreement patterns if they yield the same category of "subject" that must be allowed for Dyirbal?[8]

A similar question may be asked regarding the choice of a test as criterial within a single language. Why should different tests in the same language yield different results? What differences should we ignore and what differences should we elevate to independent levels of the grammar?

Another serious question has to do with the flexibility allowed in choosing different criterial tests in different languages for the same universal distinction. Why should we believe that a grammatical distinction "proved" by one syntactic test in one language is the same distinction that is "proved" by a different syntactic test in another language? It could just be a spurious coincidence between two unrelated phenomena that happen to converge on the same distinction.

There are counterarguments in the formalist tradition that respond to all these questions. Let us begin with the last question. If the distinction in question is universal, then it should not be surprising that two different syntactic tests, even in two different languages, should converge on the same distinction. The criterion of economy should prevent us from proposing two separate distinctions in universal grammar that are fundamentally the same. All the remaining questions regard variability in languages: either the same test in different languages produces different distinctions, or different tests in the same language produce different distinctions. First, part of the reason that some tests are "peripheral" in the eyes of universal grammar is that they *are* so highly variable: they are poor indicators of the universal grammatical distinctions that we are seeking. In the cases of significant differences among languages with respect to the criterial tests, such as conjunction reduction in Dyirbal, it does happen that a language does not always choose the same distinction in universal grammar for a given test as other languages do. (In fact, that is what is probably occurring in the noncriterial tests as well: languages are freer to use a greater variety of distinctions for such things as case marking, agreement, and some syntactic positions.) There is some flexibility in the choice of distinctions and constructs from universal grammar that apply to particular constructions; this is part of what the child has to learn. However, there are many structures and principles of universal grammar that the child should not have to learn: those are innate.

This view of universal grammar has been recently called the "parameterization" approach (Chomsky 1981). Universal grammar consists of much invariant structure but also a number of grammatical parameters. The parameters and the possible values are determined by universal grammar, but in certain cases the choice of value for a given linguistic structure can vary across languages. Included in universal grammar are the basic universal distinctions first glimpsed by traditional grammar—noun/verb, subject/object, etc.—in their modern manifestations (e.g., category feature assignments in X′ theory or phrase structure configurations for grammatical relations in Government and Binding Theory). This view is part of a general practice of accepting a good deal of language variation as essentially not all that surprising. Languages have different domains of application for different constructions, even for equivalent constructions across languages. What is of greater importance is the discovery of invariant elements of grammar across languages.

This is the compromise position that the formalist methodology makes with the universalist ideal. If the universalist ideal were true, then all the relevant tests would yield the same domain of application, that is, the same fundamental grammatical distinctions. However, the facts do not permit this. The compromise methodology cuts the link between tests (i.e., features of grammatical constructions) and their domain of application (i.e., the class of linguistic units that those features permit). Universal grammar specifies the possible domains of application, that is, the possible values on the parameters, but (up to a point) it does not specify which values on which parameters will determine the domain of application for which grammatical structures. This is true even of a concept as important as "subject," if Anderson's position on the subject in Dyirbal is accepted.

All the questions about the formalist methodology raised above essentially express doubt about the utility of cutting the link between a grammatical construction and its domain of application. The questions about the variation in results for the equivalent test across different languages suggest that one ought to see if a cross-linguistic pattern can be found for the domain of application of the test feature so that a universal characterization of the domain of application of that feature can be given. The question about the differences in results between a criterial test, such as the passive test for English direct objects, and a "peripheral" or "superficial" test, such as the positional test, suggests that the difference may be attributable to a genuinely different domain of application for the two test constructions. The question about whether the results of one test in one language can be equated with the result of a different test in a different language suggests that the domains of application of the two tests are determined by the test constructions themselves and therefore that any resemblance is at best indirect and at worst spurious. In sum, the questions addressed to the formalist methodology imply that there *is* some connection between a test construction and its domain of application, even across languages. And the functionalist methodology, and its style of argumentation, is based on the examination of the relation between a test, that is, the relevant feature(s) of a construction, and its domain of application.

Thus, the functionalist methodology rejects the compromise that the formalist methodology makes between the universalist ideal and the facts, namely, to cut the link between grammatical distinctions and the constructions used to test them. However, the discrepancy between the universalist ideal and the facts remains, and so there must be some other sort of compromise that the functionalist position makes. The compromise is the acceptance of patterns of typological variation for domains of application. It simply is true that different languages have different domains of application for equivalent constructions and features of constructions. Thus, one cannot say that the fundamental grammatical distinctions between noun and verb, subject and object, etc. are clear cut and the same across languages. The functionalist must then give up clear-cut distinctions between categories for prototypical organizations of categories (in the broad sense of "prototypical" represented in Lakoff [1987]). That is, the functionalist gives up, or at least relaxes, the requirement for universal absolute distinctions. Universality is found in *patterns of variation,* at the typological level (across languages) or at the level of a single language (across constructions), instead of in the domains of application for particular constructions in particular languages. In this way, the functionalist can preserve the universality of categories and the distinctions between categories like noun/verb while at the same time admitting the cross- and intralinguistic variation in the domains of application of the test construction(s) used to establish those categories.[9]

Of course, the formalist and the functionalist have reasons for choosing the compromises that each does; the different priorities that each has define the essential difference between the two approaches. The functionalist is primarily concerned with explaining language form in terms of language FUNCTION—that is, explaining the relation between a construction and its domain of application. That is, the semantics and pragmatics of the use of the construction define its domain of application, for example, what NPs can occur without a preposition immediately after an active verb in the active construction, what NPs a verb is going to agree with in a clause, and what NPs can be the subjects of a passive construction. This, for the functionalist, is the solution to the problem of the discrepancy between different "tests" in a single language. Instead of arguing that the different constructions are (or can be) sensitive to different parameterized values or that the differences are so minor that they are peripheral to the basic distinction, the differences are analyzed as a consequence of the distinct functions of the test constructions. Being the direct object of an active transitive construction is not the same as being the subject of a passive construction, despite the resemblance in broad syntactic distribution and semantic relation. It also should account for the similarities in the domains of applications of various constructions both within a single language and across languages: different constructions may be sensitive to the same or similar functional features, such as topicality, affectedness, volitionality, etc.

The formalist, on the other hand, is not centrally concerned with the form-function relation in language. Instead, the formalist is primarily concerned with defining structural relations in a language system so that "everything hangs together"—*tout se tient,* in Meillet's phrase. Thus, criterial definitions are central to, and probably even necessary for, a formal analysis. However, both the formalist and the functionalist are concerned with universal grammar and constraints on universal grammar. Hence, both must confront the cross-linguistic facts described above and make methodological choices ("compromises," as I have called them). The functionalist chooses to preserve the form-function relation, that is, the relation between a construction and its domain of application, and therefore must relax the category definitions to include implicational scales (hierarchies) and prototypes. The formalist chooses to preserve criterial definitions of universal grammatical categories and so loosens the link between a construction and its domain of application.

1.3 Comparing the Two Methodologies

It is more difficult to evaluate different methodologies than to evaluate two theories using the same methodology. Two theories that use the same methodology essentially view the same facts in the same way and have the same sorts of explanatory goals in mind. Thus, it is relatively easy to compare the coverage of the facts of the two theories and to assess success with respect to the explanatory goals. Comparing two theories using different methodologies is far more difficult. The facts are viewed quite differently, and the explanatory goals are different. The example of the formalist and functionalist methodologies in linguistics is typical. In the functionalist methodology, the relevant facts include typological variation for a particular construction and the semantic and pragmatic function of that construction in each language. In the formalist methodology, the facts consist of a variety of constructions, within a single language or across languages, that display the same or almost the same domains of application. The goal of the functionalist method is to establish a universal category that involves a prototype or some other complex category structure, with central functions found in most or all languages and related peripheral functions found in a subset of languages, and to account for the category and its structure in terms of the function of the construction. The goal of the formalist method is to establish universal categories with clear-cut boundaries, chiefly on a structural basis, namely, the discovery of one or more crucial or "core" grammatical phenomena that refer to that category in their domain of application.

Thus, it is difficult to compare the results of the two methods one by one and say that one covers the data better or explains the data better. This is a general problem in the comparison of different methods, that is to say, the comparison of two different paradigms. However, it does not mean that comparison is impossible. Essentially, the comparison of two different methods is "global": which one comes up with the more interesting results or looks to lead to a more fruitful research effort. This is a subjective judgment, but it is on the basis of such judgments that scientists choose paradigms to work in, and in such a fashion one paradigm might come to replace another.

In the comparison of approaches to universal grammar, however, we can combine this more general and subjective evaluation of the two methods with a more specific comparison. Both methods share certain fundamental assumptions. Both aim to uncover universal grammar, and both assume that the categories and distinctions of universal grammar can be discovered by examining the domains of application of certain types of grammatical behavior. The difference between the two, as I outlined above, is the reluctance of the formalist method to give up the concept of a universal absolute or clear-cut distinction and the reluctance of the functionalist method to give up a direct connection between a grammatical construction and its domain of application. Thus, we can try to determine what the preservation of universal clear-cut distinctions and/or the preservation of the relation between a construction and its domain of application buys us—or loses us.

In this book, I will be arguing essentially that there are important linguistic generalizations to be found in the relation between a construction and its (cross-linguistic) domain of application. In other words, the functionalist method buys us quite a bit because it allows us to capture those generalizations. More specifically, taking a functional-typological perspective allows us to solve the problem of a universal definition of nouns and verbs, with consequences that reach throughout grammar, and reveals a new and interesting way of looking at predicate-argument relations, leading us a step closer to the concept of "subject." The functionalist method leads to important results that open up large new areas for linguistic research.

The strongest argument for the functionalist method is that it gives us useful results, results such as those outlined in the rest of this volume. However, we may also examine the formalist methodology in order to see if, along with its undoubted successes, it has also begun to generate anomalies that suggest that the methodology is creating serious conceptual problems. I hasten to add that it is worth pointing out these conceptual problems only because the functionalist methodology can remedy them. In this section, I will discuss some of these conceptual problems, touch on some of the highlights of the analyses found in later chapters, and show how they bear on the problem of evaluating the competing methodologies.

I have argued that the primary difference between the formalist and functionalist methodologies is that the former focuses on finding universal clear-cut grammatical structures and distinctions while the latter focuses on the relation between a construction (i.e., some grammatical structure) and its domain of application. It is reasonable to examine what the search for clear-cut structures and distinctions has led to, and we will see that it has led to a number of interrelated problems.

The first major problem is the proliferation of "boundary cases." As various universal distinctions are proposed and their consequences are explored, almost inevitably a large class of exceptional or equivocal examples arise. It is in fact these examples for which the motto "let the grammar decide" was devised. Consider, for example, the passive test, which was suggested as a "better" test for the direct object–hood of the passive subject NP in the counterpart active construction. The passive construction itself is not entirely satisfactory. First, as has long been observed in English, there are a number of passivelike expressions that do not behave like "normal" passive constructions: these are the "adjectival" or "resultative" passives, such as *The door is closed.* These can be said to represent one type of "boundary case" of passive. The characteristic methodological problem with boundary cases is whether they should be treated as the same as the normal cases, that is, where the (supposedly clear-cut) distinction should be drawn. The obvious problem is, if the distinction or category is supposed to be clear cut, then why is it so difficult to make the distinction in so many cases?

The passive is a construction that has undergone intense investigation in English and other languages, and so a number of boundary cases have been noted. The aforementioned adjectival passives are now generally agreed not to be passives, or, at least, not the "normal" passive (see, e.g., Bolinger 1967; Wasow 1977; Bresnan 1982b; note that this in turn raises the question, Why do the adjectival passives look so much like the normal passives?). However, even excluding these passives, there are plenty of boundary cases to be found. In English, there are the so-called prepositional passives, whose subjects are the objects of prepositions in the active counterparts (see, e.g., Bolinger 1977):

(20) *George Washington slept *(in) this bed.*

(21) *This bed was slept in by George Washington.*

In other languages, the constructions that appear to be the equivalents of English passives, because they behave like English passives in the "normal" circumstances, have "abnormal" (i.e., boundary) cases that have led to differences in opinion as to their passive status. Perhaps the best known of these is the Japanese *-rare* construction, the subject of which may be an NP that is not an argument of the predicate (the so-called adversity passive; Kuno 1973: 301):[10]

(22) *John wa ame ni hur -(r)are -ta*
John TOP rain by fall -PASS -PAST
'John was rained on [lit., John was fallen by rain]."

This construction should itself be contrasted with a derivational transitive-intransitive pattern found in Japanese in which the intransitive counterpart can often be translated only as an English passive, for example, *someru/somaru* 'dye/be dyed' or *kabuseru/kabusaru* 'be covered/get covered' (Jacobsen 1982: 199–200).

Another example of a construction that may or may not be a passive is one found in Acehnese:

(23) *Lôn ka geu- côm lé- gopnyan*
1ST INCH 3RD- kiss PREP- she
'I was kissed by her.' (Durie 1988: 105)

The agent is marked by what appears to be a preposition, but the verb agrees with it and has no passive marking (cf. Lawler 1977 [pro-passive, though he has now abandoned formalist methodology] and Durie 1988 [anti-passive]). A lesser-known construction that also may or may not be a passive is one involving a coverb found in mainland Southeast Asian languages such as Vietnamese:

(24) *Nam bị Nga đánh*
Nam suffer Nga beat
'Nam was beaten by Nga.' (Siewierska 1984: 149)

The patient is the subject of the coverb, the coverb appears to be equivalent to a passive auxiliary, but it also appears that the agent plus main verb is a complement to the coverb (perhaps not unlike the nominalized clause in *My grandmother suffered the loss of both her husband and her father in the space of two years*).[11]

The problem of boundary cases in defining the major syntactic categories has not been broached as frequently, partly because of the pragmatic view toward defining the major syntactic categories in other languages (see chap. 2). Nevertheless, difficulties have arisen. Nominalizations of verbs were once treated in transformational grammar as underlying verbs; but their status in the theory shifted to nouns with the advent of lexicalism (Chomsky 1970). However, there still remain problems in capturing the behavior of nominalizations in English, at once similar to verbs but also quite different. For instance, the argument structure is essentially the same in *She replaced the vodka with water* and *the replacement of the vodka with water*. However, the direct object argument is obligatory with the verb form and optional—but if present requires the genitive *of*—in the nominalization.

Also, assignment of nominalizations firmly to the category of nouns focuses attention on the status of nonfinite verb forms, which now become the boundary cases. Are they nouns or verbs? The answer to this question has consequences for the analysis of clauses. Does a nonfinite form make up a separate clause (as its verblike character would imply) or not (as its nonverblike character would also imply)? Whereas a nonfinite verb form such as the infinite in English *I want to finish this* appears to be part of the same clause (Foley and Olson 1985), the nonfinite dependent forms found in SOV languages, such as the following Yimas example (Foley 1986: 178), appear to represent distinct clauses:

(25)	*marɨmp*	*-ɨn*	*awŋkwi*	*-mp*	*-i*	*antɨ*	*-nan*
	river	-OBL	down.in.water	-SEQ	-DEP	ground	-OBL
	yampara	*-mp*	*-i*	*ama-*	*tɨpaŋ*	*-ɨt*	
	river	-SEQ	-DEP	1SG.S-	bathe	-PERF	

'I went down into the river, stood on the ground and washed.'

Here, the structures appear to be far larger than one would expect "clauses" to be, and the semantic relation between the clauses resembles that between English conjoined finite clauses, but the verb forms are nonfinite.

Another multiple-verb construction, found particularly in languages without verbal inflections that would distinguish finite and nonfinite forms, are the verb concatenations found in, for example, Lahu, in which main verbs are strung together to form complexes with meanings normally associated with adverbs, particles, prepositions, and auxiliaries in English (Matisoff 1969: 70; the gloss lines indicate literal meaning, grammatical meaning, and English category counterpart, respectively):

(26) *ŋà-hɨ ğa qɔ̀ʔ chî tɔ̂ʔ pî ve*
we get return lift come.out give NML
OBLIG again out for
AUX ADV PRT PREP
'We had to lift (it) out again for (them).'

Again, there is a question as to whether these "serial verb" constructions should be treated as one clause or many; these are more clearly boundary cases between single and multiple clauses than conjunctive verb forms. One of the "verbal" categories of Lahu, auxiliaries, brings us back to English, where the category of auxiliary, with verblike and nonverblike behavior, is another kind of boundary case for the category "verb," sometimes included in that category (Pullum and Wilson 1977; Gazdar, Pullum, and Sag 1982) or excluded from it (e.g., Akmajian, Steele, and Wasow 1979).

The category "subject" is also surrounded by boundary cases. Cross-linguistically, the only "normal" subjects as found by most tests are certain intransitive subjects (the "actor" or "active" subjects). Ergative and active-stative systems produce "nonsubject" agreement and case-marking patterns for transitive subjects and some intransitive subjects (see the Quiché and Lakhota examples [8]–[12] above), and in some languages even behavioral evidence makes these into "nonsubjects." Another boundary case are "dative (experiencer) subjects," which have some subjectlike behavior but are coded in a nonsubject case or with a nonsubject agreement pattern:

Russian:

(27) *mne nado ujti*
1SG.DAT OBLIG leave.INF
'I have to leave.' (dative controls subject of infinitive *ujti* 'to leave')

Kannada (Anderson 1979: 13):

(28) *avanige tanna jātiyavarannu kanḍare āgadu*
3SG.DAT REFL.POSS community people.ACC loathe
'He can't stand the people of his own community.' (dative controls reflexive possessive *tanna*)

Many of these examples have been accommodated in the formalist methodology by discounting the value of case marking and agreement as indicators of subjecthood, but the problem of accounting for these patterns remains.

These examples pertain chiefly to the basic clausal and lexical phenomena that will be discussed in later chapters, but they can easily be multiplied for other areas of the grammar. Our point here is simply that the clear-cut boundaries that the formalist method seeks to discover do not appear to exist in many places, and different linguists have "let the grammar decide" in different ways. A legitimate question to ask is, Are the controversies that are generated by trying to draw a sharp distinction between, say, verb and auxiliary illuminating or obscuring the nature of language?

The functionalist answer is that they do obscure the nature of language. In the functionalist view, linguists should recognize the boundary status of the cases in question and try to understand why they are boundary cases. Boundary cases play an important role in the functionalist methodology. The major empirical fact that has led to concrete results for typology is the discovery that the cross-linguistic variation in such things as the basic grammatical distinctions is patterned. The use of concepts such as the hierarchical or prototypical organization of grammatical structures is intended to account for the patterns in the data. Both concepts are founded on the notion of a central, invariant class (the highest member of the hierarchy or the core of the prototype), with extensions to the central class that vary across languages. For example, in chapter 3 I will argue that there are central classes for the grammatical categories "noun" and "verb," defined by a combination of semantic and pragmatic features, that behave in essentially the same fashion across languages, and those combinations of semantic class and pragmatic function that are not the central types will vary across languages in their grammatical behavior.

In addition to proposing central grammatical classes and extensions to those classes, a functionalist theory can improve on the problematic formalist account by explaining how and why the boundary cases are variable or "inconsistent" in their behavior. For example, it will turn out that the minor syntactic categories fall into two general types of noncentral categories (see 3.3.3–4). "Peripheral" minor categories display synchronic variation without any diachronic implications. "Transitory" minor categories, on the other hand, have variable grammatical behavior that can be understood only in terms of diachronic processes, in particular, grammaticalization. I will also argue (see 5.5.1 and Croft 1990a) that predicates representing mental states—which have the dative experiencer subjects—display cross-linguistically variable behavior because the phenomena they denote do not fit into the prototypical causal structure of events for which case marking was "designed." In fact, we may go further to say that the ways in which mental state predicate-argument structures are expressed can be accounted for by well-motivated means by which non-prototypical causal structures are "fit" or coerced into the prototypical structure that defines the basic case relations. And, in the case of the major syntactic categories, I will propose an explanation for why certain grammatical behavior represents "good" tests for nounhood and verbhood and also a "deverbalization hierarchy" to define which verbal properties are the most verblike and hence will be found missing in nonfinite verbal constructions (sec. 2.4).

The presence of boundary cases can be handled in part by the formalist decision to take some syntactic tests (constructions) as criterial in determining universal grammatical categories such as subject and to treat the conflicting evidence of other grammatical features such as case marking and agreement as "noise" that should be ignored. This has two important effects. The first is that the data used to establish presumably universal syntactic distinctions are limited to those constructions that manifest those distinctions. It is true that, using the formalist methodology, one should first examine the full range of syntactic phenomena available in order to discover the relevant constructions. But the question remains, What should be done with the remaining constructions?[12] The second effect is that certain constructions are separated out as the ones that manifest the universal distinctions and the others are treated as "superficial."

The consequences of this aspect of the formalist methodology are most readily apparent in the discussion of the grammatical relations subject and object. In his paper, Anderson (1976) focused on the rules of equi, raising, conjunction formation, and reflexivization and discounted the evidence provided by case marking and agreement. The difference between the former and the latter set of rules has been described by Keenan (1976) as "behavior and control" versus "coding" properties. Coding properties represent the actual means by which the grammatical relation is expressed by the language. Behavior and control properties (henceforth "behavioral") represent certain aspects of grammatical behavior that do not encode the grammatical relation in question but do appear to refer to the grammatical relation in some way. Anderson's argument presents the behavioral rules as "deep" and the coding rules as "superficial."[13]

However, it is not at all obvious why behavioral rules should be treated as more basic or "deeper" than coding rules. Any language must code its grammatical relations, but not every language has the types of constructions that lead to behavioral rules sensitive to subjecthood. Many languages, such as the ones in the Balkan area, use finite constructions without missing argument phrases for their counterparts to equi and raising. Other languages such as Japanese use null anaphora (missing arguments) not just for putative subjects but for many other argument phrase types as well (cf. Anderson 1976:13). Similar facts hold for another rule that is frequently used in arguments about ergativity, relativization. While some languages allow relativization of only "subject"—A and S—other languages allow relativization of all of A, S, and P and even obliques. Finally, in the case of reflexivization, some languages such as Old English do not use pronouns distinct from the normal anaphoric pronouns for reflexives, while other languages detransitivize the verb so that the A versus P distinction is neutralized. Hence, if anything, coding rules are more basic to grammatical relations than behavioral rules—although the domains of application of behavioral rules are more uniform across languages.

A functionalist approach avoids the problem of having to ignore particular rules/constructions or to treat them as "superficial" phenomena because each construction and its domain of application is examined on its own merits.[14] Thus, coding rules can be taken as seriously as behavioral rules. In fact, one can quickly observe that the function of the rules of equi, raising, and conjunction formation is quite different from the function of the encoding devices of word order, case marking, and agreement. The former rules are interclausal COREFERENTIAL ARGUMENT rules whose primary function is to identify shared arguments across clauses and only indirectly to specify grammatical relations between arguments and predicates. Thus, one might expect case marking and verb agreement to be more central in determining the categories of grammatical relations that exist in a language for that reason as well.

The analyses in this book are addressed primarily to the coding of nouns and verbs—or, more precisely, the heads of argument phrases and predicate phrases, respectively—and the grammatical relations that hold between them. We will see that there is indeed a way to formulate universal characterizations of "noun," "verb," "subject," "object," and "oblique" on the basis of grammatical coding properties found in single clauses (though not without taking into consideration general discourse patterns in the functional explanation). The account of the major syntactic categories in chapters 2–3 is a fairly complete analysis (though it is, of course, by no means the final word on the issue). The account of the primary grammatical relations in chapters 4–6 is restricted to the coding phenomenon of case marking and voice alternations, however, and hence can be perceived only as the first step toward constructing universal concepts of "subject" and "object." Nevertheless, this is a fairly intensively explored area of grammar, and many other papers in the functionalist tradition suggest how grammatical factors other than those discussed here play a role in defining "subject" cross-linguistically. For example, DeLancey (1981, 1982), building on work by Silverstein (1976) and Dixon (1979), has given a sophisticated account that explains a great deal of the variation in case-marking, word order, and agreement patterns—the three means of encoding grammatical relations. His analysis involves a prototypical correlation between directionality of causation—the semantic factor underlying case marking, in my account—the ranking of participants in the "animacy hierarchy," and the perspective on the event defined by verbal aspect. In this account, the so-called split-ergative coding systems turn out to represent a different resolution of nonprototypical alignments of causation, animacy, and perspective than is found in most European languages.

Behavioral properties for defining grammatical relations have also been well explored. Trithart (1979) and Hawkinson and Hyman (1974) argue that the notion of topicality can be used to account for patterns of passivization, relativization, and other behavioral properties in Bantu languages. Givón (1979, chap. 4) argues that the restrictions on passivization and relativization found in some languages are complemented by rules of subject and object "promotion" that have the overall effect of allowing any argument to be expressed as a subject, with the difference that the semantic relation of the argument to the predicate is expressed on the verb (by the "promotion" morphology). In a similar argument, Heath (1979) proposes that the "deep ergativity" of Dyirbal, justified mainly for conjunction formation, actually represents the interaction of verbal antipassive morphology and case marking whose overall effect is uniquely to encode every possible coreference relation between the agent/patient of the first clause and the agent/patient of the second case. Other work on "conjunction reduction," a standard "test" for subjecthood, has revealed a complex system of cross-clausal coreference relations that now goes under the name of switch-reference (Haiman and Munro 1983). Although no unified account has yet emerged (however, see Foley and Van Valin 1984; Givón 1983a, 1983b), it appears that most of the groundwork for functional analyses of the behavioral properties of subjects has been laid, and there are many avenues for future research in this area.

In the formalist paradigm, another way in which the differences in the results of various syntactic tests can be reconciled with the notion of clear-cut universal categories without limiting the kind of evidence that can be examined is the concept of syntactic levels, components, or modules. Beginning with transformational grammar, formalist models of syntax have generally had two (or more) levels of syntactic analysis, and it is reasonable to believe that different grammatical distinctions would be found in different levels of the grammar. In particular, the universal categories would be found at one level, generally the "deep" level, and other language-specific or typologically variable categories and distinctions would be found at other levels, generally more "surface" or "superficial" levels. More recent formalist models of grammar have abandoned the derivational implication of the notion of a level, replacing it with a "component" or "module" of the grammar. I will use the term "component" as a cover term for syntactic levels or modules, each associated with certain grammatical distinctions and the constructions or rules that manifest them, regardless of whether they are linked by derivational rules.

The conceptual problem that has arisen here—at least, what is perceived by some as a conceptual problem—is the proliferation of components. I will illustrate this once again using the example of a cross-linguistic definition of "subject." In the usual two-component model of grammatical relations, the "deep" component is characterized by constructions such as conjunction formation etc. that refer to universal categories of subject and object. As we have already noted, there exist a small number of languages, of which Dyirbal is the best-known member, in which even the rules that Anderson takes to be criterial for subjecthood, particularly conjunction formation and relativization, pattern ergatively. By requiring an absolutive pattern rather than an accusative one for conjunction formation etc., Dyirbal causes difficulties for a uniform universal characterization of "subject."

Anderson accepted the Dyirbal case as an exceptional one. However, another strategy to handle this problem is to add another component or, to be more precise, add another primitive concept distinct from those at the other components to which rules may refer. This strategy was applied by Dixon (1979), who distinguishes three sets of concepts: the "deep"-level concepts, which are the three categories A, S, and P and the grouping of A and S as "subject," which is relevant for imperatives, jussives, and certain aspectual and modal verbs such as 'begin,' 'finish,' 'can,' and 'must'; the "shallow"-level concept of "pivot," which is either A + S or, in the case of Dyirbal, P + S; and the "surface" level, which (as in most other models) is a component for the many leftover factors that interact in complex ways to yield surface case marking and verb agreement. Thus, we have here three different concepts of "subject," all closely related but somewhat different in some languages, placed in three different levels. The most extreme example of this tendency in the case of defining "subject" is Perlmutter's (1982) proposal that five distinct concepts of "subject" are necessary, all derivable from the relational grammar model that has an arbitrary number of levels of derivation (more neutrally describable as "strata").

Although Perlmutter's example is considered an extreme approach to the problem of subject, it is actually not as complex in this respect as the theory of Government and Binding. The theory of Government and Binding has a large number of modules (called "theories"), many of which describe closely related but distinct concepts. For instance, rules of case assignment, theta-role assignment, phrase structure, subcategorization, and constraints on argument position all pertain to the grammatical relations held by NPs to the verb, more or less, with subtle differences used by the theory (e.g., subcategorization excludes subjects, theta-role assignment can apply to other kinds of heads than verbs, etc.). The postulation of slightly different theoretical constructs for roughly the same phenomenon then requires the postulation of principles that make the various constructs "match" most of the time. For example, in various versions of Government and Binding Theory, these matching principles have included the Projection Principle (to link subcategorization and phrase structure), the Theta Criterion (to link argument structure and theta-role assignment), the Case Filter (to link case assignment and syntactic expression of an NP), and the principle linking subcategorization and theta-role assignment described in Sells (1986:37). Government and Binding Theory also has three syntactic levels that are orthogonal to the "theories," D-structure, S-structure, and LF, each of which represents the structure of the whole sentence in some form.

The reason for the proliferation of components is not difficult to find, from the point of view of the functionalist linguist. Grammatical distinctions are justified by their relevance to certain grammatical constructions; that is, the distinction defines the domain of application of the grammatical construction used as a test. However, close examination of rules within a given language and/or equivalent rules across languages reveals that there is a great deal of variation in the domain of application. Since the components attempt to divide up the variation so that invariant clear-cut distinctions can be set up, the components proliferate until one reaches the situation of having a component for every rule or construction in the grammar.[15]

The underlying reason for the proliferation of components—not to mention the proliferation of boundary cases—is that a large number of factors interact in complex ways to determine the domain of application of a particular rule. The intensive study of grammatical rules in English has revealed a tremendous variety of subtle differences among the domains of application of individual rules, and the intensive study of certain grammatical rules across languages, such as passive and relative clause formation, suggests that the domains of application vary in many details—major as well as minor—across languages. Simple reference to "subject," "pivot," or even one of A, S, or P will not suffice to describe the domain of application of the rule correctly. This is especially clear with the "surface" rules of case marking and verb agreement, in which various concepts of animacy, definiteness, topicality, tense, aspect, volitionality, affectedness, and so on all interact in determining the actual choice of a particular case marking or agreement affix for an argument phrase. In other words, the concepts or factors that determine the domain of application of a rule all appear to interact with each other rather than dividing into coherent components. And the factors appear to be ultimately grounded in functional, that is, semantic and pragmatic, considerations.[16]

The functionalist methodology avoids this problem entirely by not dividing up the grammar into components (in the formalist sense of parallel structural representations of a sentence that are structurally related). There is only one structural representation of a sentence, which is compared to equivalent structures across languages and explained in terms of the interaction of functional factors, that is, features of the described situation or the utterance situation that are outside the structure of the sentence per se.[17]

From the functionalist point of view, one of the primary justifications for different levels of grammatical representation is to account for conflicts or mismatches in the results of different syntactic tests. This is clearly the case for the use of levels in the representation of grammatical relations. Certain constructions, the "good" (mostly behavioral) tests for subjecthood, are defined in terms of deep-level relations, while certain other constructions, chiefly the coding tests, are defined in terms of surface-level relations. Variation in the domains of application of different constructions leads to the postulation of more and more levels. The functionalist account for these phenomena divides up the problem differently, by construction rather than by domain of application, and characterizes each construction independently. This is only the starting point of functional-typological analysis, however. The additional steps that must be taken are the analysis of the typological variation in the domain of application of equivalent constructions across languages and the analysis of the variation between the domains of application of different constructions.

The postulation of levels/modules is intended to capture relations among constructions—those that are defined in terms of one level/module as opposed to those that are defined in terms of another. There are several promising ways to attack the problem of relations among constructions in a functionalist model without invoking additional levels.

First, rules interact in "conspiracies." Examples include the aforementioned analyses of the relation between relativization, passivization, and promotion described by Givón and the relation between antipassivization and conjunction in Dyirbal proposed by Heath (1979). Other examples include the relation between degree of pronominal differentiation and "strict complex ID rules" (completely constrained cross-clausal coreference rules) described by Heath (1975) and the general relations that Langacker (1974) found to hold among what were described as "movement rules" in transformational grammar. The phenomenon of "conspiracies" represents a certain type of relation among rules that could be captured in functional terms—that is, two or more "independent" features of constructions that actually interact quite closely with the purpose of encoding certain concepts in certain ways, for example, encoding certain arguments as subjects or heads of relative clauses in the case of Givón's analysis.[18]

Second, different constructions interact in such a way as to define a central category member through a prototype or a hierarchy. We will see in chapter 4 that different constructions contribute to the definition of a prototypical noun and verb, the function of the construction accounting for its role in defining the syntactic categories. The subsequent chapters will examine case marking and voice relations, which "conspire" to encode semantic and pragmatic relations of arguments to predicates. Behavioral properties of subjects will not be discussed here; this topic merits at least another book-length study. However, I will present a possible hierarchical relation among the different test constructions used for defining subjects:

> *Ergative rule hierarchy.* Ergativity—that is, a domain of application distinguishing S and P from A—in coreferential-argument rules (conjunction formation and the like) implies ergativity in focusing (extraction) rules, which in turn implies ergativity in verb agreement (if agreement exists), which in turn implies ergativity in case marking (if case marking of direct case roles exists).

This hypothesis is suggested by the languages given in table 1.1 (though gaps occur in the evidence).[19]

TABLE 1.1 *Evidence for the Ergative Rule Hierarchy*

	Coreferential Argument	**Focusing (Extraction)**	**Verb Agreement**	**Case Marking**
Dyirbal	erg	erg	erg	erg
Quiché	acc	erg	erg	N/A
Avar	acc	?	erg	erg
Warlpiri	acc	acc	acc	erg
Russian	acc	acc	acc	acc

Cole et al. (1980) suggest a diachronic interpretation of a simpler version of this implicational universal in their examination of the acquisition of subjecthood by dative experiencer argument phrases (i.e., experiencers that are case marked as indirect objects) in several languages. In the languages that they examined, the acquisition of behavioral subject properties such as conjunction formation and control historically precedes the acquisition of coding subject properties such as case marking.

Another example of a hierarchy of rules or constructions is the previously mentioned deverbalization hierarchy of finiteness for nonfinite and nominalized verb forms in 2.4, in which it is argued that ability of a nonfinite form to take "normal" (i.e., main clause) tense-aspect modality marking, subject marking, and object marking forms a hierarchy (but are independent of the ability to take case marking and adjectival, as opposed to adverbial, modifiers). Keenan's (1976) paper on subjects argues for a prototype organization of subject properties, that is, rules that are generally considered to refer to the concept "subject," and Borg and Comrie (1984) use a similar argument for direct and indirect objects.

The single-level representation of linguistic structures has an important consequence for a thoroughgoing functionalist analysis: there are no derivational rules, that is, rules relating one structure to another.[20] Instead, as we have already noted, the goal of the functionalist method is to provide an example of structural linguistic phenomena in terms of the FUNCTION of a grammatical construction, not in terms of the structure of a related construction, whether the related structure is abstract, and whether the structural relation is derivational. Thus, derivational rules are contrary to the spirit of a functionalist approach to grammar.[21] A functionalist grammatical rule is a form-function rule, that is, a rule that maps a linguistic function onto a linguistic form and vice versa, thereby modeling the processes of production and comprehension, respectively.

1.4 Preliminaries to This Study

The primary question that the remainder of this book addresses is, What is the explanation for the structure of the clause in natural languages? This section will lay some general groundwork for understanding the problem and a functionalist approach to its solution. I will take the primary function of natural language to be to COMMUNICATE INFORMATION. (There are, of course, many other functions that affect language structure, however.) I take the (not entirely uncontroversial) position that the basic structure of utterances can largely be accounted for by the primary function of language. The function of language to communicate information implies the hypothesis that both the structure of the information—semantics—and the structure of communication—pragmatics and discourse—contribute to determining basic language structure.

One can define morphosyntactic structure as being constituted by three essential components: units of various types, such as "noun," "verb," and "argument phrase"; the relations or dependencies that hold between the units; and the linear order in which those units appear in the utterance.[22] I will operate under the slight idealization that a linguistic utterance is a linear sequence of units, ignoring suprasegmentals. Of course, intonation plays a major role in determining information structure and affects the information communicated (Bolinger 1987, 1989). In fact, Chafe's most recent work uses the intonation unit as the basic discourse unit (Chafe 1984, 1987). Nevertheless, the intonation unit subsumes a variety of morphosyntactic structural types that are equally present in utterances, and intonation appears to be an independent parameter, albeit one that interacts closely with clause morphosyntactic structure.

The distinction between the two components of relations between units and linear order is still somewhat controversial since the widely accepted phrase structure model of syntactic structure combines the latter two. However, the study of so-called free word-order languages and of various other linguistic phenomena, particularly grammatical relations, argues in favor of delinking linear order from grammatical dependencies.[23]

Given this initial characterization of morphosyntactic structure, one can provisionally define the clause as a syntactic unit made up of the following smaller units: a verb or predicate,[24] one or more argument phrases that are dependent on the verb to varying degrees,[25] and, within the argument phrase, a noun and (perhaps) adjectives or other modifying expressions that are dependent on the noun.[26] This definition introduces a number of undefined concepts, namely, the basic units "verb," "noun," and "adjective" (or perhaps "modifier"). In addition, the grammatical manifestations of dependencies, in this case, the dependencies between the predicate and the arguments, must also be defined in one way or another. Continuing in this descriptive vein, we may postulate three primary morphosyntactic strategies of grammatical dependencies: linear order (as implicitly used in phrase-structure analyses), a "deictic" morphological strategy (agreement affixes and elements), and a "relational" strategy (adpositions and case markers; for discussion, see Croft 1988). The dependencies holding at the clause level, namely, those between the verb and its dependent nominal phrases, generally go under the rubric "grammatical relations" proper: subject, object, and various types of oblique phrases.

Although this description of basic clause structure is very elementary, one can already draw a number of conclusions from it from a functionalist perspective. The classification into units, relations, and linear order already implicitly suggests a relation between form and function, namely, that the information that a human being communicates is divisible into units and relations between those units, with linear order imposed by the nature of the medium (although it is also used for communicative effect). This division into units and relations, found in every human language, and the "fitting" of the world into this division, appears to be a fundamental cognitive fact about human beings. The existence of relations can be thought of as a necessary consequence of the "chunking" of the unity of experience that is represented by the linguistic units: if experience is individuated into units, then there must be relations to reassemble those units. I will not comment any further on the functional significance of the analysis of experience, but discussion of the appropriate "cuts" in experience will surface in the analysis of the commonsense semantic classes involved in the definition of the major syntactic categories in chapters 2–3 and in the analysis of verbal semantics in chapters 4–6.

The importance of clause structure in natural language is its universality: all languages have clauses, although there may be some difficulties in defining clause boundaries (see the preceding section). The most plausible external explanation that comes immediately to mind is that the clause is the minimal complete information unit. It is minimal in that larger discourse units—complex sentences, dialogues, and texts—are made up of clauses. It is complete in that the use of smaller units (appropriately called "fragments") requires the presence in the discourse context of the information that would be embodied in a full clause. For example, the fragment *No,* while not a full sentence, implies the presence of, for example, a question such as *Did you quit your job?* that provides the "missing" clause-level unit of information *I didn't quit my job.* Or the fragment *and Fred Sue* implies the presence of a preceding conjunct such as *In the movie, John loves Mary . . .* that provides the rest of the clause-level information communicated by *Fred loves Sue.* The fragment *Nice!* implies the contextually salient presence of something such as, for example, the hearer's new portable studio-quality tape deck that completes the clause-level unit of information *Your new tape deck is nice!*

These observations suggest that the clause appears to provide a linguistically universal and apparently highly significant unit of information organization. It is also likely that the clause represents some natural division of the information itself, independent of its organization for communication. The first step toward explaining this fact is the examination of the structure of clauses. By doing that, we may be able to determine what kind of information a clause contains and why it is organized in the way that it is. The question that I begin to answer in the remaining chapters is, How does the structure of the clause result from the nature of the information itself (the semantics) and the organization of that information for communication (the pragmatic structure)?

Before jumping into the empirical data and its analysis, some caveats must be issued regarding the evidence and the analyses presented in the following chapters. First, like many other functionalist analyses, this study is typological in nature, requiring examination of a large number of languages in order to formulate universal generalizations that they want to explain functionally. This makes the simple statement of the linguistic facts and lowest-level generalizations a major endeavor. I have minimized this problem here by examining only a small set of very basic and mostly absolute universals, those enumerated in this section. However, as will be seen in the analyses in this book, restricting oneself in such a way still requires a large amount of typological analysis. In addition, I have restricted myself to what Tomlin (1986) calls SYMPTOMATIC evidence. This is evidence from grammatical constraints that are hypothesized to represent conventionalized remnants of "pure" functional constraints. One reason for this limitation is that grammars of natural languages generally describe only the conventionalized constraints and not the "living" functional constraints, which can be uncovered only by extensive text analysis and informant work and so cannot be researched on a large scale. A more important justification for allowing this restriction is the hypothesis that the typological patterns found in conventionalized constraints are indeed symptomatic of patterns in the external phenomena presumed to underly them. The hypotheses developed herein can be tested against direct evidence for functional constraints.

The theoretical caveat has to do with the fact that external explanations of linguistic phenomena require models of the external facts that are used to explain them. That is, a model of the world, or the way that people commonsensically conceive the world, and a model of what goes on in discourse, that is, the act of people producing, understanding, and interacting by means of language, are prerequisites for functional explanations. These models properly come from outside linguistics proper, from related cognitively oriented disciplines such as philosophy, psychology, some parts of anthropology and sociology, and also artificial intelligence. However, these models are only beginning to be developed in these related fields and so cannot be directly used for functional explanations. Thus, I cannot say that the functional explanations found in these chapters are corroborated by nonlinguistic cognitive or social models (except in a few instances, such as in the work of Rosch [1978]). Instead, the functional explanations represent hypotheses about general human cognitive behavior that are based on linguistic evidence, which can in turn be refined by nonlinguistic evidence. In other words, linguistic structure, by virtue of its relative concreteness compared to the subject matter of the related cognitive sciences (especially philosophy, artificial intelligence, and psychology), provides generalizations that can—and ought to—be tested in nonlinguistic cognitive domains, those domains in return providing richer (and better) models of external structures by means of which one can make additional linguistic predictions. The analyses in this book should be taken in this spirit: as proposing models of language function that are intuitively plausible based on the linguistic evidence but that must be enriched by future interdisciplinary research.

2

The Cross-Linguistic Basis for Syntactic Categories

There must be something to talk about and something must be said about this subject of discourse once it is selected. This distinction is of such fundamental importance that the vast majority of languages have emphasized it by creating some sort of formal barrier between the two terms of the proposition. The subject of discourse is a noun. As the most common subject of discourse is either a person or a thing, the noun clusters about concrete concepts of that order. As the thing predicated of a subject is generally an activity in the widest sense of the word, a passage from one moment of existence to another, the form which has been set aside for the business of predicating, in other words, the verb, cluster about concepts of activity. No language wholly fails to distinguish noun and verb, though in particular cases the nature of the distinction may be an elusive one.

Sapir 1921 : 119

2.1 Background to the Problem

It is taken to be a truism, an "absolute universal" in Greenberg's sense or a "design feature of language" in Hockett's sense, that all natural language utterances are made up of distinct units that are "meaningful" and that all natural language systems divide those units into a series of two or more classes or SYNTACTIC CATEGORIES. In fact, it would be safe to say that the nature of syntactic categories is at the very heart of grammar. This accounts for the fact that, in the course of outlining a theory of syntactic categories and syntactic category membership in this and the following chapter, I will address at least in passing such diverse problems as the distinction between inflectional and derivational morphology, inherent aspect, reference, relative clauses, nonfinite verbal morphology and its semantics, functional sentence perspective, the notion of valence, restrictive versus nonrestrictive modification, the raison d'être of inflectional categories, and the arbitrariness of the semantics of complex nominal relations.

No theory of grammar would be considered adequate unless it allowed one to define a set of distinct syntactic categories in its formal structure, and every major theory allows one to do just that. No theory of grammar, however, should be considered adequate unless it provides a universal definition of the basic grammatical categories that can be applied in a straightforward fashion to any human language. It is at this point that agreement (and, often, even discussion) largely ends. For example, it is frequently claimed that there exist languages that do not have adjectives (e.g., Schachter 1985), and it is occasionally claimed that a small number of languages do not distinguish between the two major categories "noun" and "verb" (e.g., Kinkade 1983).

The simple way to put the problem is that there are essentially two methods for developing a cross-linguistically valid universal criterion for a grammatical category, language internal (also known as structural) and language external (also known as functional, or semantic/pragmatic in the realm of morphosyntax); but neither method alone can answer the question of what constitutes the major syntactic categories 'noun' and 'verb.' The traditional external definition, a semantic one, is intuitively plausible and can be applied uniformly to any human language but is not empirically adequate. The internal definition, dividing roots into categories based on grammatical behavior, can be applied in individual languages, but the results from one language to another are not strictly comparable. In this and the following chapter, I will present a theory of syntactic categories that uses both internal and external criteria that are applicable to all human languages in a uniform fashion. The internal criteria use a well-motivated typological criterion, marking theory (Greenberg 1966a), extended and combined with recent hypotheses on the structure of categories, such as prototype theory (e.g., Coleman and Kay 1981; Lakoff 1987), to develop a cross-linguistically valid criterion for determining major category membership. The external criteria to be proposed here recognize that the traditional semantic classification is basically correct but incomplete, requiring an independent external parameter, based on pragmatic or discourse function, to achieve empirical adequacy (almost exactly as Sapir describes it in the epigraph to this chapter). Not only does this yield a solution to the old problem of a universal yet adequate definition for "noun," "verb," and "adjective," but it also demonstrates the value of the functional-typological method of analysis, which promises to produce solutions to all the fundamental definitional problems described in chapter 1.

I will begin by describing the traditional semantic (external) definition of the major syntactic categories, and a more recent semantic definition, to illustrate their value and their inadequacies. After that, I will turn to the evolution of internal criteria from the standard structuralist method to more sophisticated typological methods. The latter will bring us to the typological method that allows one to compare internal (structural) linguistic criteria across languages and forms the basis of my analysis of the major syntactic categories.

The traditional definitions for the major syntactic categories are purely semantic, based on a commonsense ontology of types of entities: nouns denote persons, places, or things; adjectives denote properties or qualities; verbs denote actions. This purely semantic approach, intuitively attractive as it is, is inadequate as it stands. For example, the noun *motion* denotes an action as much as does the verb *move,* and the noun *whiteness* denotes a property or quality as much as does the adjective *white.* For this reason, the traditional definition is generally discarded. Nevertheless, its intuitive naturalness is powerful and worth salvaging. (In fact, as we will see, even the structuralists use it.)

The traditional semantic analysis is based on a commonsense ontology of the types of phenomena found in the world: things, properties, actions, etc. This commonsense ontology is a controversial issue in linguistic as well as philosophical semantics, where neither surface verbs nor adjectives denote individual entities (instead, they denote functions from individuals to truth values). More recently, philosophers such as Donald Davidson have argued that verbs, at least action verbs, must be allowed to refer to events and the theory of situation semantics (Barwise and Perry 1983) actually encourages one to speak of different ontological types such as actions and properties. Some linguists (e.g., Carlson 1984) have endorsed similar positions. Situation semantics has expressly attempted to capture the commonsense ontological classification that I am also proposing. I will use the term DENOTES to express the relation between a lexical root and the piece of the world, partial situation, etc., that the lexical root is naively considered to "mean."[1]

Prior to this recent revival of interest in a more commonsense ontological classification of phenomena in formal semantics, a slightly different definition of syntactic categories was proposed in the formal semantic literature. The categorial grammars from the Montague tradition define syntactic categories in semantic terms (see, e.g., Schmerling 1983). Categorial grammar defines its categories in terms of their combinatorics: the VALENCY (number of arguments; see 2.3) of the category and the type of its inputs and outputs are encoded in the category name. For example, the type of a transitive verb is ⟨*e*,⟨*e*,*t*⟩⟩: that is, something that combines with an entity (the direct object) and yields something that combines with another entity (the subject) and yields a truth value. This provides more semantic information than an (untyped) first-order calculus representation like $F(x, y)$, which gives only the valency of the predicate. Although this is an improvement over the purely formal approach in some ways since it provides a relation between category membership and the semantics of the member lexical item, there are difficulties in matching semantic category membership with syntactic category membership. The best-known mismatch between categorial grammar categories and natural language categories is that the single category ⟨*e*,*t*⟩ comprises (nonrelational) nouns as in *Ed is a carpenter,* adjectives that do not take complements as in *This table is heavy,* and intransitive verbs as in *She's sleeping.* Thus, ⟨*e*,*t*⟩ cus across every major natural language syntactic category. A more subtle difficulty is provided by certain complement-taking verbs and adjectives. For instance, Chierchia (1984) argues persuasively that a verb like *want* or *try* combines with a one-place predicate (its infinitival complement) to make a one-place predicate (the VP as a whole). This analysis would force one to posit separate *want*'s for (1) and (2), however:

(1) *Jan wanted to eat supper.*

(2) *Jan wanted a ribeye steak.*

It may be possible to combine the two *want*'s by proposing a phantom *to get* . . . in (2) (e.g., McCawley 1979), but this solution seems less plausible for a unified analysis of predicates like *afraid:*

(3) *John is afraid of rabbits/of explosions/that you will tell on him.*

There are other aspects of the categorial grammar representation that contribute to these difficulties, in particular, the minimal Fregean ontology of entities and truth values referred to above.

A seminal typologically oriented semantic approach to the definition of syntactic categories is Dixon's study of the syntactic category "adjective" (Dixon 1977, originally written in 1970). Unlike the categories "noun" and "verb," whose universality has rarely been questioned (but see below), the category "adjective" does not have a clear-cut grammatical status. Dixon examines a number of languages that have a small closed class of adjectives and discovered a surprising amount of semantic regularity. Languages with small adjective classes always include terms that fall in the semantic classes that Dixon defines as dimension ("big," "small"), age ("young," "new," "old"), value ("good," "bad"), and color ("white," "red," "blue"). Certain other semantic classes surface as adjectives in languages with slightly larger adjective classes, particularly human propensity ("happy," "clever," "kind"), physical property ("hard," "heavy," "hot"), and speed ("quick," "slow," "fast"—though there are interference effects from the class "adverb" in this case). Finally, the less "typical" adjectival semantic classes, human propensity and physical property, systematically fall into the other major syntactic categories when the adjective class is small, human propensity terms usually being nouns and physical property terms usually being verbs (Dixon 1977, 62).

Dixon was able to take advantage of the cross-linguistic variation in syntactic category membership of the class "adjective"—which is sometimes an open class, sometimes a small closed class, and possibly sometimes not a separate class at all, allegedly being a subclass of verbs—and use it to develop a PROTOTYPE theory of syntactic category membership. Much of this and the following chapter may be seen as extending Dixon's analysis of syntactic category membership to nouns and verbs, which are always open classes and therefore less amenable to typological analysis.

It is worth noting that Dixon's semantic definition of "adjective" is actually quite close to that of traditional grammar, in which adjectives are defined as denoting "qualities." Nevertheless, it should be pointed out that Dixon used internal grammatical criteria to obtain his results, and at bottom Dixon's discovery is that there is a significant correlation between the grammatical criteria he used—not explicitly spelled out—and the traditional semantic definition of "adjective." There still remains the problem that, in languages with an open class of adjectives, any concept can surface as an "adjective" in one way or another; for example, the denominal *vehicular* and the participle *walking* are both "adjectives," in some as yet undetermined sense of that term.[2]

In sum, the semantic virtues of the traditional semantic analysis of syntactic categories appear to be greater than those of the categorial analysis. Nevertheless, the problems of empirical adequacy are so great that the majority of linguists have turned instead to an internal analysis of syntactic categories, based on the grammatical behavior of lexical items (although Dixon's study demonstrates a significant relation between external semantic criteria and internal grammatical criteria).

The summary of parts of speech systems provided by Schachter (1985) for the series on syntactic typology and field description represents a typical modern view of the nature of syntactic categories and syntactic category membership. Schachter argues that the only criteria for determining the number of syntactic categories in a language and syntactic category membership are internal: "It is assumed here that the primary criteria for parts-of-speech classification are grammatical, not semantic." The internal criteria include distribution in sentence structure, ability to inflect for the various inflectional categories of the language, and its "syntactic functions" (Schachter 1985 : 3). The internal criteria, which are widely accepted, would lead to a purely relativistic approach to defining syntactic categories: having established categories on internal criteria, how would one identify categories from two different languages as the "same" syntactic category? Schachter provides a semantic heuristic, based on the traditional semantic analysis, for the cross-linguistic identification of categories: if the language-internal category contains words denoting actions, then call the category "verb"; if it contains words denoting persons and things, then call the category "noun"; and so on.

Another difficulty that Schachter observes in the use of purely internal criteria is the inability to distinguish syntactic SUBCLASSES from major syntactic categories, for example, intransitive versus transitive verbs as opposed to verbs in general:

> Such subclasses are not ordinarily identified as distinct parts of speech, since there are in fact properties common to the members of the different subclasses, and since the label *parts of speech* is . . . traditionally reserved for 'major classes.' . . . It must be acknowledged, however, that there is not always a clear basis for deciding whether two distinguishable open classes of words that occur in a language should be identified as different parts of speech or as subclasses of a single part of speech. . . . What this means is that there may in some cases be considerable arbitrariness in the identification of two open word classes as distinct parts of speech rather than subclasses of a single part of speech. [Schachter 1985 : 5–6]

As we will see, this is the central problem in defining the major syntactic categories. Schachter does not suggest a solution to this problem, although he points out that a source of the problem is the fact that the internal grammatical properties that distinguish syntactic categories tend to cluster around a class and do not provide necessary and sufficient conditions for category membership. In other words, there are lexical items that do not have all the grammatical properties expected of "nouns" and "verbs"; there are a variety of boundary cases (as one might expect, given the remarks in chap. 1). Schachter concludes this introduction to the methodological problems surrounding syntactic category identification pessimistically: "Some rather celebrated questions—for example, whether or not all languages make a distinction between nouns and verbs—may ultimately turn out to be more a matter of terminology than of substance" (Schachter 1985 : 6).

Schachter's view is representative of the structuralist and generative tradition, which analyzes syntactic categories as structural concepts without a necessary connection with semantic or other extralinguistic factors. Many current versions of X′ theory in generative grammar take the major categories to be noun (N), verb (V), adjective (A), and preposition (P) and decompose these categories into the binary features, usually [±N] and [±V].[3] The feature decomposition of syntactic categories was intended to capture certain generalizations of syntactic behavior that appear to cross major categories that generative (interpretive) theorists no longer thought suitable to capture by transformations or by more abstract categories such as "Predicate" that had been proposed by the generative semanticists in the late 1960s and early 1970s.

An intuitive difficulty with the X′ decomposition of features is that it gives the same syntactic category status to adpositions as to nouns, verbs, and adjectives. The latter three are generally called the OPEN classes: they are extremely large classes that can easily assimilate new items, while CLOSED classes are small classes that only slowly assimilate new items. Adpositions are always closed classes and may not even be universal (see 3.3.4). Nouns and verbs are always open classes, while adjectives are usually open classes, although sometimes they are closed classes and possibly sometimes do not exist (see 3.3.2). Nouns, verbs, and adjectives are traditionally called the "major" classes, and adpositions are never so called. These differences in category type are not predicted or even suggested by the [N, V] feature decomposition. The analysis that I will provide will account for the different behavior of nouns and verbs, adjectives, and adpositions as well as explaining some of the generalizations that syntactic category decomposition has attempted to account for.[4] As Schachter clearly demonstrates, however, the primary drawback of the structural approach to syntactic categories is that no adequate cross-linguistic definition of a syntactic category is possible since the grammatical manifestations of syntactic categories are so varied across languages.

In fact, some linguists (Kuipers 1968; Kinkade 1983) have gone so far as to argue that some languages, in particular the Salishan, Wakashan, and Chimakum languages in northwestern North America, do not even have a noun-verb distinction. Kuipers's and Kinkade's argument against the noun-verb distinction in Salishan languages rests primarily on the fact that any lexical root may be inflected with the grammatical affixes and clitics associated with predicates. (This is, in fact, the chief argument provided against the noun-verb distinction in other languages.) Likewise, any lexical root can function as the argument of a predicate. In other words, syntactic distribution suggests that any lexical root can display both nominal and verbal grammatical behavior.

However, closer examination of the evidence provided by Kuipers and Kinkade strongly suggests that there is grammatical evidence to distinguish nouns and verbs and even that their characterization of the flexibility of lexical roots as proof of the lack of the noun-verb distinction is distorting the facts somewhat. In the latter case, the problem is that the translation of a "predicated" noun or a verb (or an adjective) as "argument" is distinct from the "normal" noun and verb meaning. Consider the following examples (from Shuswap [4], [6] and Kalispel [5]: Kinkade 1983:28–29):

(4) *meˀ xméy -nt -s -t*
EXP fly -TRANS -YOU.OBJ -PASSIVE
'you'll be covered with flies'

(5) *p'oxụ́t -s*
father -his
'He is his father'

(6) *nt'əláneˀtuˀ ɬxʷ- k'ʷúl' -mn*
N. that AGENTIVE- do -INSTRUMENTAL
'It was N. who was the helper.'

In the first example, the meaning of the predicate is 'cover with flies,' not 'fly'; it is analogous to zero-derived verbs in English such as *hammer* in *I hammered the nail into the sheetrock.* The meaning changes from that denoting an object to that denoting an action. The other two cases, the predicate nominal and the equative construction for focus, are not as obviously meaning changing. Nevertheless, they do not name or denote objects: the predicate nominal identifies the subject as belonging to the category denoted by the predicate, and the equative asserts the individual identity of the subject with the predicated noun. In fact, the fact that a noun serving a predicating grammatical function can be interpreted in two ways (classifying or equating) demonstrates that some meaning is added in these constructions (see 2.3).

Other changes in meaning occur in the use of "verbs" as arguments. The use of deictic elements, usually associated with "nouns," in combination with roots denoting actions and properties results in constructions meaning, for example, 'the big one' or 'what is wrapped' (a package; Kinkade 1983 : 30). These constructions denote objects, not properties or actions, and so by the traditional definition should be "nouns." These constructions do not provide evidence for the hypothesis that nouns and verbs are not distinct.

In addition, Kuipers's and Kinkade's examples provide positive grammatical (structural) evidence that the categories "noun" and "verb" are distinct. However, since neither author addresses this evidence directly, one cannot demonstrate conclusively that strong positive evidence for the "noun"-"verb" distinction exists in these languages based solely on the evidence provided. Kuipers notes the existence of the "nominalizing" *s-* prefix in Squamish but oddly denies that it is a nominalizer of typical verbs, contrasting *s-taq°* 'water' (NML-drink) from *man* 'father' and *puš* 'cat' (Kuipers 1968 : 612). Kuipers further observes that the *s-* prefix can be attached to typical nouns, with a slight meaning change, namely, "being an N, that something is an N." This is exactly what one would expect, given the argument above that predicate nominals represent a different meaning from the simple noun. The *s-* prefix form is a nominalization of the predicative noun in the meaning of the *be* of predication. Finally, Kuipers does not consider the distinct forms of the possessive pronominal prefixes (*'n-* 'my') and the subject pronominal prefixes (*n-* 'I') as a relevant distinction, although their distribution would probably distinguish nouns and verbs in Squamish.

From the glosses provided for various examples (e.g., the Kalispel examples in Kinkade 1983 : 28), it is clear that some Salishan languages distinguish possessive pronominal affixes from subject pronominal affixes, the former used for modification by nouns and the latter in predication. Although roots denoting objects may take subject "agreement" inflections directly when predicated, no examples are given to indicate if action stems may take possessive prefixes directly.[5] The Salishan languages, like all other languages, have deictic elements that can be used for arguments only. The *s-* nominalizer is mentioned by Kinkade but argued to be identical to the stative marker, at least in Chehalis. There are also some special forms for subjects of complements: "to indicate subject of a complement, one finds, at least in some Salishan languages, dependent subject markers" (Kinkade 1983:27).

The scanty evidence provided by Kuipers and Kinkade strongly suggests that there is indeed an internal distinction between the lexical roots that we would normally call "nouns" and those that we would call "verbs." However, a more thorough analysis of these languages would be required to verify that there does indeed exist a grammatical noun-verb distinction (see, e.g., van Eijk and Hess 1986). The necessary analysis has been largely provided by Jacobsen (1979) for Makah, a Wakashan language in the same general area and displaying similar typological characteristics.[6] Jacobsen recognizes that syntactic distributional patterns can divide lexical stems into nouns, verbs, and adjectives and examines a considerable amount of evidence in that regard. On distributional criteria, Jacobsen succeeds in establishing not only the categories "noun" and "verb" but also "adjective" and a host of minor categories. The relevant evidence is briefly summarized here. Only bare lexical stems denoting objects may take the nominal inflection for possession, the nominal syntax of articles and demonstratives, and function as subjects or objects of a predicate. Suffixation of -°*iq* to actions and properties results in forms that mean 'one who . . . ,' that is, headless modifier forms (Jacobsen 1979:123), which may function as referring expressions since they refer to persons or objects; however, they cannot take all demonstratives (122). The headless modifier forms of actions may also function as modifiers (relative clauses; 123). Other relative clause forms require a prefix (unglossed; see the examples on 121, 127). Words denoting properties, unlike those denoting actions, do not require -°*iq* to function as modifiers, although it is also found (136–37). Modification by roots denoting objects requires either a possessive construction or the suffix *i:c* as an adjectivalizer (139), thereby distinguishing those roots from roots denoting properties. Any lexical root may be predicated, as in Salishan, but nominal roots can take only the durative aspect and in particular are restricted to the nonfuture tenses (140–41).[7] Thus, Makah appears to be a quite well-behaved language with respect to syntactic category membership.

Finding grammatical behavior that distinguishes the putative syntactic categories is not the real problem in identifying "nouns" and "verbs" in the Salishan and Wakashan languages—in fact, in any language. As Jacobsen has demonstrated, that is possible even in the most intractable-seeming languages. The real problem is deciding what kind of grammatical evidence justifies distinguishing the major categories "noun" and "verb," as Jacobsen argues, and what kind of evidence would merely support, say, the existence of two subclasses of a major category "predicate," as Kuipers and Kinkade would have it. After all, grammatical evidence can distinguish count nouns from mass nouns in English or stative verbs from processual verbs, but no grammarian treats these as major categories. The genuine difficulty is developing a language-independent criterion for distinguishing grammatical criteria for subclasses from grammatical criteria for major syntactic categories. The remainder of this chapter presents a solution to this problem, once I have discussed a similar solution to this problem proposed recently by Hopper and Thompson (1984).

Hopper and Thompson make an explicit attempt to link specific grammatical phenomena to a universal definition of "noun" and "verb" in a cross-linguistically uniform fashion. They proceed from the fact that the grammatical inflections and syntactic constructions that are used in internal analyses of syntactic category membership possess a meaning or discourse function, and they argue that the meanings or discourse functions of the grammatical criteria are associated with two larger discourse functions, "discourse-manipulable participant" and "reported event," that they identify with "noun" and "verb," respectively. (Actually, these descriptions combine both semantic characteristics [participant and event] and discourse functional ones ["discourse manipulable and "reported"]; see below.) The grammatical constructions and lexical classes that Hopper and Thompson analyze as non-prototypical instances of each discourse function are as follows:

Discourse-manipulable participant ("noun"):
- Nonreferential constructions:
  - Incorporation of patient
  - Incorporation of oblique
  - Compounding
  - Predicate nominals
  - Nominals in the scope of negation
- Nonmanipulable participants:
  - Anaphora: pragmatically nonreferential NPs, pronouns
  - Body part nouns

Reported event ("verb"):
- Statives:
  - Predicate adjectives
  - Attribution
  - Existential clauses
  - Copula clauses

Irrealis clauses
Negative clauses
Serial verbs
Compound verbs
Dependent clauses:
- Verb functioning as noun ("nominalizations")
- Relative clauses
- Purpose clauses
- "Absolute" construction
- Chaining construction
- Bound clauses ("complements")

Somewhat surprisingly, Hopper and Thompson appear to deny any but the loosest connection between the array of grammatical properties that they associate with "noun" and "verb" and semantic classes of lexical roots. They do state that "every language has roots whose semantic content makes them more likely to be realized as N's than V's, and other roots for which the reverse is true" (Hopper and Thompson 1984:744), and suggest that prototypical Ns are "visible (tangible, etc.) object[s]" and that properties of prototypical Vs "might similarly be considered to be visibility, movement (kinesis), and effectiveness" (707–8); but these are only suggestions. Instead, they conclude the article with the following statement:

> We should like to conclude, however, by suggesting that linguistic forms are in principle to be considered as LACKING CATEGORIALITY completely unless nounhood or verbhood is forced on them by their discourse functions. To the extent that forms can be said to have an apriori existence outside of discourse, they are characterizable as ACATEGORIAL; i.e. their categorical classification is irrelevant. Categoriality—the realization of a form as either a N or a V—is imposed on the form by discourse. Yet we have also seen that the noun/verb distinction is apparently universal: there seem to be no languages in which all stems are indifferently capable of receiving all morphology appropriate for both N's and V's. This suggests that the continua which in principle begin with acategoriality, and which end with fully implemented nounhood or fully implemented verbhood, are already partly traversed for most forms. In other words, most forms begin with a propensity or predisposition to become N's or V's; and often this momentum can be reversed by only special morphology. It nonetheless re-

> mains true that this predisposition is only a latent one, which will not be manifested unless there is pressure from the discourse for this to occur. In other words, far from being "given" aprioristically for us to build sentences out of, the categories of N and V actually manifest themselves only when the discourse requires it. [747]

It appears from this quotation that Hopper and Thompson wish to deny that there is any relation between lexical semantic category and syntactic (i.e., discourse functional) category membership, although they admit that there exists evidence for it.

Closer examination of the typological evidence that Hopper and Thompson use to support their position reveals why they do not emphasize the relation between lexical category membership ("noun" or "verb") and discourse function. Most—though not all—of the evidence that they provide involves CATEGORIALITY, that is, the functioning of a morpheme (root) as an independent syntactic unit. In fact, Hopper and Thompson repeatedly refer to their evidence as manifesting higher or lower categoriality, period, not higher or lower category membership as "noun" or "verb." Morphemes that are lower in categoriality tend to lose their status as independent syntactic units, including any inflections associated with those units, and in particular become compounded or incorporated to adjacent syntactic units. This accounts for incorporation of patients (Hopper and Thompson 1984: 711–13) and obliques (713–14), for standard noun-compounding phenomena (714–15), and also for compound verbs (735–37) and some examples of serial verbs (734–35). In these instances, it is not the case that the members of the compound form (noun-noun, noun-verb, or verb-verb) lose their nominal or verbal character so much as they lose their character as autonomous syntactic units. Instead, the compound as a whole describes a single conceptual unit (or, as Hopper and Thompson would put it, a discourse unit).[8]

These are all examples of almost completely decategorialized noun and verb roots. In addition, there is what may be called "partial" decategorialization, in which the root affected becomes dependent on a root that syntactically ought to be in a parallel position. This is generally the case in complex sentences, in which there are several verbs expressing some sequential or simultaneous set of events; one verb is "fully" categorial (the main verb), while the other verbs are expressed as dependents (subordinate clauses of various types) on the main verb. The dependent verbs are "partially" decategorialized: either they lack some or all of the main verbal inflections, or they are rendered as participles and nominalizations. In the former case, the dependent verb forms lose their general categorial character, not just their purely verbal character. In the latter case, not only do the forms lose their verbal character, but they also gain nominal character (e.g., the ability to allow case endings or adpositions; 739, 741)—but this fact is not accounted for by Hopper and Thompson's analysis. This type of partial decategorialization accounts for most of the various phenomena described by Hopper and Thompson under the rubric "dependent clauses" (739–44): purpose clauses, the "absolute" construction, chaining constructions, and bound clauses (cf. Givón 1980).

There are also a number of nominal phenomena that Hopper and Thompson describe that appear to be examples of partial decategorialization. Nouns referring to body parts tend to be incorporated, the surest test of the loss of independent syntactic status (1984 : 724). In other languages, the body part term is not incorporated outright, but it is stripped of any autonomous syntactic status—inflections and modifiers—and the possessor of the body part usurps its syntactic roles ("possessor ascension"). Again, this represents more a loss of categoriality than a loss of nominality. Likewise, nonreferential nominals in the scope of negation (717) and semantically referential but pragmatically nonreferential nominals (i.e., those mentioned once but not referred to again, as in *I read the paper* [only mention] *and went to bed;* 717–24) often lack characteristic noun markers if the language possesses them, and these too may be examples of the loss of categoriality, not the loss of nominality.

As Hopper and Thompson argue, the more distant the function of the noun root from presenting a new participant in the discourse and the more distant the function of the verb from reporting an actual event, the more likely the root is to lose its categoriality. Hopper and Thompson's typological evidence supports this position (see also Myhill 1988). Hopper and Thompson employ the functional-typological method in their analysis, using typological structural evidence and functional external evidence. That is, they (a) identify parallel structural elements across languages by functional means (i.e., what discourse [or semantic] function the morpheme, inflection, or construction performs); (b) discover a cross-linguistic pattern that forms a typological scale (continuum, cline, gradient, to cite synonymous terms used in the literature); and (c) use this to propose a general definition of "independent syntactic unit" (i.e., highly categorial root).[9]

But categoriality per se does not specify what category a lexical root is likely to appear in, and loss of categoriality is not necessarily the same as loss of nominal or verbal character. Hopper and Thompson's definitions for "noun" and "verb" are very similar discourse functionally: they both describe the presentation of a new and important or salient piece of information into the discourse, either a participant or an event (see 3.2.3). The crucial distinction between "noun" and "verb" in their "discourse-functional" definition remains a basically semantic one: "participant" or "(actual) event." In fact, some of their arguments to justify the degree of categoriality are based on the semantic part of the definition of "verb": stative constructions are low in categoriality because they are not events (processes), a semantic criterion, and purpose clauses, irrealis, and negative verb types are low in categoriality because they do not represent actual events. The problem of distinguishing (highly categorial) nouns from verbs, as opposed to distinguishing high-categorial from low-categorial syntactic units, remains.

This is most evident in Hopper and Thompon's remarks on the remaining evidence that they provide for categoriality, predicate nominals, predicate adjectives, nominalizations, and relative clauses (attributive verbs), all of which display behavior that represents genuine evidence for the noun-verb distinction.[10] Hopper and Thompson discuss the fact that predicate nominals do not display the characteristic inflections of nouns. However, in many languages, predicate nominals display the characteristic inflections of verbs, which has been taken by Kinkade, Kuipers, and others to be evidence of the absence of the noun-verb distinction. Hopper and Thompson call this "incorporation of the nominal root into the verbal affix" (Hopper and Thompson 1984 : 717); however, there is no reason to accept this analysis instead of the simpler one that the predicate nominal has acquired some verbal characteristics as well as losing most nominal ones. Likewise, Hopper and Thompson observe that a nominalized verb, as well as losing many verbal characteristics, gains nominal ones (738, 739, 741). Although Hopper and Thompson provide explanations for why lexical items lose nominal or verbal grammatical properties, they do not provide an explanation within their model as to why they would acquire the opposite grammatical properties in certain circumstances.[11]

At one significant point, however, Hopper and Thompson do suggest an explanation as to why nominalizations acquire nominal characteristics: "the function of [verbal] nominalizations is to REFER TO EVENTS. . . . A form referring to an event taken as an entity is functioning neither to report an event nor to refer to a manipulable entity; but it has elements of both" (746). Although Hopper and Thompson do not pursue this reasoning, this is indeed the correct line of attack on the noun-verb problem.[12] What is now necessary is to uncover the correct combination of typological structural factors that will justify such an analysis.

2.2 The Basic Correlations and Typological Markedness

Let us return to the traditional grammar definitions of the syntactic categories, elaborated and supported by Dixon's analysis for adjectives. As I pointed out, the traditional definitions for the major syntactic categories are empirically inadequate at first glance: the noun *motion* denotes an action as much as does the verb *move,* and the noun *whiteness* denotes a property as much as does the adjective *white.* Nevertheless, the commonsense ontology underlying the traditional definitions has some intuitive basis and in fact forms the basis of a cross-linguistic pattern that will identify the major syntactic categories.

Two things can be observed about the aforementioned putative counterexamples to the traditional semantic definition. First, the forms *motion* and *whiteness* are used when the speaker wants to REFER to an action or property itself rather than to predicate it or modify an already-named object in some way. It is important to distinguish the action of referring from denotation. The action of referring is a property of the discourse, not the semantics (i.e., the thing referred to): it is a possible function of a word in the utterance. Denotation, on the other hand, is intended to signify a relation between a word (i.e., a string of sounds) and the entity or class of entities that it names (cf. Langacker 1987a: 11–12).[13] Second, the forms *motion* and *whiteness* are morphologically complex compared to both the "real" noun *dog* and the verb *move* and the adjective *white* from which they are respectively derived: the complex forms consist of an additional nonzero morpheme.

The pattern described in the past paragraph can be made sense of by introducing the concept that Schachter and others call syntactic "function"—meaning the role that a constituent plays in the clause. These functions can be identified in all languages and thus have the potential to provide a universal basis for the major syntactic categories. The exact nature of the syntactic functions is actually quite complex, and fuller discussion will be reserved for chapter 3. For now, it will suffice to say that I will argue that syntactic functions (which, incidentally, play little role in the formal structure of a phrase-structure theory of syntax except as a by-product of the node labels[14])—have an external basis. Each syntactic function is a propositional speech act (Searle 1969) that organizes the information denoted by the lexical roots for communication and thereby conceptualizes it in a certain way (for detailed discussion, see 3.2.2). For now, I will describe these as PRAGMATIC FUNCTIONS; the reader should keep in mind that this is not a structural linguistic category but an externally motivated one. The externally defined function of a surface nominal form is REFER-

ENCE: that is, to get the hearer to identify an entity as what the speaker is talking *about.*

Turning to the other major syntactic category that is certainly universal, verbs, one finds that a similar situation holds in English. Consider treating things and properties as "verbs." This is traditionally named PREDICATION, corresponding to an externally defined function, namely, what the speaker intends to *say about* what he is talking about (the referent). While the morphology of the roots that denote objects and properties in English does not change when the concepts that they denote are predicated, the roots do require the support of the copula *be,* which carries the relevant verbal inflections. Predicated actions (i.e., "normal" verbs), on the other hand, do not require a copula. Again, the predication of things and properties in English is characterized by the presence of an additional morpheme, albeit one that is phonologically independent from the root. The predication of actions, on the other hand, is not.

Finally, turning to the last major syntactic category, adjectives, one finds a similar grammatical pattern. The externally defined function relevant here is MODIFICATION. The definition of this function is less obvious than those for reference and predication. Modification appears to be largely an accessory function to reference and predication: restrictive modification helps fix the identity of what one is talking about (reference) by narrowing the description, while nonrestrictive modification provides a secondary comment (predication) on the head that it modifies, in addition to the main predication. Nevertheless, when "atypical" semantic types function as modifiers, their surface morphosyntax displays essentially the same pattern that we have observed with respect to reference and predication.

Verbs, that is, roots denoting actions, require an additional morpheme when used for modification. This morpheme may be a bound affix, as in present participles like *the sleeping child* or passive participles like *the broken glass.* Or it may be a phonologically relatively free form, as in relative clause constructions such as *the child who was sleeping (on the couch),* where a finite predicate form is syntactically subordinated to a nominal head by some means, for example, the presence of a relativizer or relative pronoun and the altered word order in which the head precedes the other elements of the sentence regardless of its normal place in a main clause predication.

In the case of nouns, that is, lexical items, denoting objects, functioning as modifiers, a number of possibilities occur. All but one require the presence of an additional morpheme. Morphological affixation to the root may occur, such as in the denominal adjective *vehicular.*[15] The usual morphosyntactic means for expressing adnominal modification, however, is some sort of genitive construction. English has two genitives, both of which are morphosyntactically marked: the prehead genitive formed with the *-'s* clitic and the posthead genitive formed with the preposition *of*. Also, nouns can function as posthead modifiers with a large array of other prepositions as well, such as *for, with, in, by*, and so on. In all these cases, modification by lexical roots denoting objects requires nonzero morphemes not required by "adjectives" (lexical roots denoting properties).

The English examples that I have discussed so far are summarized in table 2.1, with the major semantic classes in rows and the "syntactic" functions in columns.

TABLE 2.1 *English Examples of Marked and Unmarked Correlations*

	Reference	**Modification**	**Predication**
Objects	vehicle	vehicle*'s*, vehicul*ar*, *of/in/etc.* the vehicle	*be* a/the vehicle
Properties	white*ness*	white	*be* white
Actions	destruc*tion*, *to* destroy	destroy*ing*, destroy*ed*	destroy

As the table title indicates, the pattern in grammatical structure observed here is MARKEDNESS, in the classical Prague School sense developed by Trubetzkoy, Jakobson, and Greenberg. However, this pattern is far more complex than the original conception of markedness. The original conception of markedness involved a single grammatical parameter, such as grammatical number, with two values, for example, singular and plural. The pattern in the table involves two independent grammatical parameters, lexical semantic class and "syntactic" function, each of which possesses three values rather than two. Hence, a modification of classical marking theory is required to allow us to use the traditional criteria of markedness for the analysis of syntactic categories.

The modifications to classical marking theory refine the grammatical criteria used to define typological markedness patterns and connect markedness patterns to typological hierarchies, such as the animacy hierarchy (Silverstein 1976; Dixon 1979) and the grammatical relations or "accessibility" hierarchy (Keenan and Comrie 1977). The model of typological markedness will be outlined in the remainder of this section and then applied to the problem of a cross-linguistic definition of syntactic categories in the remainder of this chapter (for a detailed discussion of the model, see Croft 1990b).

First, the concept of markedness must be able to handle multi-valued categories, and cross-category correlations. Classical marking theory defines the marked-unmarked relation as a single-category, absolute relation. If, for example, one argues that the category value "plural" is marked with respect to "singular," then one is hypothesizing that "plural" is marked in an absolute sense and that the value "plural" will be marked in every context. Formally, one can represent the markedness pattern of paradigmatic elements of a category as privileged members of a single set, the set of members of a grammatical category:

$C = \{u, m\}$ or $C = \{u, m_1, m_2, \ldots\}$
($u, m_1, m_2, \ldots$ elements of a category C).

However, "plural" behaves like the unmarked member of the category of number in comparison to "dual," leading to a hierarchy singular < plural < dual (where $X < Y$ is to be read 'X is unmarked relative to Y'). In order to accommodate hierarchical patterns such as this one, one must relax the absolute markedness constraint so that "plural" is marked only relative to "singular." This allows us to be able to state that "plural" is unmarked relative to "dual" or, more generally, that there is a HIERARCHY of values in the category of number singular < plural < dual. Formally, this is represented by a (possibly partial) ordering of the elements of the category:

$C = \{m_1 < m_2, m_3 < m_4 < \ldots\}$
(<: partial ordering so that m_1 is less marked than m_1, etc.).

The formal description given here is in the familiar form of an implicational hierarchy: given some grammatical phenomenon, one can read the hierarchy from right to left to obtain a series of implicational universals. This relation between markedness and implicational universals is not accidental and has been discussed by Greenberg (1966a:21–22). This extension to marking theory is able to characterize the typological evidence for the principal grammatical hierarchies (number, animacy, grammatical relations, etc.; see Croft 1990b, chap. 5).

The second extension to markedness involves allowing a value in a category to vary in its markedness relative to a value in some other category. In the case of the grammatical category of number, it has been observed that some lexical semantic classes of nouns in some languages have unmarked plurals (called "collective") and marked singulars ("singulative"), for example, Turkana *ŋι-ɲa*\` 'grass'/*ɛ-ɲa-ìt* 'blade of grass' (Dimmendaal 1983:228; note that, in English as well, the "plural"—mass—form is unmarked and the "singular"—partitive—requires two additional morphemes). That is to say, the markedness pattern for singular-plural depends on the lexical semantic class of noun involved; it can be reversed, as in the collective-singulative examples. This phenomenon has been called "markedness assimilation" (Andersen 1968), "local markedness" (Tiersma 1982), "marking reversal" (Witkowski and Brown 1983), and "natural correlation" (Croft 1983, 1988). The unmarked correlation corresponds to a typological prototype (see Croft 1990b, chap. 6). Formally, this can be represented as sets of ordered *n*-tuples of correlated members of different categories:

Category	Values
A	*a b*
B	*j k*
C	*x y*

⟨*a,j,x*⟩,⟨*b,k,y*⟩: unmarked (prototypical) correlations,
⟨*a,k,y*⟩,⟨*b,k,x*⟩, etc.: marked correlations.

The cases of simple markedness and hierarchies discussed above occur when there is no such markedness relation across categories.

The pattern of relation among lexical semantic classes and pragmatic functions is one of the most complex types, a three-way correlation between two parameters. There is an unmarked correlation between the semantic class of object and the function of reference so that a word denoting an object is unmarked in the function of reference but marked in the other functions. A similar pattern holds between properties and modification and between actions and predication. We may summarize the prototypical correlations suggested by the English examples in table 2.2.

TABLE 2.2 *Prototypical Correlations of Syntactic Categories*

	Syntactic Category		
	Noun	*Adjective*	*Verb*
Semantic class	Object	Property	Action
Pragmatic function	Reference	Modification	Predication

Once the concept of markedness is modified to accommodate these more complex patterns of relations among values of grammatical categories, it can be used to analyze complex phenomena such as the problem of a cross-linguistic definition for the major syntactic categories. In particular, markedness, as typologically interpreted, allows us to define which structural criteria for distinguishing syntactic categories are valid for the cross-linguistic universality of syntactic categories—namely, the markedness criteria—and which are not. In other words, marking theory allows us to use language-specific grammatical criteria to support (or reject) universal hypotheses.

The theory of markedness is based on the discovery that paradigmatic members of the same grammatical category have asymmetrical linguistic properties. The most exhaustive discussion of the linguistic properties relevant to markedness in both phonology and morphosyntax is to be found in Greenberg 1966a. The markedness properties discussed by Greenberg are as follows (P indicates a phonological property, S a syntactic one; page references are to Greenberg 1966a):[16]

Phonology

P1. In neutralized contexts, the unmarked value is realized, not the marked one (12–13).

P2. In text counts, the unmarked value has at least as great a frequency as the marked value (14).

P3. The unmarked value has at least as wide a distribution across phonological environments as the marked value (21).

P4. The unmarked value has at least as great a variety of allophonic variants as the marked value (21).

P5. There are at least as many phonemes with the unmarked feature as the number of phonemes with the marked feature (21–22).

Morphosyntax

S1. The surface realization of the unmarked versus the marked value is frequently that of zero versus nonzero morpheme (more generally, the realization of the marked value will involve at least as many morphemes as the realization of the unmarked value) (26–27).

S2. The marked member will display syncretization of its inflectional possibilities with respect to the unmarked member (i.e., there will be at least as many distinct forms in the paradigm with the unmarked value as in the paradigm with the marked value) (27).

S3. The form that normally refers to the unmarked value will refer to either value in certain contexts ("facultative" use); the "par excellence" use of the unmarked term for the supercategory including the marked and unmarked term (e.g., *man*) may also be included here (28, 25).
S4. In certain grammatical environments, only the unmarked value will appear (contextual neutralization) (28–29).
S5. An unmarked form will have at least as many allomorphs or paradigmatic irregularities as the marked form (29).
S6. An unmarked form will display at least as great a range of grammatical behavior as the marked form (defectivation) (29–30).
S7. The plural form of the unmarked gender is used to refer to collections consisting of objects of both genders ("dominance"—grammatical number only) (30–31).
S8. In text counts, the unmarked value will be at least as frequent as the marked value (31).

The array of phonological and morphosyntactic properties that are discussed by Greenberg can be analyzed as representing the four criteria of markedness listed in table 2.3 (the criteria are discussed in detail in Croft 1990b, chap. 4).

TABLE 2.3 *Standard Criteria for Markedness (based on Greenberg 1966a)*

	Phonology	**Morphosyntax**
Structural	(See below)	Zero value (S1)
Behavioral		
Inflectional	No. of phonemes (P5) No. of allophones (P4)	Syncretization (S2) No. of allomorphs (S5) Defectivation (S6)
Distributional	No. of environments (P3)	(Not discussed by Greenberg)
Frequency	Frequency (P2)	Frequency (S8)
Neutral value	Neutralization (P1)	Facultative use (S3) Contextual neutrality (S4) "Dominance" (S7)

The evidence for syntactic category membership of English lexical items presented in this section consists of manifestations of the structural criterion of markedness. All the marked combinations of semantic class and pragmatic functions are characterized by the presence of an additional morpheme (or morphemes) indicating the—marked—pragmatic function; I will call this FUNCTION-INDICATING MORPHOSYNTAX. The unmarked combinations are characterized by the lack of function-indicating morphosyntax associated with the lexical roots.

The presence of (nonzero) function-indicating morphosyntax in certain combinations of lexical semantic class and pragmatic function but not in others is POSITIVE evidence for the marked status of the former with respect to the latter. In many cases, however, there is no function-indicating morphosyntax even for the marked combinations. For example, English employs the "complex nominal" construction, which involves a zero-marked noun root functioning as a modifier: *university housing, state budget.* These examples are analogous to the case of languages that do not use a morpheme for the plural as opposed to the singular, so that both are represented by the bare root, as in Chinese *shū* 'book'/*shū* 'books' (Li and Thompson 1981 : 11).[17] Such languages as Chinese do not represent counterexamples to the hypothesis that, *typologically,* the plural is more marked than the singular. The typological pattern of markedness, like other typological patterns, represents a constraint on variation, so that some though not all language types are predicted to exist. For example, the implicational universal "If a language has Adjective-Noun (AN) word order, then it has Numeral-Noun (NumN) word order" (Greenberg 1966b : 86) does not exclude the existence of languages with NA and NumN word orders; it excludes only the existence of languages with AN and NNum word orders. Likewise, the structural criterion of markedness can be phrased as an implicational universal roughly as follows: "If a language uses a zero form for plural, then it will use a zero form for a singular," or, in the noun modifier example, "If a language uses zero function-indicating morphosyntax for lexical roots denoting objects in the pragmatic function of modification, then it will also use zero function-indicating morphosyntax for such roots in the pragmatic function of reference."[18] The language type excluded by the typological structural criterion of markedness is a language that uses nonzero function-indicating morphosyntax for lexical roots denoting objects in the pragmatic functon of reference but zero function-indicating morphosyntax for such roots in modification. This would constitute genuinely NEGATIVE evidence for the markedness pattern linking roots denoting objects and the pragmatic function of reference. The example of English zero-marked complex nominals in the modification function, combined with the zero-marked nouns in the reference function, I will call NEUTRAL evidence.

The behavioral criterion of typological markedness is the most important, but also the most complex, since it is covert, unlike the structural criterion. In general, it refers to the range of morphosyntactic behavior that the value in question has, the marked member having a smaller range of morphosyntactic behavior than the unmarked member. The behavioral criterion can be roughly divided into two types: ability to take various inflections (morphology) and ability to occur in various contexts (syntax; this distinction is only as clear as that between morphology and syntax, i.e., not very). For example, English stative verbs are marked because they do not allow the progressive forms.[19] This example can also be interpreted as a syntactic distributional fact—stative verbs do not fit in the *be* __*-ing* construction. A more "purely" syntactic fact of behavioral markedness, for example, is that mass nouns cannot appear directly after numerals or that sentential complements cannot usually be clefted (**It was that Mary left that John was surprised*).

The structural and behavioral criteria of markedness both pertain to grammatical structure. The frequency criterion, on the other hand, differs in that it pertains to the frequency of marked and unmarked members in texts. The frequency criterion states that the unmarked member will be at least as common in text counts as the marked member. For example, if the singular noun is less marked than the plural noun, then it is expected to occur more frequently in texts than the plural, as is indeed the case (Greenberg 1966a: 32).

The neutral value criterion appears to be the most tenuous one for evaluating markedness. The neutral value criterion is different from the textual, structural, and behavioral criteria in nature. The latter three all involve a relative quantitative measure of the grammatical properties of the marked and unmarked term: the marked member is expressed by at least as many morphemes as the unmarked member; the unmarked member can occur with at least as many inflectional distinctions and in at least as many syntactic contexts as the marked member, and the unmarked member is textually at least as frequent as the marked member. The neutral value criterion, on the other hand, cannot be so relativized: either the neutral value is the unmarked one or not. There are difficulties involved in defining neutralization and determining its relation to the other criterion, and it also is empirically at odds with the other criteria. For example, English *they* is used to refer to unidentified individuals regardless of number, suggesting that the plural is the neutral (unmarked) value, although the behavioral criterion (lack of gender distinctions) suggests that it is the marked value. These considerations suggest that the neutral value criterion should be excluded from the primary properties of markedness (see Croft 1990b, sec. 4.3.4).

Typological markedness involves the convergence of the structural, behavioral, and textual criteria of markedness in a cross-linguistic pattern in which only positive and neutral evidence, not negative evidence, is observed. It is normally taken to be the case that the empirical evidence for typological markedness patterns need find only positive evidence of some grammatical type (structural or behavioral) in at least some languages of the world. However, the examination of behavioral evidence where available often reveals positive evidence for markedness patterns in languages that do not display positive evidence for structural markedness. For example, there is no overt structural evidence to distinguish the markedness of stative verbs as opposed to process verbs in English, but there is behavioral evidence (inability to occur in the progressive, at least not without a significant change of meaning). Also, Jacobsen's argument for distinguishing the categories "noun" and "verb" in Nootkan, discussed in 2.1, is essentially a demonstration that nouns (lexical roots denoting objects) are behaviorally marked as predicates compared to verbs (lexical roots denoting actions). If behavioral evidence is as powerful as these examples suggest, one might propose a stronger claim: that *all* languages will display some positive evidence for a typological pattern—if not structural evidence, then behavioral evidence.

Typological markedness patterns associated with the pragmatic functions allow us to distinguish grammatical evidence supporting major category status from grammatical evidence that indicates only grammatical subclasses. Simple distributional facts indicate only grammatical subclasses, for instance, the various nominal declension classes and verbal conjugation classes of Latin. Of course, in some cases grammatical subclasses based on distributional facts coincide with major category boundaries. For example, in Yagaria predicate nominals can be distinguished from predicated verbs by the use of a different negative morpheme, *-opa* instead of *a'-*:

"Verbal" negative predicates (Renck 1975:84):

(7) *ge a- su -d -u -e*
word NEG- say -PAST -1SG -INDIC
'I did not speak.'

'Nominal' negative predicates (Renck 1975:47):

(8) *de* *-opa*
man -NEG
'It is not a man.'

Thus, one can set up two subclasses of lexical roots in Yagaria, one that uses *a*'- in predicate negation and one that uses *-opa*. Although this coincides with the noun-verb major category distinction in Yagaria, it is not in itself evidence for the noun-verb distinction as a manifestation of the universal categories noun and verb because there is no structural markedness relation: both constructions use the same number of morphemes to indicate (negative) predication, namely, one. On the other hand, the lack of verbal inflectional morphemes in the negative construction with *-opa* is (positive behavioral) evidence for the markedness pattern (roots denoting objects are more marked as predicates than roots denoting actions).

In general, language-internal distributional evidence can provide evidence only for language-particular subclasses of lexical items. Only if the distributional evidence also takes part in typological markedness patterns, or other typological patterns, can it provide evidence for universal grammatical categories. Thus, in the analysis of the universal categories noun, adjective, and verb proposed here, only if the distributional evidence relating to the pragmatic functions of reference, predication, and modification exhibits typological markedness patterns does it provide evidence for the major syntactic categories as grammatical universals.

The hypothesis of this chapter is that all languages will display some positive evidence in favor of the markedness patterns that establish the universal syntactic categories noun, verb, and adjective. In the following two sections, I will describe the structural and behavioral markedness patterns for the major syntactic categories noun, verb, and adjective that should be identifiable across languages. In support of the hypothesis, I conducted a survey of the evidence for syntactic category membership in twelve languages: English (SVO, Indo-European), Turkish (SOV, Altaic; Lewis 1967), Turkana (VSO, Nilo-Saharan; Dimmendaal 1983), Swahili (SVO, Congo-Kordofanian; Ashton 1944), Georgian (SOV, Kartvelian; Aronson 1982), Chinese (SVO, Sino-Tibetan; Chao 1968; Li and Thompson 1981; Norman 1988), Acehnese (SVO, Western Austronesian; Durie 1985), Woleaian (SVO, Eastern Austronesian; Sohn 1975; Sohn and Tawerilmang 1976), Yagaria (SOV, Indo-Pacific/Papuan; Renck 1975), Diyari (free, Australian; Austin 1981), Lakhota/Dakota (SOV/free, Siouan; Buechel

1939; Boas and Deloria 1941) and Quiché (VOS, Mayan; Mondloch 1978). These languages are areally, genetically, and typologically diverse. However, most of them were chosen because they have been supposed to present difficulties in determining syntactic category membership, particularly for adjectives.[20] In all these languages, I was able to find positive markedness evidence that established the existence of the major categories noun, verb, and adjective (although there were some gaps in the data). In addition, I performed an in-depth study of Russian lexical roots for further evidence of structural markedness, and textual frequency studies of Quiché (VOS, Mayan), Nguna (SVO, Melanesian), Soddo (SOV, Semitic), and Ute (free, Uto-Aztecan) in order to investigate the textual criterion of markedness for the major syntactic categories.

2.3 Structural Markedness and the Semantic Prototypes

In the preceding section, I presented positive evidence of the predicted structural markedness pattern for the various combinations of lexical semantic class and pragmatic function in English. The words that I have selected as examples are intended to be representative of roots denoting objects, properties, and actions. In fact, the informal definitions of "objects," "properties," and "actions" are used in virtually every grammatical description of a human language for describing the characteristic properties of nouns, adjectives, and verbs, respectively. In other words, the traditional semantic account of syntactic categories is partly correct; it correctly identifies which lexical semantic classes will be unmarked for each pragmatic function. However, it is necessary to firm up traditional grammatical intuition with a more thorough empirical study and more precise semantic definitions of "object," "property," and "action." In this section, I will present more precise definitions of the semantic classes and describe the results of a detailed empirical study of Russian lexical roots (Croft 1984, 1986) as well as the data from the twelve-language study.

The semantic definitions are the result of the identification of semantic prototypes for the major syntactic categories based on observations of a large number of languages regarding structural and behavioral markedness patterns. The semantic properties described here are not particularly surprising, virtually all of them having already been identified as possessing major grammatical significance. However, the definitions presented here will differ in some details from previously established definitions. The major semantic properties are valency, stativity, persistence, and gradability.

Valency is defined here as inherent relationality. A concept is inherently relational if its existence or presence requires the existence or presence of another entity. I will use the term ARGUMENT to refer to the additional entity or entities implied by the inherently relational entity. For example, *hit* is inherently relational because its existence requires the existence of two entities, the hitter and the object hit.[21] Likewise, *red* is inherently relational because its existence requires the existence of another entity, namely, the object that possesses the property.[22]

On this account, however, *man* is not relational: the existence of a man does not imply the existence of another entity, in the way that the existence of an instance of hitting or of redness does. As Langacker puts it: "One cannot conceptualize the [FIND] relationship without conceptualizing the two things functioning as trajector and landmark of that relation . . . but it is perfectly possible to conceptualize a man or a cat without mentally setting it in a relation with some external object" (Langacker 1988a: 103).

Thus, in terms of inherent relationality, the valency of common nouns is zero. This differs from the way that nouns are usually analyzed in the linguistic and philosophical literature, in which nouns have a valency of one. The standard analysis is based on the predicate nominal construction, translating *John is a man* as *Man(John)*. However, the relation between the predicate and the "argument" in this analysis is one of class inclusion (the individual John belongs to the class or category "man"), not to any sort of relationality as defined above. As will be seen below, defining valency consistently as inherent relationality will provide some important insights into the nature of the relation between nouns, verbs, and adjectives.

The lexical semantic class used to define prototypical adjectives consists of concepts with a valency of one, which fits Dixon's observations regarding the core adjectival concepts. (In general, the semantic definition for adjectives will be based on Dixon's [1977] typological study of "core" or "prototypical" adjectives.) Verbs, on the other hand, are represented by concepts possessing a valency of one, two, or more. Thus, there is overlap between the classes of verb and adjective in terms of valency alone; we must turn to the second semantic property to distinguish core verbs from core adjectives.

The second semantic property used to define the categories is STATIVITY, that is, the aspectual distinction between states and processes. This category represents the presence of absence of change over time in the state of affairs described by the concept. One can distinguish prototypical verbs with a valency of one from prototypical adjectives, in that the former are processes while the latter are states. This distinction also identifies prototypical nouns as stative.

The third semantic property is PERSISTENCE. This category is closely related to stativity but is not identical to it. Persistence describes how long the process or state is likely to last over time; processes or states can be persistent or transitory. This semantic feature has been identified by Carlson (1979) as the source of the difference in acceptability between the following two generic sentences:

(9) *Elephants are gray.*

(10) **Elephants are sick.*

Predicates requiring the copula can be divided into those that allow a generic bare plural subject and those that prohibit it.[23] Carlson labeled the former "object-level predicates" and the latter "stage-level predicates." The intuition that underlies the distinction is permanent versus transitory presence of the entity described by the concept. By this intuitive definition, prototypical verbs should be transitory. Verbal predicates do occur with generic subjects, as in *Bats fly at night,* but the verb must be interpreted generically (i.e., habitually) in those contexts. Carlson argues that ordinary verbal predicates (those not using the copula) with generic bare plural subjects are stage-level predicates that have been "converted" to object-level predicates by virtue of the habitual interpretation that is required of them.

Stativity and persistence have generally been conflated in the past because it so happens that they coincide very closely: all processes are transitory.[24] For example, Givón (1979:320–22) proposes a concept of "time-stability" for an external basis to syntactic categories that appears to be a combination of Aktionsart (change) and predicate level (transitoriness) since he contrasts types "that change slowly over time" with those "which involve rapid change" (Givón 1979:321). On the other hand, on the next page (322) he equates "more time-stable" with "permanent" and "less time-stable" with "temporary."

Unfortunately, Carlson's test is not completely accurate. His test yields those predicates that help define the generic type. These are always persistent properties (excluding habitual actions, of course), but not all persistent properties define the generic type. For instance, my binder may be green, and that is certainly not a transitory property of my binder, but it is not a generic property of binders. Carlson's test would fail for this property (**Binders are green*), but that contradicts our intuitions. A more suitable linguistic-semantic criterion for persistence needs to be formulated. One possibility is iterability: iteration is incompatible with the description of a persisting concept but acceptable with a transitory one since the transitory one can reasonably be expected to occur again. This test yields results that better fit the intuitive definition of persistent vesus transitory:[25]

(11) *John is always sick.*

(12) *John is always eating potato chips.*

(13) **John is always tall.*

The fourth major semantic property is GRADABILITY: if the entity denoted by the concept can be manifested in degrees (such as height, coldness, etc.), then the concept is gradable, otherwise not. Prototypical adjectives are gradable, while prototypical nouns and verbs are not.

To summarize, the semantic characteristics that are used to identify the lexical semantic categories of objects, properties, and actions are given in table 2.4.

TABLE 2.4 *Semantic Properties of Prototypical Lexical Classes*

	Objects	**Properties**	**Actions**
Valency	0	1	≥1
Stativity	state	state	process
Persistence	persistent	persistent	transitory
Gradability	nongradable	gradable	nongradable

The use of the term "prototypical" implies that the definitions of objects, properties, and actions provided here do not exhaustively classify the lexicon. For instance, mass nouns such as *syrup,* states such as *sick,* and nonrelational processes such as *rain* do not fall into any of the three categories by these definitions. I assume that the unmarked character of the three lexical semantic classes will be found only in the core of each category. Other lexical semantic classes will not display a universal (i.e., cross-linguistically valid) markedness pattern that would definitely place them into the three major syntactic categories. This is in keeping with other typological research that has indicated that unmarked members of grammatical categories such as "transitive clause" (Hopper and Thompson 1980, 1982) are restricted to a small core set of semantically (and/or pragmatically) defined types. However, as will be seen in the Russian lexicon study, the definitions provided above do cover a majority of the lexicon of basic vocabulary.

The structural markedness hypothesis was tested on the basic vocabulary of Russian (Croft 1984). An index of all the Russian lexical roots in Wolkonsky and Poltoratzky (1961) was made with a detailed semantic classification that allows one to identify which semantic classes belong to which prototype (if any). This classification differs from most other semantic classifications of the lexicon by being based primarily on semantic properties that are directly relevant to morphosyntactic behavior instead of on semantic "fields" or "domains," although the latter do play a role in the classification. Only roots were examined. This policy excluded a large amount of derived vocabulary, particularly verb + prefix combinations, but it functioned as a useful control for examining the most basic vocabulary. There remained a total of 468 roots. The roots were classified into the three prototypical categories defined above; there were 316 roots that fit the prototypes. (For examination of additional roots, see 3.3.3.) The "core" semantic category roots were examined as to whether the correlated category manifestation was the unmarked form (i.e., no nonzero derivational affixes) or among the least marked forms (i.e., no form was less marked than the correlated category form). The results are given in table 2.5.

TABLE 2.5 *Unmarked Category Status of Russian Lexical Roots*

	Nouns	**Adjectives**	**Verbs**	**Total**
Objects	128	0	0	128
Properties	1	58	0	59
Actions	0	0	129	129
Total	129	58	129	316

These results strongly support the hypothesis (the one exception will be discussed in 3.3.2). Indeed, I expect that examination of any good dictionary in which related forms are placed together will strongly support this prediction, although such studies have not been made.

The English function-indicating morphosyntax found in table 2.3, and examined in the Russian lexical root study, is actually the manifestation of construction types that are universal in natural languages. The general construction types are presented in table 2.6.

TABLE 2.6 *Function-indicating Morphosyntax*

	Reference	**Modification**	**Predication**
Objects	UNMARKED NOUNS	genitive, adjectivalizations, PP's on nouns	predicate nominals
Properties	deadjectival nouns	UNMARKED ADJECTIVES	predicate adjectives
Actions	action nominals, complements, infinitives, gerunds	participles, relative clauses	UNMARKED VERBS

The analysis of syntactic categories presented here predicts the existence of these constructions because they indicate the various combinations of lexical semantic class and pragmatic function. In addition, the analysis predicts the structural markedness of the constructions in the marked combinations of lexical class and pragmatic function: that is, that those constructions will be structurally more complex, or at least as complex, as the morphosyntax for the core category types. No other theory to my knowledge makes such a prediction.

Of course, there are other types of derivational morphology and also related syntactic constructions. These include, for instance, agent nominalizations, deriving *runner* from *run*. These types of derivational morphology often change the syntactic category membership of the derived form, so that *runner* is a noun, whereas *run* is a verb. In fact, it has been suggested that one of the distinctions between derivational morphology and inflectional morphology is that derivational morphology changes the syntactic category membership of the stem to which it is attached, whereas inflectional morphology does not. This suggestion, however, does not account for derivational forms that do not change category, such as causatives and applicatives, which change verbs into verbs, and denominal agentive nouns (*musician* < *music*) and denominal abstract nouns (*theft* < *thief*), which change nouns into nouns. The analysis of syntactic categories presented here correctly predicts that the category-changing properties of these types of derivational morphology are merely side effects of the meaning change performed. I will call such derivational morphology TYPE-CHANGING MORPHOLOGY since it changes the semantic type of the root. For example, agent nominalizations change the semantic type of the root from an action to an object (specifically, the person performing the action). Thus, an agent nominalization will be an unmarked noun and will behave more or less like an unmarked noun (i.e., require a copula for predication, participate in genitive constructions as a modifier, etc.)—hence, of course, the term "agent nominalization."[26]

I will now examine the typology and semantics of function-indicating morphosyntax on the basis of the survey of twelve languages mentioned above and also informal observations of other languages.

Nonzero (positively marked) predication is associated with lexical roots that denote objects and properties. The standard structural mark is a copula construction. A copula is used for predication of nouns (objects) and adjectives (properties) in English, Georgian, Yagaria, and Diyari and for nouns only in Turkana and Mandarin Chinese. In Swahili, a copula is used in the third person, obligatorily for nouns and optionally for adjectives; otherwise, nouns and adjectives take the subject agreement prefixes used with verbs. Turkish, Acehnese, Woleaian, Lakhota, and Quiché do not use a copula for nominal or adjectival predication; in these languages, behavioral evidence must be examined (see 2.4).

Many languages use a copula for the predication of nouns and adjectives in all but the least marked construction, that is, present positive realis predications. In the latter, predication is zero marked. This is found in Diyari and Turkana in the sample:

Turkana:

(11) *a-yɔŋ̀ ɛ-ka-pɪl-a-nì̥*
I.NOM witch
'I am a witch.' (Dimmendaal 1983 : 75)

(12) *mɛ̀ɛ̀rɛ̀ a-yɔŋ̀ ɛ-ka-pɪl-a-nì̥*
be.NEG I.NOM witch
'I am not a witch.' (Dimmendaal 1983 : 76)

Diyari:

(13) *pula- ya kintala -Ø malaɲʈi*
3DU.S- NEAR dog -ABS bad
'These dogs are bad.' (Austin 1981 : 102)

(14) *kaṇa -Ø paḷu ŋana -ṇa waṉṯi -yi*
person -ABS naked COP -PRT AUX -PRES
'People were naked long ago.' (Austin 1981 : 104)

Usually, the copula is a phonologically independent morpheme, but in Yagaria the nominal copula ("equative") is suffixed to the noun:

(15) *gayale -'a -e'*
pig -3SG -EQUATIVE
'It is his pig.' (Renck 1975 : 47)

In Yagaria, adjectival predication is marked, but in an unusual fashion. Most Yagaria nouns and adjectives have "long" and "short" forms, the long form usually adding *-na.* The distribution of long and short forms is fairly complex but follows syntactic category markedness patterns for the most part. In the case of adjectives, the short form is always used for modification, while the long form is used for predication (the existential verb is also used for a copula in some sentences):

(16) *ma- gaveda okavu' -na*
this- string blue -SUFF
'This string is blue.' (Renck 1975 : 60–61)

In general, function-indicating morphosyntax has little or no semantic effect; in fact, this is how function-indicating morphosyntax is distinguished from type-changing morphosyntax. However, there is often a subtle semantic difference involved, and, in the case of predicate nominals, there is a quite significant semantic difference. When used as predicates, some relation has to be inferred to hold between the subject and the predicate. In the case of inherently relational predicates such as core verbs and adjectives, the subject is normally the inherently implied argument.[27] Prototypical nouns, that is, objects, have a semantic valency of zero. Because of this, in any context in which they are forced to behave as if they have a valency of one, some semantic relation that will hold between the noun and its "argument" will have to be COERCED or "construed" (Langacker 1987a, 1987b) so that the predicated noun can be "about the" subject noun phrase. When predicated, the subject-predicate noun relation can be one of several semantic relations. The most common are the relation of token to its subsuming type, the "classifying *be,*" and the relation of token-token identity, the "equational *be,*" or "*be* of identity":

(17) *John is a thief.*

(18) *John is the thief.*

In Thai, this distinction is manifested in distinct copula constructions (Kuno and Wogkhomthong 1981 : 76): [28]

(19) *cɔ:n pen/*khɨ: khru:*
John is teacher
'John is a teacher.'

(20) *khon thî: chán chɔ̂:b thî sùd *pen/khɨ: cɔ:n*
person that I like most is John
'The person that I like best is John.'

In addition to these uses, there is another use, the "individualizing *be*" (Bolinger 1980b), in which the predicated noun characterizes the subject without subsuming it:

(21) *John is a thief!*

This can be translating as something like 'John acts/is acting like a thief'; that is, John has the characteristics and behavior of a thief but is not (necessarily) a thief in the professional sense. In English, the classifying and individualizing constructions are identical except in various peripheral constructions (see Bolinger 1980b; and 3.2.1), but they are distinguished in languages such as French in which classification is accomplished without the use of an article:

(22) *Jean est voleur.* (classifying)

(23) *Jean est un voleur.* (individualizing)

This does not exhaust the semantic possibilities, however. Some other types of copula constructions can be distinguished by comparing English copula types and Thai ones. For instance, in introducing a person, an English speaker uses the person's name, so that the construction resembles the equational one (*This is John*); but in "introducing" or "naming" an object, say, to someone who does not recognize it, the construction uses an indefinite article and so resembles the classifying *be* (*This is a dinosaur*). Thai uses *khɨ:* in both constructions, however (Kuno and Wogthomkhong 1981 : 86, 91), suggesting that the "*be* of naming" is a distinct relation: [29]

(24) *nî *pen/khɨ:khun cɔ:n phî:an dìchán khà*
this is Mr. John friend I POLITE
'This is my friend John.'

(25) *man khɨ: daynosǎw*
this is dinosaur
'This is a dinosaur.'
(naming object for hearer for the first time)

The fact that a noun, which in reference is zero valency, must be coerced into an inherently relational concept such as token identity or classification when used as a predicate clearly goes a long way toward accounting for why roots denoting objects are typologically marked as predicates. This will be taken up again in chapter 3.

Not surprisingly, a similar phenomenon is found in the examination of the marked combination of a noun functioning as a modifier. In English, this can be done in a structurally unmarked fashion, using the complex nominal construction:

(26) *brown jacket*

(27) *torn jacket*

(28) *record jacket*

(29) *record industry*

An inherently relational modifier like *brown* or the verbal participle *torn* has one of its arguments as its head (in a transitive modifier like *torn,* the voice morphology—in this case, passive—determines which participant is denoted by the head). Examples (26) and (27) can be paraphrased as 'a jacket that is brown' and 'a jacket that is/was torn,' respectively. Nouns as modifiers (complex nominals, including those that are denominal adjectives such as *theatrical*) can have virtually any semantic relation. If nouns had a valency of one, as the standard analysis proposes, one would expect (28) to mean 'a jacket that is a record' and (29) to mean 'an industry that is a record,' but they cannot be so paraphrased.[30] The reason for this, of course, is that there is no inherent semantic relation in the noun modifier, so any contextually appropriate semantic relation is induced in the modifier-head construction.[31]

As table 2.6 indicates, there are a variety of nominal modifier relations. The most basic nominal modifier relation is the genitive construction. There are a great variety of morphosyntactic strategies for expressing a genitive relation (for an enumeration, see Croft 1990b, chap. 2), but the construction is often characterized by the presence of at least one additional morpheme, thereby providing positive structural evidence for markedness. This is true in all the languages in the sample except Acehnese, which like some analytic languages uses simple juxtaposition for the genitive relation. Of course, the genitive construction must coerce some sort of semantic relation on the noun, such as ownership, a part-whole relation, etc. Frequently, that relation is indicated by a semantically more specific case affix or adposition, as in English *a cake* ***for*** *Nina*. As with predication of nouns, the fact that a major semantic reinterpretation of the denotation of the noun is required for noun modification indicates that core nouns are not unmarked modifiers.

Reference to properties is also marked, most frequently by derivational means. Abstract deadjectival nouns use nonzero morphemes in English (*white-**ness***), Turkish (*güzel-**lik*** 'beauty'), Turkana (*a-ŋaŋ-**aan**-ʊ̀t* 'purple-ness'), Swahili (***u**-zuri* 'beauty'), Georgian (***si**-mağl-e* 'height'), Acehnese (***neu**-laju* 'speed'), Lakhota (***wo**-wašte* 'goodness'), and Quiché (*uƚ-**īl*** 'goodness'); no data were available for Woleaian, Yagaria, and Diyari. Mandarin Chinese uses an unusual strategy for forming nouns referring to properties, combining the positive and negative antonym forms (Li and Thompson 1981 : 81):

(30) *dà- xiǎo*
big- small
'size'

(31) *gāo- ǎi*
tall- short
'height'

Even in this case, reference to properties requires an additional morpheme to the basic adjectival form; two morphemes are used to refer to the quality, whereas only one is used in modification.

It is commonly argued (e.g., Schachter 1985 : 17; Thompson 1988 : 170–71) that in many languages adjectives are identical to nouns because they use the same inflections for case, number, and gender as nouns. Although in many languages this is true, the inflections always refer to the object possessing the quality, not the quality itself—that is, the adjectival inflections "agree" with the noun (or refer to the object named by the noun if the noun itself does not inflect). This is most striking when an adjective stands alone with its inflections. In these cases, the resulting construction does not denote a quality; instead, it denotes the object that possesses the quality:

Swahili (Ashton 1944:52):

(32) *vi-* *kubwa*
CLASS- big
'(the) big ones' (cf., *vi-su* 'knives')

Quechua (Schachter 1985:17):

(33) *rikaška:* *hatun* *-kuna* *-ta*
I.saw big -PL -ACC
'I saw the big ones.' [compare (34)]

(34) *rikaška* *alkalde* *-kuna* *-ta*
I.saw mayor -PL -ACC
'I saw the mayors.'

Swahili is particularly informative in this regard. Adjectives agree with the nouns that they modify according to noun class and use the same prefixes to agree with the head noun that the nouns use themselves. In these cases, the adjective uses the noun class prefix appropriate to the noun that it modifies, and the prefix changes depending on the noun class of the head noun. If the adjectival term is used to denote the property itself, it becomes a *u-* class noun, and of course the prefix is invariant since it indicates the noun class of the property noun.

In other languages, the ability of an adjective to inflect like a noun is more a function of the syntactic distribution of the inflection. In Diyari, as in many other Australian languages, the nominal inflections are placed on only one constituent (in Diyari, the last constituent), which may be a noun or an adjective:

(35) *n̪awu* *muɲt̪a* *-ri* *-ṇa* *wara* *-yi* *ŋan̪t̪i* *t̪uŋka* *-li*
3SG.NFEM.S sick -INCH -PRT AUX -PRES meat rotten -ERG
'He became sick from the rotten meat.' (Austin 1981:120)

In Georgian, the adjective does not inflect (except for stems ending in a consonant in the ergative case; Aronson 1982:111) when it is modifying a noun, but it does use the nominal inflections if no head noun is present:[32]

(36) *ḳarg* *propesor* *-s*
good professor -DAT
'to (the) good professor'

(37) *ḳarg -s*
good -DAT
'to the good one'

In these cases, the adjective plus noun inflection refers to an object possessing the property, not the property itself. In fact, it appears that there do not exist languages with nominal inflectional morphology distinct from adjectival inflectional morphology in which the adjective(s) in a "headless" noun phrase takes the nominal inflection (Joseph Greenberg, personal communication). This fact supports the analysis of adjectival inflections as being functionally distinct from nominal inflections, even in those cases in which they are phonologically identical.

The existence of nonzero morphology to derive deadjectival nominals, and the fact that adjectives inflected like nouns either agree with nouns (if modifiers) or denote objects rather than properties (if standing alone), eliminates the arguments in favor of the interpretation of adjectives as a subclass of nouns. In languages that exhibit this pattern, it is more accurate to say that adjectives in these languages are "un-verblike" rather than "nounlike." As will be observed below, it is more difficult to distinguish adjectives from verbs using the markedness criteria.

The marked pragmatic functions for semantically prototypical verbs are modification and reference. In both these cases, there is a rich variety of grammatical constructions that are commonly found for these categories. These constructions can be divided into nonfinite and finite types. All the languages in the sample except Chinese and Woleaian form action nominalizations, and in the other languages (except for some Acehnese and Turkana forms) nonzero nominalizing morphology is used: English *walk-**ing***; Turkish *çaliş-**mak*** 'to work, working'; Swahili ***ku**-imba* 'singing'; Turkana (***a**-*)***kɪ**-ɲam`* 'to eat, eating'; Georgian *çer-**a*** 'writing [imperfect]'; Acehnese ***neu**-hëy* 'calling out'; Yagaria *fili-**te'-na*** 'death'; Diyari *kuŋka-**ni*** 'limping'; Lakhota ***wo**-gnaye* 'deception'; Quiché *pakal-**ēm*** 'climb, climbing.' Of these languages, English, Turkish, Georgian, Yagaria, and Diyari also have nonfinite participial forms, with nonzero function-indicating affixes, that can be used when a verb is modifying a noun, for example, Turkish *bekle-**y-en** misfirler* '(the) waiting guests' or Georgian *da = çer-**il**-i* [PREVERB = write-PSTPRT.NOM] 'written.' Yagaria and Diyari use the nominalized form of the verb for nonfinite modification, Yagaria using the short form without *-na: fili-**te'** yale* [die-NMNL people] 'dead people.'[33]

The phenomenon of verbal modifiers resembling verbal nominalized forms extends to finite forms as well: English *that,* for both relative clauses and complements, is an example. A more common pattern, found in Quiché and Acehnese, is the use of a nominalizing form both as a relative clause marker and as a headless relative clause denoting one of the arguments of the verb:

Quiché (Mondloch 1978: 198, 84):

(38) *xawi či' k'ō k- ēl wi lē k- ā- tixoh*
where COMP exist PRES- leave from DET PRES- 2SG- eat
'Is there somewhere where what you eat comes out?'

(39) *š- pē lē ači lē š- in- kun -ax kap̓ixīr*
PAST- come DET man DET PAST- 1SG- cure -FOC day.before.yesterday
'The man whom I cured the day before yesterday came.'

Acehnese (Durie 1985: 232):

(40) *ka= matê ureueng nyang= ji= poh baroe*
IN= dead person REL= 3= hit yesterday
'The person whom he struck yesterday is dead.'

(41) *jih' =keuh nyang= ceumeucue*
he =EMPH REL= steal
'He is the one who steals.'

The Quiché example is particularly striking since the relativizer is the determiner used with nouns. Thus, it appears that the finite verbal clause is functioning as a noun without any additional morphological alteration. The "nominal" example (also called a "headless relative clause") functions exactly like the examples of adjectives combined with nominal inflections: it refers to an object involved in the action denoted by the verb, not the action itself.[34] This pattern is also found in Lakhota, Classical Nahuatl (Andrews 1975), and Kanuri (Hutchison 1981). The Acehnese case is identical except that the relevant morpheme is not a determiner; it may be that other forms have usurped the determiner function.

One also finds lexicalized examples of the same phenomenon, such as the following Mohawk example from Mithun (1984b):

(42) *ó:nen ki' ne rahtahkón:nis tahoná:khwe'*
now just the he.shoes.makes he.got.mad
'At this point the shoemaker became angry.'

Just as in the ordinary headless relative clause, the "agent nominalization" *rahtahkón:nis* 'shoemaker' is of the same form as the finite clause 'he makes shoes,' but it denotes an individual, not the action he performs. It might be more accurately translated as 'the [one who] makes shoes.' A large number of examples of lexical roots denoting actions and properties being used as nouns without further derivation but denoting objects were found in the Russian root study (stem vowels for the verbal forms are in parentheses) (see table 2.7).

Finally, one occasionally finds that the verbal relative clause marker is identical to the nominal genitive marker, so that both marked modifier types, nominal and verbal, use the same overt mark. This is found in the sample with the Mandarin Chinese *de* and the Swahili "*-a* of relationship":

Swahili (Ashton 1944 : 145):

(43) *kiti ch- a mti*
chair CLASS- REL wood
'a wooden chair'

(44) *maneno y- a ku- pendenza*
words CLASS- REL NOM- please
'pleasing words'

Chinese (Norman 1988 : 160):

(45) *jīntiān shàngwǔ de hùi*
today morning MOD meeting
'this morning's meeting'

(46) *xǐhuan chōuyān de rén*
like smoke MOD people
'people who like to smoke'

In Swahili, the verbal construction is in fact a genitive construction since the verb is nominalized. In Chinese, the verbal construction may actually be nominal as well since Chinese is a language in which action nominalizations, and complements in general, do not have a nonzero derivational morpheme associated with them. This state of affairs is found in (mostly analytic) languages that do not distinguish nonfinite verbal forms, and in such languages one must turn to behavioral evidence to find positive evidence for markedness. Besides these cases, however, there is an obligatory or at least optional nonzero morpheme that indicates the subordinate (modifier or complement) status

TABLE 2.7 *Russian Zero Type-Changing Derivation: Actions/Properties and Objects*

Root	Action/Property	Object
voz	convey, carry (i/Ø)	cart, wagon
kol	stab, thrust (o)	stake
kos	cut, mow (i)	scythe
var	cook (i)	boiling water
pil	saw (i)	saw
ed	eat (Ø)	food
glas	say, mean (i)	voice
lom(l)	break (i)	scrap, fragment
klad	hide (Ø)	treasure
sad	plant, sit (i)	garden
plat	pay (i)	fee
prud	dam (i)	pond
pot	sweat (e)	sweat
luč	catch fish by torchlight (i)	light
mer	measure (i)	measure
par	steam (i)	steam
igr	play (a)	game
um	know how (e)	mind
p'at	go backward (i)	heel
p'atn	spot, stain (a)	spot, stain
znak	mean (i)	sign, symbol
slug	serve (i)	servant
niz	low	bottom
moroz	cold	frost

of the otherwise finite verb form in all the languages in the sample, and this represents the general pattern.

The various verbal forms used for reference have some semantic distinctions associated with them, partly by virtue of their form and partly by virtue of the verbs of which they are complements. The construction type with the least alteration of meaning is the action nominalization, which refers simply to the action denoted by the verb. This type is most easily identified as a subject of a predicate that describes some property of the action: *Skateboarding is dangerous.* In English, two other referential verbal forms have been noted in the literature: factive nominalizations, such as *Zelda's signing the contract,* and finite complements, such as *That Zelda signed the contract* (discussion and examples here are based on Langacker MS, 1.2.1; see, e.g., Lees 1960; Chomsky 1970; and Ransom 1986, who calls factive and finite complements "occurrence" and "truth" complements, respectively). Factive nominalizations denote the fact that the action took place and so do not take manner predicates:[35]

(47) **Sam's washing the windows was meticulous.*

(48) *Sam's washing the windows was a shock to everybody.*

Finite complements can characterize the reality as well as the fact of a situation and so allow predicates such as *false:*

(49) *That Zelda signed the contract is simply false.*

(50) **Zelda's signing the contract is simply false.*

Various kinds of complement-taking verbs allow only a subset of the action, factive, and reality interpretations and so limit the appropriateness of different kinds of complements (this is a very complex area and will not be discussed here; see Ransom 1985).

From the point of view of the pragmatic function of reference, however, there is no difference between the direct objects of *I want a ribeye steak* and *I want to eat supper;* they both refer to the object of desire of the subject. In the first case, that is a straightforward physical object. In the second, it is not so clear: simplemindedly, it is the action, but it may be some more abstract entity related to the action. In either case, the object in the second case is not a typical referent and is marked as such, with a syntactic marker *to* or, in many other languages, a derived infinitival or gerundive form.

It could be argued that any kind of nominalization other than a pure action nominalization is a type-changing construction, not a function-indicating construction, and so cannot be used to evaluate structural markedness hypotheses. Nevertheless, taking the more inclusive route has not given us any reason to question the markedness of verbal nominalizations.

2.4 Behavioral Markedness and the Deverbalization Hierarchy

In the preceding section, the typological survey reveals a representative and systematic set of function-indicating grammatical constructions that define structural markedness patterns for the major syntactic categories. The function-indicating constructions use nonzero morphemes for the marked combinations of lexical semantic class and pragmatic function as predicted. Nevertheless, the sample reveals certain classes of exceptions: some languages use no copula for nonverbal predications (especially adjectival ones), some languages use no genitive marker for nominal modifiers, and some languages use simple verb forms for nominalizations. In these cases, one must turn to grammatical behavior, both inflectional and syntactic, to find positive evidence for the markedness patterns underlying the cross-linguistic definitions of the major syntactic categories. In fact, one can observe behavioral markedness patterns even in cases in which nonzero function-indicating morphosyntax already indicates structural markedness.

The potential range of grammatical behavior of a lexical root is vast, especially when syntactic behavior is taken into consideration. Unfortunately, grammatical descriptions rarely discuss inflectional behavior with any thoroughness, let alone syntactic behavior. Nevertheless, enough evidence can be gathered from the twelve-language survey and more informal observations over a wider range of languages to indicate what gaps in grammatical behavior are to be expected in marked combinations of lexical semantic class and pragmatic function.

Most of the discussion in this section will pertain to inflectional behavior of lexical items. Each major syntactic category has a particular set of inflections associated with it across languages. Languages may not utilize all the inflectional possibilities, but they draw from the same set of inflections for each syntactic category, and a periphrastic means is always available to indicate the concepts indicated inflectionally in other languages. The standard inflectional categories found for each major syntactic category are listed below:

Nouns: number (countability), case, gender, size (augmentative, diminutive), shape (classifiers), definiteness (determination), alienability;

Adjectives: comparative, superlative, equative, intensive ("very Adj"), approximative ("more or less Adj" or "Adj-ish"), agreement with head;

Verbs: tense, aspect, mood and modality, agreement with subject and object(s), transitivity.

In the survey, evidence was sought for the absence in marked combinations of lexical item and pragmatic function of those inflectional categories that occurred in the unmarked combinations.

Predicated nouns and adjectives in languages that use copulas for these constructions do not inflect for any of the standard verbal inflections: instead, the copula does, as in Diyari, Turkana, Georgian, and English. In these languages, nouns (and adjectives) simply do not have forms that are inflected for tense, even if the surface structure allows another way to indicate tense—the latter fact is merely a way to "get around" the behavioral defect of predicated nouns and adjectives.

Predicate nominals and adjectives display behavioral markedness in almost all cases, including those with copulas. English predicate nominals, being stative, do not allow the progressive form; this is a general pattern, as will be seen. In Turkish, the verbal inflections are applied to the nominal and adjectival root; historically, the inflections are derived from the verb 'be.' However, nouns are not inflected for subjunctive or imperative (Lewis 1967 : 107); instead an independent verb stem *ol(-mak)* is used (Lewis 1967 : 141). Swahili inflects nouns and adjectives except in the third person, in which an invariant copula is used (Ashton 1944 : 92). Both adjectives and nouns use a single negative form, *si* (Ashton 1944 : 93); verbs use two negative forms, *ha* for indicative and *si* for subjunctive (Ashton 1944 : 70). Turkana nouns do not inflect, the inflections being carried by a copula. Turkana has "true" adjectives and also stative verbs, most of which fit the prototype of adjectives (i.e., unary valency, stative, persistent, and gradable). Stative verbs, including the copula 'be' and the stative-verb adjectives, inflect only for ± past tense (Dimmendaal 1983 : 103). True adjectives take only the habitual and stative suffixes (Dimmendaal 1983 : 332):

(51) *ɛ̀̇ mùgɩ -aan -à*
3SG- purple -HABIT -STAT
'It is purple/mauve.'

In Georgian, nouns and adjectives require the copula verb but also use an invariant clitic for the third person singular (Aronson 1982 : 65):

(52) *Davit -i kartveli ar -is*
David -NOM Georgian be -3SG.PRES
'David is a Georgian.'

(53) *Davit -i kartveli -a*
David -NOM Georgian -COP.CLITIC
'David is a Georgian.'

The copula verb has no imperfect forms (Aronson 1982 : 66).

Mandarin Chinese uses a copula, *shì,* for nominal predication. The copula does not take any aspect markers, can be negated only by *bu,* not *méi(yǒu),* and cannot take certain auxiliaries (Li and Thompson 1981 : 148). Predicate adjectives do not use a copula. However, the durative aspect marker *zài* is excluded because adjectives are stative. The perfective aspect marker *-le* is used, but only with specific meanings: either the adjective is construed as an inchoative process, or it is construed as bounded by a specified quantity (Li and Thompson 1981: 188–89, 202):

(54) *chènshān xiǎo -le sān cùn*
shirt small -PERF three inch
'The shirt got smaller [i.e., shrank] by three inches,' *or,*
'The shirt is (too) small by three inches.'

Acehnese predicate nominals and adjectives do not use a copula. However, predicated nouns do not take the clitics that cross-reference the actor or undergoer arguments of a standard verbal predicate (Durie 1985 : 107). Durie does not indicate any inflectional behavioral difference between predicated adjectives and verbal predicates. Woleaian is described similarly to Acehnese: the predicate nominal does not allow the subjective particles that cross-reference the subject and does not take any aspect markers (Sohn 1975 : 145–46). However, there does not seem to be any inflectional difference between predicated adjectives and verbal predicates. On the other hand, little evidence is present, and there may be positive syntactic evidence of the behavioral markedness of predicated adjectives, certainly concerning the distribution of verbal modifiers referring exclusively to processes.

Yagaria predicate nominals use an "equative" (copula) suffix, and adjectives use a copula and the "long" form of the adjective. It appears from the examples given that none of the standard verbal inflections, of which there are many, are used. Diyari uses a copula for both nominal and verbal inflection, so neither the noun nor the adjective is inflected for any verbal categories. No information is provided regarding inflectional restrictions of the copula. Lakhota predicate nominals and adjectives are inflected for actor and undergoer like verbs. There were no examples of predicate nominals with either the locative or the instrumental verbal prefixes in the relevant section of Boas and Deloria (1941 : 39–52). Predicate adjectives may take locative prefixes: *'i-čhą̨ze* [LOC-angry] 'be angry on account of someone' (Boas and Deloria 1941 : 42). However, instrumental prefixes construe the state as a process in most if not all cases: *ma-ka-suta* [1SG.UND-INST-hard] 'he made me hard (by striking)' or '(circumstances) have made me hard' (Boas and Deloria 1941:47). Finally, Quiché predicate nominals and adjectives take the approriate person agreement inflections but do not inflect for tense/aspect, nor do they take the voice inflections of standard (transitive) verbs.

The survey languages reveal several common patterns. In many languages, nouns and adjectives do not inflect for any verbal categories because those categories are expressed by a copula, and even the copula may not express all the standard verbal inflectional categories. Predicate nominals tend to lack tense-aspect and agreement affixes, as do predicate adjectives, though to a lesser extent. Above all, any aspectual inflection (or syntactic constructions) that refer to processes do not apply to predicate nominals or adjectives since they are stative.

Data is scantier for the other marked combinations of lexical semantic class and pragmatic function. Most genitive constructions are expressed with an overt morpheme, such as the genitive case. In those languages in which adjectives agree with their head nouns, such as Turkish, Swahili, and Turkana, the genitive modifier does not take the agreement markers. Normally, the construction lacks agreement, but in Swahili the genitive linker ('*-a* of relationship') takes the agreement prefixes, as in examples (43)–(44) above. Semantically, noun modifiers lack the extensive adjectival inflectional behavior associated with gradability. Lewis notes that Turkish nouns cannot be inflected for comparative and superlative degrees (Lewis 1967:53); this is probably true for all the other languages in the survey. Turkish also uses reduplication for intensification only for a core subset of adjectives as in *gömgök* (from *gök* 'blue') and *yepyeni* (from *yeni* 'new'; Lewis 1967:55–56).

Gradability may also distinguish adjectives from verbs used as modifiers since many verbs, particularly process verbs, are not gradable. Quiché inflects adjectives for intensification, as in *nim-alax* 'very big,' but uses a two-morpheme separate word *sip̓alax* 'very' for the intensification of verbs. In fact, inflection for intensification is restricted to adjectival modifiers: adjectives (or anything else) when predicated must also use *sip̓alax* (Mondloch 1978:94):

(55) *sip̓alax nim lē ʒ̓iʔ*
very big the dog
'The dog is very big.'

In Lakhota, adjectival modifiers are compounded with their head nouns, as in *pte-thąka* [buffalo-large] 'large buffalo' (Boas and Deloria 1941:69); however, noun-verb compounds are not nominal modifiers but represent incorporated patient nouns with verbal heads: *čhą-le* [wood-gather] means 'gather firewood' (Boas and Deloria 1941:70), not 'wood being gathered.'

Finally, reference to properties and actions lacks some characteristic nominal inflections, most notably number inflections, chiefly due to the fact that verbal nouns usually and deadjectival nouns almost always are mass nouns. Unfortunately, this is not commented on in the grammars for the languages in the sample, except for Turkana (Dimmendaal 1983:211, 270). Verbal nouns in Turkish display another sort of behavioral markedness: they do not take possessive affixes or the genitive case (Lewis 1967:167). Finite complements and many nonfinite complements generally do not allow for nominal inflections on the verbs that head them—for example, the English infinitive does not inflect for number and allows only one preposition, *to* (unlike, e.g., French), so that *to* has become the structurally marked indicator of the infinitive rather than a manifestation of its behavioral markedness.

A more striking pattern with verbal forms is their loss of verbal properties. Many nonfinite verb forms and nominalizations do inflect for various verbal categories, particularly voice and aspect, and allow the expression of subject and object. However, most of these forms use a distinct means for expressing tense, aspect, modality, voice, and subject and object than is used in verbal predication. For example, possessive constructions rather than the usual subject and object inflections are noted for nonfinite verbal forms in English, Turkish, Georgian, Woleaian, Yagaria, and Quiché in the survey sample. Thus, we may compare nonfinite verb forms by whether they express various categories and dependents in the way normally associated with verbal predicates or in some other way (usually some construction associated with nouns). The best evidence is found in languages that display a variety of nonfinite verbal forms, such as English and Quiché. The evidence in these two languages, along with evidence gathered by Comrie (1976a), suggests the existence of a deverbalization hierarchy:

> *Deverbalization Hierarchy:* If a verbal form inflects tense-aspect-modality (TAM) like a predicated verb, then it will take subject and object dependents like a predicated verb. If a verbal form takes a subject dependent like a predicated verb, then it will take an object dependent like a predicated verb.

In other words, the verb types in table 2.8 are expected, ranging from fully finite to completely nominalized (PV = predicated verb).

The deverbalization hierarchy can be used to classify different degrees of finiteness of verbal forms. For example, English infinitives,

TABLE 2.8 *Nonfinite and Nominalized Verb Form Behavior*

	Tense-Aspect-Modality	Subject	Object
Fully finite	like PV	like PV	like PV
	not like PV	like PV	like PV
	not like PV	not like PV	like PV
Fully nominalized	not like PV	not like PV	not like PV

participles, and gerunds do not take tense/aspect inflections and do not take subjects in the way that main verbs do, but they may still take direct objects in the way that main verbs do:

(56) *I made it easy for him/*he to eat/*eats/*ate this.*

(57) *The girl drawing funny faces is my niece.*

(58) *John's drinking upsets Jane.*

English nominalizations, on the other hand, cannot even take the direct object in the way that main verbs do:

(59) *Fred abhors the hunting of ducks/*the hunting ducks.* [ignore the participial reading]

The full scale can be represented by the Quiché forms in the following examples. I have provided parallels from other languages from Comrie (1976a), who discusses the full range of types with respect to nominalization (defined by him as the ability to take case affixes):

Subject and object, but not TAM like PV:

Quiché intransitive perfect:

(60) [**š-*] *ux-* *ātin* *-naq* *arētaq*
[*PAST-] 1PL.ABS- bathe -PERF when
'We had already bathed when . . .'

Tabasaran:

(61) *izu* *-s* *äγ'äjas* *du* *-γu* *kitab* *uwx* *-uw*
1SG -DAT know 3SG -ERG book.ABS read -NOM
'I know that he is reading the book.'

Object but not subject or TAM like PV:

Quiché transitive perfect:

(62) [*š-] *at-* *nu-* *c̓ukūm* *arētaq*
[*PAST-] 2SG.ABS 1SG.POSS look.for.PERF when

'I had been looking for you when . . .'

English verbal noun:

(63) *John's feeding the squirrels . . .*

Neither subject, object, nor TAM like PV:

Quiché passive nominalization:

(64) *či qa- č̓ap̓ -eš -ik*
for 1PL.POSS- speak.to -PASS -NOM

'in order to speak to us'
(lit. 'for our being spoken to')

Russian nominalization:

(65) *razruš -enie gorod -a vrag -om*
destroy -NOM city -GEN enemy -INST

'(the) destruction of the city by the enemy'

Comrie's data indicate that the verbal properties—tense-aspect-modality, subject, object—are not ordered with respect to nominalization or, rather, the one property that Comrie takes to be criterial for nominalizations, namely, the ability to take case marking. Whether properties of actions used referentially are realized as adjectives or adverbs at some point in this hierarchy or independently if it is not yet known, though variation exists: English *John's quick/quickly maneuvering;* Polish *chodzeniu cicho* [move-NMNL-LOC quiet-ADV] 'moving quietly' (Comrie 1976a). The partial ordering of nominal and verbal properties for actions functioning nonpredicationally is illustrated below:

tense/aspect/modality<subject<direct object
adverb/adjective modifier
case marking

These results are tentative and remain to be verified by a more thorough typological study. If these preliminary results prove to be correct, they are not surprising: the ability to take characteristically verbal inflections and to take subjects in the same way as main clauses are the two most important grammatical properties of predications, and one would therefore expect them to be lost first. One may thus conclude that there appear to be systematic patterns in the behavior of lexical semantic classes that shift pragmatic-functional category.

Returning to the general issue of behavioral markedness, we must discuss an important issue in the evaluation of behavioral markedness: the role of the inflectional distinctions in determining major category membership. In a number of cases in this section, I argued that behavioral markedness rested crucially on the inability of marked lexical classes to take certain inflections characteristic of certain pragmatic functions because of inherent semantic properties of the root: nouns are zero valency, predicate nominals and adjectives are stative, prototypical nominal and verbal modifiers are not gradable, and prototypical adjectival and verbal nominalizations are mass, not count. This is due to the fact that the prototypical nouns (objects), adjectives (qualities), and verbs (actions) by definition possess these semantic characteristics. The question that needs to be answered is, Why do the major pragmatic functions have characteristic inflections that select particular lexical semantic classes as the unmarked members of the class?

First, it should be pointed out that positive (not just neutral) markedness evidence that is not directly connected to lexical semantic class converges on the same lexical semantic classes as the purely semantic evidence for prototypical nouns, verbs, and adjectives. In other words, the association between pragmatic function and lexical semantic class is not accidental. But that is precisely the point: characteristically predicational inflections such as the progressive and other aspectual distinctions are present precisely because they are relevant to prototypical verbs, namely, actions. Likewise, characteristically modificational inflections such as comparison and intensification are present precisely because they are relevant to prototypical adjectives, namely, gradable properties; and nominal inflections like number are present because they are relevant to prototypical nouns, namely, individuatable (countable) objects. In general, only the core members of the syntactic category will display the full grammatical behavior characteristic of their category because only they have all the semantic characteristics that the characteristic inflections tap into. This is to say that the inflectional categories of the major syntactic categories have been "tailored" to their semantically core members. This is an example of a processing constraint: languages inflect only for those properties that are of relevance to core members of the category; they do not inflect for properties of peripheral members of the category that are not of relevance to the core members of the category.[36]

The hypothesis that the inflectional categories—and, I would guess, the relevant syntactic distributional contexts—are "tailored" to the core members of the relevant syntactic categories also contributes to the explanation for the distinction between major syntactic categories and minor subclasses that eluded Schachter. As I argued in 2.1, the major syntactic categories are those that are determined by the primary pragmatic functions. The syntactic subclasses—for example, mass versus count nouns and stative versus nonstative verbs—are byproducts of the different syntactic behavior of various peripheral semantic classes that are assimilated to the major syntactic category.

2.5 Textual Markedness

The third and last criterion for determining markedness patterns is text frequency: the element with the higher text frequency is the less marked element. Text frequency is a significant property in that it may account for the structural and behavioral markedness patterns (Greenberg 1966a; Schwartz 1980; Croft 1990b, sec. 7.2.1). By the principle of ECONOMIC MOTIVATION (Haiman 1983, 1985b, based on Zipf 1935), the more frequently occurring concept will be expressed in the shortest form—hence, it will be the structurally least-marked form. The relation between behavioral markedness and text frequency is less obvious. It may be that the less frequently occurring concept(s) will "lose," or at least lack, the characteristic inflections of the more frequent concepts simply because those forms are not used as often (cf. the usage-based grammatical storage models of Bybee [1985b] and Langacker [1988b]). However, the explanation offered in the last section—the more frequently occurring forms display a wider range of inflections because the inflections were "designed" for them (i.e., adapted to them)—may be more appropriate.

Be that as it may, the markedness pattern revealed by the text frequency criterion should be the same as the markedness pattern revealed by the structural and behaviorial criteria. However, in the case of a prototype correlation such as that underlying the major syntactic categories, there is a complication in evaluating the results. In examining, for example, the correlation between the pragmatic function of reference and the lexical semantic class of objects, one may observe whether the largest group of referring expressions is of those denoting objects or whether the largest group of expressions denoting objects is found in the referential function. Ideally, both these conditions should apply: the largest group of referring expressions should be terms denoting objects, and the largest group of terms denoting objects should be found in the referential function. It turns out that the stronger double text frequency criterion holds for the correlations establishing the categories "noun" and "verb" but not unequivocally for the correlation intended to establish the category "adjective."

Text counts were performed on texts in Quiché (VOS, Mayan),

Nguna (SVO, Austronesian), Soddo (SOV, Austroasiatic), and Ute (free, Uto-Aztecan).[37] The Quiché, Nguna, and Ute texts are oral narratives, and the Soddo text is a description of Soddo life-styles; the Ute text is lightly edited compared to the others, including more repetitions and false starts. Lexical roots were classified as in the Russian root study, with two modifications: nonphysical processes were included with physical ones, and a subcategory of object expressions for pronominal forms (including bound pronominals) was added.[38] The results are given in tables 2.9–2.12.[39]

TABLE 2.9 *Textual Distribution of Lexical Classes in Quiché*

	Reference	**Modification**	**Predication**
Objects			
Pronominal	85	16	0
Lexical	91	5	0
Properties	0	6	6
Quantifiers	0	2	0
States	1	1	2
Relations	0	0	2
Actions	12	2	108
Auxiliary	0	0	2

The text frequencies in these languages produce the expected markedness patterns for the noun and verb correlations. In all four languages, the largest number of referring expressions denote objects (as can be seen by examining the first column in each table), and the largest group of morphemes denoting objects is found in the pragmatic function of reference (as can be seen from the first two rows in each table). Likewise, the largest number of predicate expressions denote actions (the last column), and the largest group of morphemes denoting actions is found in the pragmatic function of predication (the penultimate row).

On the other hand, no clear pattern emerges for the correlation between roots denoting properties and the pragmatic function of modification that underlies the category "adjective." (In fact, the over-

TABLE 2.10 *Textual Distribution of Lexical Classes in Nguna*

	Reference	Modification	Predication
Objects			
Pronominal	131	42	0
Lexical	123	18	10
Properties	0	9	3
Quantifiers	0	7	0
States	0	2	4
Relations	0	1	32
Actions	15	3	113
Auxiliary	0	0	12

TABLE 2.11 *Textual Distribution of Lexical Classes in Soddo*

	Reference	Modification	Predication
Objects			
Pronominal	60	2	0
Lexical	123	16	8
Properties	1	5	5
Quantifiers	0	3	0
States	0	2	0
Relations	0	2	8
Actions	7	13	75
Auxiliary	0	0	0

all frequency of roots denoting properties and occurrences of modifiers is extremely low compared to the frequencies of object and action roots and of referring expressions and predications; see 3.3.2.) For this reason, roots denoting properties and modifiers of all types were counted for additional narratives in each language.[40] The results of this count are given in tables 2.13–2.16.

TABLE 2.12 *Textual Distribution of Lexical Classes in Ute*

	Reference	Modification	Predication
Objects			
Pronominal	95	6	1
Lexical	56	1	1
Properties	0	2	2
Quantifiers	0	0	0
States	0	1	4
Relations	1	1	23
Actions	2	5	156
Auxiliary	0	0	52

TABLE 2.13 *Textual Distribution of Modifiers and Property Roots in Quiché*

	Reference	Modification	Predication
Objects			
Pronominal	. . .	36	. . .
Lexical	. . .	14	. . .
Properties[41]	0	27	10
Quantifiers	. . .	8	. . .
States	. . .	2	. . .
Relations	. . .	0	. . .
Actions	. . .	2	. . .

These results still do not constitute very large numbers in each cell. However, similar patterns emerge in all four languages, which suggests that the results do have some validity.

First, it appears that the largest group of roots denoting properties is found in the pragmatic function of modification, with a significant minority found as predicate adjectives.[45] This result fits in with

TABLE 2.14 *Textual Distribution of Modifiers and Property Roots in Nguna*

	Reference	Modification	Predication
Objects			
Pronominal	. . .	58	. . .
Lexical	. . .	23	. . .
Properties	0	17	7
Quantifiers	. . .	11	. . .
States	. . .	6	. . .
Relations	. . .	1	. . .
Actions[42]	. . .	5	. . .

TABLE 2.15 *Textual Distribution of Modifiers and Property Roots in Soddo*

	Reference	Modification	Predication
Objects			
Pronominal	. . .	12	. . .
Lexical	. . .	43	. . .
Properties	1	14	7
Quantifiers	. . .	10	. . .
States	. . .	6	. . .
Relations	. . .	7	. . .
Actions	. . .	34	. . .

the expected patterns: the least marked roots denoting properties are modifiers by the textual frequency criterion. On the basis of this alone, one would expect adjectives to be least marked in the modifying function.

However, it is clearly not the case that the least marked modifiers are terms denoting properties. Roots denoting objects outnumber roots denoting properties in all four languages, and roots denoting actions outnumber roots denoting properties in one language, Soddo. Nevertheless, as we saw in the first tables, roots denoting objects are

TABLE 2.16 *Textual Distribution of Modifiers and Property Roots in Ute*

	Reference	Modification	Predication
Objects			
Pronominal	. . .	32	. . .
Lexical[43]	. . .	14	. . .
Properties[44]	0	13	5
Quantifiers	. . .	9	. . .
States	. . .	3	. . .
Relations	. . .	1	. . .
Actions	. . .	13	. . .

marked as modifiers compared to object roots used to refer; the same applies to action roots as modifiers with respect to predication. Thus, even if object and action roots outnumber property roots as modifiers, they will be marked constructions at any rate and so may turn out to be more marked than property roots as modifiers (as in fact they are, structurally and behaviorally).

But closer examination of the data suggests that most of the object roots as modifiers might be removed from the count. The largest group of modifiers in all the languages except Soddo are pronominal possessors.[46] This is actually an inflectional category in these languages (even in Nguna, which has few inflections), as in many other languages. For this reason, it may be reasonable to exclude pronominal possessors as candidates for the core or prototype of a major pragmatic function—though, on the same grounds, one should then exclude pronominal referents as well (see 3.3.1).[47] In addition, the majority of pronominal and nominal possessors modify inalienably possessed nouns. Possessors of inalienably possessed nouns are arguments of the head noun, which is inherently relational. Thus, they are semantically different from "true" modifiers such as words denoting properties: in the latter case, the modifier is relational (unary valency), and the head noun is its (nonrelational) argument. For this reason, it may be that their pragmatic function differs from that of "true" modifiers and so should be excluded from the count.[48] If we accept these two arguments, excluding all pronominal possessors and nominal possessors of inalienably possessed nouns produces the distribution for modifiers in table 2.17.

TABLE 2.17 *Distribution of Modifier Types in Four Languages*

Modifier Type	Quiché	Nguna	Soddo	Ute
Objects	1	3	13	14
Properties	27	17	14	16
Quantifiers	8	11	10	9
States	2	6	6	3
Relations	0	1	7	1
Actions	2	5	34	10
Auxiliary	0	0	0	0

Viewing the data in this way, properties play a more prominent role in the function of modification (though, in the Soddo data, there is an anomalously large number of relative clauses). If the general pattern holds out over larger numbers, it may even be argued that property roots are the most frequent and least marked modifier group, and so the double text frequency criterion is maintained.

2.6 The Major Syntactic Categories as Universals and as Language-Specific Categories

In this chapter, I have argued for an analysis of the major syntactic categories noun, verb, and adjective in terms of two independent but prototypically correlated externally defined parameters: the semantic class of the lexical root and the pragmatic function that the root plays in its manifestation in a position in the clause structure. The evidence I have provided for this analysis is based on the methodology of typological marking theory as explicated in Greenberg (1966a) and extended in Croft (1990b). Using the criteria of structural, behavioral, and textual markedness, I have compared what happens when lexical roots that are members of a syntactic category prototype appear in a pragmatic function other than their naturally correlated one. The "unnatural correlations," for example, ⟨action, reference⟩ or ⟨object, predication⟩, are typologically marked relative to the natural correlations, such as ⟨action, predication⟩ and ⟨object, reference⟩.

The evidence presented in this chapter demonstrates the existence of the syntactic categories "noun," "verb," and "adjective" as typological universals. That is, the evidence presented here represents systematic cross-linguistic patterns of variation. The patterns of variation involve the criteria of markedness. The typological universals do not predict the exact behavior of individual languages; rather, they predict that a language will fit somewhere in the pattern of variation allowed by typological marking theory. Thus, the typological universals underdetermine the structure of an individual language grammar, although they do constrain it.

In fact, marking theory does not exclude the possibility of a language that did not display any positive evidence for the prototypical status of objects, properties, and events as nouns, adjectives, and verbs, respectively—that is, evidence of an asymmetrical relation between the "natural" or "unmarked" combinations of lexical semantic class and pragmatic function and the other combinations—as long as the grammatical structure and behavior is neutral, in the sense described in 2.2. What the typological markedness analysis excludes is that a negative markedness pattern exists so that, say, lexical roots denoting objects take a nonzero function-indicating morpheme in referring expressions but not in modification or that a predicated property is inflected for more grammatical categories than a predicated action. The existence of a language displaying such patterns would be a definite counterexample to the typological universal definitions of noun, verb, and adjective presented in this chapter. No such language exists, to my knowledge.

It may also be that no language exists that has no positive evidence in favor of the markedness patterns establishing the universality of noun, verb, and adjective. For one thing, the semantic constraints underlying inflectional and syntactic behavior virtually guarantee the unmarked status of processes as verbs, gradable properties as adjectives, and countable objects as nouns (see 2.4). Nevertheless, it must not be forgotten that a typological universal pattern is almost always a pattern of variation: some languages more clearly distinguish the category "adjective" than others, by these criteria, and it may be that some languages barely distinguish the category "adjective" at all (e.g., perhaps Acehnese in the survey sample).

What is the relation between a typologically universal category such as "adjective" and an individual language grammar? The proper answer to this question can be found by treating an individual language grammar not as a fixed set of structures but as a currently more or less established set of conventions adjudicating the various external factors that constrain the linguistic system—conventions that are adhered to by an individual speaker and can change over time and even vary within a community. As I argued at the beginning of this chapter and will discuss in greater detail in the next, both lexical semantic class and pragmatic function are external factors of just this type. The typological universal pattern described in this chapter represents the constraints imposed by the relation between these two parameters. Within those constraints, individual languages—that is, speakers of a language—can vary in how and to what degree they conventionalize the relation between semantic class and pragmatic function. The relation between semantic class and pragmatic function is part of the (possibly innate) cognitive structure of every individual human language speaker, no matter to what degree it is manifested in the ever-changing conventions that govern the language that he or she speaks.

2.7 Appendix: Semantic Classification of Lexical Roots

The following is the semantic classification for the analysis of Russian roots presented in 2.3. Each class is given a descriptive name. The primary semantic features relevant to the study are listed in square brackets ("*n*-ary" refers to valency; the features are defined in 2.3). Semantic features listed under subclasses override the feature specified in the superordinate class. If the class is part of the "core" category of nouns, verbs, and adjectives, then "N," "V," or "A," respectively, are included after the list of semantic features (also, "State" is used for the state categories; see 2.5 and 3.3.3). The total number of roots in each class is listed after the semantic features, and an example of a root is presented for each class or subclass. Finally, nonobvious semantic classes are briefly defined in footnotes—note that, other than one subclass, there is no class titled "Abstract" or "Other."[49]

Naturally Individuatable (Count) Objects [0-ary, stative, not gradable; N]: 114:
- Nonrelationally defined objects:
  - Supernatural—*bog* 'god'
  - Human—*žen* 'woman'
  - Animate—*ov* 'sheep'
  - Inanimate [including plants]:[50]
    - Natural—*cvet* 'flower, color'
    - Man made—*kos* 'scythe'
    - Shapes[51]—*krug* 'circle, ring'
- Relationally defined objects [1-ary]:
  - Kinship and social relations [humans only]—*brat* 'brother'
  - Body parts:
    - Human body parts—*glaz* 'eye'
    - Animate-only body parts—*per* 'feather'

Plant/inanimate-only body parts—*kor* 'bark, rind'
Spatial orientation—*verx* 'top'
Locations [inanimate only]:
Celestial—*neb* 'sky, heavens'
Landscapes (natural locations)—*gor* 'hill, mountain'
Man-made locations—*gorod* 'city'
Time units [inanimate only]:—*god* 'year'

Not naturally individuatable (mass) objects [0-ary, stative, not gradable; N]: 14:
Substances—*med* 'honey'
Forms/materials[52]—*porox* 'powder, dust'

Groups [human only; stative, 1-ary, not gradable]: 4—*l'ud* 'people, mankind'

Collections/units[53] [stative, 1-ary, not gradable]: 4—*gromozd* 'pile, heap'

Quantifiers [stative, 1-ary, values on a (gradable) scale: 10:
Quantifiers proper—*cel* 'whole, entire'
Numerals—*vtor* 'two'

Properties [stative, 1-ary, gradable, persistent; A]: 54:
Color—*bel* 'white'
Measure (spatial)—*mal* 'small'
Time-related properties—*nov* 'new'
Other physical properties—*plosk* 'flat'
Socially defined properties—*sv'at* 'holy, sacred'

Token-related properties[54] [stative, 2-ary symmetric, normally persistent; A]: 6—*rav(n)* 'similar, equal'

Dispositions [transitory for actions, persistent for individuals; States]:[55] 17—*xitr* 'cunning, sly'

States [1-ary, stative, mostly transitory, gradable; States]:[56] 49:
Environmental states [persistent only for environments]—*xolod* 'cold'
Physical states—*golod* 'hunger'
Emotional states—*krot* 'mild, meek, gentle'
Socially/functionally defined states—*bogat* 'wealth'
States of affairs[57]—*pravd* 'true'

Spatial relations (adpositions) [2-ary, stative, transitory]: 3—*p(e)-red* 'front, before'

Weather [processual, 0-ary, transitory]: 2—*bur* 'storm'

Relations [mostly stative, 2-ary, not gradable]: 7:
- Being, being at [1- or 2-ary, persistent]—*by(t)* 'be'
- Measure[58]—*sto* 'cost'
- Possession—*im* 'possess'

"Inactive actions" [2-ary, stative but treated processually, transitory]:[59] 11:
- Living [persistent]—*ži(v)* 'live, alive'
- Position/body posture—*leg* 'lie, lie down'
- Possession/keeping—*derž* 'maintain, keep, hold, preserve, retain'

Mental relations and inactive actions: 30:
- Perception—*vid* 'see'
- Emotion (including seeking)—*xot* 'want, desire, hunt'
- Knowledge and belief—*zna* 'know'

Activities—physical [processual, 1-ary, not gradable, transitory]: 40:
- Nontranslational (bodily) motion—*nik* 'bend down, droop'
- Bodily activity—*plev* 'spit'
- Human activity—*pl'as* 'dance'
- Animate activity—*ras(t)* 'grow'
- Inanimate activity—*zvon* 'ring, sound'

Translational Motion [processual, 1-ary,[60] transitory; V]: 18—*gul* 'walk'

Cause-physical-state [processual, 2-ary, transitory; V]: 1—*lek* 'cure, heal, treat'

Cause-activity [processual, 2-ary, transitory; V]: 5:
- Cause-nontranslational motion—*vert* 'turn, spin'

Actions [processual, 2-ary, not gradable, transitory]: 92:
- Physical actions [V]:
  - Creation—*stro(j)* 'build'
  - Contact/affect:
    - Force—*klon* 'bend'

Affect—*t(e)r* 'rub, scrape, grate, wash'
Transform—*gar* 'burn, heat'
Undo—*lom(l)* 'break'
Destroy—*gub* 'destroy'
Ingest—*ed/est* 'eat'
Mental/social actions:
Speech actions [2,3-ary]—*boron* 'scold, abuse'
Other mental/social actions[61]—*ščad* 'have mercy, pardon'
Cause-relation/action [processual, 3-ary, not gradable, transitory]:
43:
Cause-physical-relation [V]:
Cause-motion—*nes* 'carry, bring, wear'
Cause-connectivity—*v'az* 'join, tie, knit'
Cause-position—*de(ž)(d)* 'place, put'
Cause-possession (transfer) [V]—*da(t)* 'give'
Cause-mental-relation:
Cause-emotional-relation [2-ary]—*pug* 'frighten'
Cause-knowledge/belief—*uk* 'teach, learn'

Modality: 5—*kaz* 'appear, seem, express'

Aspect: 4—*kon* 'end, finish'

3

Toward an External Definition of Syntactic Categories

3.1 Introduction

In the preceding chapter, I presented evidence supporting a universal definition of the major syntactic categories "noun," "verb," and "adjective," based on a typological prototype pattern using standard criteria of markedness. The establishment of the typological pattern necessitated the recognition of two independent external parameters, lexical semantic class (objects, properties, and events) and pragmatic function (reference, predication, and modification). The typological evidence reveals that specific lexical semantic classes are associated with each pragmatic function; these are the prototypical lexical classes for each function. The primary semantic parameters that define the prototypes are valency (inherent relationality), stativity (change over time), persistence over time, gradability, and boundedness (at least for objects, manifested as countability). In this chapter, I will discuss more precise definitions of the pragmatic functions and possible explanations for the correlations of lexical semantic classes with each of the pragmatic functions.

Linguistic structure is sensitive not only to the "objective" characteristics of a situation, as represented more or less by the lexical semantics of a root, but also to the way the speaker conceptualizes or perceives the situation. This is more than just a matter of selecting information to be expressed and not selecting information to be ignored. To some extent, the speaker imposes structure on a scene that may be related to the "objective" structure of the scene itself in a quite indirect way, or it may not be a structure present in the "objective" structure of the scene at all. This can be called the CONCEPTUALIZATION of a situation, a view of linguistic structure propounded by Fillmore (1975), Lakoff (1977, 1987), Talmy (1977, 1985, 1988), Langacker (1987a, 1987b), and others.

In fact, one can imagine pragmatic or discourse structure as an aspect of conceptualization. The organization of information into referring expressions, modifiers, and predications and—to look ahead to chapters 4–6—the ordering of participants as subject, object, and oblique is largely structure imposed on the scene by the speaker, although it is obviously closely intertwined with "objective" properties of the scene itself (as manifested in the grammatical choices imposed by the lexical root).[1] One can study the conceptualization of a scene in two ways: semantically, by examining how conceptualization influences the semantic structure, and pragmatically or discourse functionally, by examining what conditions in the planning and execution of discourse license a particular way of conceptualizing the scene: "Rather than being derivative one from another, both semantic and discourse-functional facts are reflections of underlying cognitive schemata, the illumination of which must be the ultimate goal of both semantics and discourse analysis" (DeLancey 1987:54).

In the next section, I will present a cognitive model of the pragmatic functions that simultaneously involves the conceptualization of the entity in the function, a speech act that defines the function, and a communicative purpose or goal of the function. Casting a lexical root as a referring expression, a modifier, or a predicate imposes a specific conceptualization (coercion, construal) of the entity denoted in accordance with the pragmatic function (Bolinger 1967; Wierzbicka 1986; Langacker 1987b). The pragmatic function itself is analogous to an illocutionary speech act, but it is a speech act that structures information inside the proposition rather than modifying the proposition as a whole (Searle 1969). Finally, the pragmatic function is deployed to carry out a goal in a larger framework of discourse, which has also been modeled in a cognitive perspective (e.g., Chafe 1979, 1980, 1987; DuBois 1987; Givón 1983a).

Most of the examples in this chapter are derived from nonprototypical lexical semantic classes. The examination of these classes both tests and enriches the cognitive model presented in this chapter. The nonprototypical examples lack some of the relevant prototypical features, and, by comparing them to the prototypes, those features can be teased out. Also, in the case of the pragmatic functions, nonprototypicality involves an "unnatural" or at least "imperfect" correlation of lexical semantic root with syntactic construction (referring expression, predication, attribution). In those cases, there will be a mixture of properties, some associated with the syntactic category expressed and some associated with the syntactic construction that the lexical semantic root is naturally correlated with. By comparing the unnatural correlations of lexical semantic class and syntactic construction with the natural correlations, the relevant discourse-functional (and cognitive semantic) features can be teased out.

3.2 Conceptualization, Pragmatics, and Discourse

Prototypes, including the lexical semantic prototypes described in chapter 2, do not exist in thin air; prototypes must have some reason for existing. In particular, this prototypical combination of semantic features must be related in some way to the function that nouns, verbs, and adjectives play, the functions that I have named reference, predication, and modification. This section will examine this far more difficult area.

3.2.1 Conceptualization

One can use the cognitive semantic perspective in order to examine the very fact of being a noun, an adjective, and a verb itself as a way to conceptualize the entity denoted by the word.

A detailed study of the distinction between noun and adjective was made by Wierzbicka (1986); prior work had been done by Bolinger (1967, 1980a, 1980b). Wierzbicka examines marginal cases (as does Bolinger), in which concepts appear to differ only in their manifestation as adjective or noun:

i. naming of concepts, e.g., *blind* (adj.) vs. *cripple* (n.);
ii. occurrence in *X is a* ____ vs. *X is* ____: *Rosemary is blond/gray* but *Rosemary is a blond/*gray;*
iii. occurrence in *a/the* ____ vs. *a/the* ____ *N: The man/*male kept shouting and screaming;*
iv. comparison of adjectives derived from nouns without a dramatic meaning change: *Jew* vs. *Jewish, friend* vs. *friendly.*

Wierzbicka characterizes the difference between nouns and adjectives as that between CLASSIFICATION (categorization) and DESCRIPTION.[2] That is, nouns place their referents into a class, with an overall set of properties (including stereotypical ones). Adjectives do not categorize the objects they describe; they simply attribute the property they denote to the object. For instance, the noun *Jew* has acquired the connotations—often negative, as in this case—that do not accrue (at least, not as much) to the adjective *Jewish,* and so the former is avoided (Bolinger 1980a: 79). The adjective *Polish* describes someone's ethnicity, but the noun *Pole* categorizes the person as "belonging to Poland" (Wierzbicka 1986: 378). In describing women, *blond* is associated with an identifiable (stereo)type and so can be used as a noun; *gray* is not associated with a particular type and so cannot be used as a noun. As Wierzbicka puts it, "Nouns embody concepts which cannot be reduced to any combination of features. They stand for categories which can be identified by means of a certain positive image, or a certain positive stereotype, but an image which transcends all enumerable features" (Wierzbicka 1986:361). Nouns name a KIND, whereas adjectives simply name a PROPERTY. When adjectives come to be used as nouns, they acquire additional features, in particular, a restriction to humans (*the poor, the blacks, the blind*). Even when used as nouns, however, adjectives will display defective grammatical behavior (Wierzbicka 1986:365):

(1)?*A white*/**A poor*/**A blind sat in the back of the bus.*

Wierzbicka also argues that the "core" adjectival concepts, which we have seen pertain to color and size (Dixon 1977), are adjectival because they are perceived as referring not to kinds but to particular individuals (Wierzbicka 1986:366–67). Also, because nouns represent a conceptualization of something as a kind, they are not gradable concepts—in the folk theory of classification, categories have reasonably clear boundaries.[3]

In the same way that Wierzbicka describes adjectives close to the borderline with nouns, Bolinger describes uses of nouns as adjectives with a quite similar distinction. Most predicate nominals require the article *a*. This is unlike the situation in most Romance languages, such as French, in which a noun can be predicated with or without the article:

(2) *Jean est voleur.*
John be thief
'John is a thief.'

(3) *Jean est un voleur.*
John be a thief
'John is a thief!'

Without the article, the predicate is describing a property of the subject, namely, being a thief. Bolinger (1980b:1) describes the use without the article as a CLASSIFYING one. With the article, the predicate is characterizing the subject as a particular individual possessing a collection of qualities belonging to the stereotypical thief, though not necessarily being a thief. Bolinger calls this an INDIVIDUALIZING use. Of course, in English there are very few remnants of the predication of nouns without articles. Bolinger (1980b) describes a great many of them; here I will point out only two that help distinguish nouns from adjectives. First, in the plural, there is still a distinction between classifying and individualizing constructions (Bolinger 1980b:2; the distinction is one of preferred interpretation, not an absolute one):

(4) *John and his brothers are thieves.*

(5) *John and his brother are a/*Ø couple of thieves.*

(6) *They're all thieves.*

(7) *They're all a/*Ø bunch of thieves.*

Second, if the concept is gradable, then it is more likely to be predicated adjectivally, without the article (Bolinger 1980b: 9):

(8) *John is Swedish.*

(9) *John is part Swede/part Swedish.*[4]

(10) *?*John is partly a Swede.*

Bolinger also refers to the description-classification distinction that Wierzbicka uses. True adjectives describe; most denominal adjectives classify. For that reason, the more nounlike predicate nominal construction with the article and *one* is preferred (Bolinger 1980b: 2):

(11) ?*George's plantation is Southern.*

(12) *George's plantation is a Southern one.*

(13) ?*The speeches in this volume are all presidential.*

(14) *The speeches in this volume are all presidential ones.*

In other words, Bolinger argues for a scale of more adjectivelike to more nounlike conceptualizations, ranging from describing to classifying to individualizing. Description is exclusively adjectival. Classifying is nominal but uses an adjectivelike predication construction in English compared to individualizing, which is exclusively nominal (or compared to the equational *be,* which is also exclusively nominal since it equates two tokens of a type).

One may add to Bolinger's examples of nouns used predicatively like adjectives examples of nouns used as unmarked modifiers. These are compounds or more compound-like in nature. Compounds are distinguished from standard genitive constructions grammatically, in that they are less marked as modifiers, and semantically, in that the modifying element in the compound no longer has specific reference, serving only to describe or characterize the head noun. Compare the different Turkish izafet constructions (Lewis 1967: 42–43) and their English translations:

(15) *üniversite -nin profesörler -i*
university -GEN professors -3PL
'the professors of the university'

(16) *üniversite profesörler -i*
university professors -3PL
'university professors'

In the "definite izafet," with the genitive case, and in the English genitive, the modifying noun still represents an independent kind that is related to the head noun in some way. In the "indefinite izafet," and the English compound, both lacking the nonzero genitive morpheme, the modifying noun is just a "qualifying" (Lewis 1967:42) property of the kind named by the head.

Langacker's cognitive definition of "noun" appears to focus on a different aspect of conceptualization of an entity. Langacker defines a noun as "a region in some domain" (Langacker 1987b:58). A domain is any sort of background structure of experience: space, time, the number scale, etc. A region, taken abstractly, is "a set of interconnected entities" (62); entities are defined as I have done, namely, anything (62–63). Entities are interconnected if they "are coordinated as components of a higher-order cognitive event" (61–62); and a cognitive event occurs with any sort of mental experience (61). Nouns are nonrelational, which Langacker points out is a matter of conceptualization (e.g., *circle* vs. *round;* 68), while adjectives and verbs are relational. Langacker writes, "A nominal predication presupposes the interconnections among a set of conceived entities, and profiles the region thus established. By contrast, a relational predication presupposes a set of entities, and it PROFILES the INTERCONNECTIONS among these entities" (68).

The presupposing of a set of entities makes nonnominals relational: the presupposed entities are related to the nonnominal predication. It appears that Langacker's definition of "noun" focuses on the *autonomy* of a concept that is expressed by a noun rather than on its classifying conceptual function.[5] His example of *circle* versus *round* illustrates well his distinction, however: a circle is an autonomous object of its own, whereas being round is something associated with an entity. This, however, creates a problem with the abstract noun *roundness,* which does not mean the same thing as *circle.* However, *roundness* appears to conceptualize a property as an autonomous entity that can be spoken of in abstraction from the entities it presupposes. For that reason, the argument to *roundness,* in fact the arguments for any nominalized relational entity, can be dropped since they are "out of focus." The conceptualization of a nominalized entity as autonomous explains why the core noun lexical semantic classes have zero valency: they can most easily be conceptualized as autonomous entities.[6]

The difference between adjective and verb in conceptualization is chiefly one of permanence versus transitoriness. Wierzbicka compares the attributive versus predicative use of adjectives in English and adjectival versus verbal forms of color words in Latin and Russian (Wierzbicka 1986 : 376):

English:

(17) *Her red cheeks radiated youth and good health.*

(18) *Her cheeks were red.*

Latin:

(19) *Rosa rubra est*
rose red [ADJ] is
'A/the rose is red.'

(20) *Rosa rubet*
rose be.red [VERB]
'A/the rose is red.'

Russian:

(21) *Parus bel*
sail white [ADJ]
'The sail is white.'

(22) *Beleet parus odinokij v tumane morja golubom*
be.white sail lonely in mist.LOC sea.GEN blue.LOC
'The lonely sail was white in the blue mist of the sea.' [Lermontov]

In both the attributive versus predicative adjective distinction and the predicate adjective versus predicate verb distinction, the former is more likely to be interpreted as representing a permanent property, and the latter is more likely to be interpreted as representing a temporary state.

In the reverse direction, English verb-object compounds cannot appear attributively unless they represent some well-established state, such as *ill-behaved* (*child*) or *woman-hating* (*man*): "[A] secretary who erases mistakes is not a *mistake-erasing secretary*, nor is a wife who wakes her husband a *husband-waking wife*. These must wait the day when we have some interest in characterizing secretaries as mistake-erasing or wives as husband-waking" (Bolinger 1967:6–7). Here Bolinger is using the phrase "characterizing" in the same way that Wierzbicka (and Bolinger himself in 1980b) use the term "describing." The description must characterize some property that is stable and salient enough to merit an attributive adjective. Bolinger uses this to account for *labeled goods/*sent goods, a scratched surface/*a scratched head, deposited money/*withdrawn money:* the participle in the first member of each pair represents a more stable characteristic of the head noun. In English, adjectives are found generally in prenominal position and verbal modifiers (participial phrases and relative clauses) in postnominal position: *a small child/the child sleeping in the crib*. Some modifiers occur in either position, but the prenominal position describes a more permanent quality than the postnominal one: *a responsible man/the man responsible* (*for the contract*) (Bolinger 1967:4). Finally, Bolinger provides an example of a three-way distinction between a verb, a predicate adjective, and a predicate nominal, with the expected associations of transitoriness,[7] isolable property, and stereotype, respectively (Bolinger 1980a:79):

(23) *Jill fusses.*

(24) *Jill is fussy.*

(25) *Jill is a fussbudget.*

Langacker's (1987b) cognitive analysis of nouns and verbs represents a somewhat different proposal for the verb-nonverb distinction. Langacker proposes that predication (the pragmatic function described here) involves sequential scanning of the concept rather than summary scanning:

> In [summary scanning], the various facets of a situation are examined in cumulative fashion, so that a more and more complex conceptualization is progressively built up; once the entire scene has been scanned, all facets of it are simultaneously available, and cohere as a single gestalt. . . . By contrast, sequential scanning involves the successive transformation of one scene into another. The various phases of an evolving situation are examined serially, in non-cumulative fashion; hence the conceptualization is dynamic, in the sense that its contents change from one instant to the next. [Langacker 1987b:72]

Langacker's analysis obviously fits for processual entities and explains why they form the verbal prototype. Langacker argues that sequential scanning also applies to stative verbs, such as *resemble, have, want, know,* and *like* (which he calls "imperfective processes"), saying that these predicates are "plausibly interpreted as describing the perpetuation through time of a static configuration" (79). Unfortunately, that description applies better to *keep* than to *have,* to *yearn for* than to *want,* to *stay* than to *be* (*at*), and to *look at* than to *see* (see Dahl 1979). The first verb in each pair occurs naturally in the progressive, conceptualizing the state of affairs as an "inactive action" (see 2.5), and contrasts with the second verb of the pair, which occurs in the simple present without generic meaning—the standard test for stativity. Thus, it is not clear how Langacker's definition extends beyond true processes.

Bolinger's and Wierzbicka's analysis of the verb-nonverb distinction supports the prototypicality of transitory predicates as verbs since they can be easily conceptualized as transitory. Langacker's analysis, if correct, supports the prototypicality of processes since they are the most easily scanned sequentially.

In addition to these examples of subtle semantic differences found in words or compounds that differ only in their (unmarked) syntactic category—details rarely described in language grammars—there are more dramatic alterations in meaning caused by the shift in syntactic category that are commonly described and appear to be widespread. The most dramatic alterations occur in the shift from noun to predicate or modifier, and vice versa. As I pointed out in 2.3, a noun used as a referring expression simply indicates the class or category of the entity referred to. If, on the other hand, the noun is predicated, then it denotes a relation, either a predicational relation (belonging to the class), an equational relation (identity of individuals), an individualizing relation (possessing the stereotypical characteristics of the class), or one of several other relations. Likewise, if the noun is a modifier, either as a genitive modifier or as a plain modifier in a complex nominal construction, it denotes a relation holding between the noun modifier and the noun head (e.g., possession by Rita in *Rita's car*). The noun is semantically converted into something that can be properly ascribed to a referred-to entity. Conversely, an adjective or a verb when used in a referring expression must be converted into something that can be properly referred to. This is done most directly by nominalization: this allows the property/action to be referred to. As was noted in 2.3, in many languages (though not in English) an adjective and/or verb can also be put directly into a noun slot in a noun phrase; that is, it can be used as a referring expression with a definite article without any explicit nominalizing morphology. In these cases, however, the resulting expression refers not to the property/action but to one of the persons or objects serving as an argument to the property/action, as in Spanish *la roja* [the.FEM red.FEM] 'the red one' or Quiché *lē k-Ø-ā(t)-tix-oh* [the PRES-3.INAN.ABS-2SG.ERG-eat-TRANS] 'what you eat.' In other words, adjectives and verbs can function as nouns directly in many languages, but only if their denotation is shifted from properties/actions to persons or objects.[8]

Bolinger's and Wierzbicka's examples illustrate two kinds of conceptualization phenomena. The first is LEXICALIZED CONCEPTUALIZATION (see Croft MS): two words that denote the same thing but differ in grammatical category, such as Russian *bel* [predicate adjective]/*belet'* [verb] 'white' or English *Polish* [adjective]/*Pole* [noun], will differ in the conceptualization of the entity denoted. The second phenomenon is COERCION (see Croft MS): the conceptualization of the denotation of a lexical item will be imposed by its grammatical context, as in ____ *hate women* [predicate]/*woman-hating* ____ [modifier]. That is, coercion represents the contribution by the grammatical construction to the semantics (conceptualization) of the lexical item as found in that construction.[9] The examples in the last paragraph exhibit a semantically more dramatic type of coercion. Coercion/conceptualization is the basic phenomenon; lexicalized conceptualizations represent a grammaticalization of the coercion relations associated with the relevant grammatical construction (they are usually found at the margins of the lexical semantic prototypes).

The conceptualizations contributed by reference, modification, and predication are as follows:

Referring creates an autonomous entity and makes it into a kind or an individual of the kind (with its attendant stereotype and connotations);
Modification makes the entity into a stable but one-dimensional description (property) of some other entity;
Predication sequentially scans an entity, making it into a transitory (and changing?) state of affairs, involving at least one participant.

Having described the conceptualization imposed by syntactic category membership, one can examine the reason why human beings conceptualize their experience in language in this way. Part of this is probably due to innate cognitive makeup. Another place to seek an answer, however, is in the function of language, communication.[10] We organize our experience, encoded by the semantics of lexical items, in a particular way in order to communicate it to our interlocutors. Thus, the ultimate goal is to understand the pragmatics, or discourse function, of reference, predication, and modification.

3.2.2 Pragmatic Function

The definitions of "noun" and "verb" that I have more or less explicitly endorsed throughout the previous chapter—nouns specify what we are talking about and verbs what we are saying about it—are rooted in the ancient definition of "subject" and "predicate." (The traditional grammar definitions for "noun" and "verb," on the other hand, are associated with the semantic classes of the prototypically nominal and verbal lexical roots.) Before describing current manifestations of these and related concepts, an important terminological ambiguity must be pointed out. The term "subject" has two distinct uses. In one use, it is contrasted with "predicate"; this use is central to distinguishing the pragmatic functions of nouns and verbs. In the other use, "subject" is contrasted with "object," "indirect object," and "oblique." In this use, one class of noun (more precisely, noun phrase in modern structural analysis) is contrasted with another. This use generally has little to say about the noun-verb distinction. Unfortunately, the same ambiguity has been replicated in the new terminology adopted by many for this concept: the term "topic" is used on the one hand to contrast with "comment" and on the other hand to contrast with "nontopic" noun phrases of various sorts.

Current work on pragmatic or discourse-functional approaches to the definitions of the major syntactic categories fall into two general groups, one in philosophy and one in linguistics, reflected by the terms each uses ("pragmatics" in philosophy, "discourse function" in linguistics). In neither tradition has the noun-verb distinction been treated as a significant pragmatic/discourse functional issue. However, important proposals have been made in both traditions that we will build on here. I will discuss the two analytical traditions in turn.

The philosophical pragmatic tradition that has the closest connection to discourse function is speech act analysis (Austin 1962; Searle 1976). Speech act analysis is a model of speech as a series of actions that the speaker plans with intended (and unintended) consequences for the hearer. More recently, the philosophical speech act tradition has been utilized in artificial intelligence research, where it fits well with the standard artificial intelligence model of rational human behavior as planning and problem solving.

Austin's original development of speech act theory, for the most part unchanged, pertains specifically to what he called ILLOCUTIONARY ACTS, such as requesting, promising, asserting, etc. These speech acts take an entire proposition in their scope, so that, for instance, the following sentences have the same proposition, although they represent different speech acts:

(26) *Fred, fix the hose.*

(27) *Will Fred fix the hose?*

(28) *I promise to fix the hose.* [spoken by Fred]

(29) *Fred will fix the hose.*

These sentences express a command, a request, a promise, and an assertion, respectively, all of the proposition *Fix*(*Fred, the hose*). Austin developed a classification of illocutionary acts into various types, a classification refined by his followers, notably Searle (1976; see also Hancher 1979).

The analysis of illocutionary acts has been the primary focus of attention for speech act analysis and as such does not pertain directly to the issue of the function of nouns and verbs in discourse. However, Searle's first major work in speech acts (Searle 1969) proposes an extension of speech act theory that applies directly to this problem. Searle proposed that there are actually three levels of speech acts that are performed every time an utterance is made (Searle 1969 : 23–24). The highest level is illocutionary acts, applied as we saw to whole propositions. The lowest level he titled UTTERANCE ACTS, that is, simply producing words and morphemes. The intermediate level acts are PROPOSITIONAL ACTS, which structure the sentence and are constituted by reference and predication: "The characteristic form of propositional acts are parts of sentences: grammatical predicates for the act of predication, and proper names, pronouns, and certain other sorts of noun phrases for reference" (25). Propositional acts (and utterance acts) are not preconditions for illocutionary acts; they are acts performed simultaneously with illocutionary acts (24).

The act of reference is that of identifying some entity, that is, the entity that the speaker intends to talk about (Searle 1969 : 85). The act of predication is the act of ascribing a property to a referred-to entity (100).[11] In fact, Searle argues that recognizing the distinction between reference and predication as acts allows one to avoid a number of philosophical paradoxes, most particularly, the attempt to distinguish 'be wise,' which represents the ascription of a property to an individual, from 'wisdom,' which refers to the same property.[12] This is, of course, the same distinction made in the last chapter between the pragmatic functions of reference and predications.[13] The sameness of 'be wise' and 'wisdom,' which philosophers had attempted to capture through the notion of "reference," is due to their having the same denotations (in the definition of "denotation" provided in 2.1; Searle [1969: 100] refers to this as "expressing a sense").

The application of speech acts to parts of the proposition by Searle helps account for one of the primary lexical semantic features that correlates with the noun-verb distinction. In 2.3, I argued that nouns differed from verbs (and adjectives) primarily in that nouns had a valency of zero and verbs (and adjectives) had a valency greater than zero. Likewise, the propositional acts of reference and predication have a valency of zero and one (or more), respectively. The referring relation holds between the identifying linguistic expression and what it denotes and so does not inherently involve any other entity. Predication, on the other hand, is the ascription of a "property" (in the broader philosophical sense) to a referred-to entity and therefore inherently involves the referred-to entity. It is for this reason that predicate nominals are conceptualized as relations, the relation of an individual belonging to a class or having a characteristic feature. The predication involves a relation between the predicate and a referent: the predication must "hold" of a referent.

Searle does not discuss modification. Modification may be a distinct propositional act. At the least, modification is a secondary version of the primary propositional acts of reference and predication, or some sort of "intermediate" category between the two (see 3.3.2). However, this does not complete the taxonomy of propositional speech acts. In addition to reference, predication, and (possibly) modification, there are acts that crosscut these three categories and are manifested in the lexical-inflectional continuum. A fuller description of the crosscutting propositional acts presented in Croft (in press a) is summarized very briefly here since these functions are orthogonal to the pragmatic functions in question. The three acts are CATEGORIZING the entity, SITUATING the entity in some background dimension, and SELECTING the entity (type-token).

Categorizing the entity is simply naming it and corresponds to the concept of denotation introduced in chapter 2. This function is performed by the lexical roots, though it is also performed by gender and classifiers for objects (nouns) and classes based on transitivity and aspect for actions (verbs).

Objects are situated with respect to a physical background dimension, space, and actions are situated in time.[14] Situating is performed grammatically in terms of a deictic framework (demonstratives, tense) or in relation to some landmark in the background dimension. The landmark itself may be indicated deictically (locative deictics for objects, temporal deictics for actions) or by name (proper names for places and times); or the landmark may itself be another entity, and some relational expression is used (spatial adpositions for objects, temporal/causal connectives for actions). Adjectives, that is, words denoting properties, appear to fit into this system as well in that qualities are measured against the background dimension of quantity. The "position" of a quality such as height is expressed absolutely, as with numerals accompanying measure expressions (*six feet tall*), or relative to the property associated with another object, as in comparatives (*Harriet is taller than Fred*). Situating of objects and events in a mental space (Fauconnier 1985) also occurs, with a human being's beliefs, desires, and obligations providing the situational framework. This "metaphysical" situating accounts for the existence of various devices for indicating the epistemological and ontological status of objects (articles, definiteness, fictional context nouns such as *my* ***idea*** *of a vaction*) and events (modals, sentential adverbs, irrealis mood, complement-taking verbs of belief, desire, etc.).

The third major crosscutting propositional speech act is selection of an entity from among its "fellows." For most concepts, there is a concept type and multiple concept tokens instantiating the type (in reality or in imagination). A speaker may select the concept type, using a generic article or other construction (e.g., the bare plural in English) for objects and the generic/habitual inflection for events. If the speaker selects a concept token, he or she must individuate it from its fellows and quantify the individuals selected. For objects that come "naturally" in units—that is, count nouns—the individual may be readily selected, or a partitive used to select a part (*top of the box, arm of a chair, a piece of the cake*), or a collective used to select a larger unit (*a bunch of grapes, a set of chairs*). Parallel inflectional forms and minor-category items perform the selection function for actions: perfective forms select a bound event, a collective construction selects a group of related actions, and imperfective, progressive, and other complement-taking verb types select parts of actions. When an individual object or action is selected, it can be quantified through numerals and quantifiers for objects (*five books, many books*) or through quantifying adverbs for actions (*do it five times, he always does it*). Finally, a selected entity must sometimes be distinguished from other selected entities, through special modifiers for objects (*the same/other/second/last book*) and actions (*she did it again/back*).

These propositional speech acts appear to account for the minor syntactic categories and inflectional categories associated with nouns, verbs, and adjectives (see Croft [in press a] for an exhaustive enumeration of types of grammatical and lexical categories).[15] Categorizing, situating (physical and "metaphysical"), and selecting apply to objects and actions alike, and also to properties in some cases (particularly physical situating), relative to the background dimensions of space, time, and quantity, respectively. A full taxonomy of propositional speech acts ought to provide a classification of the morpheme types, lexical and grammatical, found in human languages.

The functions defined by the major syntactic categories in the prototypical case are headed by the categorizing lexical roots—the nouns, verbs, and adjectives—and their dependents are the morphemes that perform the situating and selecting functions. The speaker plans his or her utterance below the clause level in terms of these propositional speech acts; for the speech acts to be successful, they must satisfy appropriate felicity conditions, as do illocutionary speech acts. In order to understand better what conditions govern the use of the propositional speech acts of reference, predication and modification, I now turn to research in discourse structure.

3.2.3 Discourse Function

The linguistic tradition of discourse analysis has largely focused on a different set of problems than those that would bear on the noun-verb issue, specifically, on those that deal with different types of noun phrases. The closest linguistic distinction to the pragmatic one of reference and predication is that of "topic" and "comment" as found in Hockett (1958). Hockett's description is very close to the traditional definition of subject and predicate: "The speaker announces a topic and then says something about it" (Hockett 1958:201). However, Hockett (like others after him) applies the topic-comment distinction to constructions other than the traditional European subject-predicate distinction, specifically, the English construction known as "topicalization" (Ross 1967; Prince 1981a) and the construction found in Mandarin Chinese and other languages known as the "topic" or "double-subject" construction:

Topicalization in English (Prince 1981a:252):

(30) *I have a recurring dream in which . . . I can't remember what I say. I usually wake up crying. This dream I've had maybe three, four times.*

"Double subjects" in Mandarin Chinese (Li and Thompson 1976: 468):

(31) *Nèike shù yèzi dà*
that tree leaves big
'That tree [topic], the leaves are big.'

The double-subject constructions may be an extension of the topic-comment structure from the canonical subject-predicate structure. In the canonical subject-predicate structure, the referent (topic) is normally the semantic argument (or one of the arguments) of the predicate (comment). This need not necessarily be the case, however, since this is only a preferred correlation of the pragmatic reference-predication (topic-comment) relation with a semantic argument-predicate relation. The double-subject constructions may be an example of a reference-predication (topic-comment) relation holding between a predicate and a nonargument referent. Nevertheless, a semantic relation of some sort is induced. Chafe (1976 : 51) suggests a translation of the Chinese example as 'That tree has big leaves,' in which the Chinese topic is rendered as the English subject. This shows how a language such as English that does not allow a nonargument "subject" can repackage the semantic content in a way that may be pragmatically similar to the Chinese sentence. Thus, it may be that the double-subject constructions represent nonprototypical topic-comment constructions that are disallowed in so-called subject-prominent languages.

Chafe, however, disagrees with this analysis, suggesting instead that the "topic" in this construction more closely resembles the scene-setting temporal or locative phrase, as in *On Saturday I went to the movies.* Evidence supporting Chafe's analysis is that tests for VP-hood of the nontopic portion of a double-subject construction fail (Li and Thompson 1976 : 487–88, n. 9). If Chafe is correct, then the double-subject construction may be better analyzed as an extension of the scene-setting construction, not as an extension of the canonical subject-predicate construction (cf. Hockett 1958 : 202–3). Perhaps it is best described as intermediate between the two since the function of scene setting ("limiting the applicability of the predicate to a certain restricted domain"; Chafe 1976 : 50) is closely related to the function of reference/"subject" as described above (limiting the applicability of a predicate to a certain individual).

Similar comments apply to the topicalization construction. The basic difficulty here, as in the double-subject construction, is that the syntactic subject is not the "topic"; unlike the double-subject construction, the "topic" is a (fronted) nonsubject argument. Prince (1981a) analyzes the function of topicalization in discourse and proposes that (i) the topic NP has to be evoked in the discourse or inferrable from an evoked entity (see below for definitions of "evoked" and "inferrable"),

(ii) the rest of the sentence except for the tonically stressed element is given information, and (iii) the tonically stressed element provides new information. As with the double-subject construction in Mandarin Chinese, the untopicalized portion of the English topicalization construction does not behave like a VP; hence, the surface structure is not analogous to a canonical predicate. Nevertheless, the English topicalized NP seems to represent "what the sentence is about" more so than does the Chinese topic NP. In sum, these two constructions might be nonprototypical topic-comment structures, using a definition such as Hockett's, signaled by the presence of a nontopic subject, but that very fact raises the issue of whether these constructions should be treated as extensions of the canonical topic-comment/subject-predicate construction type at all.

Another distinction that is a candidate for helping define the discourse functions associated with "noun" and "verb" is the THEME-RHEME distinction, also known as FUNCTIONAL SENTENCE PERSPECTIVE, used by the Prague School linguists (Firbas 1966; Mathesius 1975) and by Halliday (1967; cf. also Kuno 1972). Mathesius begins by using the "about" relation to define theme and rheme: "The element about which something is stated may be said to be the basis of the utterance or the theme, and what is stated about the basis is the nucleus of the utterance or the rheme" (Mathesius 1975:81). However, two characteristics distinguish theme and rheme from subject-predicate and topic-comment. First, theme and rheme can represent a gradient scale, a scale of COMMUNICATIVE DYNAMISM (Firbas 1966:270), so that a grammatical element may be the rheme of the preceding element and the theme for the following one. Thus, the theme-rheme relation may hold between scene-setting locatives and the rest of the sentence, as in Czech [*Na břehu jezera*] [*stál hoch*] '[On the bank of the lake] [stood a boy]' (Mathesius 1975:82). Second, as implied by the first distinction, theme-rheme is closedly related to word order, not to the subject-predicate relation: "The theme and the rheme are not the same as the grammatical subject and the grammatical predicate. . . . correspondence between functional sentence perspective and formal sentence structure is often lacking" (Mathesius 1975:84). It is worth noting that functional sentence perspective was originally developed to analyze a language (Czech) with relatively free word order; applying it to a language such as English with much less free word order potentially poses difficulties (Mathesius 1975:85). Firbas's notion of communicative dynamism combines word order ranking and a semantic scale of "salient" or "prominent" information, neither of which is associated with the noun-verb distinction.

Halliday's definition of "theme," like Firbas's and Mathesius's definitions, is more closely associated with word order than with subject-predicate (which he associates with another grammatical "system"): "Basically, the theme is what comes first in the clause. . . . the theme is assigned initial position in the clause, and all that follows is the rheme. . . . the theme is what is being talked about, the point of departure for the clause as a message" (Halliday 1967 : 212). Although Halliday also identifies theme with "what is being talked about," his second phrase, "the point of departure for the clause as a message," appears to be closer to the Prague School view of theme-rheme and also close to theories of the function of word order recently developed in the American tradition of discourse analysis of word order (DeLancey 1981; Mithun 1987). In this tradition, word order represents a ranking of information units according to a general principle not unlike Firbas's communicative dynamism: "attention flow" (DeLancey), "newsworthiness" (Mithun). On the basis of these observations, it appears that this family of discourse-functional concepts is not relevant to the subject-predicate (and, ultimately, noun-verb) distinction.[16]

By far the most thoroughly examined area in the discourse function of grammatical constructions is that involving 'givenness' and 'topicality' (in yet another guise). A detailed taxonomy of 'given'-'new' distinctions is given by Prince (1979, 1981b). Prince's taxonomy is restricted to the notion of "given" defined as "shared knowledge" or ASSUMED FAMILIARITY (to the hearer), as she more accurately calls it (Prince 1979 : 270–71; Prince 1981b : 235–37):

Evoked

(Textually) evoked: mentioned previously in the discourse: *I bought a lawnmower, but* ***it*** *was defective.*

Situationally evoked: salient member of the context, including the participants in the discourse: ***I*** *laughed.*

Inferrable

Containing inferrable: the entity is part of an NP properly contained in the containing inferrable expressions: *I'll take* ***one of those pears.***

(Noncontaining) inferrable: the entity is inferrable from general knowledge about already evoked entities: *I turned on the computer and* ***the screen*** *was blank.*

New

Unused: the entity is available to the hearer but has not been evoked: *I sent a letter to* ***George Bush.***

Brand-new

Brand-new anchored: the entity is not available to the hearer but the description properly contains an NP (or NPs) that

> refer to some other entity (at least one of which appears not ever to be brand-new itself): *I saw* ***a student of mine*** *the other day.*
>
> *Brand-new (unanchored):* the entity is not available to the hearer: ***A student*** *gave me a ride home.*

In addition to these distinctions, Prince notes that there are at least two other notions of "givenness." First, a given entity is not only known to the hearer but is in the front of the hearer's consciousness. This is the concept used extensively by Chafe and his students (e.g., Chafe 1976, 1987; DuBois 1987). The latter authors contrast "given" in this sense with "accessible" or "inactive," which appear to be inferrable entities and evoked entities that are no longer at the front of the hearer's consciousness. Second, a given entity is recoverable by the hearer from the NP used to express it or the grammatical construction in which it is expressed; this concept is used by Kuno and discussed by Givón (e.g., Givón 1983a). These notions are orthogonal to Prince's taxonomy of assumed familiarity, though they are somewhat interrelated (e.g., a brand-new entity cannot have been at the forefront of the hearer's consciousness, nor can the hearer recover its identity with some prior entity known to him or her).

The given-new taxonomy, however it is defined, is applied essentially to noun phrases, not to predicates, although it has been observed that predicates are almost always "new," and if they are not, then a marked construction occurs (altered stress and intonation, or a cleft or focus construction). A given NP is contrasted with a new NP. The reason for this can be derived from the definitions of reference and predication discussed above. Reference, the propositional act associated with nouns, is the choice by the speaker of what the clause is going to be about. Independently of this choice, perhaps after this choice has been made, the speaker must assess the familiarity and/or salience to the hearer of what the speaker has chosen to talk about and choose the wording of the noun phrase and other details of the clause (e.g., verbal voice) accordingly. Hence, the given-new cluster of discourse distinctions is associated specifically with what is being talked about.

This point is made overtly by most of the researchers in the area. Chafe's (1976) original paper outlining many of the discourse functional concepts discussed here explicitly states that his taxonomy is about nouns at the outset (cf. Lambrecht 1987 : 220). This implies that most of this research is not going to contribute to the noun-verb issue, but a remark by DuBois explaining why he excludes verbs from his analysis suggests a solution to the problem:

> Referential entities are treated by speakers as having continuous identity over time; hence new reference to non-identifiable entities involves opening a cognitive file for the referent, and references to given definite entities subsequently add information to update the file. Events, by contrast, are characteristically ephemeral and unique, so that successive verbs ordinarily do not refer back repeatedly to a single event. . . . It may be that speakers attend to new nominal information on a separate cognitive track, as it were, from new verbal information. [DuBois 1987:817]

Following DuBois's suggestion, I propose that the propositional speech act associated with nouns, reference, includes the opening of a "cognitive file" (cf. Karttunen's [1976] "discourse referents"; Heim's [1982] "discourse file"; Givón's [1983a] "topic continuity") for the referred-to entity, whereas no such file is opened in a predicational propositional act, associated with verbs. In other words, being about something involves creating a cognitive file for that thing; ascribing a "property" (in the philosophical sense) does not involve creating a file for that entity. I will provide supporting evidence for this hypothesis here and point out what sort of typological research could provide firmer support.

First of all, this hypothesis would explain the correlation of the remaining semantic properties with the discourse functions of reference and predication. As I argued above, the valency distinction of zero (nouns) versus nonzero (verbs) is accounted for by the corresponding valencies for the propositional acts (zero for reference, nonzero for predication). This leaves the state versus process and permanent versus transitory distinction, the latter also playing a major role in the conceptualization of nouns, verbs, and adjectives. Lexical semantic categorizations based on unchanging and permanent features of the entity are more likely to be used for reference because a cognitive file must be opened and its identity maintained over time. Categorizations based on changing and transitory features are conversely associated with predications since they need not be maintained. This is closely related to Givón's definition of the syntactic categories based on time stability, which combines stativity and permanence.

Second, it would account for another discourse functional feature associated chiefly with noun phrases, topic continuity (Givón 1979: 66; Givón 1983a; cf. also Hopper 1986). Topic continuity involves the maintenance of topic identity over the period of a discourse and the switching from one topic to another. Grammatical devices for topic maintenance and topic shift, like devices for "given" and "new," are associated with nouns (noun phrases), not verbs. Under the hypothesis, this is due to the fact that the cognitive files for the nouns in the discourse have to be maintained, while no such files are maintained for the verbs. Significantly, Givón uses the term "topic" in the cited work to refer to any noun phrase, not just the most prominent one in the clause; he is clearly describing a phenomenon associated with nouns in general.

Third, it would avoid some of the pitfalls of a given-new account of nominalized verb constructions and focus or cleft constructions. In this account, focus or cleft constructions have the effect of making an NP (or sometimes another constituent) the new information or the predicate. As a consequence, the backgrounded (Schachter 1973) part of the sentence, headed by the verb, is hypothesized to represent given or presupposed information. However, this is not always the case. Prince (1978) has demonstrated that the backgrounded portion of some *it*-clefts (also known as "clefts") is used to present information that is new to the hearer. Prince calls these INFORMATIVE-PRESUPPOSITION *it*-clefts, illustrated below (Prince 1978 : 898; this is a newspaper filler, so the backgrounded clause cannot possibly refer back to given information):

(32) *It was just about 50 years ago that Henry Ford gave us the weekend. On September 25, 1926, in a somewhat shocking move for that time, he decided to establish a 40-hour work week, giving his employees two days off instead of one.*

Prince notes that the purpose of the informative-presupposition *it*-cleft is to present the information in the backgrounded clause as generally known rather than totally new: had the first sentence not been clefted, it would seem that the newspaper had just discovered this fact. Prince argues that the informative-presupposition *it*-cleft functions to modify the evidentiality of the information in the backgrounded clause: simple predication commits the speaker more directly than *it*-clefting, which allows the speaker to shift epistemological responsibility onto "general knowledge." From the perspective of our hypothesis, the informative-presupposition *it*-cleft implies that the information in the backgrounded clause refers back to an already open cognitive file, namely, a file established under "generally known facts." Thus, even if the backgrounded clause is new information to the hearer, a cognitive file has already been opened for it. This is the reason for the cleft in this case. This is extremely suggestive, but it is necessary to do a more systematic survey of nominalized and complement clause types in order to see if they can plausibly be associated with the maintaining of a cognitive file for the information contained therein.

Fourth, there do seem to be some significant differences between new NPs that will become topics and (prototypically new) predicates. Many languages use some sort of existential construction for new referential-indefinite NPs, that is, noun phrases that introduce a new discourse participant that will be referred to later (i.e., have a cognitive file opened for it). However, cross-linguistically the existential construction does not render the new NP more verblike, unlike predicate nominals, which are commonly inflected just as verbs are in a language. (On the other hand, existential constructions do tend to render the rest of the clause more nounlike.) This suggests that languages do distinguish new-NP constructions from new-predicate constructions, so that nouns inflected like verbs are predicate nominals, not existential NPs.

Conversely, one can examine semantically and pragmatically nonreferential NPs. Semantically nonreferential NPs do not refer to a specific entity. Pragmatically nonreferential NPs do refer to a specific entity, but that entity is mentioned only once and then dropped from the conversation (Givón 1981:86). Givón gives the following examples from Modern Hebrew to illustrate a pragmatically nonreferential NP:

(33) *az axarey ha- avoda halaxti la- sifriya ve- yashavti*
so after DEF- work went.1ST to.the- library and- sat.1ST
sham ve- karati sefer -exad ve- ze haya sefer
there and- read.1ST book -one and- it was book
metsuyun
excellent
'So after work I went to the library, and I sat there and read a book, and it was an excellent book.'

(34) *az axarey ha- avoda halaxti la- sifriya ve- lo hay*
so after DEF- word went.1ST to.the- library and- NEG was
li ma la- asot az karati sefer ve- karati shney
to.me what to- do so read.1ST book and- read.1ST two
itonim ve- axar- kax halaxti ha- bayta
papers and- after- that went.1ST to- home
'So after work I went to the library and I had nothing to do, so I read a book, and a couple of newspapers, and then went home.'

In the first example, the book is a referential indefinite, but it is referred to again immediately ('**it** was an excellent book'); therefore, a cognitive file was opened for it. In the second example, the book is also a referential indefinite, but it is dropped after its first mention.

These are the types of NPs that a cognitive file might not be opened for. Cross-linguistically, these NPs lose their categoriality entirely, in the terms of Hopper and Thompson (1984 : 718–22).[17] More significantly, semantically nonreferential NPs are the first NP type to be incorporated into verbs (Mithun 1984a : 849; Hopper and Thompson 1984 : 711). Pragmatically nonreferential NPs are incorporated in languages with more extensive noun incorporation, what Mithun calls Type III incorporation: "Incorporated nouns are not salient constituents in themselves, whose presence might obstruct the flow of information. They simply ride along with their host V's" (Mithun 1984a : 859). This evidence suggests that those entities for which a file is not to be opened are attracted to the primary grammatical element for which a file is not opened by definition, the verb. The compounded verb represents the "ephemeral" information as a grammatical and conceptual unit.

Finally, note that Langacker's concept of sequential scanning for predications (Langacker 1987b : 72, discussed in 3.2.1) is in some ways the opposite of opening a cognitive file. In opening a cognitive file, the entity is activated as a whole (Langacker's "summary scanning," the opposite of sequential scanning) and remains active, at least for a while. In sequential scanning, however, the temporal phases of the entity are focused on and then dropped as soon as the new phase (and also as a new event) is scanned.

Further research on the grammar of existential constructions, of pragmatically nonreferential NPs, and of nominalized (or at least deverbalized) verb constructions is necessary to provide convincing support for this hypothesis. The evidence given above, however, suggests that the presence versus absence of a cognitive file for the information denoted by the constituent is the relevant discourse functional factor distinguishing nouns and verbs (opening a cognitive file is part of the propositional act, of course).

Finally, there is the matter of adjectives and modification. In a recent paper, Thompson (1988) examines the distribution of adjectives (defined on a semantic basis as "property concepts") in English and Mandarin Chinese conversation. Thompson found that adjectives are not found in definite NPs (the philosophers' favorite context)[18] but instead are found in new NPs, as predicate adjectives and as modifiers of a predicate nominal.

(35) *We used to do some awful things though* (176)

(36) *and her parents apparently weren't even that wealthy* (174)

(37) *he's a very nice guy, he's a real good person* (174)

The statistics for each use are as follows:

Modifier in a new NP	66	21%
Modifier of a predicate nominal	33	11%
Predicate adjective	209	68%
Total	308	100%

The majority of adjective uses were as predicate adjectives. Significantly, the modifier uses almost all involve a semantically uninformative or "empty" head noun (*a nice guy*). Thus, when an adjective is used as the modifier of a predicate nominal, it is essentially functioning like a predicate adjective; and when an adjective is a modifier in a new NP, it is essentially providing the contentful label to the NP. Thompson argues that a modifying adjective is used to describe a new referent while a predicating adjective is used to describe an already established referent; hence, the two functions fit the Hopper and Thompson (1984) definitions of a prototypical noun as a new referent and a prototypical verb as an assertion about an established referent (Thompson 1988: 178, 180).[19]

These results differ significantly from the results in the four-language text survey presented in 2.5. In that study, modifying adjectives outnumbered predicate adjectives by around two to one, the reverse ratio of that found by Thompson, and very few if any of the modifying adjectives were modifying a predicate nominal. Also, modifying adjectives were found being used to describe already established referents, albeit quite infrequently. Although the sample of the four-language survey is much smaller than Thompson's, the consistency of the results across the four languages is quite striking. The reason for the different proportions is possibly due to the fact that the four-language survey used oral narratives, whereas Thompson used oral conversation. However, in a recent study of informal conversational English data by Chafe, 33.5 occurrences per thousand words for attributive adjectives were found compared to 15.8 occurrences per thousand words for predicate adjectives (Chafe 1982: 41–42). This is the same proportion of attributive to predicate adjectives, around two to one, as that found in the four-language survey.

Wierzbicka's description of the function of attributive adjectives suggests an explanation for the fact that attributive adjectives are generally predicated only of newly introduced referents: "Adjectives [in attribution], which stand for single features, can be freely used to enrich the image evoked by the noun. . . . a noun . . . creates a category. . . . an adjective . . . adds a feature without creating a new category" (Wierzbicka 1986:374). Thompson's data demonstrate that the feature-adding function of attributive adjectives is largely restricted to the initial creation of a cognitive file for the referent. That is, the image of the referent, including ancillary features provided by adjectives, is established at the outset (possibly by an initial sequence of descriptive clauses, as suggested in the preceding paragraph).

At this point, we may summarize the external explanatory model of the major syntactic categories as follows. In performing a speech act, the speaker must perform a series of propositional acts. The most important of these are reference and predication. The act of reference simply identifies a referent and establishes a cognitive file for that referent. For this reason, "ideal" referring expressions are zero valency and conceptualize the entity as an autonomous unit. Since the cognitive file will last for a while and there may be several cognitive files open, the referring expression must represent the referent as a particular kind that is fairly stable and permanent—hence, the "typecasting" conceptualization of nouns and the stative and permanent features of prototypical noun roots. The act of predication ascribes something to the referent; for this reason, prototypical verb roots are ideally nonzero valency, and even zero valency noun roots must be coerced into a relational interpretation. Communication is a series of predications; none of them open a cognitive file for what is ascribed, sequentially scanning a scene instead. Predications report relatively transitory facts about the referent—hence the association of transitory and processual lexical roots with prototypical predicates. The propositional act of modification functions to enrich the nominal image by an additional feature—hence the "one-dimensional" conceptualization of adjectives. However, the nominal image, including additional features, is created at the time that the cognitive file is opened. For these reasons, "ideal" attributive adjectives are permanent—they must last as long as the nominal image—but they must be relational since they add to an existing nominal image without creating a new image themselves.

The summary presented here is tentative, as the discussion of the supporting research indicates. Nevertheless, it is a coherent model, fitting the more concrete typological evidence provided in chapter 2, and it is a useful starting point for further research.

Although most functionally oriented linguists would accept the model of syntactic categories as sufficiently general to count as an explanatory model, one might still ask, Why do human beings organize information in the way that they do? It seems that one can say only that this is simply the way people structure information in discourse (cf. Searle 1969: 119–20). This argument is parallel to that offered by Talmy (1983) for the conceptualization of space as expressed in language. Talmy argues that, no matter what sort of spatial configuration a human being is trying to describe in natural language, he must always describe it in terms of a series of figure-ground relations, with one entity (the figure) situated by means of a path expression to another entity or entities (the ground). Thus, for example, an arbitrarily complex spatial configuration such as one might find in a still life will have to be described in a series of figure-path-ground units in natural language:

(38) *In the still life, two pears are sitting next to a dish. In the dish are a bunch of grapes and a banana, and there's a dressed pheasant on the opposite side of the dish from the pears.*

The same fact appears to hold for the organization of information into clauses in discourse: no matter how complex a given situation is in terms of the number of entities involved and the number and kinds of relations that hold between them, a human being attempting to describe it in natural language must split it into a series of reference-predication pairs:

(39) *Fred was sitting on the steps, smoking a cigar. A little old lady strode up and snatched the cigar out of his mouth. Fred got angry.*

It is actually extremely difficult to imagine how one could organize information in any other way. It is possible, for example, to imagine that people could have communicated instead by simply referring to (and modifying) events:

(40) *The sitting on the steps by Fred. The smoking of a cigar by Fred. A little old lady's striding up. Her snatching the cigar out of Fred's mouth. Fred's getting angry.*

This sort of communication seems incomplete, of course, because natural language has the additional function of predication, in contrast to mere reference. Thre are also additional functions, or propositional acts, namely, modification, categorizing, selecting, and situating, described above. Assembling all these functions together provides a cognitive model of the organization of information for communication, which may provide significant evidence for the organization of the human mind.

3.2.4 Semantic and Pragmatic Conflicts

In most of the cases examined so far, the pragmatic function has "overridden" the semantic class when the two do not match: that is, a predicate nominal is a predication, a nominalization is a referring expression, etc. In the discussion of conceptualizations, however, it was observed that differences in conceptualization were maintained even when the lexical items shifted function. Thus, the conceptual difference between the nominal *He's a Jew* and the adjectival *He's Jewish* is maintained even though both are in a verbal function, namely, predication. Also, when lexical items denoting a certain semantic type are used in a function other than the one that they are naturally correlated with, they frequently retain some of the behavioral features of their naturally correlated category (see 2.4). If this is the case, one might expect to find more drastic mismatches of grammatical and pragmatic structure. Also, if the category structure of nouns, verbs, and adjectives is indeed a prototype structure, then it would be expected that neither property—semantic class nor pragmatic function—is a necessary condition of category membership, and so semantic class would sometimes "override" pragmatic function in the realization of a clause.

Such examples exist; there are examples in English. In general, a post-VP verbal adverb serves as the predication of the action denoted in the main clause. For example, I once uttered *We're going to get home pretty late* in a conversation where going home was what was being talked about. Thus, the action was being used referentially, and its lateness (a property) was the predication. That utterance is pragmatically equivalent to *Our getting home will be pretty late.* Nevertheless, the former was actually uttered and certainly sounds more natural; in that case, the semantic class of the referent (action) overrode its referential function with respect to the surface syntax.

A similar phenomenon appears to be found in Quiché, which is predicate initial, the opposite of English (Quiché is VOS). Recall that *sipalax* 'very' is the predicate intensifier (see 2.4). An adverb can precede the clause and be modified by *sipalax:*

(41) *iwir* *sipalax* *maʔtam* *š-* *ux-* *opan* *čo-* *xah*
yesterday very late PAST- 1PL.ABS- return to home
'Yesterday we got home very late.'

However, this is probably more "literally" translated by the pseudo-English cleft sentence 'It was very late that we got home,' in which the adverb is the predication and the clause is made into a complement (the immediately preceding utterance in the dialogue from which this sentence was taken was 'When did you get home last night?'). In fact, Quiché cleft (focus) constructions, which among other things are used to answer WH-questions, are formed in just this way.

Another example of semantic class overriding syntactic category is when the object or an oblique is the predication: in answer to a question like *Who did Fred marry?* the response *Fred married Hárriet* sounds reasonable, though the discourse functionally "proper" utterance would be the cleft[20] *It was Harriet that Fred married* and the one-word answer *Harriet,* presumably a simple predication (cf. *It was Harriet*) is more likely. In fact, however, it appears that, in general, actions are most resistant to changing discourse functional category, as attested by the many finite complement and relative clause constructions as well as by the adverb-predication and object-predication examples just given.

In fact, there are two very general ways in which the discourse function of syntactic categories may be at least partially overridden, leaving the syntactic structure to reflect the lexical semantic correlations: suprasegmental marking (stress and/or intonation), and word order. Contrastive stress in English can have approximately the same effect as the morphosyntactic cleft construction without changing the syntactic structure of the utterance. In languages with freer word order than English, such as Czech, the effect of English cleft constructions can be accomplished by simply reordering words in a sentence (though see the comments in 3.2.3 regarding the possibly independent discourse function of word order).

Both suprasegmental and word order marking of clause-level discourse structure bring up major issues in the analysis and representation of both syntactic structure and discourse structure that I do not intend to address here. The point of the examples is to demonstrate that one must conclude that the pragmatic function of a syntactic category is not a necessary condition of the manifestation of that category in nonprototypical cases.

3.3 Other Semantic Classes of Lexical Roots

A good test of the semantic, conceptual, pragmatic, and discourse functional factors that play a role in the definitions of the major syntactic category prototypes is the examination of additional semantic classes of lexical roots. The analysis presented in 3.2 gains additional support to the extent that it provides explanations for why these lexical semantic classes are special in various ways.

3.3.1 Pronouns and "Superprototypicality"

Personal pronouns display the properties of being behaviorally unmarked relative even to core or prototypical nouns. They have underived (or at least synchronically underived) morphological structure. They are also textually extremely frequent (see 2.5). In particular, with respect to the topic of this section, personal pronouns have an even greater variety of morphosyntactic inflectional behavior. Personal pronouns distinguish at least as many categories in number as do common nouns: "In general, pronominal categories tend to be more differentiated than those of the noun" (Greenberg 1966b:96). One of Greenberg's universals is that pronouns distinguish at least two numbers in every language (Greenberg 1966b, universal 42). More specifically, Greenberg proposed his universal 43: "If a language has gender categories in the noun, it has gender categories in the pronoun" (Greenberg 1966b:96; counterexamples do exist, however, e.g., Hindi). Other examples can be found as nearby as English, where the first- and third-person pronouns distinguish case, although common nouns do not. Demonstrative pronouns are similar in their variety of syntactic behavior, although they are sometimes morphologically complex, being the demonstrative adjective plus an "empty noun" root.

Thus, one may conclude that personal pronouns indeed appear to be even more prototypical "nouns" (referring expressions) than common nouns since they are textually more frequent and display characteristic nominal inflection more often than common nouns do. The reasons are fairly clear. First, pronouns refer almost solely to an individual; they do not classify a referent as belonging to a type.[21] Thus, they are purely referring expressions, in contrast to common nouns, and so are more "nounlike" than nouns (cf. Bolinger 1967:23: "Nouns . . . both name classes and designate individuals, often doing both things at once"). Nevertheless, common nouns, which classify objects into taxonomic types, are the closest to prototypical nouns after pronouns; taxonomic classification of a referent under a type seems to be sufficient for reference in the appropriate context (for more discussion of the relation between pronominal and nominal reference, see Bolinger 1979). In addition, pronouns are paradigm examples of referring expressions that stand for entities for which a cognitive file has been opened; they *must* go back to previous reference to the same entity. Hence, their "superprototypicality" as members of the category "noun."[22]

Another factor that may influence degree of prototypicality for nouns with respect to grammatical behavior is animacy. Pronouns are found at the "top" of the animacy hierarchy in most accounts (e.g., Silverstein 1976; Dixon 1979). Nouns denoting humans are more likely to bear number and case inflections than nouns denoting animates, let alone inanimates (e.g., see the evidence presented in Croft

1990b, 5.3.3). Nouns denoting humans are also more likely to express sex-gender distinctions than nouns denoting animals. A possible explanation for this universal typological pattern is that the (human) speaker is more likely to take note of human referents and maintain cognitive files for them (though no studies have compared human, animate, and inanimate referent tracking, to my knowledge).

There is considerable evidence that some semantic subclasses of properties are "more adjectival" than others. Dixon reports that antonym pairs for physical dimensions, age/maturity, and quality ("good"-"bad"), and also color terms, are the entities included in the small closed adjective classes in some languages. Evidence from the sample survey confirms Dixon's results for the languages with small adjective classes (Swahili, Turkana), even for languages with larger adjective classes. A subset of Turkish adjectives allows reduplication for intensification (Lewis 1967 : 55–56); Lewis's list of the commonest of these includes basic color terms, 'quick,' 'new,' and 'long' as well as less prototypical adjectives. In Georgian, suppletive comparative and superlative forms are found for 'good,' 'bad,' 'a little,' and 'many' (antonyms for quantity; Aronson 1982 : 246). English also has suppletive comparative and superlatives for *good* and *bad;* and, although the morphological comparatives in *-er* and superlatives in *-est* are distributed largely on phonological grounds, they include all Dixon's core adjective concepts. Finally, Quiché adjectives normally do not inflect for number, but special number inflections are found for *nimaˀq* 'big.PL' and *c̉utiˀq* 'small.PL.' A possible explanation for the "superprototypicality" of Dixon's core adjective types is that properties like size and color are useful for distinguishing individuals of the same type since those properties tend to crosscut the biological, functional, and shape-based taxonomies that are used for animate, man-made, and inanimate object classes, respectively.

It is more difficult to identify a "superprototypical" verb class since the division of verbs into grammatical subclasses generally does not display any markedness pattern. One example of a verbal classification utilizing a markedness distinction is found in Kanuri (Nilo-Saharan). Class 1 verbs are inflected by means of a person affix (prefixed for third person, suffixed for first and second person) and an aspect suffix, in the simplest inflection: *bú-k-ìn* [eat-1SG-IMPF] 'I am eating' (Hutchison 1981 : 97). Class 2 verbs are inflected with the class 1 affixes and an additional morpheme, *-n-: lè + n + k + ìn* (*lĕngìn*)[go-N-1SG-IMPF] 'I am going' (95). Historically, the class 2 verbs consist of the verb root plus the inflected form of the class 1 verb *n+* 'say, think'; synchronically, however, this means that class 1 verbs are less marked than class 2 verbs. Hutchison lists about one hundred class 1 verbs (98–101), divided into five groups.[23] Although they include some nonprototypical verbs (such as the transitive stative verbs **ràg+* 'want, love, like' and *yàsə̀ra+* 'believe,' the stative *yìmbàr+* 'be tired,' and the existential verb *də̀g+* 'live, stay, exist'), the vast majority of them are 2-ary valency (transitive) processes, and most of the rest are intransitive processes (see table 3.1). In 6.4, I will argue, based on Croft (in press b), that "superprototypical" verbs are transitive processes.

TABLE 3.1 *Kanuri Class 1 Verbs by Semantic Type and Conjugation Group*

	Groups 1–4	**Group 5**
2-ary process	70	0
1-ary process	13	8
2-ary stative	4	0
1-ary stative	1	1
Auxiliary	0	1
Total	88	10

Group 5 in Kanuri has been separated in table 3.1 because it is extremely irregular (Hutchison 1981 : 101), and resembles the category "auxiliary." One frequently finds that the inflectionally least marked verbs are auxiliary verbs. These originated historically with verbs that originally meant such prototypical processes as 'go,' 'come,' 'do,' 'make,' 'get,' and 'give' but also (as in Kanuri class 1 group 5 verbs) such unprototypical statives and semistatives as 'stay, exist,' 'be,' 'have,' 'want,' 'like,' and 'be able.' Actually, the cross-linguistic behavior of auxiliaries with respect to verbal inflection is highly variable. For example, English *be* and *have* are the least marked verbs inflectionally in the language, but the modal auxiliaries are invariant. Cross-linguistically also, auxiliaries range from the most inflected verbal types to the least. This has in part to do with the fact that auxiliaries represent an intermediate or "transitory" stage in a grammaticalization path (see 3.3.4). However, it should also be pointed out that some of the verbal inflectional categories, particularly mood and tense, are more typically sentential than verbal and are less closely associated with the verb than has been assumed here (for a summary of degrees of semantic closeness of various verbal inflections to verbal semantic content, see Bybee 1985a, 1985b).

3.3.2 Adjectives as a Less Prototypical Class

In chapter 2, I argued that adjectives, like nouns and verbs, constitute one of the major syntactic categories of human languages and provided evidence demonstrating that adjectives represent an unmarked or prototypical correlation between the lexical semantic class of unary valency, stative, persistent gradable properties and the grammatical function of modification.

However, adjectives are definitely not in the same class as nouns and verbs. That is, in some sense, adjectives are "nonprototypical" or even "marked" relative to nouns and verbs. There is considerable typological evidence to support this view. First, as Dixon noted, there are many languages that have a very small, closed adjective class (see also 3.3.1). Nouns and verbs, on the other hand, are always open classes in human languages. There is also frequency evidence that demonstrates the marked character of adjectives in comparison to nouns and verbs. In the Russian root study in 2.3, there were far fewer basic adjectival roots (i.e., roots denoting properties) than basic nominal (object) or verbal (action) roots. And the text frequency counts reported in 2.5 show that the prototypical adjective class is far less frequent than the prototypical noun or verb classes and that modifiers are far less frequent than predications and referring expressions.

Moreover, not only are adjectives less basic than verbs and nouns, but they are also intermediate in grammatical characteristics. The twelve-language survey reported in chapter 2 reveals some important patterns that suggest the intermediate status of adjectives with respect to nouns and verbs. Predicate adjectives fall between nouns and verbs in structural markedness: predicate nouns are more likely to be structurally marked (with a copula) than predicate adjectives. In fact, the following implicational universal holds for the sample and probably holds more broadly: if the predicate nominal construction does not use a copula, then the predicate adjective construction does not also. In some cases, a more subtle gradation of properties is found. In Swahili, predicate nominals inflect with verbal agreement prefixes in first and second person, but third-person constructions use the copula. Predicate adjectives also use the first- and second-person agreement prefixes, but in the third person they may use either the nominal copula or the verbal agreement prefixes (Ashton 1944:93).

Another implicational hierarchy pertains to the grammatical function correlated with adjectives, modification. In the sample, the following implicational universal holds: if a language has a morphological means to indicate verbal modification (i.e., if a language has participles), then it has a morphological means to indicate verbal reference (i.e., a language has nominalized verb forms). In fact, as I noted in 2.3, some languages use nominalized forms for verbal modification. This indicates that participles are more marked than nominalizations since they are less widespread, they can be replaced by nominalizations, and their existence depends on the existence of nominalizations.

The most obvious evidence for the intermediate status of adjectives with respect to verbs and nouns is the sharing of morphological inflections with one or the other of those categories. All the languages in the sample that use a copula for both nominal and adjectival predication except Yagaria use the same copula for both; this reflects a widespread cross-linguistic pattern. Although adjectival agreement performs a distinct function from nominal gender, number, and case marking, the morphological forms are nevertheless similar or identical, as in Turkish and Swahili. Adjectives also generally take the same agreement affixes as verbs in those languages in which predicate adjectives are inflected directly (though it must be pointed out that nouns also do if they are inflected as predicates). In other cases, adjectives share some properties with nouns and some with verbs in the same language. For example, in Turkana, the number inflections resemble those of nouns, while the agreement/modification markers are the same as those used for verbs (Dimmendaal 1983 : 332). In Japanese, by contrast, adjectives more or less resemble verbs: the adjective resembles the verb in predication in two of the four levels of politeness, while the noun requires the copula in all levels of politeness, and in modification both adjective and verb directly modify the head noun while a nominal modifier requires the particle *no*.[24]

There are some plausible semantic and pragmatic explanations for the subsidiary and intermediate character of adjectives. Modification is an ancillary function to reference and predication: modifiers help either to characterize the referent (so-called restrictive modification), or to say something additional about the referent (nonrestrictive modification). As noted above, adjectives either enrich the image of a noun or function commonly as predicates, in fact being somewhat difficult to distinguish clearly from verbs. Thus, modifiers appear to have a secondary pragmatic function (hence the marked status of the prototypical modifiers, adjectives) and, moreover, that function mimics either reference or predication (hence the intermediate status of adjectives). Nevertheless, it appears that no language fails to provide the distinction between "primary" and "secondary" information that is embodied in the difference between reference and predication on the one hand and restrictive/nonrestrictive modification on the other.

Turning to the semantic characteristics of the prototypical lexical semantic classes for noun, verb, and adjective, it is quite clear that prototypical adjectives are intermediate between prototypical nouns and verbs in a semantic sense also, as can be seen from table 3.2 (reproduced from section 2.3).

TABLE 3.2 *Major Semantic Properties of Core Lexical Classes*

	Objects	**Properties**	**Actions**
Valence	zero	nonzero	nonzero
Stativity	stative	stative	processual
Persistence	persistent	persistent	transitory
Gradability	nongradable	gradable	nongradable

Excluding the unique feature of properties, gradability, prototypical adjectives share a nonzero valency with actions and the two temporally oriented features, stative and persistent, with nouns. (It is worth noting here also that the fundamental noun-verb semantic distinction, like the subject-object distinction, fits Rosch's [1978] theory of prototypes in that adjacent prototypes tend to contrast maximally in their defining properties.)

Gradability provides the unique characteristic of prototypical adjectives. Most properties, in particular the core physical properties, are gradable scales, and this fact accounts for the inflectional categories of comparison, equatives (*as . . . as*) and intensification (English *very,* the Quiché adjectival suffix *-alax*), all of which express the measurability of scales. Although some objects and actions can be coerced into representing a gradable scale (*He is more of a singer than she is*), the scale referred to is generally that of a property associated with the object class rather than the object class itself (in this case, quality of singing, not occupation).[25] All the characteristic inflections of modifiers except for agreement are associated with gradability. Presumably, there is some intimate association between the pragmatic function of modification (as a function distinct from reference and predication) and semantic gradability.

Closer analysis of the pragmatic function of modification demonstrates that it resembles both of the primary pragmatic functions in its two faces (restrictive and nonrestrictive). Closer analysis of the semantic class of properties demonstrates that it shares characteristics of actions (nonzero valency) and of objects (stativity and persistence). Thus, one may conclude that adjectives are semantically and pragmatically intermediate between nouns and verbs, which are themselves semantically and pragmatically highly distinct. This fact is reflected in their morphosyntactically intermediate status in natural languages and also in the fact that lexical items denoting all but the most "core" adjectival types are assimilated to the open classes of noun and verb.[26] This type of situation leaves only a small closed class of adjectives. However, the distinctive characteristics of adjectives, specifically their "secondary" discourse function and their semantics of gradable scales, appear to be sufficiently important or salient features to the speaker that there is always a grammatical manifestation of a distinct adjective class, small though it may be. Finally, one may conclude from the evidence concerning adjectives that the structure of prototype categories is hierarchical: the adjective prototype is at a lower level than the noun and verb prototypes and can be partly if not completely assimilated to the higher two prototypes.

3.3.3 Numerals, States, and Other Peripheral Lexical Classes

There are many other lexical semantic classes than those which make up the prototypes. I will use the term PERIPHERAL class or category to cover these nonprototypical cases and discuss some of the more important peripheral classes in this section. This section is not intended to be a thorough evaluation of the problems in these areas; instead, it should indicate the direction that the theory of syntactic categories that I have proposed must go in order to account satisfactorily for the range of major and minor syntactic categories in natural languages (see also Croft in press a).

Numerals and quantifiers are the classic example of an intermediate syntactic category. They behave quite straightforwardly as if they were between adjectives and nouns. Comrie (1981 : 101–4, after Corbett 1978) points out that one can describe a cline or graudal shift from adjective to noun from the lower numerals to the higher ones in Russian, with *odin* 'one' functioning like an ordinary adjective on the basis of the seven grammatical criteria that Comrie uses, *million* 'million' functioning like an ordinary noun, and the intermediate numbers functioning partly like one category and partly like the other. The scale of adjectival morphosyntax for smaller numerals and nominal morphosyntax for larger numerals is a general fact (Greenberg 1978:285, universal 47). Quantifiers display a similar split to numerals, but apparently along different lines: those describing totalities (*all*) or units (*each, a*) are more like adjectives, the others more like nouns. In Russian, the words for 'all' (*ves'*) and 'each' (*každyj*) inflect like adjectives and do not govern the case of their heads, while other quantifiers such as *mnogo* 'many' do not inflect adjectivally and govern the genitive case of their "head." In the latter type, however, the nominal behavior is due to the quantifiers (or numerals) functioning as HEAD nouns, with the object quantified as a dependent, rather than the other way around, as one might expect.

The semantics of quantity provides some clues for the treatment of numerals partly as adjectives and partly as (head) nouns. Quantities, like adjectives, fall on a single gradable scale, that of amount or cardinality. Thus, they share the most significant semantic characteristic of properties. Unlike properties, however, quantities are more discrete. Terms describing values of gradable properties, such as *tall/short, large/small,* etc., are relative extent terms that come in pairs and indicate only a direction on a scale, "up" or "down." Quantities do indicate more or less specific values on the scale, precise in the case of numerals and vague in the case of quantifiers such as *a few, many.* Since quantifiers and numerals name specific values, they are more likely to be realized as nouns. More important from the point of view of nominality is that quantifiers, by naming values, can be conceptualized as referring to units, that is, aggregates of individuals taken as a whole.[27] As such, they denote objects or, more precisely, aggregates of objects. The conflict is between conceptual focus on the aggregate or on the individuals that make it up as the relevant unit(s). The individuals that make up the whole are more salient in smaller quantities, simply because there are fewer of them and more attention can be focused on each. In this case, the quantifier or numeral is more likely to be conceived of as a descriptive property of the individual(s) involved (e.g., *two eggs*). In larger quantities, the individuals are less salient by themselves, and the aggregate is more salient, by virtue of its size: one does not focus on the individuals when looking at *hundreds of marbles,* for instance. In that case, the numeral or quantifier is more likely to be conceived of as a unit in its own right, expressed as a noun or nounlike form and taking the type of the individuals as a genitival modifier (*a gross of eggs*).

The conceptualization of nouns and adjectives also accounts for the fact that numeral-noun constructions often change over time from syntactically noun-genitive ($\text{numeral}_{\text{noun}}$ $\text{object}_{\text{genitive}}$) constructions to syntactically adjective-noun ($\text{numeral}_{\text{adjective}}$ $\text{object}_{\text{noun}}$) constructions.

Nouns represent an entity as belonging to a kind; it is under the kind label that the cognitive file is opened. A word denoting a quantity does not provide a useful kind label under which to open a cognitive file for a referent, even if semantically the quantity is a sort of object and the type of object quantified can be thought of as a "property" of the object, as discussed in the preceding paragraph. On the other hand, the type of object quantified can better play that role, leaving the quantity as an "enriching" descriptor of the entity selected (i.e., describing the cardinality of the selected entity group); and syntactic reanalysis assigns the syntactic categories and relations accordingly. This phenomenon occurs also with other quantity constructions, such as the partitive for mass nouns:

(42) *Harry drank four cans of beer.*

(43) ?*Harry crushed four cans of beer.*

(44) *Harry crushed four beer cans.*

The entity referred to in the direct object of the first sentence is the beer, which is the genitive dependent, not the head. Use of a verb that requires the direct object to be what is denoted by the head noun can result in questionable acceptability. At best, this sentence can be interpreted as Harry crushing cans full of beer; the sentence cannot be interpreted as referring to cans that are characterized by their normally containing beer but that are not presently containing beer. The latter interpretation requires a complex nominal construction, in which 'beer' is clearly a modifier with the associated conceptualization of an incidental property, as in the third sentence.

The mass noun *beer* as a modifier is an appropriate example of another peripheral category, substances and materials. The roots denoting substances and materials, that is, unbounded, homogeneous, and not naturally individuatable entities, are usually categorized as mass nouns. Mass nouns are most commonly nouns, but cross-linguistically they occasionally display unmarked modifier properties. In the twelve-language survey discussed in chapter 2, Turkish treats mass nouns referring to materials as structurally unmarked modifiers, like adjectives but contrasting with the normal izafet construction used with other noun modifiers (as in exx. [15]–[16] above; the following examples are from Lewis 1967 : 42–43):

(45) *altın bilezik*
gold bracelet
'gold bracelet'

(46) *uzun yol*
long road
'long road'

In Lakhota, mass nouns denoting materials form compounds with the nouns they modify, rather than using a genitive construction (Boas and Deloria 1941 : 68):

(47) *makha- thipi*
earth house
'earth lodge'

Substances resemble properties as opposed to individuatable objects (i.e., count nouns) in that both are homogeneous in internal structure and without sharp boundaries, but they differ in that they are not found in antonym sets (i.e., they are not purely "one dimensional"). Most core adjectives are not only one dimensional; they indicate just positive or negative direction on the scale they denote (length, height, age, speed): *tall/short, big/little, fast/slow, new/old.* The single exception to this generalization is color terms. Although colors generally belong to the very core of the adjectival category, they differ semantically from the other categories in that they do not form antonym pairs on a single dimension. Instead, color terms generally denote regions in the color scale with fuzzy boundaries (Berlin and Kay 1969). In that respect, colors are more like substances than other properties, and in fact alone among the core adjectival semantic classes they display some unmarked nounlike behavior. English color terms can be used as mass nouns without the abstract deadjectival morphology normally associated with properties in referring expressions: *I like red, but not blue.* In all the languages that I have examined on the issue of the existence of the syntactic category "adjective," I have found only one or two instances in which a property root in a nominal construction is said to refer to the quality itself rather than an object denoting the quality, and those instances were colors, like English.

The largest commonsense lexical semantic class outside those defining the three major syntactic categories—in fact, equal in size to the class of adjectives, using the rough measure of the number of basic Russian roots—is that of states. States include physical states such as *hot, cold, hungry,* mental states such as *angry, happy, sad,* and other states such as *peace(ful), right, poor.* Semantically, they differ from properties in being transitory, not persistent. Thus, states appear to be semantically intermediate between properties and actions, though much closer to adjectives, as can be seen from table 3.3.

TABLE 3.3 *Major Semantic Properties of States and Core Lexical Classes*

	Objects	Properties	States	Actions
Valence	zero	nonzero	nonzero	nonzero
Stativity	stative	stative	stative	processual
Persistence	persistent	persistent	transitory	transitory

This pattern is borne out in the text frequency patterns described in 2.5. States pattern closely with adjectives, in that predicated states are quite common along with states as modifiers. However, the structural and behavioral evidence implies that states are intermediate between adjectives and nouns, if anything. The structural markedness of states in the Russian lexicon was examined. The results are given in table 3.4.

TABLE 3.4 *Unmarked Category Status of Russian Roots including States*

	Nouns	Adjectives	Verbs	Total
Objects	128	0	0	128
States	31	28	7	66
Properties	1	58	0	59
Actions	0	0	129	129

One would expect that structurally zero-marked states would be relatively randomly distributed between N, V, and A since they are an intermediate class, differing from the core members of all three categories. It appears that states are intermediate between objects and properties and also to actions to a lesser extent; that is, although there are not the unambiguous correlations found for nouns, adjectives, and verbs,[28] it is clear that, in Russian at least, there is a nonrandom distribution of states across the three categories. Although there are a fair number of basic verb roots among states, approximately half the roots are basic nouns. If one returns to English, one observes that this tendency is present here as well, as seen in the examples in table 3.5.[29]

TABLE 3.5 *Some English Adjectival and Nominal State Roots*

Noun	Indeterminate	Adjective
hunger	cold	happy
thirst	hot/heat	sad
anger		smart
joy		stupid
peace		sick
harmony		ill
health		empty
wealth		rich

Evidence from Kanuri also suggests that lexical items of the same semantic class tend to surface as nouns at least as often as adjectives. For example, the word *kə̀nâ* 'hunger,' like its English translation, is a noun, unlike *gànà* 'small.' Compare the two words in reference, modification, and predication (Hutchison 1983:55, 199, 171, respectively):

(48) *kənâ* 'hunger'

(49) *nə̀m-gànà* 'smallness'

(50) *tádà kə̀nâ -à*
child hunger -ASSOC
'a hungry child'

(51) *tádà gànà*
child small
'a small child'

(52) *shíllowù ngáwúré -à*
star tail -ASSOC
'a star with a tail [shooting star]'

(53) *Módù gànà*
Modu small
'Modu is small.'

(54) *Módù kə̀nâ -à*
Modu hunger -ASSOC
'Modu is hungry.'

(55) *Módù kèké -à*
Modu bicycle -ASSOC
'Modu has a bicycle.'

The least marked form of 'hunger' is in the function of reference, whereas, when it is a modifier and a predicate, it requires the associative suffix ("with . . .") like a typical noun such as 'tail' or 'bicycle.' In contrast, the least marked form of 'small' is as a modifier (and also predicate, in the simple present), whereas when it is referring to the quality it requires a nominalizing prefix.

Finally, Dixon, in his survey of semantic classes of adjectives, says that states, which are largely what Dixon classifies as "human propensity" terms, are very frequently basic nouns if they are not basic adjectives (Dixon 1977 : 56). On the other hand, Chinese states are verbs (or, at least, resemble verbs as much as Chinese adjectives do).

I do not have a solution to this anomaly, but I can suggest some promising clues. First, it appears that verbhood abhors stativity. In English, the only stative verbs have a valency of (at least) two: intransitive statives are not realized as verbs, and even some transitive statives have adjectival counterparts: *fear/afraid of, like/fond of.*[30] This appears to be true of other languages as well (although still others have special "stative verb" conjugations that on closer inspection usually turn out to be adjectives). Although many expressions denoting states are derived from verbs denoting the process of entering the state (or of causing something to enter the state), for example, *surprised, excited, confused,* these are type-changing derivations, from a process to a state. In some languages such as Classical Nahuatl (Andrews 1975), these roots (as well as roots denoting object-level properties) are ambiguous between the stative and the process (inceptive or inchoative) interpretations, so one cannot determine which is more basic.

There is one possible explanation for the fact that more states than properties are nouns. If a state is a root noun, then the modifier construction it will use will frequently be a possessive construction, for example, Spanish *tengo hambre* [I.have hunger] 'I am hungry.' It may be that for some reason the relation between a state and the possessor of the state is more amenable to metaphoric expression as a possession relation than the relations between a property and the possessor of the property. One possible reason comes to mind. Possession, specifically the ALIENABLE possession of ownership, is transitory. So is spatial location, often the identical construction to possession (that is, the way to say '*X* has *Y*' is '*Y* be_{loc} (at) *X*'; see Clark 1978; cf. *She is in love/in a bad mood*). Thus, the transitory possession of a physical or emotional state may be more easily expressed by a possessive construction, with the state being expressed as a basic noun, than the more permanent possession of a property. Of course, possessive constructions are used to express INALIENABLE possession as well, which is more permanent. However, most languages distinguish between alienable and inalienable possession constructions, albeit in sometimes subtle ways. A strong confirmation of this hypothesis would be to find that languages that have both states and properties as basic nouns and have distinct alienable (or ownership-derived) and inalienable possessive constructions express modification by states with the alienable (ownership) construction and modification by properties with the inalienable construction.

The topic of inalienable possession brings us to another intermediate category: inherently relational nouns, such as kinship terms and body parts. I included these in the Russian root count under basic nouns, but they merit some discussion. The inherent relationality of relational nouns is somewhat different from that of (transitive) actions. Consider the kinship term 'father.' In predicate logic, it is normally translated into a two-place predicate *Father(x,y),* indicating a valency of two, as in the transitive action *Hit(x,y).* However, 'hit' denotes the relation itself, whereas 'father' denotes the second argument of the relation *Father,* in this case the range of the function. That argument is an object, in this case a human. The object is itself not inherently relational in the way I have defined it, but the word 'father' defines the object in terms of the relation that holds between it and some other object, namely, the child.[31]

In this manner, relational nouns resemble nominalizations of verb arguments such as agent nominalizations like *shoemaker.* Since agent nominalizations are quite verblike in some languages, reflecting the relationality of the description of the object qua participant in the action, one might expect a similar phenomenon for relational nouns proper. Davis (1964) analyzes Santa Ana Keresan relational nouns (specifically, kinship terms, body parts, and some social roles like "friend") as morphosyntactically intransitive verbs: valency overrides other factors (relational nouns make up a suspiciously unique inflectional class, but the person agreement inflections are fused with a full range of modal/evidential meanings). The intransitive subject is the possessor, but, if kinship terms are referred to as subject or object in the phrase, they are frequently followed by a nominalizing clitic (Davis 1964 : 123):

(56) *séẓ-* *ánaisdyʊ* *-šɛ*
1PL.INDIC- father -NOM
'our father; the one who is a father to us'

When a relational noun is predicated, that is, when the speaker is predicating the relation, the relational noun is transitivized (Davis 1964:113):

(57) *śa-* *uḳî* *-ni*
2/1PL- friend -TRANS
'you are my friend/I am your friend'

These examples probably ought to be analyzed as headless modifier expressions, as the alternative glosses suggest. In Santa Ana Keresan, then, it appears that the root does indeed denote the relation, and not an argument of the relation, since no type-changing derivation is involved, only function-indicating ones (the nominalizer). In fact, the Russian relational root *drug* could also be interpreted in a similar manner since along with the unmarked noun *drug* 'friend' one finds the more or less unmarked verb *družit'* 'be a friend with, be friends.'[32]

Another interesting semantic class with anomalous semantic characteristics is that including terms describing the weather. These are stage-level processes like verbs, but they have a valency of zero like nouns since weather is a characteristic of the environment. Thus, one might expect a tension between assignment of unmarked weather expressions to verbs or nouns. A cursory examination of some weather expressions in English, Russian, Spanish, Quiché, Lakhota, and Woleaian suggests that the situation is rather complicated. Roots denoting precipitation appear to be predominantly nominal:

Russian:

(58) *idët* *dožd'/sneg*
go.3SG rain/snow
'it is raining/snowing'

Lakhota:

(59) *wa-* *pa*
snow- fall
'it is snowing'

Quiché:

(60) *š-* *ok* *aq̇ap̂*
PAST- come dew
'the dew has come [evening greeting].'

However, in all these cases the phrase itself uses a (processual) verb of motion in combination with a noun. The noun appears to denote the precipitation itself, that is, the water (compare Lakhota *mnimni* 'sprinkle,' a reduplication of *mni* 'water'), although it could also denote the process, as in English *The rain will stop soon.* It is more common to find a zero-derivation, as in English *rain/snow* or Lakhota *p̄o* 'fog/be foggy'; the only strong case of an unmarked verb form that I have found is Spanish *llov-* 'rain (v.)' *lluv-i-* 'rain (n.).'[33] The best cases are those words that must denote the event rather than some product of the event (the precipitation); interestingly, the two examples in the Russian root study are unmarked nouns, while the unmarked forms of their English counterparts, 'storm' and 'thunder,' can function as nouns or a verbs, both denoting the event. Finally, some languages coerce the "zero-valency" weather expressions into unary predications and express them as intransitive verbs. Woleaian makes an argument out of the location (Sohn and Tawerilmang 1976:81, 92; the nouns are zero derived, however):

(61) *ye* *langi/maliumel* *Weleya*
3SG typhoon/storm Woleai
'Woleai is being struck by a typhoon/is having a storm.'

One weather expression in Classical Greek, *hýei* [rain.3SG] 'it is raining,' sometimes takes the supernatural figure Zeus as the subject: *Zeus hýei,* literally 'Zeus is raining' (Joseph Greenberg, personal communication).

In conclusion, there exists typological variation in the expression of weather events between nounlike and verblike constructions (or unmarked forms that are both nominal and verbal) that one can attribute to weather events falling semantically between the prototypes for nouns and verbs.

3.3.4 Auxiliaries, adpositions and other transitory categories

A considerable debate has gone on over the status of auxiliaries. On the basis of typological evidence, Steele and others have proposed that "auxiliary" (that is, AUX) is a universal syntactic category (Steele 1978; Akmajian, Steele, and Wasow 1979). Steele uses semantic criteria as evidence for the status of auxiliary as a universal, namely, the expression of tense, aspect, and various types of modality in auxiliaries. However, Steele is using a slightly different definition of "universal" than the one generally used in typological analyses: instead of meaning something present in all human languages, like nouns and verbs, Steele means something "available" to human languages, that is, possibly rather than necessarily occurring in human languages.

It is possible that in every natural language one will find certain verbs in the semantic range that Steele linked with auxiliaries with morphosyntactic peculiarities and also perhaps certain adverbs or other forms (e.g., English *better* in *He better leave*) with positional peculiarities and the same semantic range. But the most verblike auxiliaries, such as the "standard" auxiliaries in English, appear to be simply behaviorally defective verbs in one way or another, as would be expected from the semantic nonprototypicality of the meanings that they express with respect to the category "verb." It is true that finite inflections are sometimes associated with the less verblike auxiliary forms or distributed across the auxiliary and the main verb, such as the second-position particles in Warlpiri (Hale 1973) and Papago (Zepeda 1983), but this reflects the sentential status of most of the inflections and also (in the more verblike cases) synchronic uncertainty as to whether the main verb of the utterance is the "auxiliary" or the main verb.[34]

A historical explanation is the most plausible one for the status of auxiliaries in natural languages. Auxiliaries represent a diachronically as well as semantically intermediate category: they are forms that once functioned as full verbs (or adverbs) and will presumably eventually become verbal affixes. Their "in-between" status is as much a result of historical intermediacy as of their semantic nonprototypicality. I will call diachronically intermediate categories TRANSITORY categories. It may turn out that the diachronic grammaticalization cycle (Lehmann 1982, 1985; Heine and Reh 1984) of verb > auxiliary > affix is sufficiently frequent in occurrence and unstable in duration that there is no language that does not have at least one lexical item in the intermediate category "auxiliary."[35] Another consequence of the diachronic nature of transitory categories is that they do not possess a "core" definable in terms of syntactic behavior. Instead, the members of a transitory category display more of a cline or scale, ranging from the grammatical properties associated with a full-fledged lexical item to those associated with a particle on its way to being an affix. This is found, with numerous complications,[36] when comparing the different English auxiliaries and "semiauxiliaries" in their grammatical behavior with respect to various grammatical constructions (see table 3.6).

The present-day English auxiliaries have undergone a varied history, including loss of other tense forms (*used to, ought to, must,* [*be*] *going to*), split of present and past forms to distinct functions (*can/could, will/would, may/might, shall/should*), loss of ability to take a direct object noun phrase (*can, ought, shall, will*), and some variation on the ability to take *to* + infinitive (*dare, need, ought*).[37]

It should be clear that the explanation for the existence of a transitory category such as auxiliaries is a completely different kind of expla-

TABLE 3.6 *Behavior of English Auxiliaries and Semiauxiliaries*

	Preg-Neg Position	**Question Inversion**	**No *to* + Infinitive**	**No Tense Inflection**
can, must, will	Y	Y	Y	Y
(have) better	Y	?	Y	Y
ought to	(Y)	Y	N	Y
need	Y/N	Y/N	Y/N	Y
dare	Y/N	Y/N	Y/N	N
used to	N	N	N	Y
be going to, be about to, have to	N	N	N	N
be, have	Y	Y	N.A.	N
make X	N	N	Y	N

nation for a (putative) universal category. Rather than reflecting some basic pragmatic propositional function, a transitory category owes its existence to a diachronically unstable universal process and displays a cline of grammatical behavior rather than a prototypical core.

Another very similar case that has been proposed for major category status is adpositions. As was mentioned in section 2.1, adpositions fill out the binary category features [N, V] in one version of X′ theory. I will argue here that, although adpositions are definitely a distinct semantic class and they do perform a certain type of propositional pragmatic function, they do not merit the status of a major syntactic category in the way that "noun," "verb," and (to a lesser extent) "adjective" do.

First, the category adposition may not be universal. It is possible that there are languages without adpositions at all: that is, the function of adpositions is taken by verbs, relational nouns, or case affixes. Virtually all adpositional relations in Yoruba (Rowlands 1969) and Igbo (Green and Igwe 1963) are carried out behaviorally by "serial verbs"; each language has only one general locative preposition. Mandarin Chinese also uses only verbs, called coverbs, for most adpositional relations (Li and Thompson 1981, 366):

(62) *wǒ gěi nǐ dào chá*
I give you pour tea
'I'll pour you some tea.'

However, some of these coverbs are used only in adpositional relations, not as full verbs, and these may properly be called "adpositions." Other languages, for example, Mesoamerican Indian languages, use relational nouns based mostly on body parts for adpositional relations, as in Quiché:

(63) *č- u- pām lē kosiʔn*
at- 3SG.POSS- belly the kitchen
'inside the kitchen'

However, Quiché also has two true prepositions, both of general locative nature, one found in example (63). Finally, some languages such as Maricopa (Gordon 1986) appear to have only affixes to express spatial and other adposition-like relations, though Maricopa has "locational nouns" used for more specific spatial relations (Gordon 1986:46). If it is true that languages without adpositions as independent words exist, then "adposition" is not a universal category in the way that "noun," "verb," or even "adjective" are.

Of course, the reason for this is diachronic once more: verbs and relational nouns represent the origins of adpositions and case affixes their demise as independent syntactic units. Like auxiliaries, adpositions are transitory categories, between the lexical verbs, nouns, and deictic directionals they come from and the inflectional affixes they become. Most languages preserve several layers of adpositional markers, and a cline in grammatical behavior can be observed. In general, one can observe the following adposition types in English: "pure" adpositions in the form of simple prepositions and the sources of new adpositions in the complex prepositions consisting of some combination of "pure" prepositions and a relational noun or adverb (*inside* [*of*], *in front of, out of*). Recent entries into the category "adposition" began as relational nouns requiring the construction *Prep the* [*relational noun*] *of NP* (e.g., *yn the side of* 'inside'; 1613, *Oxford English Dictionary*). All these have lost first the preceding preposition and/or the determiner and finally (if it has happened yet) the genitive *of* (see table 3.7).

The origin of adpositions in nouns provides a diachronic explanation for the phenomenon that has led some linguists to argue for the status of adposition as a major category: government of NPs by adpositions. Government of NPs by adpositions, as in Russian, is due to a historically newer layer of adpositions co-occurring with a historically

TABLE 3.7 *Evolution of the Grammatical Behavior of Selected English Prepositions (in terms of centuries)*

	Origin	Loss of *the*	Loss of Prep	Loss of *of*
outside	16	17–19	17–19(?)	19–20
inside (of)	16	17–19	17–19	19–?
in front of	17	19	?	?
on top of	17	19–20	?	?

Note: ? = not yet.

older layer, namely, the case affixes. In fact, in some Uralic and Altaic languages the newer and the older adpositions have both become suffixes, so that nouns are double suffixed. The commonness of this phenomenon is due to the diachronic rapidity of the adposition renewal process.[38] As with auxiliaries, diachronic renewal is so rapid that most languages have at least one lexical item in the class "adposition" (e.g., Palauan, Yoruba, and Igbo have one, and Quiché has two), but again the synchronic universal would be clearly due to a diachronic process, not a universal pragmatic function.

Finally, adpositions, like auxiliaries, are always a closed class and so contrast with nouns and verbs, which are always open classes, and with adjectives, which are frequently (although not always) open classes. Transitory categories in general are not large categories because the stage of grammaticalization that they represent is one that already has limited membership to a small number of elements, each of which denotes a general semantic value (see Heine and Reh 1984).

3.4 Conclusion

The analysis of major syntactic categories offered in these two chapters, if correct, has far-reaching consequences for current views of grammar. The correlation of semantic and pragmatic properties, and the separation of semantic valency from the valency of propositional speech acts, succeeds in explaining certain cross-linguistic patterns of syntactic category membership and behavior that cannot be explained in either the traditional semantic account or the categorial semantic account. This analysis also stands as an argument for allowing semantics and pragmatics to interact closely with each other since their separation would prevent the generalizations in these chapters from being captured. The results also indicate that attempts to separate "grammar" from lexical semantics are counterproductive: lexical semantics provides a major insight into the structure and behavior of lexical items in different surface-syntactic functions.

This analysis also provides a significant portion of the necessary argument for the functionalist approach outlined in chapter 1. I have argued that syntactic categories do have a cross-linguistically valid external basis, and, in fact, the analysis I have proposed also provides a functional basis for certain other "core" grammatical phenomena such as derivational morphology, predicate nominals and adjectives, and relative clauses. These categories and constructions, which have generally been treated as purely arbitrary and thus amenable only to formal syntactic treatment, are founded on basic principles of commonsense ontological classification of the world and of presumably very deep principles of organizing information. In addition, I have argued that cognitive semantic and discourse functional explanations of syntactic phenomena are not mutually incompatible. A cognitive semantic account explains how the placement of a lexical item in a particular grammatical category or construction determines (or at least affects) the conceptualization of the experience denoted by that item; a discourse functional account explains why one would want to conceptualize the experience in that way in order to communicate it to one's interlocutors.

The functional basis of the major syntactic categories that make up the primary units of the clause having been established, one can now turn to the grammatical relations that hold the clause together. This is a much larger task, and only a part of it will be taken on here: the grammatical relations of the clause level, those that hold between a main verb and its arguments. The reason for focusing on this aspect of the problem, besides its undoubted importance, is that it arises from a putative "problem" in the analysis of syntactic categories given here.

As the reader has certainly noticed, there is a mismatch with respect to valency between the semantic class of actions and the propositional act of predication that actions prototypically correlate with. The semantic valency of unmarked verb roots is often two or more, while the valency of predication (subject-predicate) is only one. This fact was temporarily set aside by suggesting that the most fundamental distinction between objects/reference on the one hand and actions/predications on the other was the distinction between zero and nonzero valency, that is, between inherent relationality and the lack thereof.

This mismatch implies that there is a conflict between the need of semantic structure to express multiple referents and the apparent lack of a place for them in the pragmatic structure of the clause (proposition). This mismatch is in fact responsible for much interesting morphosyntax. First, the unique and privileged status of the subject/"topic" and the plausibility of the verb phrase as a surface constituent—that is, the classical distinction between "subject" and "predicate"—can be attributed to the pragmatic structure, which requires that one referent be "the" primary referent and that the other participants and modifying material be subsumed under a predication unit headed by the verb. The semantic structure of the clause, however, attributes equal status to every argument and also argues for the predicate (normally, the main verb) as the head of the clause. Thus, in other morphosyntactic respects argument phrases are treated alike, in particular, in their internal (phrasal) morphosyntactic structure, while the verb as head of the clause attracts the "sentential" inflections such as tense, modality, speaker attitude, and speech act type.

From the point of view of pragmatic structure and semantic structure, there is the need to distinguish multiple semantic arguments. This is accomplished by the strategies of case marking and agreement as well as by word order. I argued in chapter 1 (and in Croft 1988) that, of these surface-structural strategies for indicating grammatical relations, case marking is the strategy that represents or denotes the relation itself that holds between the main verb and its arguments. Hence, it is most likely that the semantics and pragmatics of case marking will hold the key to a semantic and pragmatic analysis of clause-level grammatical relations. This analysis is developed in the next three chapters.

4

Thematic Roles, Verbal Semantics, and Causal Structure

4.1 Introduction

The analysis in the preceding chapters demonstrates that a prototype approach to cross-linguistic grammatical patterns (the typological markedness patterns) allows us to develop a universal definition of the major syntactic categories that is not constrained to the quirks of a particular language, as a purely structural analysis would be. The acceptance of the prototype approach permits us to account for the existence of numerous boundary cases, a perennial difficulty for the formalist approach. In keeping with the functionalist goals in linguistic explanation, the analysis revealed a pattern based on the meanings of lexical roots and suggested a motivation for this pattern in cognitive conceptualization and pragmatic function.

In this and the following chapters, I will examine a problem that emerged directly from the syntactic category analysis: accounting for the ways of distinguishing different arguments of a predicate, in particular, those arguments other than the subject. This is directly related to a major issue in contemporary linguistic theory: the status of the grammatical relations "subject," "object," and "oblique" in universal grammar. In this section, I will restrict myself to a narrower topic that sheds considerable light on the issue: the function of case marking (prepositions, postpositions, and case affixes; chap. 5) and the closely associated verbal forms (voice, causatives, and applicatives; chap. 6). The reason for doing so is a principled one: to examine the domain of application of a single rule, or rather a single closely related pair of rules, case assignment and voice. As I noted in chapter 1, generative arguments for subjecthood have utilized an array of constructions, most of which involve interclausal relations—control of nonfinite complements, deletion of coreferential arguments in conjoined clauses, the relation between a relative clause and its head noun in the main clause, reflexivization across clause boundaries, etc. From the functionalist point of view, each construction has its own semantic and pragmatic conditions governing its domain of application, though the domains of application will coincide to the extent that they refer to the same functional concept (e.g., topicality). However, the first stage of analysis is determining the domain of application of an individual construction.

I have chosen to focus on case marking and voice for two reasons. First, case marking and voice constitute one of the fundamental ways in which a clause is organized grammatically: they characterize predicate-argument relations. Second, as I will argue, case marking and voice are closely related to lexical meaning, particularly, verbal semantics. Nevertheless, as with syntactic categories, the relevance of verbal semantics to grammatical structure is motivated by conceptual and pragmatic factors. Also as with syntactic categories, the pragmatic factors are logically independent of the semantic ones: just as almost any concept can be expressed as a noun, almost any argument can be expressed as a subject (or object), depending on the choice of verb and voice. Unlike the preceding chapters, however, this chapter will concentrate solely on the semantic and conceptual consequences of pragmatic choices of subject and object. The pragmatics of subject and object choice is a well-researched area and will be briefly summarized in 4.2. However, the relation of pragmatics to semantics in this area has been a vexing problem, and it is this problem that I will address here.

4.2 Pragmatic and Conceptual Factors in Subject and Object Choice

Actually, the ability to express any argument of a predicate as the subject of a clause appears to be more limited than the ability to express any concept as, for example, a noun. Flexibility in subject and object selection is dependent on two major factors: the existence of a verb that allows the relevant NP to be the subject or the object and the existence of a construction type such as the passive that allows a "reassignment"[1] of argument NPs from the unmarked configuration of grammatical relations to the desired one. Thus, the ability to make the NP referring to a hole the subject of a clause describing a digging event is dependent on both the existence of a verb *dig* that makes *the hole* the direct object and the existence of the passive voice construction that allows a "reassignment" of *the hole* to subject:

(1) The hole was dug by a stray dog.

In some languages, inflexibility in the assignment of an NP to subject or object is gotten around by flexibility in word order, so that a similar pragmatic function to, say, passive or "dative shift" is achieved through reordering the NPs without reassignment of case relations or verbal voice (cf., e.g., Givón 1984: 158; or the " topicalization" in English described by Prince 1981a). In languages such as English in which both NP reordering and NP reassignment ("relation-changing") constructions exist, there is most likely a pragmatic differentiation. In this chapter (and the following ones), however, I will concern myself only with reassignment constructions, or as they are popularly called, "relation-changing rules."

Whenever there is flexibility in the assignment of NP to subject or object, one may compare constructions that differ only in NP assignment in order to determine the pragmatic conditions underlying subjecthood and objecthood. Most discourse analysts agree that, when a choice for subject is involved, topicality governs the choice, and that, when a choice is not involved, the NP that is grammatically required to fill the subject slot is a "natural topic" (Hawkinson and Hyman 1974). That is, the active voice construction is used when the agent is more topical than the patient, but the passive voice construction is used when the patient is more topical than the agent (Givón 1984a: 177). "Natural topicality" refers to the preference to assign topicality to NPs higher in the animacy hierarchy (Silverstein 1976; Dixon 1979), a ranking that includes NP type as well as animacy proper: first/second person < third-person pronoun < proper name < human common noun < animate common noun < inanimate common noun. Also, topical NPs are generally definite, as are subject NPs (Givón 1979: 51). Before turning to definitions of "topicality," it is worth pointing out that, where there is a choice available between (zero-marked) object and (case-marked) oblique, it appears that the more topical NP is assigned to object position (Trithart 1979; Givón 1984a). Thus, the grammatical relations hierarchy, subject < object < oblique,[2] is a topicality hierarchy: subjects are more topical than objects, which are in turn more topical than obliques.

The majority of the evidence presented for the topicality hierarchy has been based on "natural topics," that is, grammatical constraints that require that the more animate/more definite NP be made an object instead of an oblique or a subject instead of an object. Givón (1983b) has proposed a gradient concept of TOPIC CONTINUITY for a grammar-independent definition of topic (see 3.2.3). Topic continuity is measured in terms of "referential distance" (how many clauses back to the previous mention of the NP), "persistence" (how many clauses forward the NP is mentioned), and "referential ambiguity" (competition between potential topic NPs). Givón uses the concept of topic continuity to characterize word order alternations and other grammatical devices than case assignment and voice,[3] so his definition cannot be solely a definition of "subject" (or, rather, that aspect of subjecthood that is not subject to semantic or other constraints). Nevertheless, quantitative text studies of voice in Chamorro (Cooreman 1983) and Nez Perce (Rude 1988) suggest that topic continuity does govern subject choice (cf. Givón 1983b: 57). Finally, it is worth noting that if topic continuity—that is, opening a cognitive file—underlies nounhood, as I suggested in 3.2.3, then it is not surprising that it also underlies the ranking of NPs: the most active cognitive file is the primary NP in the clause.

Of more direct relevance to the problem addressed here is the relation between topicality (more precisely, the manifestation of topicality in the grammatical relations hierarchy) and semantic relations between NPs and verbs. Semantic relations were first described in traditional grammar under the heading of "uses of the cases," and in an important recent revival, that by Fillmore (1968), the semantic predicate-argument relations are titled "case roles."[4] The case roles, now generally called THEMATIC ROLES, will be discussed in detail in 4.3, but for now we will focus on the relation between the well-established case roles of agent, patient, instrumental, dative/benefactive, and assignment to subject or object. Fillmore proposes a subject selection hierarchy: "If there is an A[gent in the clause], it becomes the subject; otherwise, if there is an I[nstrument], it becomes the subject; otherwise, the subject is the O[bject]" (Fillmore 1968: 33). Fillmore supports his hierarchy by the following examples:

(2) *John opened the door.*

(3) *The key opened the door.*

(4) *The door opened.*

However, the position of instrumentals in the subject selection is somewhat shaky since, in many languages, instrumentals cannot be assigned directly to subject position if an agent is missing from the clause (see, e.g., DeLancey 1984a: 186).

Givón (1976: 152; and later work) proposes an alternative *topic* selection hierarchy: agent < dative/benefactive < accusative/patient. Givón supports his topic selection hierarchy by the preference of subjects to be agents and, for objects, the preference of dative/benefactive NPs to be unmarked objects if a "dative-shift" or "promotion to object" construction is available in the language (Givón 1984a). If topicality is closely related to subjecthood, then somehow Fillmore's and Givón's case selection hierarchies must be reconciled. However, it should be noted that they are not as different as they appear: the problematic status of the instrumental has already been noted, and a significant component of the topicality of dative/benefactive NPs is that they are overwhelmingly human, whereas patient NPs often are not (see the English text counts in Givón [1979, chap. 2]).

Fillmore's view of the subject selection problem underwent a significant shift. Fillmore's best-known article following his original case grammar proposal (Fillmore 1977) discusses the relation between semantic role and subject choice in terms of "perspective on a scene." The basic concept is that a SCENE—what is being described—is an arbitrarily complex entity, containing all sorts of participants at various levels of detail. When a speaker chooses to describe a scene, however, he or she must select only certain aspects of the scene, by virtue of doing so emphasizing certain aspects of the scene, including certain participants of the scene, relative to other aspects of and participants in the scene.[5] This selection process is the selection of a main verb and the selection of certain participants as subject, object, and so on.

This method of describing verbs and scenes works best with complex situations such as the commercial situation, in which there are different lexical items such as *buy, sell, pay,* and *cost* that allow different participants to be subject and object (and also allow different participants to be obligatorily present, optional, or obligatorily absent). In less complex situations, there are fewer lexical choices, but that is made up for to some extent by certain inflectional choices, namely, the different voice forms.

Fillmore's notion of perspective on a scene represents the conceptualization by the speaker of an external, nonlinguistic situation that the speaker is describing. As in the case of the major syntactic categories, we may examine subject and object assignment to determine what semantic effects they have on thematic relations that are otherwise determined by the verb.

A study of Hare, Newari, and English by DeLancey (1984a) suggests some coercion or construal patterns for subjecthood. In Hare, instrumental NPs cannot normally be (transitive) subjects; however, inanimate nonvolitional NPs can be transitive subjects if they represent an ultimate cause, without any external agent (De Lancey 1984a : 187):

(5) *féku ye- wékhj*
gun 3OBJ- killed
'The/a gun killed him/her/it.'

This sentence is not acceptable unless interpreted that the gun went off spontaneously without human interference. In English, it appears that, while instrumental subjects may allow a proximate cause interpretation, as in *The key opened the door* and *The bullet killed him instantly,* they are also usable as ultimate causes, without human responsibility involved. Volitional causation, at least in the "normal" commonsense construal, is an ultimate cause, without an outside source. Other Hare data, and data from Newari as well, suggest that subjecthood also assigns direct causation: the subject brought about the action without a mediating cause. In Newari, the normal transitive clause has a subject marked with the ergative case; it contrasts with a sentence with the suffix *-yana;* note the English translations (DeLancey 1984a: 195):

(6) *harsa -nɔ̃ wo misa -yatɔ siat -ɔ*
H. -ERG the woman -DAT kill -PERF
'Harsha killed the woman.'

(7) *harsa -nɔ̃ -yana wo misa sit -ɔ̃*
H. -ERG -'CAUSE' the woman die -PERF
'Because of Harsha, the woman died.'

DeLancey notes that there are a variety of situations that the two sentences could describe; for example, (6) could be used for a situation in which Harsha physically assaulted the woman without intending to kill her, and (7) could be used for a situation in which Harsha told a third party something that caused the third party to kill the woman. This conceptualization of subjects as direct causers appears to involve not simply subjecthood but the fact that a simple clause with a simple transitive verb is used since indirect causation is expressed by complex clauses in some languages. That is, expression of the action with a single verb as much as assignment of the causer to subject role influences the conceptualization of direct causation.

The semantic effect of assignment of an NP to object position instead of an oblique—conceptualizing an entity as an object—has been observed widely. This is the fact that, in an alternation between object and oblique, the object in the construction is the more AFFECTED entity (Fillmore 1968; Anderson 1970; cf. Wierzbicka 1980: 70–74):

(8) *I shot the sheriff.* [sheriff hit]

(9) *I shot at the sheriff.* [sheriff probably not hit]

(10) *Gary sprayed the paint on the wall.* [all the paint used, but perhaps not all the wall covered]

(11) *Gary sprayed the wall with the paint.*[all the wall covered, but perhaps not all the paint used]

In other words, other things being equal, the object NP is conceptualized as being more affected by the action than the oblique NP.[6]

It does not appear that the semantic conceptualization effects just described relate directly to high topicality (subjects) or "medium" topicality (objects). The relation between conceptualization of objects and pragmatic or discourse function seems the clearer one. If an entity is more affected by the action denoted by the verb, then it is more centrally involved in what is being asserted than a less affected entity. It seems reasonable to assume that a more involved entity is more topical than a less involved one; otherwise, a different predication (or a different verbal form, not requiring the NP to be an object) would have been chosen. The relation between conceptualization of subjects and discourse function appears to be a bit different. An ultimate, direct cause of the action denoted by the main verb is not going to have any competitors for main topic, such as other involved agents. Another factor contributing to the topicality of subjects is animacy. Prototypical agents are volitional; hence, they are most likely human, or at least animate. As we noted, high animacy correlates with high topicality. It has been suggested that subject position also correlates with the participant with which the speaker empathizes most closely (Kuno and Kaburaki 1977; DeLancey 1981). The speaker will empathize with participants higher on the animacy hierarchy (including maximal empathy with the speaker himself or herself and the hearer). Similar arguments apply to the selection of more animate thematic roles such as benefactive as objects (Givón 1976, cited above; Dryer 1986; see also 5.4.2 and 6.1). However, the primary explanation for the conceptualization of subjects and objects is based on the conceptualization of verbs (see 6.4).

I now turn to the issue to be addressed in the following chapters: the relation between subject and object choice, however it is assigned, as well as the conceptualization it imposes on the situation, and the thematic roles that make up the semantics of predicate-argument relations. There are several general problems in the literature that these chapters will address. First, there is the definition of the thematic roles themselves. Second, there is the status of the "subject/object selection hierarchies." Finally, there is the problem of defining the range of thematic roles allowable for subjects and objects and for various oblique adpositions or case markers. This and the following chapters will offer solutions to all these problems.

4.3 Problems with Case (Thematic) Roles

The various approaches to the analysis of grammatical relations, to use that term to cover any proposal for the structure into which to fit the main verb and the noun phrases and adpositional phrases that make up the main verb's surface arguments, mirror the approaches to syntactic categories. The structural and generative tradition analyzes grammatical relations independently of extralinguistic factors. The plausibility of this approach is due to the fact that the connection between semantic role and choice of grammatical relation is not at all obvious, if it even exists. It is extremely difficult to say what the subject of *John killed the rat* and *John likes Beethoven* have in common semantically. If one adds the passive *The rat was killed by John*, then there seems to be no basis for a semantic analysis of subject. Instead, much of the debate in the structural and generative tradition has focused on how to represent the structure of the clause, including subject and object: phrase structure, as the generative tradition has consistently maintained; dependency relations, as relational grammar (Perlmutter 1983) and a number of European syntactic theories (Tesnière 1959; Halliday 1976; Hudson 1976; Dik 1981; Mel'čuk 1979) have advocated; or a combination of both, as lexical functional grammar (Bresnan 1982a) has proposed.

Despite the apparent lack of relation between subject and semantic role illustrated above, the thematic roles holding between the main verb and its arguments play a major role in most contemporary theories of grammar. This is particularly true of the oblique grammatical relations but also of the direct ones (subject, direct object, and, possibly, indirect object). The seminal works that brought this interest to the foreground were Gruber's dissertation (Gruber 1976, originally written in 1965) and Fillmore's original paper on case grammar (Fillmore 1968). The case and thematic role theories that have followed Fillmore's have several important features that are not present in traditional grammatical accounts of case uses (although it is difficult to interpret the traditional grammatical analyses owing to their frequent imprecision). The three most significant features are as follows.

i. Thematic (case) roles are defined as semantic primitives (i.e., semantically unanalyzable).
ii. Thematic roles are defined independent of the semantics of the verb, which is also left unanalyzed (primitive).
iii. There are only a small finite number of thematic roles.

These three features lead to a REDUCTIONIST approach to thematic role definitions that attempts to minimize the number of thematic roles that would have to be cited by grammatical rules.[7] The most extreme version of the reductionist approach is the "strict interpretation" of the localist hypothesis in which nonlocal thematic roles are reduced to source, location, and goal.[8] Unfortunately, the reductionistic approaches all share the problem of vagueness and overgenerality in attempting to account for the richness of typological data. In the remainder of this section, I will argue that all three of these assumptions of modern case/thematic role analysis should be abandoned and that their abandonment will in fact permit us to develop a much more adequate theory of relation between surface case marking and semantic relations.

Let us turn to the first assumption, that thematic roles are semantically primitive. A reductionist approach to case analysis will necessarily have to subsume a number of semantically distinct though related participant roles into a single unanalyzed thematic role. For example, one often finds a role called "Goal," which is intended to subsume the traditional allative, recipient, and benefactive roles. However, natural language data show that these three roles must be both distinguished from one another and related to each other as well. Consider the three major subtypes of the "goal" thematic role in English:

(12) *I gave my ticket to the girl.* [recipient]

(13) *I walked to the church.* [allative]

(14) *Carol sewed up the pocket for me.* [benefactive]

These three roles cannot be subsumed unequivocally under a single thematic role because that would not account for the preposition *for* in (14) as opposed to *to* in (12)–(13). On the other hand, these three roles are *related:* the same preposition is used in (12) and (13). The examination of other languages would confirm that these three grammatical roles are related yet distinct: for example, Russian has one case form for (12) and (14) and a distinct form for (13), while Mokilese has the same form for all three.

In addition to examples such as the "goal" role, which subsumes a number of linguistically distinct but typologically related participant roles, there are other case relations that have not yet been accounted for in the case literature to my knowledge, such as the following pattern with English *with* (cf. Nilsen 1972:21):[9]

(15) *I went to Dyerville Flats with my brother.* [comitative]

(16) *John tickled her with a feather.* [instrument]

(17) *Mary played the Rondo with great sensitivity.* [manner]

(18) *Fred loaded the wagon with hay.* ["objective"]

The relationship between the thematic roles found with English *with* is not obvious, but the typologically quite widespread combination or SYNCRETISM[10] of these thematic roles under a single surface case marker must be accounted for.

A theory that considers thematic roles to be unanalyzable primitives will not be able to handle this data. What is necessary is a semantic analysis that will allow us to decompose the semantics of thematic roles in a way that will capture the fact that allative, benefactive, and recipient are related to each other but not to instrumental, comitative, and manner. The question is, How?

The answer to that question lies in the abandonment of assumption (ii), that there is no relation between thematic roles and verb meaning and that the latter is left unanalyzed. The best way to see this fact is to examine assumption (iii), that there is a small finite number of thematic roles, critically. The greatest objection to the reductionist research program in case grammar is the tremendous variety of semantic roles that have to be accounted for. It is difficult to see how one could fit the following examples into a reductionist system:[11]

(19)	Negative quality	*A man without humor*
	Function	*I used the stick as a club.*
	Reference	*We talked about the war.*
	Price	*I bought it for five dollars.*
	Extent	*He ran (for) two miles.*

The only way in order to begin to account for the wide variety of thematic roles found with different surface predicates is to analyze the meaning of the verbs that they are associated with. The more difficult to handle thematic roles are associated with very small but semantically coherent classes of verbs, such as verbs of commercial exchange for the price role. In fact, taken to its logical conclusion, a fine-grained analysis of thematic roles will result in a unique case frame for almost every verb in a natural language. I believe that this reductio ad absurdum is the correct grounding point for the analysis of case, however: what it implies is that the definitions of the thematic roles must mesh in some natural way with the lexical semantics of the verbs that govern them. It is obvious that, although semantic thematic ROLES may be verb specific, surface morphosyntactic case MARKINGS in natural languages gather together large classes of thematic roles since there are thousands of verbs with thousands of roles but never more than fifty to eighty case markers and at the very most just a dozen or so case markers other than the spatiotemporal ones. Thus, surface case marking imposes structure on thematic relations to an even more abstract degree than verb roots impose structure on the human experience of events.

It is less obvious that verbal semantics will provide a way out of this problem. To do so, one must hypothesize that verbal semantics itself is quite structured and that only certain crucial aspects of verbal semantic structure are relevant to surface case marking. In the next section I will argue that the causal structure of events will provide the relevant semantic features for case analysis.

4.4 Verbal Decomposition and the Individuation of Events

4.4.1 Causal Structure and Verbal Semantic Analysis

In the preceding section, I argued that among other things an adequate theory of thematic roles would have to link the definitions of those roles directly to the meanings of the verbs that require them. I also argued that, if that is true, then regularities in the semantics of thematic roles would reflect regularities in verbal semantics. In other words, what a single lexical verb in a natural language may denote does not vary in arbitrarily many ways, and in fact there are systematic regularities that cover verbal semantics and in turn (partially) determine thematic roles.

Verbs denote events, that is, processes (actions) or states. Although linguists have not explored lexical semantics very thoroughly, philosophers have debated about the structure of events for many years. Some have proposed that spatiotemporal extension defines events. This proposal runs into difficulties, however, because spatiotemporal extension is neither a necessary nor a sufficient condition for defining events. Simultaneous colocated events, such as a ball spinning and getting hot at the same time or a jogger running and sweating at the same time, demonstrate that spatiotemporal extension is not a sufficient condition for individuating events. There are also a few examples that suggest that spatial location is not a necessary condition. The action of being widowed, for example, cannot be located at either the location of the person dying or that of the person being widowed.[12] This is manifested in the unacceptability of the following sentence:[13]

(20) **Mrs. Woodland was widowed in Las Vegas.*

A somewhat different type of example of the inability of locating certain kinds of events in a spatial region, also from the philosophical literature, is that of a killing by stabbing in which the victim's death occurs far away from the location of the stabbing (and also long after the time of the stabbing). One does not want to say that the killing occurred at either location (or time, for that matter) alone or in a combination of both. In fact, natural language expressions of the spatial location of events (so-called external locatives) appear simply to describe a spatial region in which the event occurred. With events such as widowing or the drawn-out killing example, in which no single connected spatial region can plausibly include the event, these expressions are unacceptable. Temporal expressions appear to function in the same way: they describe an interval that includes the occurrence of the event. Although the drawn-out stabbing example provides problems for temporal expressions, it is difficult to find a candidate for an event analogous to widowing on the temporal plane.

In a paper titled "The Individuation of Events" (1980a) first published in 1969, Donald Davidson criticized the spatiotemporal approach and argued instead that causal structure defines events.[14] Davidson concludes his article with this passage: "Events are identical if and only if they have exactly the same causes and effects. Events have a unique position in the framework of causal relations between events in somewhat the way objects have a unique position in the spatial framework of objects" (Davidson 1980a: 179).

The criterion of causality in individuating events applies to individual lexical items as well: individual lexical items appear to denote only causally linked events. Consider the well-known example of verbs whose semantics combines a "manner" or activity as well as a path of motion (cf. Talmy 1972):

(21) *The boat sailed into the cave.*

The activity of sailing and the motion into the cave can be combined only because the activity of sailing *causes* the motion to come about. If the activity does not cause the motion to come about, the sentence is unacceptable:

(22) **The boat burned into the cave.*

This sentence cannot even mean 'the boat was burning while entering the cave': that would be combining two causally unrelated, albeit simultaneous and spatially co-occurring, events into a single clause. In fact, if one does want to describe two causally unrelated events that are simultaneous and possibly also spatially co-occurring, then one must use two separate verbs in separate clauses, linked coordinately or subordinately:

(23) *The top spun* **and** *got hot* **at the same time**.

(24) *The boat was burning* **as** *it entered the cave.*

This is not simply a case of an incompatibility between *burn* and *into* in the latter sentence; the combination is acceptable just when the burning causes the motion:[15]

(25) *The branding iron burned into the calf's skin.*

That the lexical semantics of verbs should follow the same principles as the philosophical analysis of events is not altogether surprising since—from the perspective of the surface structure of natural languages expressing cognitive reality fairly directly—the verbal lexicon constitutes an encoding of what human beings perceive and consider to be individual events. But it provides the fundamental basis of the analysis to be presented here: that verbs reflect segments of causal structure, not any other kind of structure.

The question now is, How is causal structure to be represented? The standard philosophical technique is to represent causality in terms of events causing events:

Sail(e_1, boat) & Enter(e_2, boat, cave) & Cause(e_1, e_2).

There are two difficulties with the philosophical-logical representation. First, the thematic roles of the participants are not expressed at all. The notation could be modified, as Castañeda suggested in a modification of Davidson's (1980b) original proposal, in the following way:

Enter(e_2) & Theme (e_2, boat) & Goal (e_2, cave).

However, this notation does not indicate any relation between the verb (the unary predicate of e_2) and the thematic role type; both are still unanalyzed. Another drawback is that there is no a priori reason to exclude the possibility of one event causing another event without any participants being shared between the two events, a situation excluded by the commonsense intuitive notion of causation:

Dance(e_1, Mary) & Enter(e_2, boat, cave) & Cause (e_1, e_2).

An alternative approach to decomposing events is in terms of individual arguments combined with propositional arguments, such as the following analysis of the word *break:*

Cause (x, Become(y, Broken(y))).

These analyses are directly related to the generative semantic decompositions of verbs in structure (of which one of the first and best is Gruber [1976]), although they are intended to be semantic rather than syntactic representations. The best-worked-out analysis of verbal semantics in these terms is Dowty (1979), in a Montague grammar framework (see also Foley and Van Valin 1989); Jackendoff (1983), in his own mentalist conceptual structure framework; and Gawron (1983), in a frame-semantics framework. Dowty uses both Vendler's (1967) classification of aspectual types and generative semantic lexical decompositions to construct a Montague grammar semantic fragment. Although Dowty's analysis of verbal semantics is concerned chiefly with the interaction of verbs and temporal expressions, the decompositions are very close to those to be proposed here, in which inherent aspect (or Aktionsart) and causal relations are perhaps the two most important components of lexical analysis. Lexical decomposition is often criticized, largely because it is combined with, and confused with, a reductionist approach to the number of primitive subunits used for verbal analysis. It should be clear from the comments in 4.3 that I am not advocating a reductionist approach in linguistic analysis (see also 4.4.2–3).

Nevertheless, the propositional-argument representations, in which an individual is related to an event, has its drawbacks. It suffers from the same defect as the philosophical representations in which an event is related to an event, namely, that there is no necessary connection between participants involved and events related: [16]

Become(x, Broken(y)).

Another problem is that there is no thematic role that is consistently associated with the participant that is extracted to be the individual argument, as opposed to the participants that remain in the propositional argument. The thematic role associated with each argument is a combination of the predicate type and its position in the argument structure (e.g., an agent role would be defined as the argument position "x" in Cause(x, P(y)).

I believe that these two objections are relatively minor and can be patched up at least in part by advocates of these means of representing causal structure. However, the major objection to this approach is that there is a third way to represent causation that allows us to capture a large number of linguistic generalizations. This is to represent causation as individuals acting on individuals, with some notion of transmission of force determining which participant is "first" in the causal order or causal chain. This form of representation was first proposed by Talmy (Talmy 1972, 1976) and has begun to be employed by linguists for causal analysis (e.g., DeLancey 1985; Lichtenberk 1985; Langacker 1987a; Klaiman 1982a, 1982b, 1988; see also Barber 1975). The advantage of the representation of causal relations in terms of individuals acting on individuals are twofold. First, it requires that causally related events share individuals since the individual at the endpoint of one event is the initiator of the next, causally connected, event (x, y, z = participants):

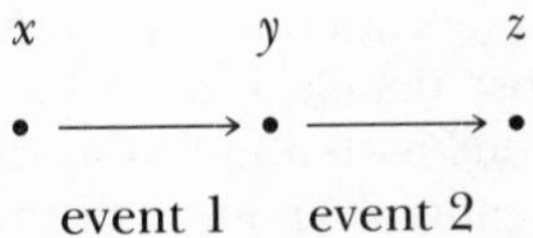

The second advantage is that it imposes a (possibly partial) ordering of participants in the causal chain of events: x precedes y in the causal chain, and y precedes z in the causal chain. This will prove to be a crucial feature in formulating linguistic universals, and it is absent from the other two representations of causation.[17]

4.4.2 Semantic Primitives and Granularity

At this point, it appears that we are defining a system of semantic primitives not unlike other systems that have been proposed (e.g., Schank 1972). The notion of semantic primitive is attractive but also extremely problematic. The two most important problems are that primitives seem always to be further analyzable and that a finite set of primitives may not succeed in capturing the complexity of our experience (and, as a consequence, the linguistic expression of experience). We may avoid these problems by recognizing that a "semantic primitive" describes a conceptualization of experience, not the complex structure of experience itself; the conceptual processes of granularity and idealization account for the abstraction to "primitives."

I will illustrate the problem of potentially infinite analyzability and its solution in this section. One may define causes and effects in increasingly fine detail, and so the problem of individuating events arises again, not on the level of what principles structure events, but on the issue of reaching an atomic level of analysis of the causal structure of events. For example, the sentence in (25) can be expanded into the complex but causally linked sequence of events in (26):

(25) *John was sick.*

(26) *The virus attacked John's throat, which became inflamed, resulting in laryngitis, until the immune system succeeded in destroying the infection.*

The solution to this problem is the notion of GRANULARITY (Hobbs 1985; Croft MS). This is the idea that there are different levels of precision in conceptualization, so that some concepts are conceptualized as irreducible at one level even if they are reducible at another, more "fine-grained" level. Thus, details and distinctions below the more "coarse-grained" level can be ignored at that level of granularity. However, one may shift one's attention to a more fine-grained level of granularity at which those details and distinctions become relevant. Likewise, one can shift one's attention to a still more coarse-grained level at which one may ignore even more distinctions.

Example (25) is at a coarser level of granularity of causal structure than example (26), although both sentences are describing the same "objective" event. Example (25) describes the event as a property of an individual human being as a whole: the human being as a whole is treated as an atomic entity. Example (26), on the other hand, describes the event as a series of events at a level considerably below that of the individual, who is no longer an atomic unit but instead a complex whole made up of many parts, including an entity (the virus) that is not part of John but is relevant (or "distinguishable") at the finer level of granularity in (25). At this level of granularity, the irreducible, atomic event in (26) becomes, not surprisingly, a causal sequence of many events.[18]

The concept of levels of granularity in conceptualizing "objective" reality allows one to "ignore" finer-level semantic details in lexical analysis when they are irrelevant to the conceptualization of the event, without committing oneself to a single-level system of unanalyzable primitives. Sometimes it is necessary to treat primitives as being themselves complex, and at other times the primitives are too fine grained for the relevant situation. Although the concept of granularity allows us to avoid these problems, there remains the problem of what can be a proper level of granularity.

There is an "easy" solution to this problem. Levels of granularity are partly determined by the types of entities that the speaker wishes to talk about, that is, the arguments of the verb. That is, what kinds of things a speaker can say about (predicate of) something depend on what kinds of things the speaker is talking about (referring to). Of course, the types of entities the speaker is talking about in turn have their own level of granularity. The distribution of referring expressions (nouns) in levels of granularity presumably has to be accounted for by a theory of perceptual and conceptual structuring of those chunks of reality that lend themselves to human conceptual individuation and classification as objects of various kinds. Developing such a theory is an important task for any cognitive approach to linguistic analysis, but it is beyond the scope of this volume.

The important feature of granularity for this model is that the granularity levels of the arguments must be matched with the granularity level of the predicate, and so choice of the granularity level of one determines choice of the granularity level of the other. This can be stated in more traditional linguistic terms: there are selectional restrictions that hold between predicates and arguments that are determined by level of granularity as well as by other semantic factors. However, there is no a priori directionality between predicates and arguments in one determining the level of granularity of the other. That is, the speaker may have decided what he is going to talk about (the referent), and that determines the way in which he will express the predication. Or, the speaker may already have an event in mind that he wishes to report, its level of granularity already determined, and that in turn determines the level of granularity of the arguments to the predicate denoting that event.

4.4.3 Ideal Models and Criteria for Atomic Events

The second problem with semantic primitives is that they cannot capture the richness of experience. In general, language does not capture the full range of experience because it has only finite means. Therefore, it must simplify or idealize its cognitive model of experience. For example, Lakoff (1987:70) notes that the definition of *bachelor* as 'adult unmarried male' is not wrong because it cannot account for the status of the pope, Tarzan, a man living with his girlfriend, a member of a gay couple, etc. It is in fact the correct definition of *bachelor;* the problem is the fit of the cognitive model of maturity, sexuality, and marriage with the variety of experience illustrated by the anomalous examples given above. Idealization, along with granularity, allows human beings to handle the complexity of experience for the purposes of linguistic communication (and, presumably, other purposes as well).

In this section, I will propose a set of criteria that represent the first steps toward an IDEALIZED COGNITIVE MODEL (Lakoff 1987) of individual events, where "individual event" is the semantic entity corresponding to a simple verb. In later sections, I will discuss some modifications to and problematic cases with the criteria given below; the problematic cases represent events that do not fit the idealized cognitive model in roughly the same way that the pope does not fit the idealized cognitive model of *bachelor.* The full idealized cognitive model of events will be presented in 6.4.

Criterion 1. An atomic event must be of only one causation type.
Criterion 2. An atomic event must be of a single inherent aspectual type, specifically a state or process.
Criterion 3. An atomic event containing two participants must

have those participants aligned in the direction of "transmission of force."

Criterion 4. An atomic event must be a single qualitative unit.

I will illustrate these four criteria by arguing that the causal sequence in (27) is correctly decomposed into the atomic events illustrated by the diagram immediately below it (making certain additional assumptions about the action described that are not explicit in the example sentence).[19]

(27) *John broke the boulder with a hammer.*

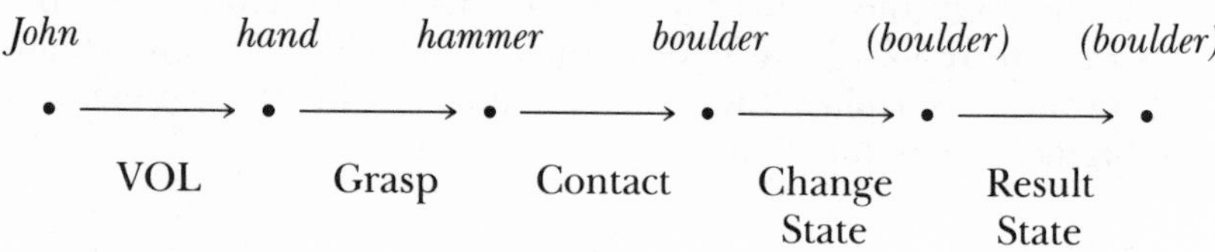

Criterion 1: Causal Type The first criterion is based on an analysis of causation types developed by Talmy (1972, 1976). Talmy points out that causation is a relation between events, but he argues that the relevant classification of causation types is based on the status of and change in the entities that participate in the event. The analysis that Talmy uses is based on the ability to speak of one object acting on or entering into a causal relation with another object and that other object being affected by the first object.[20]

Talmy distinguishes four kinds of causation:

Physical causation: physical object acting on physical object;
Volitional causation: volitional entity acting on physical object;
Affective causation: physical object "acting on" entity with mental states;
Inducive causation: volitional entity acting on entity with mental states.

The classic action verbs such as *hit* or *break* fall under the example of physical or volitional causation, depending on the animacy and control of the INITIATOR (a volition-neutral term for the "agent"/"cause"). The mental verbs of emotion, cognition, and perception fall under affective causation, with certain qualifications (see 5.5.1). The verbs called "mental/social" in 2.7 (including the verbs controlling Equi), such as *persuade, convince, force,* etc., fall under the category of inducive causation.

Talmy's four causation types can be analyzed further as an exhaustive listing of causation types based on a commonsense ontology that is dualist, that is, distinguishes between the mental and the physical. This analysis is illustrated in table 4.1.

TABLE 4.1 *Analysis of Talmy's Four Basic Causation Types*

Initiator (Acting On)	**Endpoint (Acted On)**	**Causation Type**
Physical	Physical	Physical
Mental	Physical	Volitional
Physical	Mental	Affective
Mental	Mental	Inductive

Physical causation is the interaction of two nonvolitional, nonsentient entities such that one affects the other. Volitional causation involves an initiator possessing *and* exercising his mental capacity (through planning, intending, etc.) acting on a physical object. Affective causation involves a physical object or state of affairs changing the mental (emotional, cognitive, perceptual) state of an entity; therefore, the latter must possess a mental capacity. Finally, inducive causation involves an initiator possessing mental capacity exercising it (through communication, persuasion, authority, etc.) to alter the mental state of the endpoint entity (so that he or she will act in some further way).

There is some more detail involved in the commonsense theory of dualism that must be outlined here. First, there is a basic asymmetry in the causation types, which results from a commonsense metaphysics axiom stating roughly, "No telepathy and no telekinesis outside one's own body."[21] This is illustrated in figure 4.1.

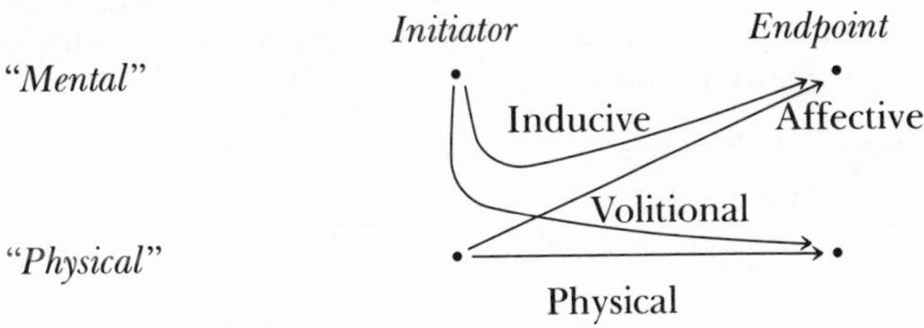

FIGURE 1. *Asymmetries in causation types*

Any causation type that involves an initiating "mental"-level entity must be mediated by a physical entity, specifically, the mental-level entity's own body. Thus, the arrow (arc) for volitional and inducive causation extends "down" to the physical level before reaching the endpoint. This asymmetry does not apply to endpoints: physical objects (or states of affairs) can alter mental states as well as act on other physical objects.

It should be clear that the mental-physical level distinction harks back to the animacy hierarchies. In fact, it introduces a subtle distinction among the class of humans (and, of course, speech act participants) since humans are dual entities that can act as physical objects (the body) or as mentally capable individuals (the usual case). This distinction is well known in the case of volitional versus nonvolitional subjects, manifested in the two interpretations possible for *John hit the wall* or *John fell.* Less well known is the fact that this distinction is also present for objects as well. In *The king showed his daughter to the knight,* the knight must be using his mental ability, namely his perceptual ability, while all that matters about the king's daughter is her perceptible physical reality, not any mental capability that she has. Thus, the mental-level entity is not just any role that may be occupied by a human being but one *exercising* his mental abilities in the action in question. This is the sense in which the indirect object roles of hearer (in *tell*), perceiver (in *show*), and recipient (in *give;* ownership is actually a social concept, but it still requires mental capacity) are *always* higher in animacy than the patient (which leads to the tendency of these roles to "usurp" object agreement; see 5.4.2).

If the mental-physical distinction does reflect the animacy hierarchy, then the unmarked causation type should be volitional causation with a mental initiator and a physical endpoint, and that certainly is the case (cf. the natural correlations mentioned in 2.2 and discussed in Croft [1988]).[22] An example of a split case-marking system that appears to reflect the mental-physical distinction directly is found in Northern Pomo (Dahlstrom 1983). Northern Pomo has an animacy/volitionality split just at the point that one would expect: the unmarked human participants are agentive, and the unmarked nonhuman participants are nonagentive (table 4.2; A = transitive subject, S = intransitive subject, P = transitive object).

TABLE 4.2 *Northern Pomo Case Marking Split*

	A, S (Active)	**S (Stative), P**
Human	-Ø	*-al*
Nonhuman	*ya'*	-Ø

The most marked type is the inversion of volitional causation, namely, affective causation, represented by mental experience verbs with thematic roles normally referred to as "experiencer" and "stimulus." The markedness of the "unnatural" correlation involved in affective causation is reflected in the typological variation of the case marking of mental verbs—that is, the use of subject-experiencer or object-experiencer constructions and the frequency of governed obliques instead of simple direct objects (see 5.5.1, Croft 1990a). However, here I am crucially interested in the unmarked case, namely, volitional causation, because the unmarked member of a category provides the core or model type for the relevant linguistic behavior (in this case, case marking) and because the behavior of the marked types is based on or derived from that of the unmarked types (see 2.4). This prediction will be made more precise in 5.4 and 5.5.

At any rate, figure 4.1 provides the basic notation that I have already used in example (27) and will continue to use throughout the remainder of this book. Atomic events will be represented by directed arcs, and the participants will be represented by nodes linking arcs. The notation is intended to reflect the fact that events, at least those that I hypothesize to constitute the core types, have causal directionality, and they can be linked into a series of causally related events such that the endpoint or affected entity of the causally preceding atomic event is the initiator of the next atomic causal event. This series I will call a CAUSAL CHAIN; any subpiece of the causal chain I will call a CAUSAL SEGMENT or simply a SEGMENT of the causal chain. The minimal segment I will generally refer to as an ARC of the causal chain.

Having explicated and analyzed Talmy's quadripartite division of causation types, one may return to example (27) and determine which arcs are atomic by virtue of the first criterion (distinct causation types imply distinct arcs). The first criterion distinguishes only the first arc from the second. The first arc is an act of volitional causation by the agent, John, onto a physical object, the hammer. Actually, to be completely precise, one must include an intermediate participant, namely, a body part of John's such as his hand, because the commonsense ontology prohibits telekinesis outside the body. This allows the acceptability of sentences such as *He shot the beer can on the fence with his left hand,* meaning that he used his left hand to handle the instrument (e.g., a pistol). On the other hand, such instruments are commonly conceptualized as extensions of the agent's body, and the type of sentence just given is quite rare. The usual meaning of an instrumental expression with a body part is that the body part itself accomplished the action, as in *He broke the boulder with his left hand.* For this reason, in future diagrams I will leave out the body part "grasp" arc, unless the body part is explicitly expressed as an object or instrument.

Criterion 2: Aspectual Type. The second criterion is based on the classification of inherent aspectual types, also known as Aktionsarten. Although various aspectual categories have been observed to be linguistically significant, the distinction that is relevant here—as in the analysis of syntactic categories in chapters 2–3—is that between a STATE and a PROCESS, the latter property being common among the last three.

Distinguishing states and processes allows the separation of a process from its resulting state even though same participant (or participants) is involved. For example, the intransitive inchoative verb *break* in *The boulder broke* covers a different part of the causal chain from the adjectival stative *broken* in *The boulder is broken:* the former includes the breaking process as well as the resulting state, while the latter covers only the resulting state. This distinction is captured by representing the process and the state as separate arcs:

• ——→ (•) ——→ (•)

break(intr.)

broken

The last two arcs in the example are distinguished by this criterion. (In order to distinguish states from processes, no arrow will be placed at the end of an arc indicating a state; see criterion 4.)

Criterion 3: Transmission of Force. The third criterion is intended to distinguish the "grasp," "contact," and "change state" arcs in the example. All three arcs involve physical causation and are processes, so the first two criteria cannot distinguish them. However, in the grasp arc, John (more accurately, John's hand) is acting on the hammer; in the contact arc, the hammer is acting on the boulder; and, in the change state arc, the boulder is acting (changing state) "on its own." What has happened is a TRANSMISSION OF FORCE from John (his hand) to the hammer and from the hammer to the boulder. Each shift in the "force" from one participant to another represents a new segment in the causal chain.

The basic concepts that must be captured by an adequate definition of the third criterion are (a) that a transmission of force from one entity to another involves the end of one causal arc and the beginning of another and (b) that the directionality of the causal chain is determined by the direction of "force." That is to say, one must be able to decompose purely causal sequences into sequences of one entity acting on another entity, which acts on a third, and so on; in this case, the sequence of entities is John, hand, hammer, boulder. This requires a model of volitional and physical action based on a notion of "force" that remains to be formalized—it would be part of the richer qualitative definitions of the causal arcs.

The difference between direct object and oblique assignment is the difference between conceptualizing the event as a transitive ACTION that transfers "force" from one participant to the other and as an intransitive ACTIVITY involving only one participant directly, though with some reference to another event, such as the goal of an unfinished activity or the direction of a gaze or shot. (This underlies the conceptualization of an entity as an object vs. an oblique described in 4.2.) Clearly, one criterion for transfer of force is whether the object undergoes a change of state or at least a complete change of state (just the criteria for object-oblique choice in most languages). The boundary of the two conceptualizations is not a sharp one, and one expects that to be reflected in typological variation in object-oblique case frames for the boundary cases. But by distinguishing between the arbitrarily complex "objective" event and the necessarily simplifying conceptualization of it, as well as the conventionalization of the distinction (subject of course to historical change), one can successfully abstract the generalization that direct object choice will always align itself with the more affected entity.

The theory of volitional action appears to be quite simple. As I argued earlier, the commonsense model requires a mind-body distinction. The link between volition and physical action is quite restricted, being a relation between a volitional entity and that entity's body (or part thereof). The VOL link translates will (intention) into physical force. The will is the source (ultimate cause; see 4.2) of the force and therefore is clearly the initiator, not the endpoint.

Criterion 4: Qualitative Semantic Differences. Consider again the aforementioned example of John running and sweating[23] or the example of falling and breaking (the latter example is oversimplified in its representation here):

(28) *John ran, sweating all the way.*

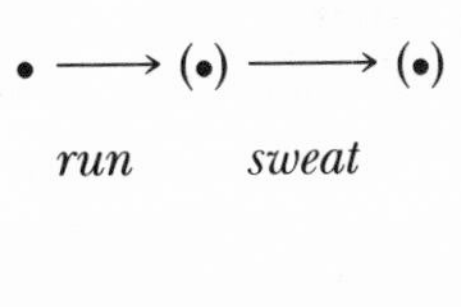

John

• ⟶ (•) ⟶ (•)

run *sweat*

(29) *The vase fell and broke.*

vase

• ⟶ (•) ⟶ (•)

fall *break*

Although it is intuitively natural to distinguish two separate atomic causal segments here, on the basis of the first three criteria one cannot distinguish them. In each example, both segments involve physical causation, both segments are processes, and both segments have the same participant. Therefore, "transmission of force" is the same (more accurately, there is no transmission of force). However, English separates the two causal segments by expressing them as separate verbs. Running and sweating, or falling and breaking, are two qualitatively different actions, and thus qualitative differences not captured by the first three criteria also suffice to distinguish causal segments as conceptually (i.e., lexically) distinct entities. Unfortunately, this criterion is not as precise as the first three; however, it will not significantly affect the analyses to be discussed below.

4.3.4 The Definition of Verb Meaning and Thematic Roles

The causal structures defined in the preceding section are actually more complex than the example used suggests. Causal chains extend indefinitely into the past and the future. Causal chains can be circular, so that an initiator may cause something to happen to himself or herself, as in shaving oneself. There are processes that do not affect other entities, such as the boulder breaking. Some relations appear to be symmetrical. This is due to mutual transmission of force, as in two persons wrestling or two moving vehicles colliding. Or it may be due to the fact that a noncausal relation holds between entities, such as one entity being located with respect to another or one entity possessing another.

This tremendous complexity of causal structure in human experience must be simplified into verbs and thematic roles, that is, the predicate-argument structure of a clause. This is accomplished, as with syntactic categories, through the conceptualization of events in a specific fashion. In Croft (in press b; see also 6.4), I argue that the conceptual model (or idealized cognitive model, to use Lakoff's [1987] term) for a simple event—that is, an event denoted by a verb exclusive of voice, causative, or applicative derivation—includes the following features:

a) a simple event is a (not necessarily atomic) segment of the causal network;
b) simple events are nonbranching causal chains;
c) a simple event involves transmission of force;
d) transmission of force is asymmetric, with distinct participants as initiator and endpoint (these terms are defined below).

The prototypical event type that fits this model is unmediated volitional causation that brings about a change in the entity acted on (i.e., the manifestation of the transmission of force), that is, the prototypical transitive event (for an early statement of the prototype, cf. Lakoff [1977]; for typological data in support of it, Hopper and Thompson [1980]; and for a contemporary cognitive statement of it, Rice [1987, sec. 2.5]). Other event types must be "coerced" into this model. A substantial amount of clause-internal syntax (viewed typologically, of course) is a manifestation of the coercion and conceptualization process and is the topic of the following two chapters. The remainder of this section will describe the consequences of this cognitive model of event structure, in particular a–c, on the linguistic issues raised so far in this chapter.

My proposal for the representation of the relation between a clause—the verb and its arguments—and the situation that it describes is actually quite simple to state. A verb denotes a segment of a causal chain, called here the VERBAL SEGMENT. This is condition a, specified further by conditions b–c, and the basis for the analysis in this volume. The subject and the object (if there is one) are at each end of the segment of the causal chain, the subject causally preceding the object (causal ordering in mental states will be discussed in 5.5.1). The causally prior end of the verbal segment represents the INITIATOR and the causally later end the ENDPOINT of the verbal segment. That is to say, subject and object delimit the verbal segment of the causal chain. Thus, a simple sentence like *Fred ate the banana* would be represented as follows (using ### as verb segment delimiters):

(30) *Fred ate the banana.*

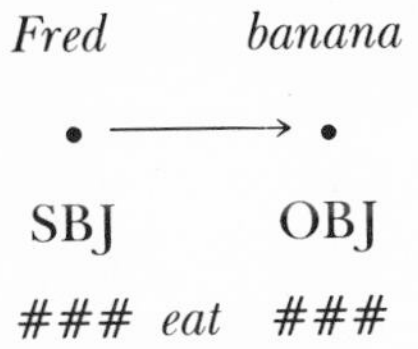

Fred		*banana*
•	⟶	•
SBJ		OBJ
###	*eat*	###

This allows us to have our cake and eat it too with respect to the thematic roles borne by subjects and objects: this is a semantic model of "subject" and "object,"[24] but the range of thematic roles allowable by subject and object (in the unmarked, simple active voice case) is defined by the semantic structure of the lexical entries for verbs (see 6.4).

Conditions a, c, and d have been (and will be) discussed in detail. Condition b of the conceptualization of an event specifies that it involves nonbranching causal chains. This is manifested linguistically in various ways (Croft, in press a). First, if the two causal chains are parallel, so that a single initiator acts on two endpoints or two initiators act on a single endpoint, then conjoined NPs can be used: *I chopped both the carrot and the cucumber; Carol and I disassembled the shed.* This represents conceptualization of the two parallel events as a single event.[25] In most cases, however, two separate clauses, representing conceptualization as two separate events that happen to share participants, are used: *I cut the cucumber when I chopped the carrot.* This is especially true if the intention of a volitional initiator toward the two actions is different, as in *I cut my finger when I chopped the carrot.* More important, nonbranching and asymmetrical causal chains clearly distinguish subject from object semantically, so that grammatical and pragmatic asymmetries between subject and object are clearly relatable to their semantic roles.[26]

I will now illustrate the range of possibilities afforded by the verbal lexicon in describing an "objective" event and affecting the choice of subject and object. Consider a fairly complicated situation, namely, communication. (This example is rich but problematic, as complex examples usually are.) The speaker engages in an activity that creates sound, that is, an utterance, that is heard by the hearer. This situation type and the segments denoted by different verbs are illustrated in figure 4.2.

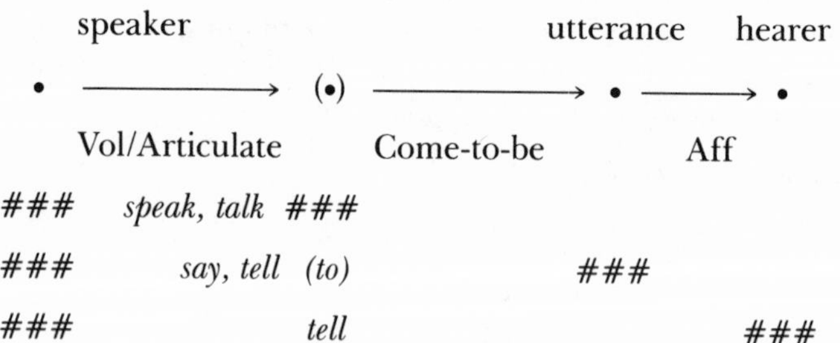

FIGURE 4.2. *Different lexicalizations of the speech event*

English has two verbs that describe just the first part of communication, the speaker's activity: *speak* and *talk.* Both these verbs allow arguments describing the other "participants" of the complex situation, namely, the hearer and the utterance (or rather the content of the utterance): *speak/talk to X about Z.* However, these additional arguments are optional and oblique. In other words, they do not delimit the segment of the causal chain denoted by the verb, and so one may say that the causal chain does not extend beyond the (unary) activity of the speaker that causes the utterance to come to be. That is, these verbs conceptualize the speaker's activity as a relatively autonomous simple event, without necessary transmission of information, as can be seen by their usage compared with another communication verb like *tell:*

(31) *He's talking, but no one's listening.*

(32) ??*He's telling them, but no one's listening.*

(33) *Be quiet; let me speak!*

(34) ?**Be quiet; let me tell you!*

Instead, there are other verbs that delimit that larger segment: *say* and *tell* (*to*). Both these verbs allow the utterance as a direct object or complement in some form:

(35) *He said "I love you"/that he loved her/a spell.*

(36) *She told a story.*

In both cases, the hearer is an oblique argument, which indicates that it does not delimit the endpoint of the verbal causal segment, and is optional, though under slightly different conditions. Finally, the hearer functions as the endpoint in the case of the "dative-shifted" case frame of *tell*—but so can the utterance, although the content may appear as an oblique (*tell Z "X"/that X; tell Z about X*). This example illustrates a number of interesting issues in the relation between causal segments denoted by verbs and the representation of events. First, the complex decomposition of the communication event type into the arcs and nodes in figure 4.2 allows one to distinguish the different verbs on a systematic semantic basis. Second, owing to the richness of the verbal lexicon in this domain and the passive voice (which, I will argue in 6.2, allows the possibility to choose the endpoint rather than the initiator as the subject), any one of the participants can be selected as the subject by the speaker.[27]

There are two important residual issues whose resolution is crucial for the development and verification of this theory of verbal semantics and thematic roles, which will be briefly described here.

The first issue is the problem of the optionality of surface-structure arguments: some objects are optional, and some obliques are obligatory. Various factors, including the genericness of the object and the pragmatic recoverability of the subject or object, allow the "obligatory" object argument (and also subject argument in certain cases and in certain languages) to be "optional" (see, e.g., Fillmore 1986; Rice 1987, sec. 5.4). That is, various factors, including pragmatic ones, determine optionality of objects and subjects, and it is not clear exactly how they interact with the causal analysis.

Obligatory obliques, as in *look for a book,* are a more direct problem for the causal structure analysis. If the verb meaning is just the causal chain between the subject (initiator) and object (endpoint), then an obligatory oblique is an anomaly. One plausible explanation for this is that the semantic conceptual conditions governing verb structure and objecthood are actually quite narrow, so that in some cases a unaffected "object" cannot be conceptualized (i.e., expressed) as a grammatical object under any circumstances. This will account for most if not all obligatory obliques since they represent unaffected "objects." However, there is some degree of conventionalization since some unaffected "objects" are grammatical objects (e.g., *seek*) whereas others are not (*look for*).

The primary motivation behind the analysis of verbal semantics in terms of causal structure given in the preceding sections is to provide a semantic framework in which to define thematic roles. Assuming that a main verb, that is, a verbal causal segment, has been selected, and consequently also the subject and object have been selected, then one can redefine the major oblique thematic roles that have been proposed in the case grammar literature.

The major oblique thematic roles can be generally described in terms of the ordering of participants in the causal chain, *relative to the choice of subject and object* (i.e., relative to the choice of verb, including verbal voice form). This is not the case for the "direct" thematic roles, those that normally become subject and object (or occasionally indirect object): agent, patient, experiencer, stimulus.[28] These thematic roles appear to be defined primarily in terms of the causation types of the arcs of which they are the initiators or endpoints. The following definitions can be used for the direct thematic roles:

Agent: the initiator of an act of volitional causation (a VOL arc);
Patient: the endpoint of an act of physical causation (a PHYS arc; recall that acts of volitional causation must be mediated by a physical entity that physically acts on the patient);
Experiencer: the endpoint of an act of affective causation (an AFF arc);

Stimulus: the initiator of an act of affective causation (an AFF arc).

The often-noted priority of these thematic roles in subject and object choice is due to the semantic structure of the verbal lexicon, namely, that verbal causal segments tend to begin with VOL arcs and end with PHYS and AFF arcs.

The oblique thematic roles, on the other hand, are defined in terms of the relation between nodes and the segment of the causal chain denoted by a verb, although, as will be seen, the causation type or at least the ontological status of the participant (mental level or physical level) sometimes plays a role. I will introduce some terms to allow us to describe positions (modes) in a causal chain more precisely:

> *X* PRECEDES *Y* and *Y* FOLLOWS *X* in a causal chain if and only if there exists a causal segment of the causal chain such that *X* is the initiator and *Y* is the endpoint. *Z* is BETWEEN *X* and *Y* in a causal chain if and only if the causal segment bounded by *X* and *Y* includes *Z*.

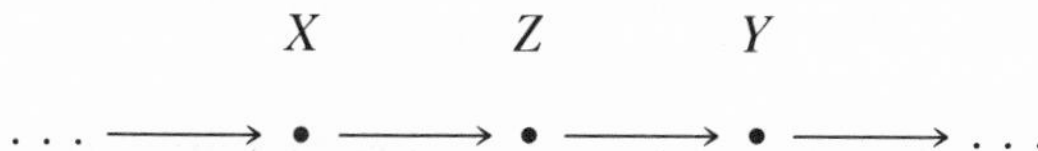

The terms "precede" and "follow" will also be applied to causal segments, so that one may say that a causal segment precedes or follows another causal segment (or a participant). A causal segment IMMEDIATELY precedes another causal segment if its endpoint is identical with the initiator of the following causal segment, and vice versa for "immediately follows."

I will illustrate the definitions of thematic roles with a slightly elaborated, somewhat contrived version of the "break" sentence, intended to illustrate most of the oblique thematic roles in a single clause.

(32) *I broke the boulder with Greg for Mary by hitting it sharply with a hammer.*

Greg	*I*		*hammer*		*boulder*			*Mary*
•	•	⟶	•	⟶	•	⟶	(•) ⟶	•
		Vol		Hit		Break	Aff	
OBL	SBJ		OBL				OBJ	OBL
	###				*break*		###	

In (32), the subject and object are *I* and *the boulder,* respectively, and thus the verbal segment extends from the VOL arc to the BREAK arc. I will begin with the participants that are objects or persons (prototypical nouns). *Mary* is a benefactive participant; her position in the causal chain is following the endpoint of the verbal causal segment. *The hammer* is an instrument; its position in the causal chain is between the initiator and the endpoint of the verbal causal segment. *Greg* is in a comitative-role; his position in the causal chain is roughly the same as the initiator of the verbal causal segment. The manner adverbial phrase *sharply* is a property of the verbal causal segment; the adverbial phrase could just as easily have been a prepositional phrase such as *with some difficulty.* The manner role is similar to the instrument because it applies to that part of the segment that is between the initiator and the endpoint, but it differs in that it denotes a property, not an object. Likewise, the means phrase also lies between the initiator and the endpoint of the verbal causal segment, but it denotes an action, specifically, an action that is a proper subsegment of the verbal causal segment and has the same initiator as the main verbal causal segment.

I offer the following definitions of the oblique thematic roles illustrated in the example:

Comitative: An entity that participates in a causal chain at the same point and in the same role as the subject of the main verb. It is likely that the comitative role also requires that the subject be the initiator of an act of volitional causation (a VOL arc).

Instrument: An entity that is intermediate in a causal chain between the subject (initiator) and the direct object (final affected entity). The instrument may have to be further restricted in that it may not be the initiator of an act of volitional causation (Levin [1979] argues in essence that the instrument must in fact be preceded by a VOL arc in the verbal causal segment), but that may in turn fall out of a more general restriction on root verbal causal segments against internal VOL arcs (see 6.1).

Manner: A property holding of some or all of the verbal causal segment. The manner role can be represented by an adverb or a manner PP; I will direct my attention to the case marking found on the last type.

Means: A proper subsegment of the main verb causal segment that shares the same initiator as the main verb. It appears that the means clause must begin with a VOL arc—that is, it must be a volition action, presumably involving a plan of which the means covers all but the last step—and must be at least one arc longer than a VOL arc to a body part or "instrument." The latter constraint may exist simply in order to make the means clause "informative."

Benefactive (or "malefactive"): The endpoint of an action that causally follows the verbal causal segment. The participant is normally a mental-level entity ontologically, that is, the endpoint of an act of affective or perhaps inducive causation (though the term "causee" is normally applied to the latter), but in some cases a more general definition appears to be suitable (see 5.6.1). I also include the recipient as a benefactive-type oblique thematic role in the evidence to be provided in the next chapter, although the similarity between the two role types requires some additional justification, which will be provided in 5.4.

In addition to the oblique thematic roles found in example (32), one may also define the following thematic roles, these being definable in the model of causal structure as it has been explicated so far:

Cause: An event (action or state) that causally immediately precedes the event sequence denoted by the main verb: for example, *He did it out of love* or *He died from an overdose/the auto accident.*

Passive agent: An entity that precedes the subject in the causal chain, when the main verb describes the event that results in the subject's present state. The passive agent somewhat resembles a cause except that it is an object or person and it is technically the initiator of the active version of the verbal causal segment. Again, it is introduced here because it figures in the evidence in the next chapter, but it will be discussed more thoroughly in 6.2.

Result: An event (action or state) that causally immediately follows the event sequence denoted by the main verb, for example, *He choked to death.*

Purpose: An event that is intended by an agentive initiator of the main verb causal segment to follow causally from the event denoted by the main verb causal segment. This role is technically on a different semantic plane from causal structure since intentions are completely different in semantic type from results. However, I include purpose in the evidence in the next chapter because the purpose is closely related to a result and appears to represent a (planned) causal segment that is not necessarily going to come about.

All the definitions of oblique thematic roles have in common the fact that they crucially refer to the position of the subject and the object, that is, the initiator and endpoint of the verbal causal segment, in the causal chain. Their definitions are RELATIVIZED to the assignment of subject and object. Thus, if a different lexical item is used, then the thematic role will also differ. Consider the following alternative descriptions of the scene in (32), or of part of it:

(33) *Greg and I hit the boulder with a hammer (breaking it).*

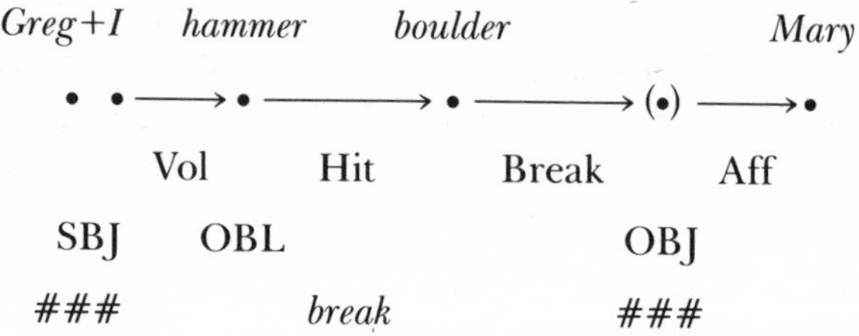

In (33), the two agents *Greg* and *I* have been conceptualized as a single conjoined subject, thus removing the possible comitative role. The verb *hit* covers a shorter causal segment than *break,* but, since *the boulder* is still the endpoint of that causal segment, it remains the direct object.[29] Likewise, *the hammer* remains the instrument since it is still between the initiator and the endpoint of *hit*'s causal segment.

(34) *A hammer was used by Greg and me to break the boulder for Mary.*

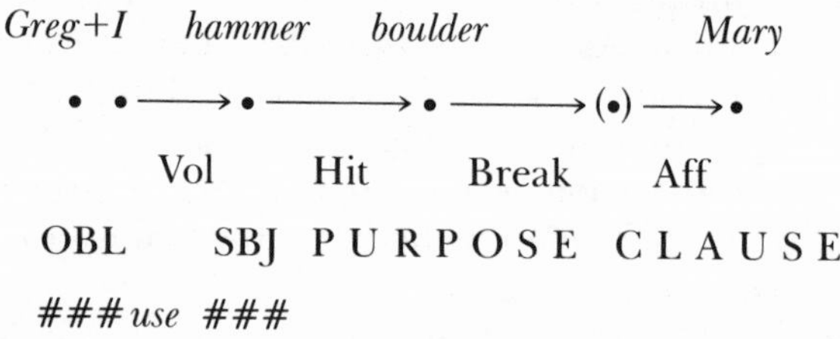

In (34), the hammer is the endpoint of the passivized main verb causal segment. Since the verb is passivized, the endpoint *the hammer* is the subject, and the initiator(s) are in the passive agent role. The purpose clause *to break the boulder for Mary* covers the main verb causal segment and in addition all the following arcs illustrated in (32). Finally, *Mary* remains the benefactive participant in the purpose clause since she follows the direct object *the boulder* in the causal chain.

(35) *The boulder broke into two pieces from the impact of the hammer.*

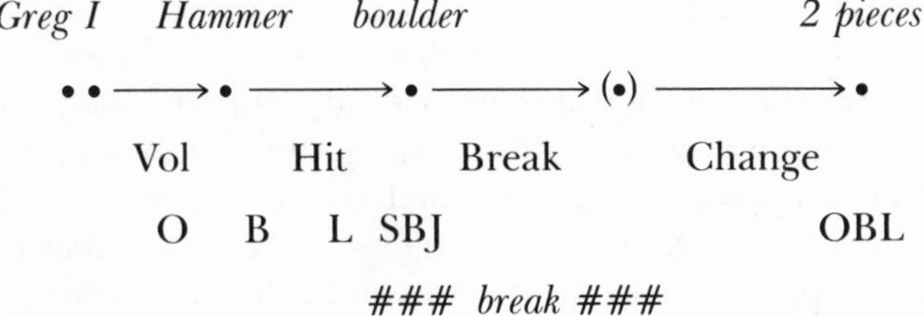

In (35), the only segment covered by the lexical verb *break* is the BREAK segment in (32).[30] The boulder is the subject since it is the "initiator" (in a nonvolitional sense, of course, and as if ignoring the external cause). The phrase *into two pieces* is a result phrase, describing a stative arc following the BREAK arc in (32). The phrase *the impact of the hammer* describes the cause—the causal segment labeled HIT in (32).

4.5 Conclusion

In this chapter, I presented pragmatic (discourse functional) and cognitive factors affecting choice of subject and object and turned to the relation between subject and object choice and the semantic relation (thematic role) of the argument to the verb (predicate). I argued against reductionist approaches to the analysis of the semantics of thematic roles and argued for linking the definitions of the thematic roles, as well as the "subject" and "object" definitions and selection hierarchies, to the semantics of the verb. An analysis of verbal semantics was proposed in terms of causal structure, based on the notion of a participant acting on another participant in an event. This model provides a vocabulary rich enough to define the major thematic roles that have been proposed by case grammarians over the last twenty years and longer. I have also argued that subject and object choice is semantically highly underdetermined and governed largely by the aforementioned pragmatic and conceptual factors and ultimately by the verbal causal segments available in the lexicon and by the voice forms available in the grammar. Thus, the thematic roles generally thought to underlie subjects and objects—at least the roles applying in the "prototypical" causal types that I have been analyzing—are defined largely by causation type, that being determined by verbal semantics. The oblique thematic roles on the other hand are defined largely by position in the causal chain with respect to the subject and the object. Hence, the definitions of the oblique thematic roles are formulated relative to subject and object choice in the causal chain, not in absolute semantic terms.

The one problem broached at the end of 3.2 not yet addressed here is the relation between thematic roles and surface case marking. The thematic roles, as usually conceived, have been used by case grammarians to analyze surface case marking, with mixed success. The obvious question to ask is, Does the causal structure model of verbal semantics provide a way of describing generalizations that are valid for surface-structure phenomena such as case marking and voice as well in a better way than the usual analysis by means of thematic roles? The next chapter argues that the answer to that question is yes.

5

Case Marking and the Causal Order of Participants

5.1 Introduction

In the last chapter, I developed a semantic analysis of events that was used to define verbs, subjects, objects, and thematic roles. I now turn to the definition of the surface case markers that allow the hearer to determine what role the participant denoted by the noun phrase is playing in the event denoted by the main verb. That is, I will propose a method for *defining* the surface case markers of a natural language.

This method involves certain assumptions concerning the proper analysis of the meaning of words and grammatical morphemes. These assumptions form the basis of the so-called POLYSEMY or USAGE-TYPE approach to defining natural language categories. The polysemy approach has been pursued by a number of researchers and can be found in such varied works as Haiman (1974, 1978), Dahl (1979), Herskovits (1982), Lindner (1981), Lakoff (1987, who calls this "radial category structure"), Brugman (1983), Lichtenberk (1985), Langacker (1988b, who calls this the "network category model"), Bybee and Pagliuca (1988), and Croft, Shyldkrot, and Kemmer (1988). In this approach, it is presumed that most natural language words have more than one USE, that is, a specific meaning that can be defined precisely. In most cases, the distinct uses of a particular natural language morpheme, such as the English word *with,* are semantically related to each other. It is further hypothesized that the relations among uses fall into a relatively small set of semantic functions linking those uses, three of which are illustrated in the following sections. Finally, the sum total of semantically related uses that fall under one natural language word do not necessarily add up to a single necessary-and-sufficient definition of that word. For example, although the following sections will argue that (among other case forms) the various uses of the English word *with* are semantically related, one cannot provide a single abstract meaning or Gesamtbedeutung that will cover all and only the uses of *with.* This approach is particularly attractive for typological analysis. It renders surface grammatical categories comparable across languages, even if the range of semantic uses is not identical from language to language, by distinguishing semantic uses and relations among uses and mapping surface forms onto the network of uses.

The central concept around which the meanings (uses) of surface case markings are organized is the position of the participant in the verbal segment (i.e., the causal segment denoted by the verb). This concept has already been employed in the definitions of thematic roles, which represent the most important uses of case markings, found in 4.4.4. In this chapter, I demonstrate that the grouping of thematic roles under surface case markers also follows this principle. In particular, oblique case markings divide themselves into two types: those that represent participants that precede the object in the causal chain and those that represent participants that follow it (in the senses of "precede" and "follow" defined in 4.4.4). This division pervades the morphosyntax of obliques, just as the initiator-endpoint distinction forms the basis of the morphosyntax of the "direct" cases.

5.2 The Causal Order Hypothesis

The first and simplest of the possible semantic relations that can hold among the uses or meanings of a given surface grammatical element (such as a case marker) is SPREAD. Spread is the extension of a form from one element (use) in a semantic domain to a semantically contiguous or "nearby" element in the same domain. This corresponds to Lakoff's "radial" categories (Lakoff 1987, chap. 6) and Langacker's notion of "extension" (Langacker 1988b: 134). It is actually a specific type of the general phenomenon of extension to semantically "near" or "contiguous" uses/situations that drives the polysemy model of natural language semantics. However, I consider spread to be a well-defined specific type of extension, namely, spread within a single DOMAIN, in this case the domain of causal structure.[1]

In order to motivate spread, one must have a model of semantic "nearness"; in the case of causality, this model is provided by the definitions of the thematic roles in terms of the structure of the causal chain. The position of participants in the causal chain with respect to the subject and the direct object is illustrated in figure 5.1, based on the definitions for thematic roles offered in 4.4.4. Similarity of meaning is determined by nearness on the causal chain of the participants referred to by the thematic roles.

However, it turns out that spread by and large respects a sharp boundary between participants that precede the object in the causal chain and those that follow. The following are examples of oblique NPs that precede and follow the object with two standard examples, *for* and *with*.

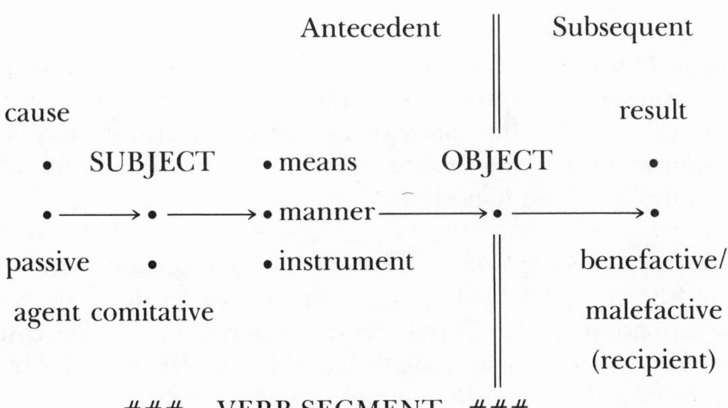

FIGURE 5.1 *Distribution of thematic roles in the causal chain*

(1) *Sam baked a cake for Jan.*

Sam *cake* *Jan*

• ——→ • ——→ •

SBJ OBJ OBL

bake

(2) *Sam whipped the eggs with a fork.*

Sam *fork* *egg*

• ——→ • ——→ •

SBJ OBL OBJ

whip

In (1), the verb *bake* makes the cake the object by virtue of its lexical semantics (and active voice form). The benefactor, Jan, marked by the preposition *for,* follows the cake in the causal chain; the creation of the cake brings about some benefit that affects Jan. In (2), the verb *whip* makes the eggs the object; but the instrument, the fork, marked by the preposition *with,* precedes the eggs in the causal chain: Sam acts on the fork, which in turn acts on the eggs. Using the causal chain diagram, I will call the benefactive thematic role a SUBSEQUENT role since it follows the object in the causal chain and the instrumental thematic role an ANTECEDENT role since it precedes it.[2] Likewise, the oblique case marker *for* will be called a "subsequent oblique/marker" and *with* an "antecedent oblique/marker."

The vertical line in figure 5.1 divides the subsequent roles from the antecedent roles. A large number of typological phenomena suggest that this is the appropriate dividing line among thematic roles. The central role that the subsequent-antecedent distinction plays in the organization of surface case-marked arguments in a clause is captured by the following hypothesis:

> *The causal order hypothesis:* The grammatical relations hierarchy SBJ < OBJ < $\text{OBL}_{\text{subsequent}}$ corresponds to the order of participation in the causal chain. (Antecedent oblique case markers are used to indicate that the oblique NP does *not* "fit" in the causal chain as the hierarchy would imply.)
> *Subsequent roles:* benefactive, recipient, result.
> *Antecedent roles:* instrumental, manner, means, comitative, passive agent, ergative,[3] cause.

The object must always be the endpoint, that is, follow the subject in the causal chain (see also 6.2); hence, SBJ < OBJ. The (subsequent) obliques follow the object in the causal chain; hence, OBJ < OBL. The grammatical relations hierarchy SBJ < OBJ < OBL, manifested in a larger number of grammatical phenomena, is essentially a reflection of the order of participation in the causal chain. This is an unmarked correlation between the lexical semantics of the verb, represented by the causal chain, and the cognitive-pragmatic factors that determine subject and object choice (see 4.2)—the same sort of phenomenon found in the definition of the major syntactic categories. The causal chain model and the causal order hypothesis—essentially a statement of correlation between causal ordering and the grammatical relations hierarchy—take the place of the "subject/object selection hierarchies" of thematic roles proposed in other models.

Of course, there are also the antecedent oblique markers, which violate the correlation of the causal order with the grammatical relations hierarchy. It appears that antecedent oblique markers must exist out of necessity: the nonexistence of antecedent markers would greatly restrict the semantic expressiveness of the clause. The subsequent-antecedent distinction is exactly the division between those oblique case markers that preserve the causal order SBJ < OBJ < OBL, that is, the causal order hypothesis, and those that violate it. That is to say, the subsequent-antecedent distinction is the way in which natural languages handle those situations in which assignment of object and oblique status on the basis of the factors discussed in 4.2 does not match the "natural" directionality of causation of object and oblique (cf. DeLancey's [1981, 1982] analysis of the "mismatch" between animacy, aspect, and causal directionality). Mismatches between subject assignment and causal order for subjects and objects is handled by voice (see 6.2). Thus, any evidence supporting the subsequent-antecedent distinction as the primary distinction among thematic role types in surface case marking also supports the relevance of the causal order hypothesis to grammatical structure and thus is also further support for the relevance of the grammatical relations hierarchy SBJ < OBJ < OBL and causal structure to grammatical theory in general. One would also want typological markedness evidence to demonstrate that the SBJ < OBJ < OBL hierarchy is the unmarked one with respect to causal sequence; this will be demonstrated in 6.2.

The basic form of the evidence that I will provide supporting the subsequent-antecedent distinction is that syncretism of thematic roles will occur so that no surface case marker will subsume both subsequent and antecedent thematic roles (hence the appropriateness of speaking of antecedent and subsequent case markers as well as thematic roles). English provides supporting evidence for this hypothesis. There are two subsequent case markers, the prepositions *to,* which governs the recipient and the result, and *for,* which governs the benefactive. However, only *to* provides positive evidence for the hypothesis since *for* covers only one thematic role.[4] The antecedent case markers *with* and *by* both provide positive evidence because each covers more than one thematic role, *with* subsuming instrument, manner, and comitative and *by* subsuming means and passive agent. I will consider English to represent three positive pieces of evidence in favor of the subsequent-antecedent distinction since there are three separate syncretisms involved: recipient-result, instrument-manner-comitative and means–passive agent.

This is perhaps a conservative appraisal of the evidence since the synchronic syncretism represented by *with* presumably represents a diachronic spread of the use of *with* from one thematic role to a second and then a third. However, even on the basis of a conservative evaluation of the facts, the typological evidence supporting the hypothesis is very strong. A survey of the case marking of the oblique thematic roles of forty languages was made (see the app. in 5.8). The number of syncretisms among subsequent and antecedent thematic roles was tallied in the same way as was described for English in the preceding paragraph: the subsumption of any number (greater than one) of subsequent or antecedent thematic roles under a single case marker was treated as one instance of a syncretism. The results are given in table 5.1.

TABLE 5.1 *Case Syncretisms among Subsequent and Antecedent Thematic Roles*

Syncretisms among antecedent thematic roles	39
Syncretisms among subsequent thematic roles	30
No directionality in the case system	5
Syncretisms across subsequent and antecedent roles	2
Number of languages surveyed	40

The evidence strongly supports the hypothesis, although there are a few questionable cases (the "no directionality" row) and two outright exceptions, to be discussed below. In fact, this study tends to confirm the general intuitions of typologists on the basis of the examination of a much larger number of languages that thematic roles such as cause, passive agent, manner, comitative, and instrument tend to "go together," as do recipient, benefactive, and result. For example, Blake (1977 : 60–61) found the syncretisms ergative-instrumental-cause and dative (recipient)-benefactive-genitive to be quite common among Australian languages.

The questionable cases all involve a massive amount of syncretism to the point at which the subsequent-antecedent distinction itself appears to be abolished. The clearest cases of these appear to be a number of East Asian and West African languages in which one adposition does all or almost all the work of the various subsequent and antecedent case markers of other languages. The best example of this that I am aware of is an Austronesian language, Palauan, which has just one oblique preposition *ęr*. In the sample, the nondirectional system is found in Lahu, Yapese, and Woleaian. The reason I have labeled these "no directionality" is that in these languages not only is there no causal directionality expressed in the case marking system but there is also no spatial directionality expressed in the cases involving motion (the parallelism between direction of causation and direction of motion will be discussed in the next section). Instead, direction of motion is found in the deictic orientation of motion verbs, and a single case marker is used for ablative and allative and often also location.

Other examples of the loss of causal directionality in the oblique case system are found in languages in which the case system appears to be collapsing. In these languages, the case markings cover a large number of uses and appear to be just beginning to break down the subsequent-antecedent distinction. In the sample, these languages are Attic Greek and Classical Mongolian. The analysis of these "exceptions" is as follows. It is a fact that there are systems in which case markings fairly neatly divide between subsequent and antecedent types; that there are systems in which there is only one basic case marking that no longer has any causal directionality in its semantic content; and that languages can historically shift from one system to the other. This transition will involve incremental spread of case markers and some variation in usage during the transition from a "directional" to a "nondirectional" system. Therefore, some synchronic apparent exceptions are to be expected in languages in the process of transition.

The difficulty is determining independently that a language is in the process of transition from one type of system to the next. Apart from attested historical stages where it is known that the transition took place, such as in the history of Greek, there are very few independent criteria, and they may be largely heuristic. The first criterion is massive syncretism: if only, say, two cases are being used to cover the entire range of oblique thematic roles, it is likely that the system is decaying and the paradigmatic semantic distinctions are being blurred.[5] The second criterion is what I call LAYERING. In virtually every natural language, at any given historical stage there are several historically distinct layers of grammatical constructions performing the same function (see 3.3.4). Typical examples of different layers are the prepositions and cases of Russian and the simple prepositions and relational nouns of Quiché. In both cases, the historically older layer (cases in Russian, simple prepositions in Quiché) is semantically less specific and paradigmatically less numerous than the historically newer layer. The older layer is in fact carrying little semantic load and thus may be more likely to violate semantic constraints like the subsequent-antecedent distinction. In Quiché, the oldest layer consists of the nondirectional ablative-allative-locative preposition *pa* and the preposition-complementizer *či* used in subsequent, antecedent, and locative expressions. Even the next layer, *či* plus the reduced relational noun *e*, is used for both subsequent and antecedent roles. Only the most recent "layer," consisting of the relational nouns *umal* "passive agent–cause," *uk'* "comitative," and *wač* "benefactive-hearer [communicative verbs]," obeys the subsequent-antecedent distinction.

In addition to the borderline cases of stable nondirectional systems and collapsing directional systems, there were two genuine apparent exceptions to the hypothesis in the sample, both involving the use of a subsequent case marker for a single antecedent role (the antecedent role is in italics):

Allative/recipient/purposive/*causee:* Turkish (sometimes); Recipient/benefactive/allative/purposive/*cause:* Koṇḍa (also accusative).

I will discuss the former exception in 6.1. The latter exception, also noted in Blake (1977) and apparently rather frequent, is a problematic exception that will not be discussed here, although I believe that it has a diachronic explanation.[6]

As I stated before, the general support that the results of the typological study of syncretism provide for the subsequent-antecedent distinction confirms general intuitions that are not surprising to the average working typologist. More interesting and perhaps stronger supporting evidence for the hypothesis comes from systems that display a typologically rather unusual distribution of case forms but still obey the causal order hypothesis. An example of such a system is provided by Chechen-Ingush (Nichols 1984: 188–92). Chechen-Ingush, a north central Caucasian language, has an ergative/absolutive ("nominative") case marking system for its core thematic roles, and for most verbs it has typical subsequent and antecedent case markings, such as the subsequent dative case, used for recipients among other thematic roles, or the instrumental case, used for some instrumentals:

(3) *cuo cunna a:xča delira*
he.ERG him.DAT money.NOM gave
'He gave him money.'

(4) *husam da:s ürsaca kuotam jι:ra*
house father.ERG knife.INST chicken.NOM killed
'The host [lit. "house father"] killed the chicken with a knife.'

However, for a small class of verbs denoting physical contact, what a case grammarian would normally call an "instrument" is expressed as a direct object (nominative case), and the erstwhile "patient" is expressed in the subsequent oblique dative case:

(5) *da:s woʔa: γam j-iett*
father.ERG son-DAT stick beats
'(The) father beats (his) son with a stick.'

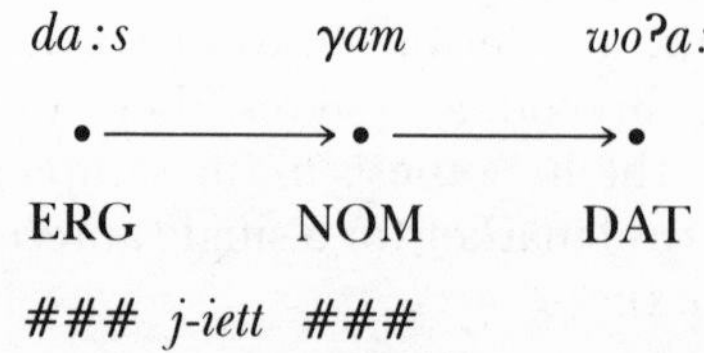

The causal structure diagram in (5) reveals quite clearly that, despite the atypical expression of "instrument" and "patient," the case marking in the example obeys the causal order hypothesis: the son causally follows the stick, which has been selected as the direct object, and therefore is assigned a subsequent oblique case.

Another rather atypical expression of verbal arguments also supports the causal order hypothesis. A number of languages allow the incorporation of a noun argument, which sometimes allows another participant to become the direct object; Mithun (1984a) calls this the Type II function of noun incorporation. It would be plausible to conclude that the incorporated noun is "between" the subject and the object since it has become part of the verb, so to speak. This turns out to be the case; the instrumental incorporation in (6) is from Huahtla Nahuatl (Mithun 1984a:861, from Merlan 1976), and the patient incorporation in (7) is from Mohawk (Mithun 1984a:868; this is possible only if the benefactive/malefactive participant is more affected than the patient):

(6) *ya'ki-* *kočillo-* *tete'ki* *panci*
he(he)it- knife- cut bread
'He cut the bread with it (the knife).'

ya' *kočillo-* *panci*
• ———→ • ———→ •
SBJ INC OBJ
tete'ki

(7) *wa-* *hi-* *'sereht-* *anv́hsko*
PAST- he/me car- steal
'He stole my car.' [Or: 'He stole my car on me.']

There are some languages in which the instrumental case is used for direct objects under certain conditions. In Hausa, the instrumental preposition is used for the direct objects of certain verbs taking recipients when the recipient is absent from the clause (for examples and a possible alternative account, see 5.4). West Greenlandic Eskimo antipassivizes the transitive verb under various conditions (including indefinite object; see above); in those cases, the patient is realized in the instrumental case (which is itself distinct from the ergative/possessive case; Sadock 1980). A similar phenomenon occurs in Dyirbal, where the displaced object of an antipassive construction is placed into the dative *or* the instrumental case. These cases must be weighed against the typologically much more common pattern of marking direct objects with the (subsequent) dative case marker under certain conditions. Both types of cases provide indirect support of the direct object as the correct boundary point between the two case marking types, subsequent and antecedent: when the direct object does acquire a case marking, it can be from either "side" of the boundary (although subsequent markers are more common).

These examples argue for causal ordering analysis over the traditional definitions of "instrument" and "patient," which attempt to pin down the causation type on more specific qualitative facts about the role played by the participant, for cross-linguistically valid generalizations concerning the semantics of surface case markings. The definition of the uses covered by the nominative case in Chechen-Ingush would have to cover both traditionally defined "instruments" and "patients" (not to mention intransitive subjects), and the uses covered by the dative case would have to cover both other "patients" and recipients. One would have to stipulate which "patients" would be realized as absolutives and which as datives and conversely which "instruments" would be realized as instrumentals and which as nominatives. Similar problems arise with Type II noun incorporation. In the causal structure analysis, however, this would fall out directly from the representation of the lexical semantics of the verbs: the verb meaning 'beat' is represented as denoting the causal segment covering only the first arc in the diagram in example (5), whereas the verb meaning 'kill' is represented as denoting the segment covering the causal chain from the killer to the victim. The endpoints are realized as nominatives, and the obliques are subsequent or antecedent, depending on their position in the causal chain. The causal structure analysis elegantly treats a distribution of cases that would cause difficulties for a traditional case grammarian.

5.3 Space and Causality

Up to this point, I have not discussed the role of motion and location in space in case marking. Nevertheless, locative and directional markers are probably the ultimate historical source of most case marking,[7] and the localist hypothesis seeks to reduce nonlocal roles to local ones in synchronic analysis as well (see references cited in Anderson 1971: 5–6). Although the localist hypothesis posits too strong a relation between local and nonlocal roles, there is still a close relation between causal and locative-directional thematic roles. In fact, there are several distinct relations, and they will be discussed in this section and the next.

The most important relation between causal and locative-directional roles is that of DOMAIN SHIFT OF METAPHOR. Domain shift/metaphor is perhaps as important a relation between the uses of a polysemous surface form as spread. Metaphor, in this technical definition, describes the situation in which the form used for an element in one semantic domain is extended to apply to a "parallel" or "similar" element of another semantic domain (an extensive discussion of metaphor in this sense as it plays a role in basic linguistic expressions can be found in Lakoff and Johnson [1980]). Metaphor differs from a natural correlation in that, in the metaphorical situation, the source semantic domain need not be a component of the target semantic domain, whereas, with a prototypical correlation, elements of both semantic domains are always present in the relevant situations. For example, in the natural correlation between ontological status and causal directionality, both semantic parameters always co-occur in a specific causal situation. What the prototypical correlation indicates is that the pairings of values <mental, initiator> and <physical, endpoint> are unmarked whereas the pairings <physical, initiator> and <mental, endpoint> are not.

On the other hand, when, say, a form denoting a spatial relation is transferred to describe a causal relation, such as the allative *to* as a resultative as in *The house burned to cinders,* no specific spatial relation between cause and result need hold and in fact does not in the example cited.[8] Instead, a more abstract isomorphism between motion and causality must be present, namely, the directionality of both motion and causation.

Finally, metaphor implies that the two domains in question, the source and target domain, are distinct. The two domains that I will discuss in this section, spatial relations and causal relations, are defined over different parameters. A spatial relation between two entities does not imply a causal relation between them, and vice versa.

There are several metaphorical relations that hold between causality and motion (and between causality and possession, as will be seen in the next section). The fact that there is more than one relation between space and causality illustrates the need to separate these two dimensions as independent semantic domains since there are conflicting metaphorical relations. This section will devote itself to those relations that are "purely" metaphorical, that is, involve a transfer of case markings from one domain, space, to another domain, causality. The next section will discuss a "coerced" metaphor, in which the integration of motion and possession events into the causal chain requires "coercion" of motion and spatial relations into causal directionality.

There is one primary metaphorical relation and two less-common ones found in "pure" metaphorical relations between space and causality. All of them involve transferring direction of motion to direction of causation. The primary metaphorical relation, which I will call the OBJECT-LOCATION metaphor, maps the "vantage point" (the figure, in the terms of Talmy [1972, 1983]) of the path of motion into the object. The object-location mataphor is described in figure 5.2.

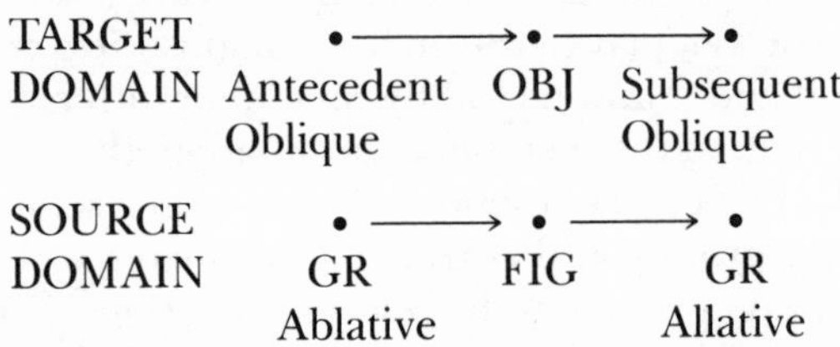

FIGURE 5.2 *The object-location metaphor*

The object-location metaphor predicts that ablative forms be used for antecedent oblique functions and allative forms for subsequent oblique functions, as they indeed are in the following English examples:

(8) *Harry came back from the party at one o'clock.*

party (Ground) — *Harry* (Figure)

• ————→ • ————→ (•)

OBL Abl SBJ

come back

(9) *The rabbit died from thirst.*

thirst — *rabbit*

• ————→ • ————→ (•)

OBL SBJ

die

(10) *I walked to the grocery store.*

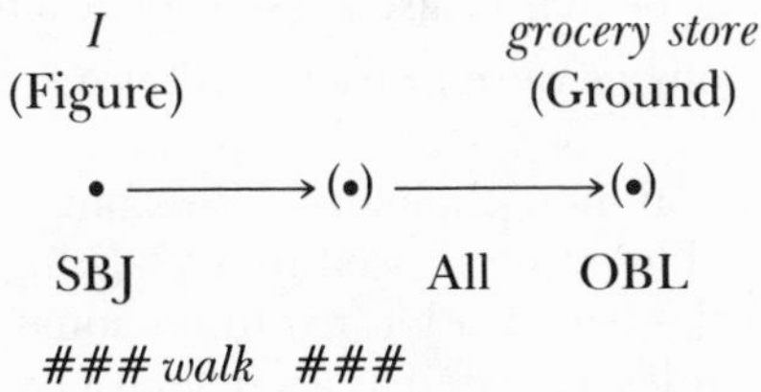

(11) *The house burned to cinders.*

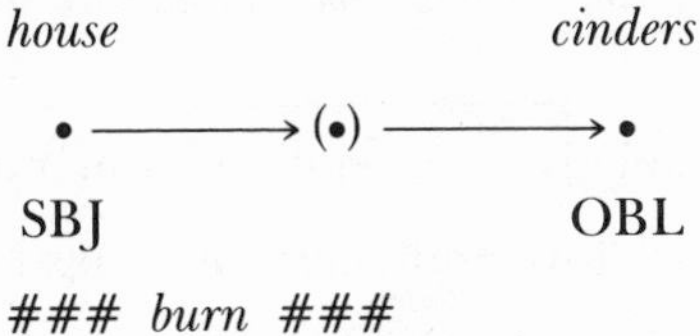

The English examples represent relatively peripheral causal thematic roles, cause and result. In many other languages, the relation between motion and causation is visible in the synchronic range of uses of the major oblique case markers. In Romanian, for example, the old Latin case system is being superseded by the use of directional and locative prepositions (Nandris 1945: 131, 182–83), a process that is already virtually complete in the other modern Romance languages. The entry of the spatial prepositions into the causal domain follows the object-location metaphor. The locative preposition *pe* 'on' is coming to be used for direct objects, albeit only those that are higher in animacy and definiteness, such as God:

(12) *Lăudăm pe Dumnezeu*
praise.1PL on God
'We praise God.'

The allative preposition *la* 'to' has come to be used for some subsequent oblique functions such as the hearer ("recipient") of verbs of communication:

(13) *N'a spus la nimeni că pleacă*
NEG.3SG.AUX say to anyone COMP go
'He did not tell anybody he was going.'

Finally, the ablative preposition *de* 'from' has come to be used for some antecedent oblique functions, such as the passive agent:

(14) *Elevii* *sunt* *lăudați* *de* *învățătorul* *lor*
schoolboys be.3PL praise.PASS from teacher.DET 3PL.POSS
'The schoolboys were praised by their teacher.'

The object-location metaphor was also examined in the language sample used in 5.2. The same procedure of tallying instances of syncretisms was used: the use of a locative/directional case marking for one or more causal roles was cited as a single instance of a syncretism. The results are given in table 5.2.

TABLE 5.2 *Syncretisms among Spatial and Causal Thematic Roles*

Syncretism between ablative and antecedent marking	13
Syncretism between locative and object marking	1
Syncretism between allative and subsequent marking	15
Exceptional syncretisms	3
Number of languages surveyed	40

The hypothesis is strongly supported by the evidence from the sample. Again, this fits with Blake's (1977) study of Australian case systems, in which syncretism of allative-dative-benefactive-genitive and ablative-cause were common. Curiously, the three exceptions all involved the same syncretism, that of the Allative and the Manner roles: Modern Irish, Finnish (a few isolated instances of allative case adverbials), and Kanuri. The areal and genetic diversity of the three languages that display the exceptional behavior suggests strongly that some nonrandom process is at work here, although I do not know what that process is and it is in conflict with the otherwise quite widespread object-location metaphor.

Other languages that happened not to be in the sample suggest two other purely metaphoric motion-causality relations. A number of languages use locative rather than ablative expressions for those participants that fall *between* the initiator and the endpoint of the causal chain, including also the initiator. For example, the ergative case or passive agent is expressive by a locative case (Keenan 1985: 263–64); Blake (1977) observes a common locative-instrumental syncretism in Australia.[9] This metaphor resembles the object-location metaphor quite closely except that location is mapped onto the verbal causal segment as a whole (and thus all the roles included in it) instead of onto just the object. I will call this the EVENT-LOCATION metaphor.[10]

There is a minor metaphor found in some Germanic languages in which the event is conceptualized as a conduit rather than a linear path. The isomorphism of directionality of motion and directionality of causation is preserved, but the figure-ground perspective is one of moving along the causal chain and passing *through* the event (the verbal causal segment). This leads to the use of 'through' for roles such as the passive agent in Old English and in Modern German (under certain conditions). I will call this the EVENT-CONDUIT metaphor.

Finally, there is another, much more common metaphor that relates the comitative thematic role to a spatial relation, the COMITATIVE-PROXIMITY metaphor, in which a spatial expression of colocation such as 'near' or 'among' develops into a comitative form. The isomorphism is one of colocation in space mapping onto colocation in the causal chain, the comitative being the only oblique thematic role that involves colocation in the causal chain. This is the source of, for example, the Old English antecedent marker *mid.*

The fact that there are at least three spatial metaphors that govern the use of case markings originally denoting location and direction for causal thematic roles demonstrates that one cannot simply *equate* certain spatial relations with certain causal ones. There is a single semantic isomorphism that governs all three metaphors, the mapping of directionality of motion onto directionality of causation, but the assignment of the locus of the figure varies from one mapping to another (at the object vs. at the verbal segment vs. moving along the verbal segment). Only a theory that defines the spatial and causal roles as distinct but related will be able to characterize the typological facts adequately.

On the other hand, one must also note that there is an experiential relation between motion and causation that strongly suggests the path-based metaphors in which direction of motion is extended to direction of causation. I have argued that physical actions, that is, events of physical contact in which an initiator comes into contact with an endpoint and transfers force to the endpoint, possibly causing a change of state to the endpoint, are the prototypical actions, those around which case marking was "designed." The typical physical action generally involves the initiator moving into contact with the endpoint, not the other way around: thus, direction of motion is parallel with the direction of transfer of force. This natural correlation implies that a metaphor in which the direction of motion were the *opposite* of the direction of causation would be highly counterintuitive; the actually attested metaphors instead conform to the natural correlation. It is also worth noting that the two major metaphors (object-location and event-location) place the figure, which is the cognitively more prominent member of the spatial figure-ground pair, at the cognitively most prominent parts of the clause, namely, the event denoted by the main verb and its "culmination" (the endpoint).

5.4 The Integration of Space and Possession into Causal Structure

One of the most significant categories of nonprototypical event types is that in which there is no transmission of force and therefore no obvious causal directionality. The two most important noncausal relations found in the verbal lexicon are spatial relations and possessive relations. There is no a priori causal relation that holds between a figure and its ground or the possessed thing and its possessor; specifically, there is no transmission of force from one participant to the other as there is between initiator and endpoint in a genuine causal relation (see 4.4). It is essential to realize that the causal, spatial, and possession semantic domains are independent, although they are related very systematically across languages. Nevertheless, spatial relations and possession relations do enter into causal relations, and thus the problem of integrating these noncausal two-argument relations into the causal chain arises and must be solved in the grammar of a language. This is accomplished by COERCION (see 3.2.1), that is, conceptualization of the spatial and possessive relations as if they did possess an asymmetry like that between a causally defined initiator and endpoint.

5.4.1 Spatial Configuration

One of the linguistically most important set of relations between participants is spatial configuration. Talmy (1972, 1983) argues that natural languages organize spatial configurations into binary asymmetrical relations between a figure and a ground, the relation being described as a path whether or not motion is involved (see 3.2.3). Normally, the path is an adpositional expression that governs the ground. It is important to observe that figure-ground configurations are noncausal relations: the figure plus path plus ground is a single unit that functions as a node in the causal structure. A causally accurate representation of an action causing a motion/location event would be as in figure 5.3.

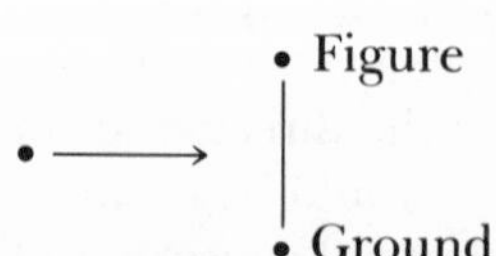

FIGURE 5.3. *Representation of spatial relations in causal structure*

For example, in the following example, the causal structure is that the subject is the initiator who brings about the figure-ground spatial configuration denoted by the combination of the direct object and the oblique expression (direct object and oblique choice and the part of the structure covered by the verb will be discussed shortly):

(15) *John put the tomato in the refrigerator.*

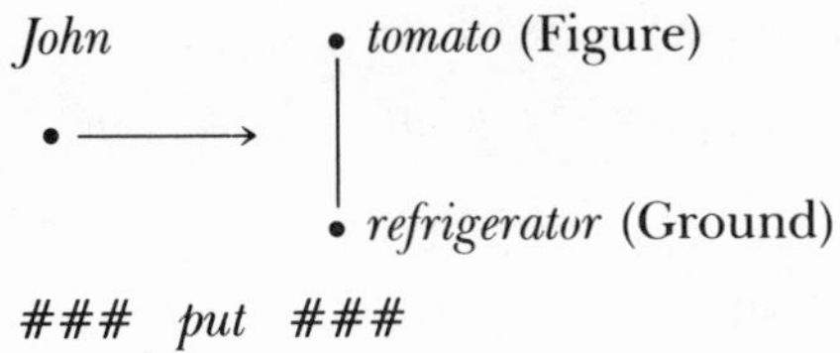

One might consider that a "causally pure" expression of the situation in (15) would be to construct a periphrastic causative expression with a complement of the form 'figure *be* path ground.' But in fact languages do not normally represent the structure as a periphrastic causative governing a clause describing motion but instead incorporate the figure and ground into the causal sequence.[11] If the figure and ground are incorporated into the causal sequence, then a "causal" ordering must be imposed on them; that is, they must be *coerced* into an ordering that is not semantically present. The ordering imposed is always figure < ground. I will call this the FIGURE-FIRST coercion.

The figure-first coercion differs from the object-location metaphor. First, the two apply to different phenomena. The object-location metaphor is a transfer of spatial relations to the domain of causal relations. The figure-first coercion is an integration of spatial relations into the causal chain; the spatial relation is part of the causal chain, not a metaphor for it. In the object-location metaphor, the object is always the figure, but the ground may either precede or follow the object in the causal chain, depending on whether the *path* is ablative or allative. In the figure-first coercion, however, the figure-ground relation becomes a directed cause-result relation: the ground *always* follows the figure in causal directionality.

The figure-first coercion predicts that, when the figure is the object, the corresponding ground is governed by the normal path expression; but, when the ground is the direct object, the corresponding figure has an antecedent oblique form, *with*, as in the following well-known examples:[12]

(16) *Jane sprayed paint on the wall.*

Jane		*paint*		*wall*
•	⟶	•	⟶	•
SBJ		OBJ		OBL
###	*spray*	###		

(17) *Jane sprayed the wall with paint.*

Jane		*paint*		*wall*
•	⟶	•	⟶	•
SBJ		OBL		OBJ
###		*spray*		###

The preceding example represents an alternation involving a single verb, *spray*. Other verbs take only one pattern or the other, forming complementary sets, although with some qualitative differences in meaning:

(18) *John put the blanket over the sofa.*

John		*blanket*		*sofa*
•	⟶	•	⟶	•
SBJ		OBJ		OBL
###	*put*	###		

(19) *John covered the sofa with the blanket.*

John		*blanket*		*sofa*
•	⟶	•	⟶	•
SBJ		OBL		OBJ
###		*cover*		###

Put is considerably more general than *cover*. An example of semantically much closer verbs is the well-known pair *pour* and *fill*. The possible case frames for different verbs are encoded by the causal segment(s) that the verb denotes in the lexicon.

There is some positive evidence for the figure-first coercion in other Indo-European languages, such as Modern Irish ([20]; Conor

Rafferty, personal communication), German ([21]–[22]; Wunderlich 1983), and Russian ([23]–[24]; Comrie 1985:314), and also in Hungarian ([25]–[26]; Moravcsik 1978:248):

(20) *Bhí an báin clūdaithe le blāthanna*
was the field covered with flowers
'The field was covered with flowers.'

(21) *Er gießt Wasser über die Blumen*
he pours water over the flowers
'He pours water on the flowers.'

(22) *Er über-/be- gießt die Blumen mit Wasser*
he APPL- pours the flowers with water
'He pours water on the flowers.'

(23) *Ivan sejet pšenic -u v pol -e*
John sows wheat -ACC in field -LOC
'John sows wheat in the field.'

(24) *Ivan zaseivajet pol pšenic -ej*
John sows field(ACC) wheat -INST
'John sows wheat in the field.'

(25) *János fák -at ültett a kert -be*
John trees -ACC plant the garden -into
'John planted trees in the garden.'

(26) *János be- ültette a kerte -t fák -kal*
John APPL- planted the garden -ACC trees -with
'John planted the garden with trees.'

Finally, the phenomenon of Type II noun incorporation cited in 5.2 also supports the figure-first coercion; the following example is from Yucatec Maya (Mithun 1984a:858, from Bricker 1978):

(27) *ki-' in- wek -ha'a -t -ik*
INCOMP- I- spill -water -TRANS -IMPF
'I splash him [. . . with water]'

In the few cases that I am aware of outside the European area, selection of the ground as the direct object displaces the direct object but does not mark it with an antecedent marker. This is the closest example to the "proper" causal representation, in which both the figure and the ground are endpoints of the verbal causal segment, at least for the purposes of case marking;[13] the examples are from Kinyarwanda (Kimenyi 1980:89):

(28) *Umugóre y- oohere -jé umubooyi ku'- iisóko*
woman she- send -ASP cook to- market
'The woman sent the cook to the market.'

(29) *Umugóre y- oohere -jé -ho isóko umubooyi*
woman she- send -ASP -to market cook
'The woman sent the cook to the market.'

Actually, the examples of the figure-first coercion also involve a mapping of path as well. In all the examples, the path between figure and ground resulted in the figure going to or toward the ground (allative path). However, Hook (1983) points out that there is a distinct form used when the figure is moving away from the ground (ablative path):

(30) *They stripped the bark from the trees.*

(31) *They stripped the trees of bark.*

Hook compares the situation in Latin, Sanskrit, and Old English, where instrumental and genitive or ablative compete for marking either path. In my analysis, both instrument and ablative are antecedent roles, and so syncretism of their case marking with that of a nonobject figure is to be expected. The syncretism of genitive with nonobject figure is expected if the genitive is itself based on an ablative, but, as will be seen in the next section, the position of the genitive is ambivalent.

The figure-first coercion plays a role in defining the representation of simple verbs of motion. Simple motion involves an activity performed by the initiator that results in a spatial configuration defined by the path of motion of the initiator/figure, the initiator and the figure being of course the same individual (see fig. 5.4).[14]

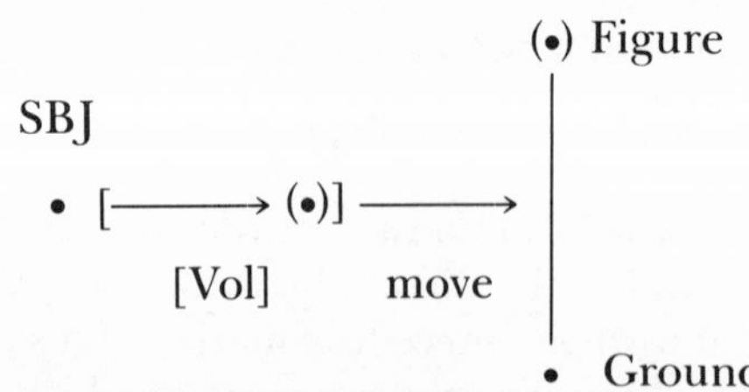

FIGURE 5.4. *Representation of a motion event*

Verbs of motion fall into two major types, according to Talmy (1985), which he calls manner incorporating and path incorporating.[15] Manner-incorporating verbs describe the activity that brings about the motion, such as *run, fly,* or *sail* and the more general verbs *come* and *go.* Path-incorporating verbs describe the path as well and include *enter, leave,* and *cross.* One can describe the difference in terms of the figure-first coercion and the number of causal arcs in the verbal causal segment:

(32) *The boat sailed into the cave.*

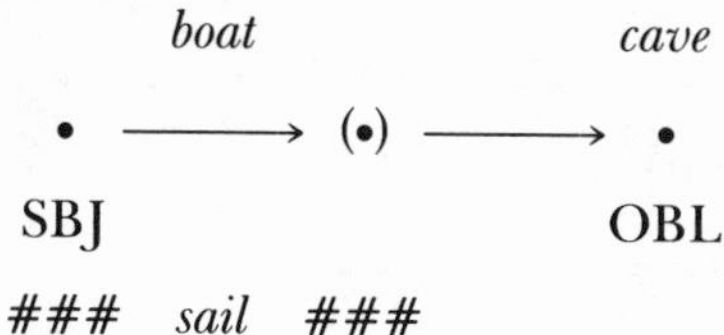

(33) *The boat entered the cave.*

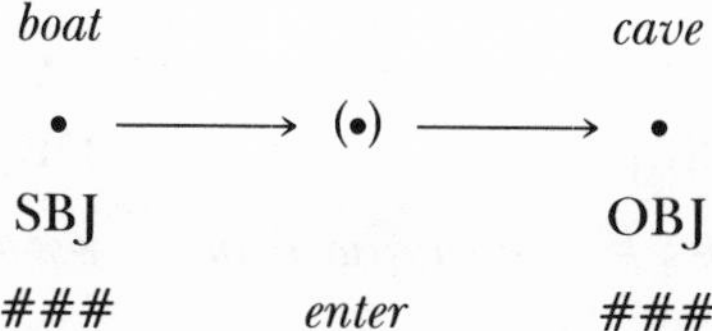

The manner-incorporating verbs denote only the first segment; therefore, the verb is intransitive, and the subsequent oblique ground uses a normal path expression. The path-incorporating verbs denote both segments, and therefore they are transitive verbs with the ground as the direct object.

One may test the analysis as follows. If the path-incorporating verb of motion involves two causal arcs, then it should allow a means expression since means expressions denote proper subsegments of the verbal causal segment. The manner-incorporating verbs, on the other hand, should not since they involve a single segment.[16] That appears to be the case:[17]

(34) *John entered the room by breaking down the door.*

(35) **John walked into the room by breaking down the door.*

The analysis of location verbs parallels that of simple motion verbs, except that the "move" arc is replaced by a "be_{loc}" arc. The existence of the stative arc, rather than simply allowing the path arc to be the "verbal" arc, is supported by the following facts. If the path arc in a sentence like *John is in New York* were the main verbal (coerced) causal segment,[18] then its endpoint, the ground, would be by definition a direct object. But the ground functions very much like an oblique and the path expression like an adposition in these expressions. More significantly, the stative "be_{loc}" arc allows one to capture the following alternations, which closely resemble the *go in/enter* alternation:[19]

(36) *The meat is in the freezer.*

meat *freezer*

• ———→ (•) ———→ •

SBJ

be

(37) *The meat occupies/takes up the (entire) freezer.*

meat *freezer*

• ———→ (•) ———→ •

SBJ OBJ

occupy/take up

(38) *The natives live in the outlying areas.*

(39) *The natives inhabit the outlying areas.*

Verbs of carrying and throwing or sending follow the expected pattern:

(40) *I took the terminal to my apartment.*

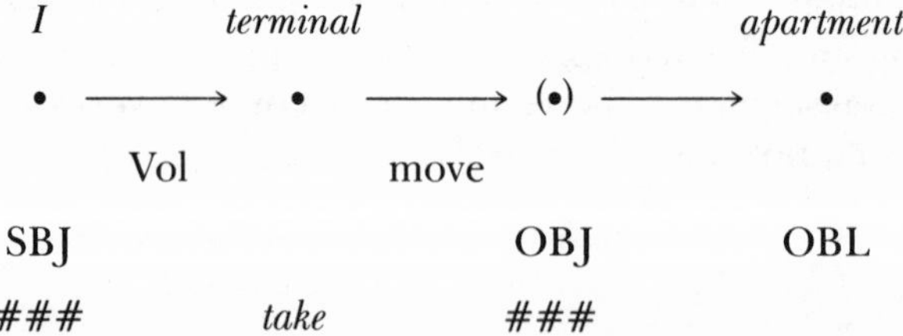

None of these verbs alternates in such a way as to give rise to an antecedent oblique marker. However, verbs of sending and throwing (in which the initiator does not go along with the figure) allow a double object construction if the ground is also a recipient (see the next section):

(41) *I sent the letter to John/Kansas City.*

(42) *I sent John/*Kansas City*[20] *the letter.*

(43) *I threw the ball to John/the back of the yard.*

(44) *I threw John/*the back of the yard the ball.*

There is one intransitive verb class that does allow the ground to become a subject, namely, verbs that roughly denote activities that are restricted to the location described by the ground.[21] They are represented by another well-known pair of examples, which have the predicted alternation between the normal path preposition and the antecedent oblique marker *with* (analyzed like the passive with antecedent marking for the nonsubject initiator; see 6.2):

(45) *Bees swarmed in the garden.*

bees *garden*

• ⟶ (•) ⟶ •

SBJ OBL

swarm ### LOC

(46) *The garden was swarming with bees.*

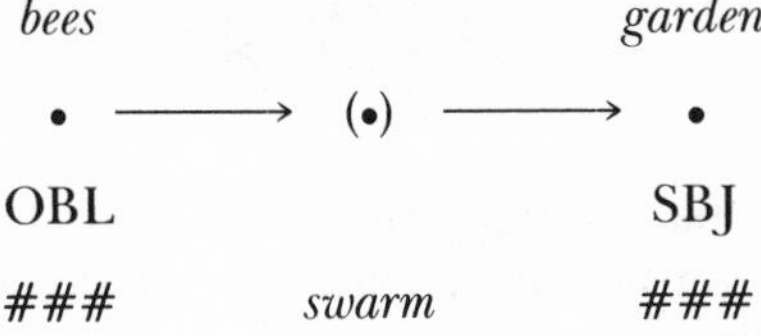

Thus, in the subject-ground examples as well as in the object-ground examples, the antecedent marker is licensed by the fact that the figure precedes the ground in the causal chain, by virtue of the figure-first coercion.

There is a problem with the analysis of the subject-ground examples, however. I have analyzed them as having the following causal structure: the swarming of the bees causes the bees to be (or stay) in the garden. An alternative semantic analysis would be to treat the garden as playing the role of an "external locative," having the entire action under its scope—to put it in Talmy's terms, the entire action is the figure, not the bees. If this latter analysis is correct, then the inversion construction would be highly unusual: external locatives do not participate in such alternations otherwise. Either semantic analysis is plausible, but even with the analysis I have used in the preceding example this construction is quite unusual and restricted to a particular class of verbs. For example, verbs of motion and body posture verbs cannot undergo a similar inversion.[22]

Although I have assumed that object choice between figure and ground is essentially free, it is a well-known fact that the semantic factor of affectedness, as a gradable property of the candidate object, is perhaps the single most important factor determining object choice (see 4.2). However, here I am concerned only with the type of oblique case marking, not the conditions under which it is used.

Finally, it is not an accident that the figure is coerced to "precede" the ground in the causal chain because in the typical situation in which some figure-ground relation is brought about it is the figure that is directly acted on by the initiator or, in the case of volitional motion, it is the figure itself that initiates the action. Though the ground as well as the figure is usually affected to some degree by the action, it is typically affected by virtue of the figure's being located at it (or removed from it), rather than by the initiator directly. In other words, there is a natural correlation between figure-ground order and causal sequence, not unlike that holding between direction of motion and direction of causation. It would be quite counterintuitive to have the coercion be the reverse, so that the ground causally preceded the figure.

I now turn to a very similar example of coercion, namely, possession relations.

5.4.2 Possession

Possession, like spatial configuration, is an asymmetrical binary relation between two participants, which I will call the possessor and possessed. Also like spatial configurations, a possession relation is noncausal: in the following example, the subject is the agent that causes the possession relation holding between the direct object and the indirect object to come about:

(47) *John gave the pie to Jane.*

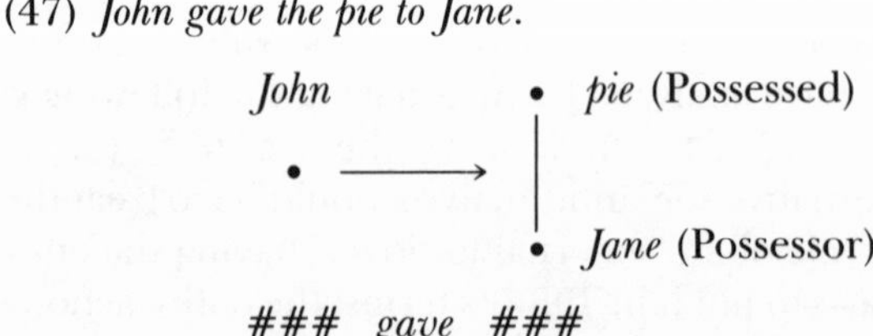

Finally, also like spatial relations, there is a "bias" or natural correlation between causal order and the noncausal relation of possession. It is the possessed item that is typically directly acted on by the initiator. Even more so than the ground in spatial relations, the possessor is affected mainly by virtue of his or her coming to have (or, in the removal type, losing) the possessed item and not by the initiator directly. Thus, one would expect a coercion in which the possessed "causally precedes" the possessor.

Nevertheless, the variation in the typological expression of this configuration is considerably greater than the variation in the expression of spatial relations in causal structures. There does exist the expected POSSESSED-FIRST coercion that is parallel to the figure-first coercion. The presence of the possessed-first coercion is frequently obscured by the fact that in most languages the basic transfer of possession verbs, 'give' and 'send,' do not have the expected antecedent forms, but there are a number of verbs that do have the same sort of alternation:

(48) *The dean presented an award to the valedictorian.*

dean		*award*		*valedictorian*
•	⟶	•	⟶	•
SBJ		OBJ		OBL
###	*present*	###		

(49) *The dean presented the valedictorian with an award.*

dean		*award*		*valedictorian*
•	⟶	•	⟶	•
SBJ		OBL		OBJ
###		*present*		###

(50) *Czechoslovakia supplied small arms to Cuba.*

(51) *Czechoslovakia supplied Cuba with small arms.*

Blansitt (1984:41) cites examples of antecedent-marked possessed with direct object possessors in Latin (ex. [52]) and Mandak (Austronesian; ex. [53], actually using the basic verb 'give'):

(52) *Rubrium* *corōnā* *dōnāstī*
Rubrius.ACC crown.ABL present.2SG
'You presented Rubrius with a crown.'

(53) *di ga raba i mi la- mani*
3PL PAST give 3SG.ACC with the- money
'They gave him the money.'

There is also a related pattern with loss of possession (examples from Hook 1983), with English *of* and the Russian genitive playing the "ablative" counterpart of English *with:*

(54) *Vlasti liši -li nas graždanstv -a*
authorities deprive 3PL.PAST 1PL.ACC citizenship -GEN
'The authorities deprived us of our citizenship.'

The former possessor is analogous to the ablative ground.[23]

Type II noun incorporation behaves in the expected manner; the following example is from Chukchi (Mithun 1984a:862, citing Bogoras 1910):

(55) *ġŭmnín ékık qä- kalê'tol- lpınrı -gın*
my son you- money- give -him
'Give my son some money.'

With many verbs of transfer of possession, however, like the Kinyarwanda spatial example in the previous section, the possessed is not placed in an (antecedent) oblique case when the possessor is the direct object. Instead, one quite frequently finds the possessor as the direct object and the possessed as an uncasemarked NP:

(56) *I gave the book to Carol.*

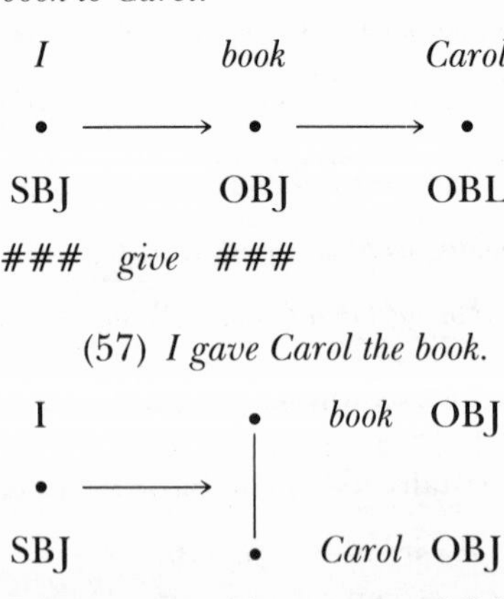

Here, it appears that the lack of causal directionality between possessor and possessed is realized directly in the direct object case marking for both roles. The double-object construction is typologically more common for possession than for spatial relations probably because the high animacy of the possessor role causes it to be selected as direct object, especially for the purposes of verbal agreement, for pragmatic reasons—especially with the "basic indirect-object" verbs *give, send, show,* and *tell* (Borg and Comrie 1984).[24]

Hausa has a rather unusual set of case frames for the verb *bā* 'give' (Cowan and Schuh 1976: 137). If both possessor and possessed are present, a double-object construction is used, with the uncasemarked possessor preceding the uncasemarked possessed, occupying the position immediately following the verb:

(58) *yā bā nì kuɗī*
he gave me money
'He gave me money.'

Either object may be dropped if unspecified. If the possessed is dropped, the case marking of the possessor, or rather the lack of it, does not change; but if the possessor is dropped, then the possessed must take the preposition *dà* 'with':

(59) *yā bā nì*
he gave me
'He gave me [something].'

(60) *yā bā dà kuɗī*
he gave with money
'He gave money [to someone].'

The patterns with unspecified object suggest that, even though the possessed is not casemarked when both possessor and possessed are expressed, the possessed can never occupy the immediately postverbal direct object position even when the possessor is absent from the clause. This is accomplished by rendering *kuɗī* an oblique in (60). Thus, the verb *bā* should be analyzed with the possessor as the endpoint.[25] What is of interest here is not only the "rule conspiracy" (see 1.3) that prevents *kuɗī* from ever being the "true" direct object of *bā* but also the fact that the preposition used is the antecedent oblique *dà*, as I would predict.

In fact, some languages keep the possession structure quite distinct from the causal structure: the possessor is still an adnominal dependent on the possessed, which is a direct object (see Croft 1985). In the spatial domain, this would be the equivalent of analyzing *the book on the kitchen table* in *I put the book on the kitchen table* as a single syntactic constituent. Although this is syntactically incorrect, the *morphology* of the two constructions is the same, and in fact the parallelism between the object-oblique relation and the head(-adnominal) modifier relation is actually quite close, as will be seen in the next section.

It is fairly clear what the source of the possessed-first coercion is. As has been noted frequently in the literature (Anderson 1971 : 107, and references cited therein), the possessor is consistently treated as the ground typologically, governed by a subsequent case marking, as can be seen from the stative verb forms:[26]

(61) *This book belongs to me.*

(62) *Mihi* *liber* *est*
1SG.DAT book.NOM be.3SG.PRES
'I have a book.'

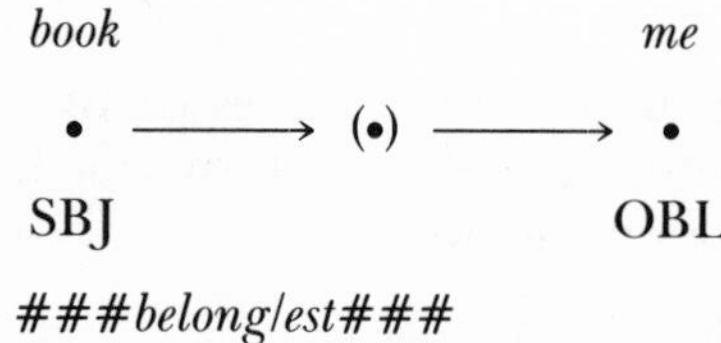

Contrast the Hausa construction for the predication of possession, in which the possessor is the head and the possessed is placed in an antecedent oblique case:[27]

(63) *yanā dà àlkalàmī*
he.is with pen
'He has a pen.'

pen → he → (•)

OBL SBJ

be

Thus, one may treat the possessed-first coercion as structurally identical to the figure-first coercion (though not absolutely identical to it since it is not the case that the possessed-first coercion is manifested every time that the figure-first coercion is).

The experiential motivation for the possessed-first coercion is quite similar to that for the figure-first coercion. Change of possession, whether giving or obtaining, involves acting on the possessed rather than on the possessor and (re)moving the possessed object relative to the possessor. Thus, the agent (initiator) acts on the possessed item rather than the possessor. The possessor is of course affected by the change of state of the possessed item—either gaining or losing possession of it—and so is "acted on" by the possessed in the same way that the benefactive/malefactive argument is acted on by the patient in standard causal actions.

One can now state the semantic patterns that underlie the "goal" category proposed by many case grammarians. The path-based object-location metaphor permits the syncretism between the allative and the benefactive case marking, and the possessed-first coercion permits the syncretism between the allative/benefactive case marking and the recipient case marking. Allative, benefactive, and recipient are all related to each other through a series of typologically general (and typologically common) semantic relations, all of which are themselves strengthened by natural correlations between the domains of spatial relations, causality, and possession.

There is one problematic genitive type that appears to violate this general pattern, but it too has its basis in a motivated coercion to a causal pattern, and the "inconsistency" is due to spread. Typologically, one finds another source for genitive markers: the ablative. This is an apparent counterexample to the coercion pattern because the ablative is an antecedent thematic role. However, it appears to have its origin in a different sort of genitive construction, the "material genitive" of traditional grammar. The semantic relation is between a creation and the material that makes it up; the common coercion is creation first. This can be illustrated with verbs of creation in English:

(64) *He made the candle out of beeswax.*

he		*beeswax*		*candle*
•	⟶	•	⟶	•
SBJ		OBL		OBJ
###		*make*		###

The experiential motivation for the ablative-material genitive is quite straightforward: the agent/initiator acts on the material to create the new object; hence, the material immediately follows the initiator (ignoring instruments).

The ablative-material genitive pattern is well attested in the forty-language sample: there are five examples of the ablative–material genitive syncretism, and no counterexamples (i.e., no allative–material genitive). In contrast, whenever the genitive uses the spatial metaphor of allative, it also includes recipient and or benefactive. In other words, it appears that the genitive conforms to the subsequent pattern of syncretisms only if it is associated with benefactive and recipient. Presumably, this association is due to the spread of a recipient/benefactive pattern to the genitive of possession. The subsequent convergence of the genitive of possession and the material (and also partitive) genitive into a single genitive case gives rise to the apparent assignment of genitive to both subsequent and antecedent forms cross-linguistically. For example, English, unlike many of the languages in the sample, uses the antecedent form *of* (formerly an ablative) for many genitives. Nevertheless, even in English, ownership is usually expressed with *'s*, and predication of ownership involves *'s* or the Recipient form *to: This book is Fred's; This book belongs to Fred.*

Dixon (1980) provides evidence in support of this analysis from Australian languages. He notes an element *-ŋu* commonly found in Australia ablative-clause cases (312–13) and observes that, among those languages that do not use a purposive-benefactive-dative case marker for the genitive, *-ŋu* is commonly found instead (314–15). The hypothesis presented here suggests that the two *-ŋu* forms are related[28] and that the two genitive patterns in Australian languages are due to convergence on a single genitive form from different sources.

5.5 Extension to the Rest of the Verbal Lexicon

The analysis of case marking and the types of meaning relations of case markers depends crucially on the hypothesis that causal relations, and specifically the volitional causation type of causal relation, are the semantically most basic verbal type. This hypothesis has two typological reflexes. First, there will be no variation across languages in the morphosyntactic expression of volitional causation in terms of subject and object choice: the initiator of an action of volitional causation will carry the usual subject marking (including ergative marking in those languages that employ it), and the endpoint will carry the usual direct object marking. Second, typological variation will be found in the expression of other types of causation, or in noncausal relations, because they do not "fit" the prototype verbal semantic structure as well as the volitional causation type. For example, there is typological variation in the expression of the figure and ground and possessor and possessed in causal relations across languages, although it follows the general principles of coercion.

The hypothesis also predicts that the extent to which noncausal relations are coerced into subject-object structures "designed" for volitional causation (in the same sense that I argued in 2.4 that major category inflections were "designed" for the core members) will reflect the extent to which the causal prototype can fit in the coerced domain. For example, in the figure-first and possessed-first coercions, there are asymmetric relations (figure-ground and possessed-possessor) that could easily be mapped into the asymmetric relation initiator-endpoint. Moreover, there is an experientially motivated reason for placing the figure first and the possessor first, in the sense that, roughly, transfer of location and transfer of possession are isomorphic to transfer of force. Also, the spatial or possession relation fits in at a specific point in the causal chain; this is reflected in the fact that both figure and ground and possessed and possessor are objects, not subjects.

The next step in lexical semantic research along the lines outlined in this book is to examine typologically the whole range of noncausal relations that become embedded in causal structures and/or expressed by verbs. In this section, I will provide examples of analyses of two well-known and difficult cases.

5.5.1 Mental Verbs

Of the causation types other than volitional causation, two are assimilated fairly well into the prototype, and the third is not. The alteration of the expression of physical and inducive causation is minor. The relative nonprototypicality of the physical initiator in physical causation is manifested by certain restrictions on its occurrence as a subject in many languages. As noted in 4.2, the initiator of a physical causation event may be the subject of a transitive verb only if it is a "spontaneous" or "ultimate" cause; that is, the causal chain cannot be (easily) traced back to some other entity. As for the mental endpoint in inducive causation, its nonprototypicality is more obviously manifested in its being placed in a subsequent oblique case (the dative), as is done fairly systematically in Spanish (e.g., with the inducive causation verbs *mandar* 'order' and *permitir* 'permit').

Affective causation, represented in the lexicon by MENTAL VERBS of perception, cognition, and emotion, is another matter entirely. There is a considerable amount of cross-linguistic variation in subject and object assignment for mental verbs. This is in striking contrast to the cross-linguistic uniformity in subject and object assignment (in the active or unmarked voice) for verbs denoting volitional causation and as such poses a challenge for the analysis of case marking, subject and object assignment, and verbal semantics presented here. However, there are specific characteristics of the semantics of mental verbs that can account for the variation in subject-object assignment.

Variation in subject-object assignment is found both across languages and within a single language. For example, many verbs in Russian assign the experiencer to the dative case ("indirect object"), while the English counterparts assign the experiencer to subject position (cf. Talmy 1985, 100–101; see the definitions of "experiencer" and "stimulus" in 4.4.4). Compare the Russian original to the English translation in the following example:

(65) *Mne* *nado* *ujti*
1SG.DAT need go.INF
'I need to go.'

Even English has some apparently synonymous verbs, one that assigns the experiencer to subject position and another that assigns the experiencer to object position.

(66) *I like classical music.*

(67) *Classical music pleases me.*

(68) *Ed fears the police.*

(69) *The police frighten Ed.*

However, some semantic differences appear in closer examination of the types of verbs that assign the experiencer to subject position ("experiencer-subject" verbs) and those that assign it to object position (either direct or indirect object position; "experiencer-object" verbs). The following examples from four languages illustrate the pattern; experiencer-subject verbs are given in (a) and experiencer-object verbs in (b):

English:[29]

(a) *like, admire, detest, fear, despise, enjoy, hate, honor, love, esteem*
(b) *please, scare, frighten, amuse, bore, astonish, surprise, terrify, thrill*

Russian:

(a) *xotet'* 'want,' *ljubit'* 'love,' *nenavisit'* 'hate,' *bojat'-sja* 'fear'
(b) (i) Accusative: *udivljat'* 'surprise,' *zabavljat'* 'amuse,' *pugat'* 'frighten'
(ii) Dative: *nravit'-sja* 'like,' *nado* 'need'

Lakhota:

(a) *waštelaka* 'like,' *chį* 'want,' *inihą* 'fear,' *phila* 'be glad'
(b) *yazą* 'hurt,' *inihą-ya* 'astonish, scare,' *phila-ya* 'please'

Classical Nahuatl:

(a) *mati* 'enjoy,' *tlazotla* 'love,' *m-izahuia* 'be amused,' *mahu-i* 'fear'
(b) *ahmana* 'disturb, upset,' *te-izahuia* 'amaze,' *mauh-tia* 'frighten'

The verbs in category (b) in all four languages (category [b][i] in Russian) represent a different causal-aspectual type from the verbs in category (a). The experiencer-object verbs are causative: the stimulus causes the experiencer to enter the mental state. This is particularly noticeable in Lakhota and Classical Nahuatl, in which the causative suffixes *-ya* and *-tia,* respectively, occur on some of the roots in (b), but on none of the roots in (a), and in fact derive (b) forms from (a) forms. The experiencer-subject verbs (and the dative-experiencer verbs in Russian), on the other hand, are purely stative: the experiencer is characterized as simply being in a mental state regarding the stimulus. This is revealed in the morphology in Classical Nahuatl and Russian. In Classical Nahuatl, the *m-* prefix is the detransitivizing ("reflexive") counterpart of the transitive *te-* (cf. 'be amazed' and 'amaze'). In Russian, the detransitivizing ("reflexive") suffix *-sja* is found on some roots in (a) and (b)(ii), but not in (b)(i), and adjectival forms such as *nado* 'be needed' are prevalent in (b)(ii), but not in (b)(i).

The richer morphology of Russian, Lakhota, and Classical Nahuatl reveals this difference between causative and stative roots for mental verbs, but syntactic and semantic differences distinguish them in English as well. The stative verbs do not allow means clauses, a characteristic of causative verb types (see 4.4.4):

(70) *John pleased his boss by coming in early every day.*

(71) **John's boss liked him by coming in early every day.*

(72) **John was liked by his boss by coming in early every day.*

Instead, a stative verb requires a causal clause:

(73) *John's boss liked him because he* [= John] *came in early every day.*

Part of the difference between a causative verb such as *please* and a stative verb such as *like* is obscured by the fact that the causative verb is quite punctual, making it difficult to use in the progressive, a good test for stative versus process verbs. However, contexts can be created in which the progressive is possible for causative mental verbs:

(74) *While the adults were chatting, the clown was amazing the children with his acrobatics.*

Also, English distinguishes process passives, which allow an agentive *by*-phrase, from stative (adjectival) passives, which do not. Many stative mental "verbs" in English are actually stative passives derived from causative mental verbs (e.g., *surprise* → *be surprised*). The two can be distinguished by the way that the experiencer is expressed: the process passive of a causative uses the agentive *by*-phrase, while the stative passive uses some other oblique expression:

(75) *Mary was surprised by John.* [process passive]

(76) *Mary was surprised at John.* [stative passive]

The process passive allows the progressive (though, again, it is difficult to create an appropriate context) and requires a habitual reading when used in the simple present, both indicators of a process verb. The stative passive disallows the progressive and does not require a habitual reading for the simple present, both indicators of stativity:

(77) (*Where's Mary?*) *She's being surprised by John for her birthday.*

(78) **Mary was being surprised at John.*

(79) *Mary is surprised by John at her birthday every year.* [habitual]

(80) *Mary is surprised at John.*

The difference between causative and stative mental verbs can be accounted for by the causal structure analysis of the two types:

Causative mental verbs

```
Stimulus        Experiencer          (Exp)        (St)
   +    ———————————→ • ———————————→  (•)   ———— (+)
  SBJ    Cause               Become  OBJ   Like
  ###            please              ###
```

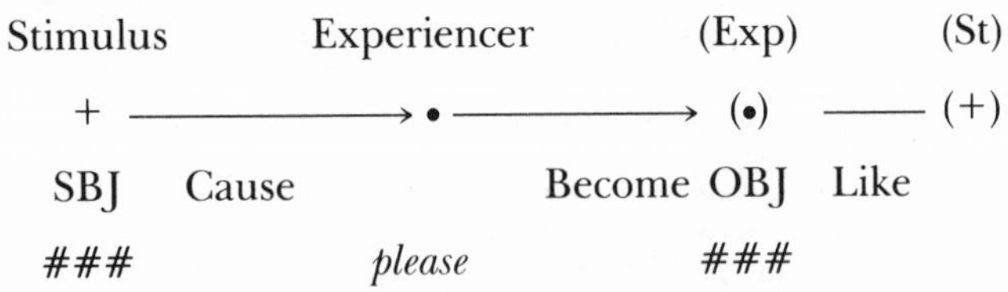

Stative mental verbs

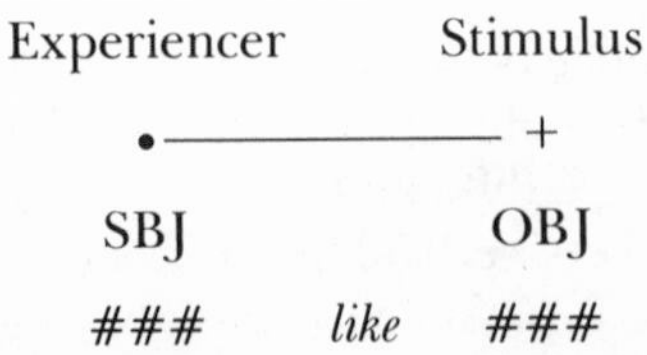

```
Experiencer      Stimulus
     • ——————————————— +
    SBJ                OBJ
    ###      like      ###
```

Experiencer		Stimulus
•	———— - - -	+
SBJ		OBL
###	*be surprised at*	###

The causative mental verbs are processes because the "cause" and "become" arcs make the verbal segment a process. They allow means clauses because means clauses are proper subsegments of the verbal segment (see 4.4.4); since the causative mental verb consists of three atomic causal segments, a means clause can be constructed. Finally, since the "cause" arc represents transmission of force, it requires the stimulus to be the subject and the experiencer to be the object—apparently the universal pattern.

The stative mental verbs consist of only a single stative segment. For that reason, it represents a state, and it cannot take means clauses, instead requiring a causal clause (see the definition of the causal thematic role in 4.4.4). Since the stative relation does not involve transmission of force, the stimulus is not affected by the experiencer, and so it frequently is found in a governed oblique case, as with other less-affected or unaffected "objects" (see 4.4.4). Above all, there is no inherent directionality of causation, and, for that reason, there is cross-linguistic variation in the assignment of the experiencer to subject or object status. Although in the languages described here most of the experiencers of stative mental verbs are assigned to subject position, Russian illustrates a pattern (common in the European, Caucasian, and South Asian areas) in which the experiencer of some stative mental verbs is assigned to an object position (often dative since the experiencer is human and is not the endpoint of a transmission of force relation with the stimulus).[30] Even in English, the nonagentive character of mental state verbs is manifested by the preference for the dative preposition *to* rather than the agentive *by* in the passive (in consequence, the passive is stative):

(81) ?**Tom's teaching ability is known by all his colleagues.*

(82) *Tom's teaching ability is known to all his colleagues.*

There is a third aspectual type of mental state verb, one that has not figured in discussion of subject and object assignment: mental activity verbs such as *think* (*about*), *wonder* (*about*), *consider*, etc. These verbs assign the experiencer to subject position. The reason for this is that the experiencer is engaging in an activity over which he or she has some volition or control; hence, the experiencer is the initiator of the action. Again, the stimulus is often a governed oblique because it is not affected by the action of the initiator/experiencer.

The fourth and final mental verb type is the inchoative mental verb, generally expressed in English by *get* + adjective: *get mad at, get bored with,* etc. Inchoative mental verbs take experiencer subjects. This appears to be true whether the verb is derived from a subject-experiencer mental state verb, as in the English inceptive interpretations of *see, know, remember* (*I suddenly saw John/knew the answer/remembered where my umbrella was*), or is derived from an object-experiencer causative verb, as in Spanish *enojarse* 'get angry' or *aburrirse* 'get bored' (from *enojar* 'anger someone' and *aburrir* 'bore someone,' respectively). This can be predicted from the causal structure:

Stimulus		Experiencer		(Exp)		(St)
+	——→	•	——→	(•)	——	(+)
	Cause		Become		State	
SBJ				OBJ		
###		*enojar*		###		
				SBJ		OBL
				###		###
					be angry at	

Stimulus		Experiencer		(Exp)		(St)
+	——→	•	——→	(•)	——	(+)
	Cause		Become		State	
		SBJ				OBL
		###		*enojarse*		###
		###		*get angry*		###

Thus, the causal structure predicts that there will not be typological variation in subject and object assignment of experiencer and stimulus for causative, inchoative, and activity mental verbs. Causative mental verbs are object-experiencer, while inchoative and activity mental verbs are subject-experiencer, because of the causal structure of a mental state-inducing event. The only type of mental verb that admits typological variation in subject and object assignment is the mental state verb. I now turn to that verbal type.

Mental states are noncausal relations like figure-ground and possessed-possessor, having no a priori causal directionality. Unlike figure-ground and possessed-possessor, though, the stative experiencer-stimulus relation does not appear to have a typologically universal coercion function determining subject and object choice. In 5.4, I argued that the figure-first and possessed-first coercions are based on the fact that changes in figure-ground and possessed-possessor relations are typically brought about by the agent/initiator acting on the figure/possessed; the coercion pattern incorporates this fact. Closer examination of the semantics of mental states, however, suggests why no such coercion pattern is universal. There are two processes involved in possessing a mental state (and changing a mental state): the experiencer must direct his or her attention to the stimulus, and then the stimulus (or some property of it) causes the experiencer to be (or enter into) a certain mental state. Thus, a mental state is actually a two-way causal relation and is better represented as follows:

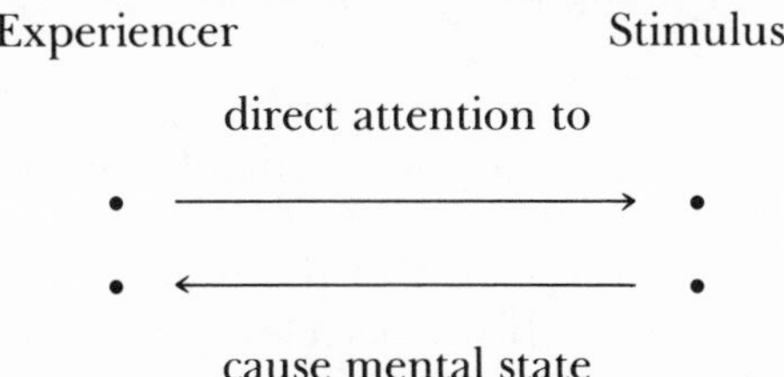

This analysis of the "internal" causal structure of mental states implies that three typological patterns should be found. First, there is no inherently typical coercion of mental states, so that some mental state verbs in some languages are object-experiencer and other mental state verbs in the same or other languages are subject-experiencer. This has been amply documented and has already been illustrated in the preceding examples. Second, if a mental state can be expressed as either a subject-experiencer form or an object-experiencer form in a given language, then the subject-experiencer version is interpreted as implying more volition or direction of attention to the stimulus than the object-experiencer version. The reason for this is that the subject is conceptualized as having control, or at least more control, over the state of affairs denoted by the verb; in mental state verbs, this means more control in directing one's attention to the stimulus. Third, there should exist languages in which mental state verbs more directly manifest the bidirectionality of the mental state causal structure: either experiencer and stimulus are casemarked identically, or one of the arguments (usually the experiencer) is assigned a "neutral" case marking (neither initiator nor endpoint). The reason for this is that, since experiencer and stimulus are both simultaneously initiator and endpoint, they are identical in causal structure; also, they are like neither the prototypical initiator nor the prototypical endpoint. Both these latter predictions are borne out; examples of each will be illustrated in the remainder of this section.

English provides an example of variable subject assignment with subtle differences in semantic interpretation (i.e., differences in conceptualization). English expresses perceptual relations with two different constructions, *see* and *be visible to.* The following examples illustrate the differences in interpretation between the two:

(83) *This peak is visible for hundreds of miles.*

(84) ?*I can see the peak for hundreds of miles.*

(85) *John can see the peak from here, but my eyes aren't good enough.*

(86) ?*The peak is visible to John from here, but my eyes aren't good enough.*

The adjectival *be visible to* with a stimulus subject is preferred when the perceptual relation is attributed to some property of the stimulus, for example, the height of the peak, as is implied by the phrase *for hundreds of miles.* If the perceptual relation is attributed to some property of the experiencer, for example, the experiencer's good eyesight (implied by the *but* clause), *see,* with the experiencer subject, is preferred. Thus, the presumed cause of the perceptual relation is made the subject, that is, initiator.

In Spanish, the verb *olvidar* 'forget' has three possible ways of assigning the experiencer: the experiencer can be made the subject (the active form), it can be made the subject and the object (the reflexive form), or it can be made a dative object (the impersonal form):

(87) *Olvidé* *hacer* *-lo*
forget.1SG.PAST do.INF -3SG
'I forgot to do it.' [experiencer = subject]

(88) *Me* *olvidé* *de* *hacer* *-lo*
1SG.REFL forget.1SG.PAST of do.INF -3SG
'I forgot to do it.' [experiencer = subject & object]

(89) *Se* *me* *olvidé* *hacer* *-lo*
3REFL 1SG.DAT forget.3SG.PAST do.INF -3SG
'I forgot to do it.' [experiencer = object]

The degree of "subjecthood" of the experiencer is matched by the degree of control over the mental relation of not knowing/remembering: the active form is used if the experiencer intentionally forgot; the reflexive form is used when the forgetting is unintentional but the experiencer is nevertheless responsible; and the impersonal form is used when the forgetting is unintentional but the experiencer is not responsible.[31]

Finally, Yoruba presents a more systematic pattern of variation between subject-experiencer and object-experiencer forms. Many Yoruba verbs of emotion normally have an experiencer object and a stimulus subject, the latter often denoting the emotion itself and occurring in an idiomatic combination with the verb (Rowlands 1969: 127; *bi* is not used in any other context):

(90) *inú* *bi* *mi*
inside anger 1SG.OBJ
'I feel/felt angry.'

However, the experiencer may also occur as subject, with the stimulus/emotion occurring as object:

(91) *mo* *bínú*
1SG.SBJ anger.inside
'I am angry.'

Rowlands (1969, 127) states: "The difference in meaning is that where the person is the grammatical object the emotion is thought of as coming on him of its own volition, as it were, while where the person is the subject he is thought of as summoning up the emotion, which is entirely under his control."

A good example is found in the following pair: the first means that the believer chooses to fear God, while the second means that the believer is afraid of God, presumably for some specific reason (Rowlands 1969: 127):

(92) *ẹ̀rù* *Olọ́rùn'* *bà* *á*
fear God fall.on 3SG.OBJ
'The fear of God is upon him.'

(93) *ó* *bẹ̀rù* *Ọlọ́rùn*
3SG.SBJ fall.on.fear God
'He fears God.'

Finally, it is not surprising that the subject-experiencer forms are more commonly used to express imperatives since imperatives imply control of the action being commanded on the part of the addressee/experiencer (Rowlands 1969: 127):

(94) *ma* *bẹ̀rù*
NEG.IMPER fall.on.fear
'Don't be afraid.'

The third prediction of the causal structure analysis is that case marking for mental state verbs would be "bidirectional" (experiencer and stimulus are assigned the same case marking) or "nondirectional" (some causally neutral form of case assignment is used). Bidirectional case marking appears to be quite rare. In Eastern Pomo, double patient marking is found with (at least?) pronominal arguments for some mental state verbs (McLendon 1978: 3):

(95) *bé:kal* *wí* *pʰi:lémka*
3PL.PAT 1SG.PAT love
'I miss them.'

(96) *mí:ral* *wí* *ma:rá*
3SG.PAT 1SG.PAT love
'I love her.'

In Japanese, *ga* is used for both experiencer and stimulus (Kuno 1973: 79–95). This is obscured by the fact that, in most grammatical contexts, either experiencer of stimulus is marked with *wa*. Both *ga*'s appear in focus ("extraction") constructions, such as WH-questions:[32]

(97) *Dare ga* *eiga* *ga* *suki* *desu ka*
who NOM movie NOM fond.of is INTERR
'Who likes movies?'

In some instances, experiencer-subject and experiencer-object constructions are found with the same verb, without any clear semantic difference. For instance, Spanish allows both the experiencer-object *Me gusta María* 'I [Obj] like Maria' and the experiencer-subject *Gusto de María* 'I like [1sg.Sbj] Maria' (with the preposition *de* for the unaffected stimulus). In Mandarin Chinese, an expression for intense emotion is interpreted "bidirectionally":

(98) *wǒ aì* *ší* *tā* *le*
I love die he PERF
'I love him/he loves me extremely'

However, the bidirectionality here may have to do with ambivalence in the interpretation of the subject of 'die' (either 'I' or 'he').[33]

Nondirectional or neutral case marking is found in languages with an otherwise "active-stative" or "actor-undergoer" system (Foley and Van Valin 1984). In these languages, the initiator of a volitional causation event is consistently assigned on case marking (or one set of agreement affixes), the "active" or "actor" marking, and the endpoint is consistently assigned the "stative" or "undergoer" marking. However, intransitive events are assigned either an active or a stative marking, on the basis of various semantic factors including volitionality/affectedness and aspect (stativity; see DeLancey 1985; Merlan 1985). This is not surprising, in itself: intransitive verbs do not have two participants and so do not participate in the causal asymmetry that determines "subject"-"object" choice. The case marking of intransitive arguments is thus more variable, sometimes assimilated to the transitive subject ("accusative" systems), sometimes to the transitive object ("ergative" systems), and sometimes divided between the two ("active-stative" systems).

In some active-stative systems, there is a third class of verbs that either take actor or undergoer case marking or take a neutral marking. In Cupeño, there is a "natural," unmarked (-Ø) form, and "most verbs for states of mind are in the -Ø class only" (Hill 1969 : 353), for example:

cáŋnewe-Ø	'be angry'
hemáne-Ø	'be embarassed, ashamed'
ʔáyelu-Ø	'be crazy, delirious'
ʔáyewe-Ø	'want, like'

In Acehnese (Durie 1985), intransitive verbs take agent cross-referencing only, patient (undergoer) cross-referencing only, or are variable. Emotional states are distributed across all three categories but in particular are frequent among the variable type (comments in quotations are Durie's):

Agent only ("some emotions"):
chên 'love, feel sympathy for'
dam 'envy, hate'
keumeung 'want, like'
têm 'want, like'

Variable ("many emotions"):
banci 'hate'
beungeh 'angry'

cinta 'love'
galak 'like'
gasêh 'love, favor'
inseueh 'feel compassion'
luwat 'disgusted'
peureumeun 'care'
rila 'content, satisfied, feel ready'
sayang 'like, feel sympathy for'
susah 'unhappy, find things difficult'
takôt 'afraid'
weueh 'feel moved by'

Undergoer ("many emotions"):
beureuhi 'desire'
deungki 'envy'
êk 'like, feel inclined'
kanjay 'ashamed'
ku'eh 'envy'
napsu 'desire, lust'
seudêh 'sad'
seugan 'not want to'
seunang 'happy'
teugiyan 'desire'

Also, some stative cognition verbs are variable, while others are agent only:

Variable:
syök 'suspect'
thee 'know how to, intuit'
tuwö 'forget'
yakin 'believe, be sincere'

Agent only:
agak 'guess, suppose'
ingat 'think of, remember'
pham 'understand'
rasa 'think, suppose'
tepeue 'know what'

tusoe 'know who'
tupat 'know where'

In sum, the causal structure model allows us to divide the mental verbs into those that vary in their subject-object assignment cross-linguistically (mental states) and those that do not (all other types). Moreover, a finer-grained causal analysis of mental states allows us to explain both why they vary more than other noncausal relations do and what kinds of variation in subject-object assignment are found.[34]

5.5.2 Exchange and the Commercial Situation

The project of determining the coercion functions that assimilate all the *noncausal* semantic relations expressed by lexical verbs in natural language is much vaster than examining just the three nonprototypical causation types. I will take only one well-known and problematic example, verbs of exchange and the commercial situation.

First, consider the situation of two entities that are similar in function and so are substitutible. The substitution situation consists of an initiator, the old entity, and a new entity, illustrated in figure 5.5.

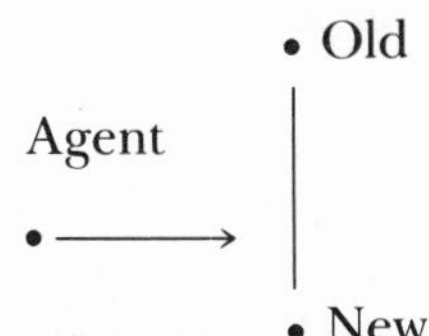

FIGURE 5.5. *Representation of substitution events*

The problem is, What is the appropriate directionality of coercion for the old and new arguments in coercing them to the causal structure? As with mental states, there is no intuitively obvious coercion, and there is variation in the linguistic expression of the old-new relation. For example, in English there is a lexical set, made up of *substitute* and *replace*, that uses a new-first coercion strategy:

(99) *The director substituted Cindy for Jane in the Virgin's part.*

director		*Cindy* (New)		*Jane* (Old)
•	⟶	•	⟷	•
SBJ		OBJ		OBL
###	*substitute*	###		

(100) *The director replaced Jane with Cindy in the Virgin's part.*

director		*Cindy* (New)		*Jane* (Old)
•	⟶	•	⟷	•
SBJ		OBL		OBJ
###		*replace*		###

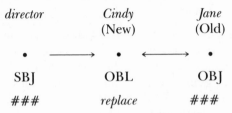

However, there is another very similar verb class, verbs of exchange such as *trade* and *exchange*, which occur only in the subsequent-oblique form and appear to have an old-first coercion strategy:

(101) *I exchanged/traded my Volvo for a Datsun.*

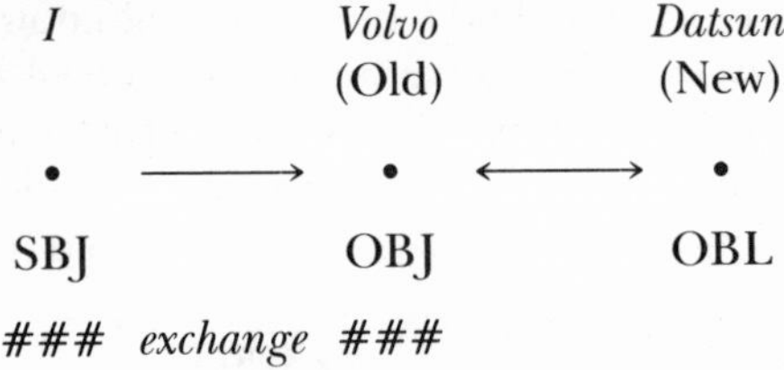

This different coercion strategy is part of a more general phenomenon involving the well-known commercial transaction situation.[35]

The involvement of a volitional seller in the commercial situation makes it different from the exchange situation and also turns it into a complex causally symmetric structure (for discussion of symmetric relations, see 6.3). This is illustrated in figure 5.6 (cf. Lawler MS, a detailed study of this verb class).

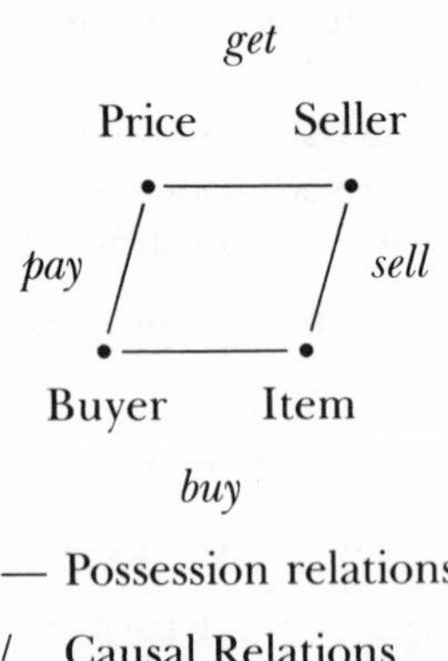

FIGURE 5.6. *Representation of commercial situation verbs*

In the commercial transaction situation, both the buyer and the seller are mental-level entities, both functioning as givers and as receivers. The old-new roles differ for the buyer and the seller: for the buyer, the item is new, and the price (money exchanged) is Old; for the seller, the item is old, and the price is new. One would expect complexity and variation in the case marking of this system, and that is exactly what one gets.

Although typological study of the marking of the participants in the commercial situation is necessary before arriving at conclusions concerning the case marking of participants, the modern English coercions can be illustrated. Each arc is represented by a separate English verb:

(102) *Fred sold a TV to John for fifty dollars.* [seller-item]

(103) *John bought a TV from Fred for fifty dollars.* [buyer-item]

(104) *John paid fifty dollars to Fred for the TV.* [buyer-price]

(105) *Fred got fifty dollars from John for the TV.* [seller-price]

The nonsubject volitional participant in all cases is coerced to be the ground, as is usual in possession situations, the preposition being allative or ablative depending on whether or not the participant obtains or parts with the direct object/figure. In the allative metaphor cases, the double object construction is possible, presumably since the resulting relation is new possessor-possessed, not former possessor-possessed, and only the former relation permits double objects in English (see 5.4.2, n. 23):

(106) *Fred sold John the TV for fifty dollars.*

(107) *John paid Fred fifty dollars for the TV.*

The entity other than the direct object that changes hands is uniformly marked as a subsequent oblique. This can be justified for *sell* and *pay* because the purpose of the action is for the initiator to come into possession of the entity governed by *for*, but that argument does not apply to *buy* or *get*. (However, the marking of this argument has varied in English historically, and it would be worth investigating this further in other languages.) On the other hand, if the buyer is the initiator—typically the correct point to enter into the causal cycle represented by the commercial situation—the physical object of payment exchanged for the item does appear as an instrumental expression:

(108) *John bought the TV with his birthday money.*

(109) *John paid cash for the TV.*

(110) *John paid for the TV with cash.*

These constructions use the old-first coercion strategy that was found with *exchange.*

The causal analysis can account for most, though not all, of the case marking in the expression of the commercial situation in English. As I stated before, however, there is a sufficient amount of variation in the history of English alone to suggest that the situation is more complex than this analysis implies. Unfortunately, little typological research has been done on verbs of commercial situation; further research is necessary before safe conclusions concerning the coercion of the commercial situation into causal structure can be drawn.

5.6 The Subsequent-Antecedent Distinction in Other Grammatical Domains

In the preceding sections, I have presented a large amount of evidence, including extensive typological evidence, supporting the existence of a subsequent-antecedent distinction among thematic roles in verb-argument relations. It is plausible to ask if the subsequent-antecedent distinction plays a significant role in other grammatical domains in which thematic roles define grammatical distinctions. This appears to be the case in at least two domains, adnominal relations and verb-related derivational morphology.

5.6.1 Adnominal Relations

One might expect to find similar semantic behavior to the types of metaphor and coercion patterns just discussed in adnominal modification in argument phrases. The same semantic relations—causal directionality, spatial relation, possession—must be expressed, but the object-oblique relation is replaced by the head-modifier relation. The head-modifier relation behaves in the same way as the object-oblique relation: the case marking of the modifier NP is subsequent or antecedent—often, in fact, the same subsequent and antecedent case markers found in the object-oblique relation—depending on the metaphors and coercions already described.

In English, the subsequent oblique *for* and the antecedent oblique *with* used in predicate-argument relations are also used in adnominal relations. The situation with adnominal relations is essentially parallel to that of predicate-argument relations. The adnominal *for* NP is used when the characteristic action linking the head to the dependent has the head as a figure, while the associative adnominal *with* is used when the characteristic action linking the head to the dependent has the head as a ground. Compare (111) and (112): for both, the characteristic action is putting the lid on the jar, where the lid is the figure and the jar is the ground. In (111), the figure is the head; in (112), the ground is the head.[36]

(111) *the lid for the jar*

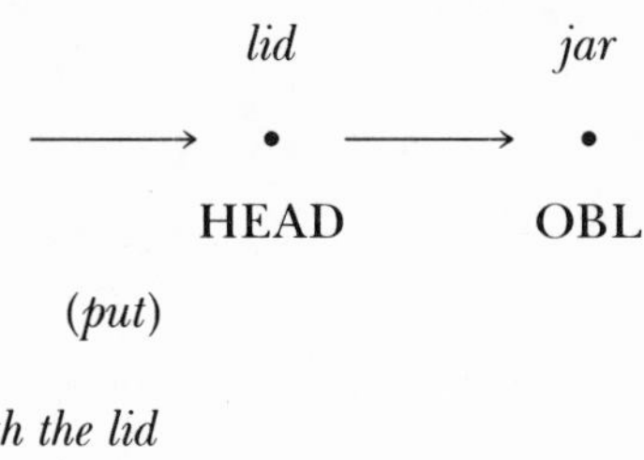

(112) *the jar with the lid*

lid *jar*

——→ • ——→ •

OBL HEAD

(*put*)

This generalization holds for possession relations also, using the possessed-first coercion; compare (113)–(115):

(113) *the food for the cats*

food *cats*

——→ • ——→ •

HEAD OBL

(*give*)

(114) *the piper with the broken finger*

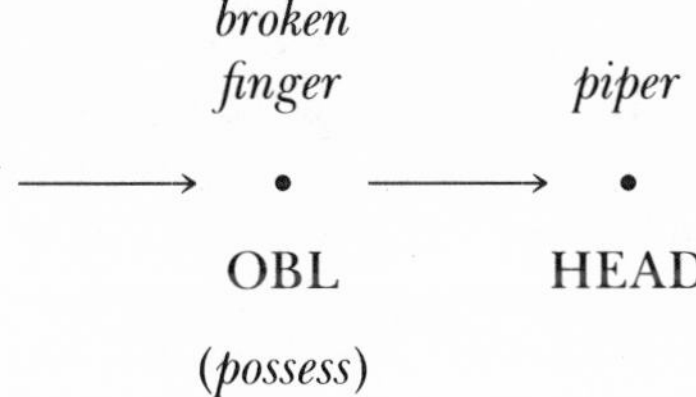

(115) *the man with the knife*

In English, the normal possessive construction uses the *'s* clitic, but, in many other languages, the case that encodes an adnominal possessor is the same as the case that encodes the recipient argument (i.e., a subsequent oblique case).

Finally, one also finds cases of genuine causal relations governing choice of at least the subsequent oblique *for* in adnominal relations (for some reason, corresponding antecedent oblique constructions are odd):

(116) *This kind of gun is for large animals and that one, for small game.*

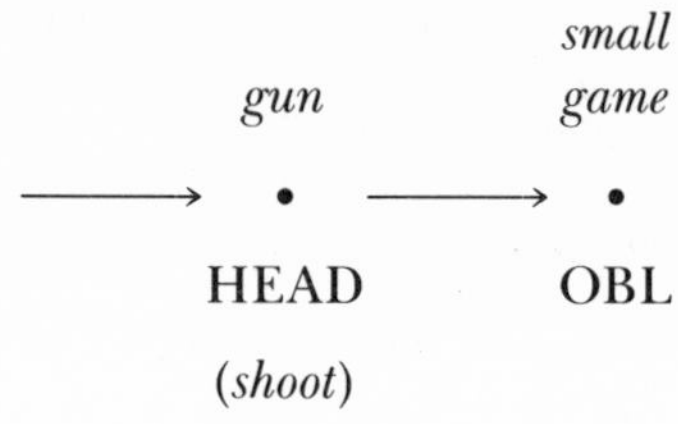

These examples demonstrate that the preposition *for* in English is a more general subsequent oblique form than the mental-level benefactive definition proposed in 4.4.4. This does not mean that there is no grammatically relevant distinction between mental-level and physical-level subsequent obliques, however, since it appears that the animacy of benefactives does determine grammatical behavior in some languages—for example, the use of double-object constructions. The benefactive type and the two genitive types, which also divide between mental-level (ownership) and physical-level (partitive and material genitive), merit further research as to the significance of the ontological distinction.[37]

The coercion of figure to head of an adnominal construction is also motivated by a correlation of pragmatic functions. The head of an adnominal construction is the referent that the hearer must identify, and the adnominal modifier is additional information deemed useful by the speaker for helping identify the referent of the head; that is the function of restrictive modification (see chap. 3). Likewise, in spatial configurations the figure is the object whose position must be identified, and the ground is the object that functions as a reference point by means of which the figure's position can be determined. The function of the figure is parallel to that of the head of the adnominal construction, and the function of the ground is parallel to that of the modifier. Again, it would be highly counterintuitive to have a coercion in which the ground was coerced to the head of the adnominal construction. The correlation is somewhat weaker with possession and direct objects, but it still appears to exist. The possessor appears to be "normally" definite, though this impression needs to be confirmed by text frequency studies, and so is more likely to function as a modifier helping fix reference rather than as a head requiring identification. The direct object, on the other hand, is more likely to be indefinite (Givón 1979:51–52) and so tends to correlate with the head, being the referent needing to be identified.

5.6.2 Derivational Morphology

In addition to figuring in the definitions of surface case markers in clauses and noun phrases, thematic roles also play a part in certain morphologically derived verb forms, in particular, the derivation of nouns denoting the argument of a verb and the derivation of verbs from nouns denoting one of their arguments.

Languages derive deverbal nouns that denote one or more roles of the verb; here, as in case marking, there is syncretism, and the syncretism follows expected patterns. One of the most common is the syncretism of agent and instrument nominalizations, as in Diola (Comrie and Thompson 1985:354; cf. the English translations): *-lib-* 'make slices' > *ɛlib-a* 'slicer'; *-tɛp-* 'build' > *atɛb-a* 'builder.' This syncretism respects the subsequent-antecedent distinction. The other most common syncretism reflects the event-location metaphor: the combination of instrument and location nominalizations (e.g., in Quiché *kun-* 'cure' > *kuni-ɓal* 'medicine' and *k̓ay-* 'sell' > *k̓ayi-ɓal* 'market') or the combination of agent, instrument, and location nominalizations as in Hungarian *ír* 'write' > *ír-ó* 'writer,' *hegyez* 'sharpen' > *hegyez-ö* '(pencil) sharpener,' and *társalog* 'converse' > *társalog-ö* 'parlor' (Comrie and Thompson 1985:355; Comrie and Thompson note no other syncretisms of role nominalizations).

Turning to verbs derived from nouns, the incorporation of nominals in oblique thematic roles that are causally intermediate between the subject and the object of the verb suggest that the causal structure analysis provides some motivation for the frequent formation of verbs from instrument nouns and other intermediate thematic roles. Denominal verbs formed from instruments form by far the largest list of denominal verbs in Clark and Clark (e.g., *yacht, nail;* 1979, list 8, 776–77). The second largest list is deverbal nouns formed from figures (e.g., *salt, tile;* list 1, 770–71). On the other hand, Clark and Clark found other classes of denominal verbs that appear to behave in the opposite way that one would expect on the basis of the causal structure analysis, in particular, denominal verbs from grounds where the figure is the direct object (e.g., *lodge, berth;* list 2, 772–73) and denominal verbs from goals—actually resultative states—where the possessor of the state is the direct object (e.g., *powder, cripple;* list 6, 774–75). In the latter case, a causative analysis would perhaps be appropriate, so that the endpoint of the denominal verb is the endpoint of the resulting state, as in the normal causative *sicken* (make *X* sick). The same analysis could be applied to denominal verbs from grounds. That would suggest that different semantic motivations would yield apparently contradictory results—causative formation producing verbs from grounds and simple causal order producing verbs from figures. I believe that this is the correct analysis, although it smacks of being able to predict anything, at least in this limited domain.

Finally, one finds APPLICATIVE derived verb forms, in which a participant that is expressed as an oblique with the underived verb form is instead expressed as a direct object. There are a number of languages that have applicative morphemes that are used to express more than one thematic role as a direct object; in other words, they display role syncretisms as well. In general, the applicatives for subsequent roles remain distinct from the applicatives for antecedent roles. In Fula, the instrument, manner, means, and locative applicatives fall under a single form, although it is distinct from the comitative applicative (Arnott 1970 : 348–53). The Kinyarwanda manner applicative is the same form as the comitative (Givón 1984b : 178). However, Wolof has a single suffix *-al* that is used for dative, benefactive, comitative, and also the causative, suggesting no directionality (Comrie 1985 : 316, 329–30); but Wolof also has a distinct instrument applicative form (Comrie 1985 : 318). Finally, Malay also has a single prefix that has causative, subsequent applicative, and antecedent applicative functions.

The syncretism of the causative with certain applicative forms, and the general analysis of applicatives and causatives in altering verbal segments, will be discussed in 6.1.

5.6.3 Compound Verbs and Causal Order

All the evidence reviewed in this chapter concerned the relation between participant roles and the causal structure of events. A reasonable question to ask is whether there is evidence in verb structure itself for the representation of verbal semantics as segments of a causal chain. I will be examining some evidence of that in terms of voice alternations in the next chapter, but here I will be examining a typologically more restricted phenomenon that appears to provide stronger evidence for the notion of causal sequences.

A number of languages, particularly in the Southeast Asian and Oceanic area, have verb concatenation (Matisoff 1969) or compound verb (Li and Thompson 1981) constructions, in which two or more verbs are concatenated to yield a constituent that is translated into a single verb (or a verb plus a particle) in languages like English.[38]

Compound verbs appear to reflect directly a decomposition of events normally denoted by single verbs in other languages and thus provide a test of the decomposition of events proposed in the preceding chapter. In the languages that I have examined, the decompositions that I have proposed pass the test. I will begin by illustrating with examples from Yao (Mien; Lombard 1968).[39]

Yao has a number of compound verbs that represent a combination of a verb indicating transmission of force with its result, such as a contact event or a change of state:

(117) *pwɔ́n zù'*
shoot hit
'shoot (and hit)'

(118) *pwɔ́n tɛ̀i*
shoot die
'shoot fatally, shoot to death'

• ——→ • ——→ •

pwɔ́n ### *zù'/tɛ̀i*

Still other compound verbs, those denoting motion, represent the manner or means verb followed by a verb indicating the path, an event type that is usually expressed in English with a verb plus a preposition:

(119) *pwɔ́n piɛ̀'*
blow enter
'blow into'

(120) *pwɔ́n baŋ*
blow fall over/collapse
'blow over, blow down'

• ——→ • ——→ •

pwɔ́n ###*piɛ̀'/baŋ*###

Each of these compound verb types decomposes the event into units that correspond to subsegments of the causal sequence denoted by a single verb or by a verb plus preposition in languages like English. This pattern supports the notion that verbs can be semantically analyzed into causal units since in languages like Yao they are analyzed morphologically in just that way.

In addition, the order of the verbs that make up the compound verbs in Yao is the same as the causal order of the subsegments that they denote. That is, the order of verbs in the compounds of Yao is ICONIC OF ICONICALLY MOTIVATED by the causal order of events in the world. This is not unlike the phenomenon described by Haiman (1980) in which the temporal order of conjoined clauses reflects the temporal order of events in the world. If we can assume that order in compound verbs iconically reflects the order of events in the world, then this can function as an argument in favor of the analysis of events in which causal sequence is essential, that is, the analysis of events as individuals acting of individuals used here. This analysis was contrasted with an analysis in which result expressions were embedded under the predicate denoting the cause, as in Shoot(*x*, Die(*y*)) or Become(*x*, Big (*x*)) (4.4.1). Now, if the embedded predicate analysis of compound verbs were correct, one would expect the iconic order of verbs in SVO languages such as Yao; but one would expect the *opposite* order in SOV languages since in such languages the syntactic complements of main verbs precede the main verbs themselves. Hence, one would expect an order like (*x* (*y* Die) Shoot) or, for the verb in question, 'Die Shoot' instead of 'Shoot Die.' Thus, SOV languages provide a test for the validity of the causal sequence analysis, implying an iconic order, and the embedded predicate analysis, implying the reverse order. The iconic order is found in the SOV languages that I have examined, Lahu (Matisoff 1969) and Kalam (Pawley 1987), as well as in a "mixed" SVO language, Mandarin Chinese (Li and Thompson 1981; bare objects follow the verb but objects marked with *bǎ* precede). Examples are provided below:

Action = Force + Contact + Result State:

(121) *kab añañ ap yap pk-e-k pag-p ok*
stone glass come fall it-having.hit-DS it-has-broken that
'A stone broke the glass.' (Kalam; Pawley 1987 : 329)

(122) *b tw dy, mon tb lak-p*
man axe having.taken wood cut he.split
'The man split the wood with an axe.' (Kalam; Pawley 1987 : 354)

(123) *jû' cí*
stab stick
'stab home, stab so it sticks' (Lahu; Matisoff 1969 : 75)

(124) *te* *tɛ*
set up put
'set up permanently (= so it stays put)' (Lahu; Matisoff 1969:95)

(125) *tú* *tò'*
kindle catch.fire
'light' (Lahu; Matisoff 1969:76)

(126) *qǐng* *nǐ* *tuī* *kāi* *zhei* *-ge* *mén*
please you push open this -CLASS door
'Please push this door open.' (Mandarin; Li and Thompson 1981:61)

Motion = Manner + Path:

(127) *ap* *yap*
come descend
'fall' (= 'come down'; Kalam; Pawley 1987:346)

(128) *dad* *ap*
carry come
'bring' (= 'carry to'; Kalam; Pawley 1987:346)

(129) *ce* *lò'*
fall enter
'fall into' (Lahu; Matisoff 1969:89)

(130) *bɔ̂'* *ce*
shoot fall
'shoot down' (Lahu; Matisoff 1969:91)

(131) *wǒ* *fàng* *xià* *wǒ* *-de* *shūbāo* *le*
1SG put descend 1SG -GEN satchel CRS
'I put down my satchel.' (Mandarin; Li and Thompson 1981:60)

I hasten to point out that the argument from the iconic relation between compound verb order and causal sequence can apply only to causal segments that are or can be lexicalized as root verbs. Sequences of events that are expressed periphrastically in languages with explicit subordinating morphology (such as English has) fall into the usual "reversed order" pattern in SOV languages. However, these sequences of events can also be of any type: simple temporal sequence, other non-causal relations, and of course tense, aspect, and modality.[40] I might add that, if anything, the iconically motivated causal sequences in SOV are related to coordinate constructions, in which the (iconically motivated) temporal sequence has an invited inference of causal relation, as in this Lahu example (compare the Kalam example [121] above):

(132) *tê pɔ̂' tí nâ' bɔ̂'* *hɛ̂' šɩ e ve yò*
shoot hit die

'All of a sudden he shot the rifle, hit (the animal), and (it) died.' (Lahu; Matisoff 1973 : 204, remainder unglossed)

Within the domain of verbal segments, however, the order of compound verbs in both SVO and SOV languages strongly supports the hypothesis that causal order is crucial in the linguistic representation of events as well as in surface case marking and other related constructions described in this section. Also, I would maintain that, even in the periphrastic case, there is a one-to-one mapping between causal segments and explicit verbs, a relation between form and meaning that Haiman (1980) calls ISOMORPHISM. This hypothesis, which has no exceptions as far as I am aware, supports the way in which I have decomposed events in the theory espoused in this book.

5.7 Conclusion

The analysis of the use of subsequent and antecedent markers, particularly English *for* and *with,* the coercion of possession and spatial relations, and the parallel between the object-oblique and head-adnominal modifier constructions depends crucially on the causal ordering relations proposed. A traditional case analysis, not using the causal ordering, is not able to define perspicuously the types of roles covered by a preposition such as the English *with.* In addition, the causal structure model captures the relation between subject selection, object selection, and the case assignment of obliques in a natural way. In a traditional case grammar analysis, the relation between thematic roles, such as recipient and instrument, and surface case markers always has to be qualified by a statement of the form ". . . unless it is selected as subject or direct object." Subject and object selection then has to be stipulated as part of the subcategorization frames of the verb. Instead of the subject and object being autonomous from the thematic roles, in the causal structure model subject and object selection interact directly with the semantics of the described situation and the surface case markers. The thematic roles, and the surface case markers that express them, are defined with respect to the position of the subject and object in the causal chain, so that case assignment depends directly on subject and object choice. Although subject and object choice is motivated by cognitive and pragmatic factors, they must be in a fixed relation with the lexical semantic representation of the verb (namely, the initiator and endpoint of the verbal causal segment, respectively). The only qualification to this strict correspondence that is possible is due to voice and verbal derivation, to be discussed in the next chapter.

5.8 Appendix: Table of Case Syncretisms

The table that follows gives the case syncretisms—that is, the thematic roles subsumed under a single case form—for the forty-language sample discussed in this chapter. The thematic role abbreviations can be summarized as follows:

> *Thematic roles:* P(passive) A(gent), Caus(e), Inst(rument), Mann(er), Means, Assoc(iative), Com(itative), Abl(ative), Loc(ative), All(ative), Acc(usative), Rec(ipient), Ben(efactor), Purp(ose), Causee, Mat(erial) Gen(itive), Circ(umstantial) [about . . .], Comp(ensation) [value].

The syncretized thematic roles are given by slashes. In certain languages, such as Russian and Attic Greek, the case syncretisms are supplemented by the adposition associated with the particular thematic role. For example, the comitative in Russian takes the instrumental case, as do the passive agent, instrument, and manner thematic roles; but it also requires the preposition *s*, unlike the other thematic roles requiring the instrumental case. Such language forms are cited in italics. Additional qualifying comments are in paretheses, for example, the distinction in Latvian between predicated possession and nonpredicative (modifying, i.e., genitival) possession.

Alawa	Erg/Inst/Loc, Ben/Gen/Purp, Abs/Dat
Gulf Arabic	Rec/Ben/Gen (ownership)
Mandarin Chinese	Rec/Ben
English	Com/Inst/Mann/Assoc, PA/Means, All/Rec/Result, Abl/MatGen/Cause, Ben/Comp
Finnish	Adessive/Mann/Means, All/Rec/Ben/Mann, Abl/Cause, Elative/Comp/MatGen/Part/Cause, Ill/Purp, Part/MatGen
Attic Greek	Gen/PA *hypo*/Abl *ex*/Com *syn,meta*/Inst *syn*/Rec/Ben/Mal/Loc *en*/PA

Gumbayngir	Erg/Inst, Rec/All
Guugu Yimidhirr	Erg/Inst, Abl/Cause, Rec/Ben/Gen/All/Loc, Ben/Purp
Hausa	Com/Inst/Mann/Assoc/Gen (pred), PA/ "Assoc," Rec/Ben
Hua	Inst/Abl, Com/Causee, Ben/'on behalf of'
Modern Irish	Com/Inst/Assoc/Purp (some), Ben/Rec/Purp, Gen/Loc, All/Manner
Kalkatungu	Erg/Inst, Rec/Gen/Purp, Cause/Advers (= Erg + *ngu*), All = Rec + *nha,* Abl = Loc + *ngu*
Kanuri	Loc/Abl/Inst/Means/MatGen/Mann, Rec/Ben/ All/Mann/Reason/Purp
Koṇḍa/Kubi	Rec/Ben/Acc/All/Purp/Cause, Inst/Abl/Mann
Kunjen	Erg/Inst/Loc, Rec/All/Purp
Lahu	Com/Assoc?/Inst (body parts)/Abl/All
Latin	Loc *in*/Abl *de*/PA *ab*/Com *cum*/Inst *cum*/Cause, Rec/Ben/Gen (pred)/All (poetic/Purp
Latvian	Com/Inst (*ar*), Rec/Gen (pred), Abl/Gen (nonpred) GenMat (*no*)
Malay	Com/Inst/Assoc/Means/Mann
Mam	PA/Inst/Caus, Com/Instr (< accompany), Rec/ Ben/Gen
Mokilese	Rec/Ben/All
Classical Mongolian	Com (some)/Inst/PA (some)/Manner/Means/ MatGen/Cause, Rec/Loc/Purp/PA?, Abl/ Cause/Part/Comp
Pitta-Pitta	Erg/Inst, Ben/Gen/Purp
Punjabi	Causee/Abl, Causee/Loc
Ayacucho Quechua	PA/Com/Inst, Rec/All/Purp, Abl/Circ, Ben/ Purp
Rumanian	Abl/Gen/PA, All/Rec, Loc/Acc
Russian	PA/Com *s*/Inst/Mann, Rec/Ben/Mal

Sre	Com/Inst, Rec/Ben
Turkish	Com/Inst, All/Rec/Purp/Causee, Abl/Cause/MatGen/Part, Ben/Purp/Circ/Cause, Mann/PA *-de*)
Urdu	Rec/Ben, Com and Inst related
Modern Welsh	Rec/Ben/Gen (some)
Woleaian	PA/Rec/Ben/Means/Causee, Com/Inst (< accompaniment)
Yapese	Inst/Rec/Ben/Loc/All/Abl, Loc/Abl
Yaygir	Erg/Inst, Abl/Cause, Rec/All, Gen/Ben/Purp?
Yokuts	Gen/PA, All/Loc, but Inst/physical endpoint (*-ni*)

Note: No syncretisms among thematic roles mentioned: Amharic, Manam, Twi, Yoruba.

6

Verb Forms and the Conceptualization of Events

6.1 Applicatives, Causatives, and Primary Objects

In 4.4.4, I pointed out that the description of events, and thus also subject and object choice, is constrained by what verbs are available to describe those events. Most if not all languages get around this constraint to some extent by the use of verbal derivational forms, in particular, causatives and applicatives. This section will briefly describe the analysis of causatives and applicatives in the causal structure model.

The analysis of causatives and applicatives in this model is in essence quite simple. If an initiator preceding the segment of the causal chain denoted by the verb is made subject, then the verb is causativized; if an endpoint following the segment of the causal chain denoted by the verb is made object, then the verb is applied (adds an applicative affix). I will begin by briefly discussing applicative affixes and a difficulty found with applicatives. A solution to that difficulty will require an examination of causatives. Finally, another difficulty with case marking in causative constructions will lead to the examination of an alternative strategy in assigning object and oblique status to participants in an event.

If applicatives add arcs causally following the verbal causal segment, then it would be expected that applicatives would always extend to subsequent oblique thematic roles. For the most part, applicatives do. One is most likely to find applicative forms for recipients and benefactives; indeed, the verb must be an applied form if a benefactive participant is present in many Bantu languages such as Kinyarwanda (ex. [1]; Kimenyi 1980:31) and if a recipient is present in Tzotzil (ex. [2]; Aissen 1983:272):

(1)	*umukoôwa*	*a-*	*ra-*	*som*	*-er/*-Ø*	*umuhuûngu*	*igitabo*
	girl	3SG-	PRES-	read	-APPL	boy	book

'The girl is reading a book for the boy.'

(2)	*ʔi-*	*Ø-*	*h-*	*čon*	*-be/*-Ø*	*čitom*	*li*	*Šun*
	ASP-	3SG.ABS	3SG.ERG	sell	-APPL	pig	the	Šun

'I sold (the) pigs to Šun.'

One also frequently finds applicatives for spatial grounds if the path is allative, as in Kinyarwanda (Kimenyi 1980:89):

(3) *Úmwáana y- a- taa -yé -mo ámáazi igitabo*
child he- PAST- throw -ASP -APPL water book
'The child has thrown the book into the water.'

In fact, the English examples with verbs such as *spray, present,* and *supply* could be called zero applicatives: in some of the other languages that I cited, such as the German, Russian, and Hungarian examples in 5.4.1, the forms that add the path arc to the verbal causal segment have an applicative affix that indicates that the path arc has been added. One also frequently finds possessors of patients as direct objects,[1] with the verb in an applied form, for example, in Kinyarwanda, Acoma (Keresan), and Awa (Indo-Pacific). One also rarely finds applicatives of event locatives, that is, phrases that describe the location in which the action took place, as opposed to the location of an argument after the action took place (*He put the book on the table; He sent Mary to the back of the classroom*). I do not know exactly how such examples ought to be analyzed. It appears that one may make the following rough generalization on types of causal segments that can be added to morphologically simple verbs: an applicative suffix can add only the coerced endpoints of noncausal stative relations, the initiator of which is the endpoint of the root verb, or the endpoint of an event of affective causation, possibly with no mental-level entities intervening.

The case marking of applicatives has largely been discussed already in 5.4. Sometimes the "patient"—the entity that is usually the endpoint but is between the subject and the object in the causal chain in the applied form—is put into the instrumental case; sometimes it is not, particularly with mental-level participants. An example of a construction in which the "patient" is put into the instrumental case is the Hausa "causative" *-ar.* This suffix is a causative but may also simultaneously be an applicative. In that case, it allows a direct object benefactive and requires an antecedent oblique for the "patient" (Kraft and Kirk-Greene 1973: 151):

(4) *Sun shayar manà dà shānū*
they drink.CAUS/APPL us with cattle
'They watered the cattle for us.'

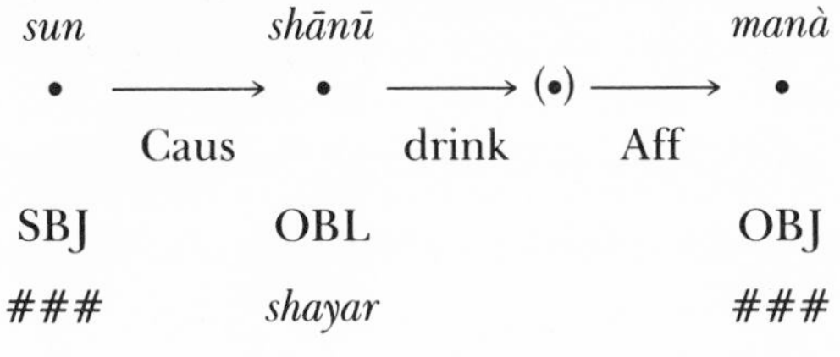

sun		*shānū*				*manà*
•	⟶	•	⟶	(•)	⟶	•
	Caus		drink		Aff	
SBJ		OBL				OBJ
###		*shayar*				###

(5) *Nā sauker* *masà dà* *kāyansà*
I descend.CAUS/APPL him with loads
'I set his loads down for him.'

The double direct object constructions frequently encountered with applicatives can be explained in all cases except the benefactive as essentially ignoring the figure-first and possessed-first coercions in case marking (although the coercions manifest themselves in the unmarked figure-object and possessed-object verb forms as opposed to the marked [applied] ground-object and possessor-object verb forms). This explanation, however, does not apply to the double objects in the benefactive applicative case since the causal order is not explicit. It is not surprising that the higher animacy of the benefactive participant leads to it being selected as a direct object instead of an oblique, but the "patient" is clearly in an antecedent role and yet frequently is not placed in an antecedent case (unlike the Hausa example above).

In all these cases, though, the "patient" (direct object in the unapplied form) often lacks some or all of its "object properties." This is not totally unexpected since the applied form's endpoint is almost always animate (a recipient, benefactive, or possessor of a patient) and "object properties"—verb agreement, relativization, passivization—are all properties associated with topicality and focus (see Hawkinson and Hyman 1974; Givón 1976; Trithart 1979). Application often is just the first step to subjectivization of an oblique via passivization (see Wunderlich 1983; and the next section), that is, a strategy for topicalizing a mental-level entity that normally cannot be a subject.

More rarely, one finds antecedent forms, specifically manner and instrumentals with "applicative" affixes. The causal analysis of verbal semantics provides a striking explanation for many of the instances of instrumental applicatives that I am aware of (though not all). According to the causal structure theory, applied forms creating instrumental direct objects "shrink" the length of the causal chain. If this is true, one would expect the instrumental applicative to be somewhat different from the subsequent applicatives. In fact, in three cases that I am aware of, Kinyarwanda, Malay, and Dyirbal, the instrumental applicative affix is the causative affix.[2] But the causal structure of the two constructions is exactly the same (example from Kinyarwanda; Kimenyi 1980: 164):

(6) *Umugabo a- ra- andik -iiš -a umugabo íbárúwa*
man 3SG- PRES- write -CAUS -ASP man letter
'The man is making the man write a letter.'

(7) *Umugabo a- ra- andik -iiš -a íkárámu íbárúwa*
man 3SG- PRES- write -"APPL" -ASP pen letter
'The man is writing a letter with a pen.'

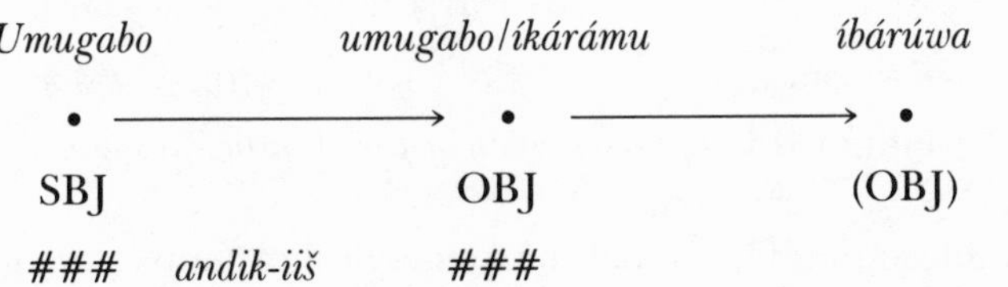

In the first example, the causative, the "causer" or new agent, is made the subject, as is normal; the causee (the second man) is made the direct object, which is one of three types of causative structures found in the world's languages (see below); and the "patient" remains uncasemarked (one would expect it to be a subsequent oblique, but Kinyarwanda does not casemark any of its non-direct-object "patients"). Thus, if one assumes the new initiator as a given, the causative construction "shrinks" the verbal causal segment so that the intermediate participant, the causee, is direct object. The same process occurs with the instrumental applicative, though without adding a new initiator: the verbal causal segment is shrunk so that the intermediate participant, the instrument, is direct object. In both instances, the mapping between the three participants in the event and the verb form and case markings is the same, although the third participant is introduced in a different position in the two constructions (at the beginning for the causative, in the middle for the instrumental applicative).[3]

The interaction of instrumental applicatives and causatives leads to the discussion of causative structures in general and their position in the causal analysis of case marking and voice. Causatives, like passives, have been studied quite a lot, and their structural characteristics are fairly well known. A typology of causative constructions would yield three morphosyntactic types:

1. Periphrastic causatives
2. Morphological causatives:
   a. Causee is direct object
   b. Patient, if present, is direct object; causee varies in case marking

Periphrastic causatives follow the causal structure in having a separate verb for the segment added, the causee functioning as endpoint in the causal verb clause, initiator in the source verb clause, or both. This is illustrated in figure 6.1.

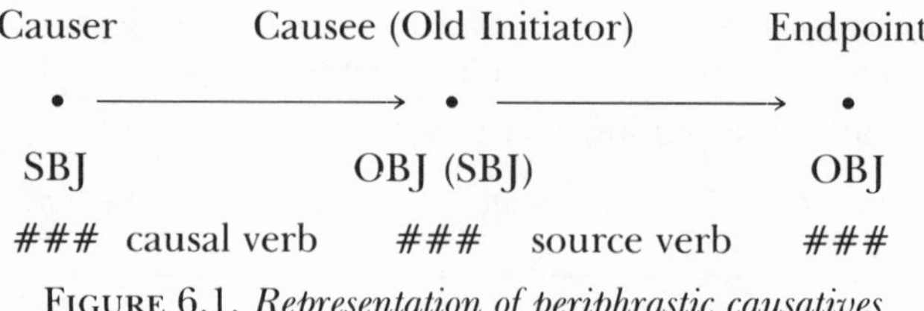

FIGURE 6.1. *Representation of periphrastic causatives*

An interesting fact is that morphological causatives are generally used for intransitives, especially nonagentive intransitives, but not for transitives, while periphrastic causatives (or sometimes a distinct morphological causative) are used for transitives, in which the added causal segment is generally inducive causation. In other words, causatives almost always add mental-level initiators, and the new segment is one of volitional causation when added to intransitives or one of inducive causation when added to transitives: for example, Turkish *piş* 'cook (intr.)' → *piş-ir* 'cook (tr.)' → *piş-ir-t* 'make/have [someone] cook [something]' (Lewis 1967 : 146). This fact will become important below.

The causatives in which the causee is direct object are counterexamples to Comrie's (1976b) "paradigm case" of causative formation based on the hierarchy of DO < IO < oblique, which is based on the third type of causative (patient remains direct object).[4] In this type, the case marking of the causee varies, apparently owing to the presence of patients and recipients and a prohibition of two arguments of the same grammatical relation. Comrie proposes essentially that the causee occupies the highest position available on the case hierarchy. In the case of causative of intransitives, both Comrie's paradigm case and the causal structure hypothesis make the same prediction: the causee becomes direct object, it being affected by the causer's action. In the rare case of the causative of ditransitives, the causee is placed in a case that is usually the passive agent (antecedent) case: that also conforms to the causal order hypothesis. In the case of the causative of transitives, Comrie's paradigm case does not match the causal structure hypothesis: it predicts a (subsequent) indirect object case, while the causal order hypothesis predicts an antecedent oblique case. The typological evidence is equivocal. The causee of a transitive verb sometimes appears in the dative (e.g., Turkish and French), as Comrie's paradigm case predicts; I will return to these cases in the next paragraph. The causee of a transitive verb also frequently appears as the direct object: this is the second type of causative, already discussed. Finally, the causee sometime appears in an antecedent oblique case; in my sample, they included Hua (comitative) and Punjabi (ablative) (cf. Comrie

1985:339; Comrie also cites Sanskrit and Finnish). Cole (1983) also observes this fact and points out that some languages actually vary with respect to the case marking assigned to the causee of a transitive verb regardless of the presence of other object or oblique arguments. The facts are complicated, but Cole's basic conclusion is that the direct object causees are found when direct force is applied, instrumental causees are found when indirect causation is involved, and dative causees are frequently found when the verb is a cognitive verb—that is, the experiencer is placed in the dative case, part of the general inversion pattern of affective causation (see 5.5.1), but realized only in causative structures in these languages.

The cases in which the causee of a causativized transitive verb is realized in the dative case, such as Turkish and French,[5] must still be accounted for. However, it appears that, in these languages, the dative-causee construction is allowed only if the causee is a mental-level participant and is therefore the endpoint of an action of inducive causation:

(8) *Charles a cassé le vase.*
'Charles broke the vase.'

(9) *La statue a cassé le vase.*
'The statue broke the vase.'

(10) *J'ai fait casser le vase à Charles.*
'I made Charles break the vase.'

(11) **J'ai fait casser le vase à la statue.*
'*I made the statue break the vase.'
[not acceptable as an alternative for 'I broke the vase with the statue.']

French appears to place any mental-level participant causally following the initiator in the dative case, regardless of its position in the causal chain relative to the direct object, as long as it follows the subject in the causal chain.

This is also true for Yokuts (Newman 1944:201), where mental-level endpoints are made into direct objects rather than datives. This pattern is called the PRIMARY OBJECT pattern by Dryer (1986): the primary object is the "direct object" (patient, theme, etc.) of a transitive verb and the "indirect object" (recipient, benefactor—in general, any mental-level endpoint) of a ditransitive verb. A SECONDARY OBJECT is the "direct object" ("theme") of a ditransitive verb. The primary object pattern is much more common with agreement: the verb agrees with the recipient/benefactor instead of the patient/theme. Our concern, however, is with case marking that follows the primary-secondary object distinction, with a nonzero case marking for the secondary object. In Yokuts, mental-level endpoints are primary objects, whether they follow the patient causally (recipients and benefactive participants) or precede it (causees), and the "patient" is placed in an oblique case *-ni:*

(12) *'ama'* *nan* *wan* *-xo'* *k'exa* *-ni* *nim*
3SG.NOM 1SG.ACC give -DUR money -OBL 1SG.POSS
'He gives me my money.'

(13) *'os* *-sut* *-su* *na'* *mam* *'edaw* *-ŋi*
steal -INDIR -AOR 1SG.NOM 2SG.ACC flower -OBL
'I stole the flowers for you/I stole you the flowers.'

(14) *c'om* *-la* *-'* *na'* *ṭan* *hi'* *xata* *-ni*
devour -CAUS -FUT I him FUT food -OBL
'I will make him devour the food.'

If there is no mental-level participant other than the patient, the patient is the endpoint, and the same *-ni* oblique case is used for instrumentals:

(15) *'ama'* *dadaṭ'* *nim* *ṭ'ik'a'an* *nan* *wọšọk* *-ni* *'amin*
and bind my foot me belt -OBL his
'and (he) is binding my foot with his belt'

The *-ni* oblique is an antecedent marker, as demonstrated by the instrumental construction (also, it is possibly related to the ablative *-nit*). In most cases, the secondary object actually is in an antecedent thematic role, but it is not in the causative construction. This indicates that the ontological status overrides causal order in the object-oblique distinction in Yokuts.[6]

Primary-secondary object case marking is found in Yoruba with the preposition/serial verb *ní* 'have, on, etc.' (which changes to *l'* when preceding a word beginning with a nonhigh vowel; Rowlands 1969:21):

(16) *ó* *fún* *mi* *l'-* *ówó*
he give 1SG.OBJ 'on'- money
'He gave me money.'

Again, the secondary object case marker is an antecedent oblique marker, being used with instruments (though it competes with another serial verb, *fi;* Rowlands 1969:85):

(17) *ó lù mí ní kùmọ̀*
he hit 1SG.OBJ 'on' stick
'He hit me with a stick.'

However, Yoruba uses a distinct construction for causatives, so the conflict between causal sequence and ontological status of the endpoint (mental-level vs. physical-level) does not arise.

The French and Yokuts systems appear to be a typologically attested if very rare alternative way to express the arguments following the initiator if there is more than one: distinguish mental-level participants from physical-level participants, whichever causal order they have (as long as both follow the subject in the causal chain). This alternative way of organizing the nonsubject arguments of a predicate is animacy based rather than causally based. The French and Yokuts systems demonstrate that, in the case assignment of objects and obliques, causal structure can sometimes be overriden by animacy (this is also true of the "inverse" constructions discussed in the next section).

6.2 Passive Voice and Markedness Patterns in Causal Structures

In chapter 5, I introduced the causal order hypothesis: that there is a correlation between the pragmatic ranking of the arguments of a verb in terms of topicality (Givón) or some related discourse function (see 4.2) and the causal ordering of the arguments in the event denoted by the verb. In that chapter, I presented extensive evidence regarding the "object-oblique" half of the causal order hypothesis, demonstrating that oblique case marking is divided between those that govern obliques that follow the object in the causal sequence in accordance with the causal order hypothesis (the subsequent obliques) and those that precede, in apparent violation of the hypothesis (the antecedent obliques). In this section, I will describe how the passive voice, as it is commonly analyzed, fits into the causal structure model as a means to "violate" the subject-object causal order. I will then demonstrate that the "violations" represent marked constructions compared to the normal correlation, which thus establishes the causal order hypothesis—and the definitions of grammatical relations "subject," "object," and "oblique" underlying it—as a typological universal of the same standing as the definitions of "noun," "verb," and "adjective" argued for in chapters 2 and 3.

Voice, in the narrow sense, applies to the distinctions "active," "passive," and also "middle."[7] The active/passive distinction has been analyzed as a derivational relation in generative grammar; however, this has led to problems and difficulties with certain kinds of "impersonal" passives (see Siewierska 1984) and with the middle voice. Traditional grammarians analyzed voice in terms of affectedness, and this analysis has been revived by Barber (1975) and Klaiman (1981, 1982a, 1982b, 1988). This analysis can be summarized as follows: in the active voice, the subject is controller of the action but not affected by it; in the passive, the subject is affected by the action but not controller of it; in the middle, the subject is both the controller of the action and affected by it. These definitions clearly are harmonious with the causal structure analysis, and I will present an analysis that is essentially the traditional analysis, cast in the terms of the model of causal structure presented in chapter 4.

The passive voice is the strategy for handling situations in which the subject chosen by the speaker (for whatever pragmatic purposes) does not precede the ("normal") object in the causal chain expressed by the verb, just as the subsequent-antecedent case-marking distinction is the strategy for handling situations in which the object does not precede the oblique in the causal chain. The passive construction is one in which the endpoint instead of the initiator of the verbal segment is the subject. What happens to the participant corresponding to the subject in this construction? The answer is that in most languages the initiator cannot be a direct object—this would be an outright violation of the causal order hypothesis—but instead has to be an oblique, usually called the PASSIVE AGENT.

The prediction that the passive agent thematic role uses an antecedent case marking, since it precedes the subject/endpoint in the causal chain, generally holds. Keenan (1985:263–64) observes that passive agents are usually instruments or "locatives" (ablative or locative, depending on the choice of metaphor, object location or event location).[8] There are a small number of exceptions. Classical (and Modern) Mongolian uses the dative case for the passive agent; however, its dative case covers a wide range of uses, and it seems to be a language whose case system is collapsing into a nondirectional type (see 5.2).[9]

In addition to predicting the use of antecedent oblique marking for passive agents, the causal analysis allows one to distinguish stative (resultative, "adjectival") passives from process passives. Resultative passives describe only the resulting state of the affected entity. Process passives describe the same process as the corresponding active but from the perspective of the affected entity rather than the agent/initiator. In some languages, including English, the resultative passive cannot take the usual oblique expression for the agent, although indirect cause expressions such as *thanks to, due to,* or *on account of* allow the introduction of an agent. The resultative passive also cannot take means expressions, unlike process passives. These differences can be accounted for by the causal structure model as follows. The process passive covers the same segment of the causal chain as the active, with the endpoint as subject:

(18) *John unlocked the door (by disabling the latch).*

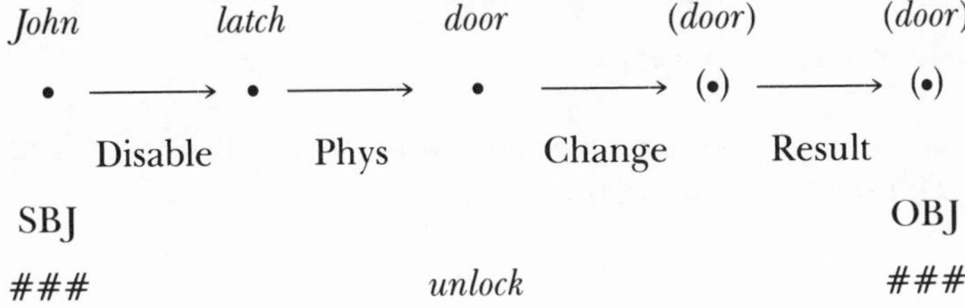

(19) *The door was unlocked (by John/by disabling the latch).*

John *latch* *door* *(door)* *(door)*

• ——→ • ——→ • ——→ (•) ——→ (•)

Disable Phys Change Result

OBL SBJ

unlocked

The resultative passive covers only the resulting state ("result") arc of the causal chain. Since it lacks internal structure, the means clause is not possible, and, since the agent is not at the beginning of the main verb causal segment, it cannot take the usual passive oblique construction, taking instead some other surface indicator of cause (cf. the discussion of causative and stative mental verbs in 6.5.1.):[10]

(20) *The door is unlocked (*by John/*by disabling the latch/thanks to John).*

John *latch* *door* *(door)* *(door)*

• ——→ • ——→ • ——→ (•) ——→ (•)

Disable Phys Change Result

SBJ

###*unlocked*###

The process passive allows the progressive (although contexts are difficult to construe) and has a habitual interpretation in the simple present, while the stative passive prohibits the progressive and does not have a habitual interpretation in the simple present:

(21) *The door is being unlocked by the robot at this very moment.*

(22) *The door is unlocked by the robot every day at 8 A.M.* [habitual]

(23)**The door is being unlocked.* [*in result passive reading]

(24) *The door is unlocked.*

The general difference between process passives and result passives is illustrated in figure 6.2.

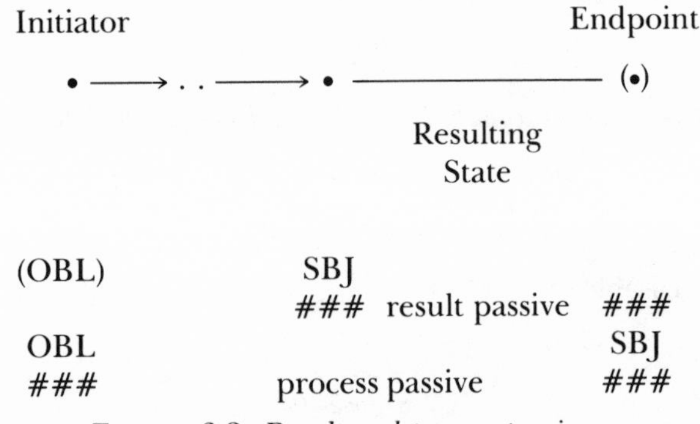

FIGURE 6.2. *Result and process passives*

Interestingly, the process passive yields a parallelism between the means clause and the passive agent that is not present in the active but may explain the syncretism of case marking: both the passive agent and the means clause are part of the causal chain denoted by the main verb (i.e., the process passive) when the subject is the *endpoint* of the main verb.[11]

There are two other linguistic phenomena that appear to have the same effect on the causal structure as the process passive—making the normal endpoint the subject—one of which is rather rare and the other quite common.

The rarer of the two is a construction that resembles the true passive but appears to violate the causal order hypothesis. It is found in a small number of languages, including Navajo, Cree, and Ayacucho Quechua, and is usually called the INVERSE construction. In these languages, whichever of the initiator or endpoint is higher in animacy is selected as "subject," the other is selected as "object," and an inverse marker is placed on the verb if the animacy ordering conflicts with the causal ordering. However, in none of these languages (that I am aware of) is there any case marking involved; the only nominal inflections involved have to do with pragmatic nonrelational properties such as obviation in Cree.[12] Instead, verb agreement, frequently a fused morpheme indicating '*x* acting on *y*,' is the relevant relational morphosyntax, with the inverse marker some other verbal affix. As one would expect, the unmarked construction is the one in which the animacy ordering is in harmony with the causal ordering. It appears that, in these constructions, the animacy ordering overrides the causal ordering for the purposes of surface verb agreement—as with the object-oblique case marking in Yokuts and Yoruba.

The second, more widespread phenomenon, is what I will call REVERSE verbs: verbs that appear to denote the same causal chain as other verbs but have the expected endpoint as subject and are not passive. The verbs make up a small set and are listed in table 6.1.

TABLE 6.1 *Reverse Verbs*

Domain	**English Reverse Verb**	**Normal Counterpart**
Space	*include, contain*	*occupy*
Possession	*have, own*	*belong to* (?)
Communication	*hear*	*tell*
Transfer (poss.)	*receive, get* [nonvol.]	*send, give*
Causality	*suffer, undergo*	. . .

The reverse verbs are problematic no matter what solution is offered for them, though some solutions are better than others. The reverse verbs fall into two classes, the stative reverse verbs and the causal reverse verbs.

The stative reverse verbs differ from the process passives in that they are all stative. This means that the transfer verbs are not really reverses of their normal counterparts, which are processes. I will examine the locative and possessive reverse verbs first. In 5.4.1, I analyzed the normal counterpart of the locative reverse verbs, *occupy*, as covering both the stative segment and the coerced figure-ground segment. Another way to analyze *occupy* is to use the uncoerced representation, given in figure 6.3.

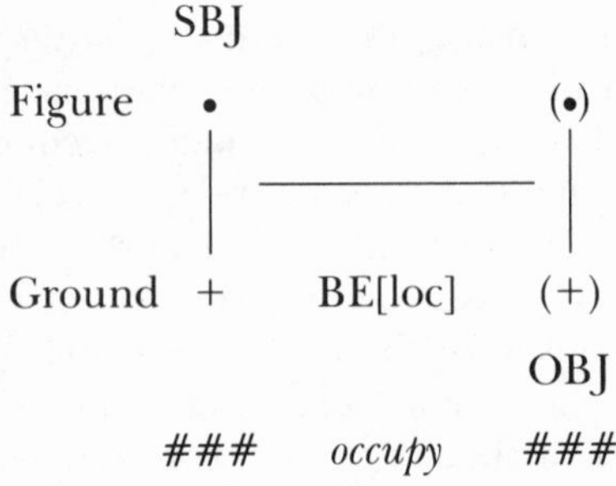

FIGURE 6.3. *Representation of* occupy

In this analysis, *occupy* selects the figure as subject and the ground as direct object in a rather arbitrary division of labor between subject and object that happens to obey the figure-first coercion. If the figure-first coercion is ruled out as irrelevant in this type of construction, which is plausible since it is intended to apply only to the creation of *new,* noncausal arcs, then one can argue that *occupy* simply takes one possible subject-object choice and *include* and *contain* take the other. Likewise, *have* may be analyzed as based on the same structure, dividing subject and object between possessor and possessed, as in figure 6.4.

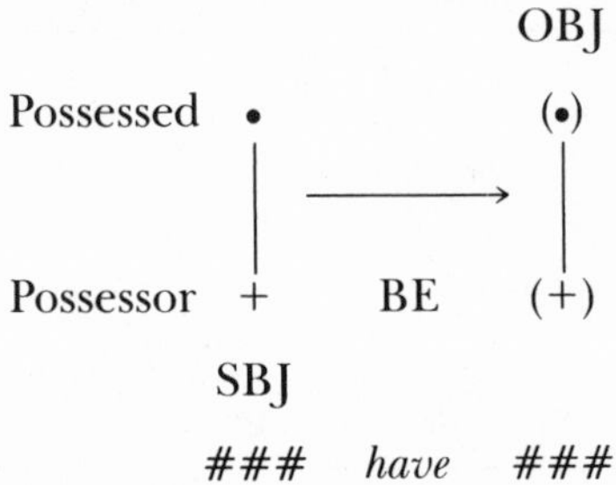

FIGURE 6.4. *Representation of* have

Finally, *receive* and *get* (in its involuntary reading) may be subjected to the same analysis by treating them as "result passives," not unlike *like* or *be surprised at,* of uncoerced versions of their normal counterparts *give* or *send* (and *hear,* in a similar fashion). This solution is not particularly palatable, but it provides an acceptable analysis within the framework without weakening or jeopardizing the extensive results already gained by it.

There is no complementary counterpart to *have* in the way that *occupy* is the counterpart to *contain,* although *belong,* taking a subsequent oblique possessor, is very close. However, *have* also has the virtue of respecting the animacy hierarchy in subject-object choice. It may even be appropriate to think of *have* as a stative subject-experiencer verb, like other English subject-experiencer verbs (see 5.5.1). Affectedness (i.e., being the endpoint rather than initiator of an AFF arc), not possession, underlies the following extended use of nonvolitional *have:*

(25) *I had my paper rejected.*

(26) *I had my insurance renewed.*

The causal reverse verbs differ from the others in two ways, however: they appear to be processes rather than states, and their second argument must denote the action of which the subject is the endpoint, not the initiator. The second argument may be a direct object, or it may be governed by the (expected) antecedent oblique:

(27) *John suffered the loss of all his family in the war.*

(28) *The office is undergoing renovation.*

(29) *Mary is suffering from arthritis.*

The "affective" *have* also appears to be an activity verb rather than a state, unlike its reverse-possession source:

(30) *Fred is having his wisdom teeth removed.*

The causal reverse verbs are probably a catchall means to describe any action from the point of view of the "patient," as in figure 6.5.

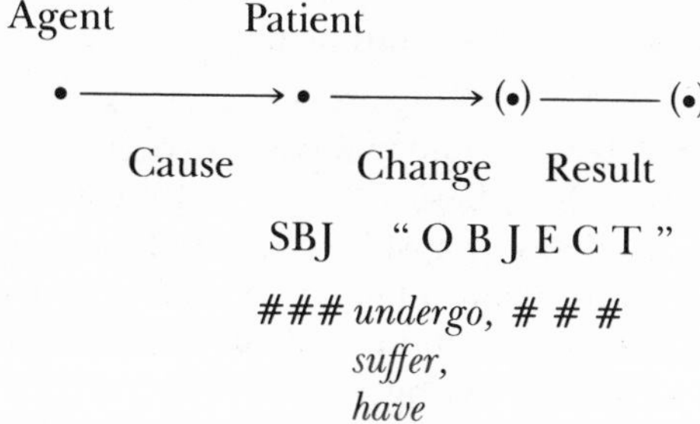

FIGURE 6.5. *Representation of causal reverse verbs*

The causal reverse verbs such as *undergo, suffer,* and affective *have* simply describe the fact of the "patient" being at the starting point of the causal chain at which patient undergoes the change described by the action, which is the object of the causal reverse verb.[13]

Having described the function of the passive voice in the causal structure model, we may turn to the problem of the markedness relations between active and passive voice and between subsequent and antecedent obliques. I have described antecedent oblique phrases and the passive voice as means to represent "unnatural" or "atypical" combinations of causal ordering and topicality, just as the function-indicating morphosyntactic constructions described in 2.3 represent the "unnatural" or "atypical" combinations of lexical semantic class and pragmatic function. In order to demonstrate that the correlation described by the causal order hypothesis is the "natural" one, one must present evidence that that correlation is typologically unmarked.

It has been widely observed that the active voice construction is unmarked compared to the passive construction. The passive almost always involves the addition of a nonzero derivational morpheme to the active verb form (Keenan 1985:250–61). Behaviorally, there are frequently restrictions on passives with respect to the animacy of the agentive phrase. That is, the agentive phrase cannot be higher in animacy than the (patient) subject in a passive, whereas the patient may be higher in animacy than the agent in the active, as in the Quiché examples (Mondloch 1978:47, 59; cf. DeLancey 1981:638, who notes that the English counterpart is not that good either):

(25) *k-* *in-* *ki-* *¢uk* *-ux*
PRES- 1SG.ABS- 3PL.ERG- look.for -TRANS
'They are looking for me.'

(26) **š-* *kun* *-aš* *lē* *yawāp̂* *w-* *umal*
PAST- cure -PASS the sick.one 1SG.POSS- by
'?The sick one was cured by me.'

Finally, text counts demonstrate that passives occur in much lower frequency than actives (Greenberg 1966a:45–46; Givón 1979:58).

There is also evidence that subsequent oblique thematic roles are less marked than antecedent oblique roles. In most cases, both are structurally marked since both are oblique phrases. However, it may be that the frequently occurring primary objects of ditransitives described in 6.1, and the double objects of some Bantu languages, represent structurally unmarked subsequent obliques (the problem with this argument is that they are no longer obliques but actually objects in these constructions). Behaviorally, many more languages have applicative verbal forms for subsequent obliques than for antecedent obliques, and, if a language has an antecedent applicative (instrument or manner), then it has a subsequent applicative (benefactive, recipient, locative "goal"). Finally, subsequent and antecedent oblique thematic roles were counted in the Quiché, Nguna, Soddo, and Ute texts used for the modifier counts in 2.5, and the subsequent obliques were more frequent than the antecedent obliques in all four languages (although, as with the modifiers, the numbers are low; see table 6.2).

TABLE 6.2 *Text Frequency of Subsequent and Antecedent Oblique Thematic Roles*

	Quiché	Nguna	Soddo	Ute
Number of subsequent oblique phrases	34	81	33	32
Number of antecedent oblique phrases	14	13	22	17

Thus, the causal order hypothesis does represent the typologically unmarked correlation between causal sequence and topicality and underlies the grammatical relations hierarchy. The analysis of subjects, objects, and obliques presented in chapters 4–6 is therefore directly comparable to the analysis of nouns, verbs, and adjectives presented in chapters 2 and 3.

6.3 Reflexive, Middle, and Other "Voice" Constructions

The middle voice, and the reflexive construction from which it is frequently derived, has a different function from the passive voice. Whereas the passive voice indicates a marked correlation between causal sequence and topicality, the reflexive and middle voice constructions are used for yet another nonprototypical causal type.

Another characteristic of the prototypical causal structure is that distinct roles are played by distinct individuals in a single arc of the causal chain. Of course, situations exist that do not possess this characteristic. One type is the intransitive verb: states and processes that are undergone by a single individual do not generally have a distinct initiator and endpoint because the role is actually neither. As was mentioned in 5.5.1, for this reason there is a lot of typological variation in the assignment of the intransitive subject: as "subject" (nominative), as absolutive, or split between "actor" ("active"), "undergoer" ("stative"), and even a variable or neutral case marking. I have expressed the mixed status of intransitive subjects by using a parenthesized node (•) at the end of a causal arc for an intransitive process or state.

The other common example of nondistinct arguments in distinct roles are found when one individual plays two roles in the causal chain, introducing "feedback loops" into the chain. The classic example is what I will call the DIRECT REFLEXIVE, such as *John killed himself,* in which the endpoint of the nonreflexive (basic) verb causal segment is identical to the initiator of the basic verb causal segment. These situation types are the ones that give rise to what has been called the "middle" voice. This voice form indicates that the participant expressed as subject is both the initiator and the endpoint in a causal chain (although it is also extended to other uses as well).

Typologically, one finds middle-voice constructions in a large number of situation types in which the subject is initiator and endpoint of causal segments larger than the basic verb causal segment, in semantic verb classes that describe "inherently middle" actions (such as verbs of obtaining in which the initiator is automatically also a benefactive participant by virtue of coming into possession of the endpoint), and even in intransitive verb forms. An overview of the argument for this characterization of the middle voice, and its relation to the direct reflexive construction, can be found in Croft, Shyldkrot, and Kemmer (1988) and Kemmer (1988; cf. Faltz 1985; and Lichtenberk 1985, the latter studying a closely related phenomenon, reciprocals, in a usage type semantic framework). In this section, I will present evidence that middle voice types are marked (nonprototypical) constructions.

The fact that these situations are nonprototypical is supported by evidence that the expression of these situation types—unlike the distinct-argument situation types but like intransitive "subject"—is typologically variable. That is to say, they are encoded in surface morphosyntactic structure in a number of fundamentally different ways in different languages and even in the same language. This contrasts with the expression of a prototypical situation, which will be typologically invariant along the relevant parameters. Thus, for example, I would expect transitive verbs with two clearly distinct participants to be encoded in essentially the same way across natural languages in terms of the causal structure and subject/object choice (though of course there will be variation as to which encoding strategy, case, agreement, and/or order is used).

I will illustrate the different surface structure strategies with the example of symmetric predicates in English, both normally symmetric predicates such as *meet* and reciprocal situations with normally nonsymmetric predicates such as *talk* (*to*). The first encoding strategy is to express the situation type with an active transitive form, arbitrarily making one of the participants the subject and the other the object:

(28) *Don met Sam.*

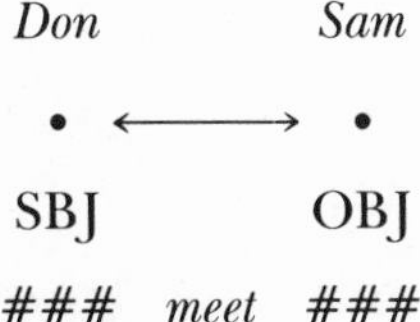

Of course, in nonsymmetric predicates, the reciprocity is lost:

(29) *Susan talked to Brian.*

Susan [utterance] *Brian*

• ⟶ [•] ⟶ •

SBJ OBL

talk

The second strategy for encoding the symmetrical double roles is to express the situation type as a transitive form, but conjoining the two participants as subjects and using a "pseudo-object" that has the syntactic position and morphological structure of an appropriate direct object or oblique but is actually an indicator of the reciprocity of the action. In English, this is accomplished by *each other;* English has a separate "pseudo-object" form for reflexives, but many languages have the same form.

(30) *Don and Sam met each other.*

Don • *each other*

Sam • ⟷ •

SBJ "OBJ"

meet

(31) *Susan and Brian talked to each other.*

The third strategy is to express the reciprocal action as an intransitive form. This strategy reflects the fact that the two participants are in the same role, or rather roles, with respect to the action. The intransitive form may be in the active voice, as in English, or in some sort of middle-voice expression (using a reflexive or a middle/mediopassive verbal form):

(32) *Don and Sam met.*

Don • ⟶ (•) (*Sam*)

Sam • ⟶ (•) (*Don*)

SBJ

meet

(33) *Susan and Brian talked.*

The conjoined subject intransitive encoding strategy can alternate with an intransitive encoding strategy with a single subject and a comitative oblique since in the intransitive coercion of the situation type the second participant is at the same position in the causal chain:[14]

(34) *Don met with Sam.*

Sam *Don*

• • ⟶ (•)

OBL SBJ

meet

(35) *Susan talked with Brian.*

The various reciprocal strategies are also found with the verbs of exchange discussed in 5.5.2. Unlike the other verbs describing the commercial situation, which describe different segments of it, the verbs of exchange express the reciprocality of the whole transaction situation (see the diagram below). The two individuals involved are both initiators since they cooperate to bring about the commercial transaction (note that the items exchanged must be conflated as well), and so the whole situation is reciprocal:

(36) *John and Fred exchanged/traded cars with each other.*

(37) *John and Fred exchanged/traded cars.*

(38) *John exchanged/traded cars with Fred.*

Agent 1 • ⟶ • Item 1

Agent 2 • ⟵ • Item 2

exchange/trade

The range of strategies reflects a vacillation between treating the nonprototypical middle situation as a transitive form (to the extent that the initiator and endpoint are distinct roles) or as an intransitive one (to the extent that they are identical). The ability to vary between transitive and intransitive forms suggests that the parenthetical-node notation for intransitives is not simply a notational hack to fit intransitives into the transitive action notation but in fact reflects an ambivalence in the conceptualization of actions with nondistinct arguments that is reflected in the typological variation in their encoding in surface structure.

Another, very different sort of construction that has been called "middle" and certainly is found with middle voice forms in many languages is the one illustrated by *This book sells well.* Van Oosten (1977, 1986) and Lakoff (1977) argue that this construction, which van Oosten calls "patient-subject" construction, is used when the action (selling, or selling well) is the result of some property of the "patient" (e.g., the trendiness of the book). The causal representation of this analysis, given below, would account for both the appearance of the "patient" as the subject and the presence of the middle voice marker (due to the subject/initiator also being the endpoint):

(39) *The book sells well.*

book			(stores)		(*book*)
•	⟶	(•) ⟶	•	⟶	(•)
	(Be-Popular)	Cause-Be-Able		Sell	
SBJ					
###		*sell*(-MIDDLE)			###

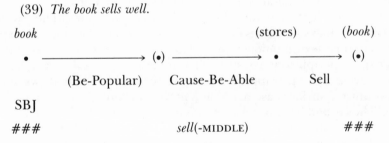

The interesting question here is why the middle form has spread to include just these causal arc types.

Finally, there are two other "voice" alternations that must be described in the causal structure model: antipassive and impersonal passive. The antipassive is largely used to render normal objects/endpoints pragmatically optional and correlates with very high topicality of the initiator relative to the endpoint (e.g., in Nez Perce [Rude 1988] and in Chamorro [Cooreman 1988]). The antipassive has the semantic effect of allowing events normally conceptualized as transitive actions to be alternatively conceptualized as intransitive activities (cf. 4.2 on affectedness)—that is, they are the functional inverse of applicatives on intransitives, and might be better called "antiapplicatives" (see

Heath [1976], who discusses several functions of this type for the antipassive as well as others). This in turn appears to have the effect of placing more pragmatic attention on the action since the endpoint of the action is completely "out of focus" (see Cooreman [1988, 587] on Tagalog and Mondloch [1978:66] on Quiché).

Impersonal passives—often middle in form—include both transitive and intransitive verbs in which the subject is absent or manifests itself as a passive agent, the verb is passivized, and (in the case of transitives) the direct object remains a direct object (see Comrie 1977). Thus, in the transitive case at least, the impersonal passive does not appear to signify a shift in pragmatic prominence from the initiator to the endpoint since the endpoint does not become subject. Instead, there is a shift of emphasis away from the subject (optional, and normally absent) to the action itself: hence its use in intransitives as well as transitives. Thus, antipassives and impersonal passives have rather similar pragmatic functions: rather than reflecting shifts in the topicality of the participants, they reflect a shift in pragmatic attention away from all participants to the action itself.

6.4 What Is a Possible Verb?

In the last three chapters, I have proposed a model of verbal semantics independent of natural language verbal predicates. The causal structure analysis analyzes events in terms of criteria that are independent of their lexicalization as individual verbs, verbs with affixes, serial verbs, or periphrastic constructions in various natural languages. I have argued that this approach to verbal semantic analysis allows us to account for surface case marking patterns, including subject and object choice, and have sketched its application to voice, valency-increasing affixes, noun incorporation, and certain derivational processes.

In the same way as we found in the analysis of syntactic categories, the best account of the cross-linguistic evidence is via an analysis in which semantic factors and pragmatic factors interact to yield the attested surface case relations as expressed chiefly by case marking and voice. I have focused on the semantic factors in the last three chapters. In conclusion, I wish to focus on the final significant semantic factor in subject-object choice, case marking, and voice: the nature of the verb itself. From a semantic perspective, the primary constraint on subject-object choice in the linguistic expression of an event is whether the verb semantics allows it. Thus, the question, What is a possible verb? is a central one in understanding how subjects and objects are chosen in grammar and, consequently, in cognition.

The problem of possible verbs requires a cognitive approach to semantic analysis even more directly than the similar problem of determining what are possible nouns (i.e., possible categorizations of objects). The reason for this is simple: most objects come already individuated. The external world spatially isolates objects, and objects move or can be manipulated in space as autonomous entities. Thus, a crucial prerequisite for categorization is already satisfied in most cases without any necessary appeal to cognition, other than our mental receptiveness to this external fact. Consequently, cognitive semantic analyses of nouns have focused mainly on the higher-level issue of the grouping of individuated objects into similarity sets ("classification") and on those objects for which individuation is problematic, such as mass nouns and pluralia tanta (see Wierzbicka 1985) and relational nouns.

Verbs, on the other hand, are a much more difficult problem from the point of view of categorization. Verbs represent a categorization of events. Events do not come clearly individuated in space or time (the latter dimension being relevant for events but much less so for objects). The world is made up of an extremely complex causal network of which we encounter just fragments (see 4.4.4). Nor can events be physically manipulated, in space or in time, in the way that objects can. Thus, the two basic criteria for individuating objects cannot be used to individuate events. The individuation of events becomes the first problem that must be addressed in this realm of linguistic and cognitive categorization. Because the individuation of events does not "come naturally," it is likely that there is a strong cognitive element to the individuation of events: that is, the process of isolating a fragment of the causal chain and naming it with a verb involves more cognitive processing than the isolation of an object and naming it with a noun.

I have already raised certain fundamental issues in the cognitive semantics of verbs in chapter 4. In particular, in 4.4.4 I argued that—in the spirit of this whole volume—verb meaning represents a conceptualization of events so that a particular event class is a privileged one, the prototype, and other event types, such as those described in section 6.3 just above, are nonprototypical but must be coerced into the "idealized cognitive model" (ICM; see Lakoff 1987; and below) that is best represented by the prototype. In most of the rest of the chapters on verbal semantics, I have concentrated on the prototypical event as that of volitional causation and described various nonvolitional, noncausal relations that must be expressed in human languages and the principles that govern their expression. Now I turn to the more general problem of verbhood.

In 4.4.4, I defined a verb as denoting a segment of a causal chain—in some sense, a "single event." The following properties were proposed for the ICM of a simple event:

a) events are segments of the causal network;
b) events involve individuals acting on other individuals (transmission of force);
c) transmission of force is asymmetric;
d) simple events are nonbranching causal chains.

The prototype effects, in particular, typological variation in the expression of nonprototypical events and the coercion of nonprototypical event types into the single causal chain model, have been illustrated quite extensively here.

If we turn to the question of what is a possible verb, then we must examine the internal structure of events, that is, the atomic causal arcs that make them up. As I argued in 4.4.3, the major properties that structure the internal structure of verbs are causal relations (transmission of force) and aspect (stative vs. processual). Using the criteria presented in 4.4.3, one can classify events into EVENT TYPES: causative, inchoative, stative, etc. The classification of events into event types crosscuts the classification of events by semantic domain such as posture, motion, etc. The latter will be called EVENT CLASSES.

In a number of places in the causal structure analysis, in particular, the discussion of mental verbs in 5.5.1, I have identified three common causal-aspectual verb types: CAUSATIVE, INCHOATIVE, and STATIVE. The three types are illustrated by the following sentences and their accompanying causal chains:

Causative:

(40) *The rock broke the window.*

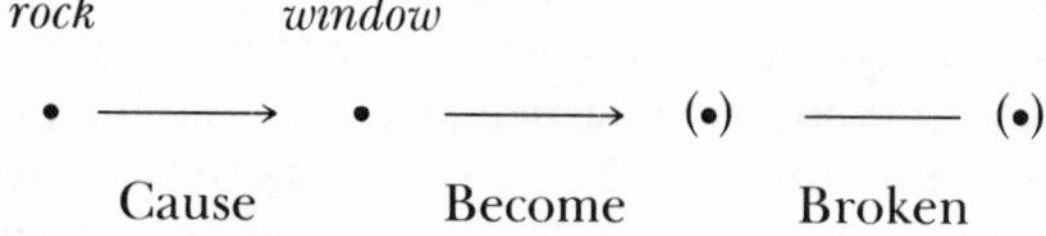

Inchoative:

(41) *The window broke.*

window

• ——→ (•) —— (•)

Become Broken

Stative:

(42) *The window is broken.*

window

• ———— (•)

Broken

This tripartite classification is quite a familiar one, representing a semantic version of the major syntactic division between stative "verbs" (i.e., adjectives; see 2.3 and below) and processual verbs and a division of the latter into transitive and intransitive verbs. One would expect that these major syntactic divisions would have some cognitive semantic basis; in fact, we have already examined evidence in chapters 2 and 3 that adjectives and verbs are cognitively significant categories. I propose that these three causal-aspectual event types are the prototypical event types. That is to say, causatives, inchoatives, and statives provide the idealized cognitive model for the *internal* structure of simple events.

I say "model" in the singular because the causal chain model shows us that the causative, inchoative, and stative event types are not independent. The causal chain of the inchoative type is simply the second and third arcs of the causative event type, and the causal chain of the stative type is simply the third (last) arc of the causative type. In fact, the causal chain model allows us to unify these three event types into one. The causal chain model reveals that the simple event ICM is really an ICM for a single event structure, the causative-inchoative-stative structure represented in full by the causative type. The three types are subsets of the idealized event structure, oriented toward the endpoint of the event: the last arc (stative), the last two arcs (inchoative), and the whole event type (causative). I will call these the three VIEWS of a simple event, or EVENT VIEWS.

In order to demonstrate that the three event views and the single endpoint-oriented cause-become-state structure that defines them represent the ICM, two hypotheses must be supported. The first is that other possible event types are coerced into the cause-become-state structure. The second is that any event has the potential to be conceptualized as a causative, an inchoative, and a stative.

There are three other possible event types: transitive statives, ditransitives, and "activity" (in Vendler's terms) or "middle" verb types. The first two have already been accounted for. Transitive stative verbs, specifically, stative expressions of location and possession, can be subsumed under the stative type, by virtue of the coercions described in

5.4. Ditransitive verbs are causative versions of the transitive stative verbs (causing a locative, possessive, or other stative relation to come about, as in *put, give,* and *show,* respectively) and so can be subsumed under the causative type. The last verb type that is attested, the activity verbs, will be seen to fall under the inchoative type.

The second hypothesis that must be supported is that any event can be expressed, that is to say conceptualized, as a causative, an inchoative, or a stative. This appears to go against common belief, which is that some verbs can be categorized as causative, some inchoative and some stative, based on their ability to occur in one but not the other two constructions. But the truth is that any verb (or adjective) can indeed be placed in a construction that is either causative, inchoative, or stative and be interpreted as denoting a causative, inchoative, or stative event view.

Some roots can do this without alteration. For example, the English verb *break* is either a causative or an inchoative verb and is one of a large class of such verbs in English. There are even some roots, such as *open,* which can be either causative, inchoative, or stative:

(43) *I opened the door.*

(44) *The door opened.*

(45) *The door is open.*

This phenomenon is generally analyzed as representing an ambiguity in the lexical items *break* and *open* and their brethren. However, the ambiguity analysis is unattractive in this case because the ambiguity is systematic (although not perfectly so). In the cognitive semantic analysis, the event type denoted by the root is coerced into one or another of the three simple event views, and the interpretation of the whole—verb root plus attendant grammatical properties indicating transitivizing, passivizing, or stativizing morphology or syntactic constructions. This grammatical process I call SHIFT (Croft MS, following bedded. In other words, *open* in a transitive case frame is causative, *open* in an intransitive case frame is inchoative, and *open* in a stative copula construction is stative.

For most verbs in English, and in other languages, the coercion is accomplished by means of ancillary morphosyntax: causativizing, detransitivizing, passivizing, or stativizing morphology or syntactic constructions. This grammatical process I call SHIFT (Croft MSb, following Talmy 1977).[15] The noncognitive semantic analysis of shift morphology is that the root is inherently causative, stative, or whatever and the morphosyntax changes the meaning so that it "fits" the construction (causative, inchoative, stative). However, shift is essentially the same process as coercion, where a root is placed into a grammatical construction without any "extra" morphosyntax, namely, the conceptualization of whatever is denoted by the root in the fashion implied by the grammatical construction. In a cognitive semantic analysis, the presence of shift morphosyntax is an indicator of something else, namely, the prototypicality—unmarkedness—of the root's being found in the grammatical construction in question. This will be discussed further below.

Therefore, one need demonstrate only that virtually any verbal (or adjectival) ROOT can be embedded in a causative, inchoative, or stative construction, with or without shift. This is fairly straightforward to demonstrate because most languages, like English, have productive shift morphosyntax. In English, the most straightforward cases are stative expressions:

(46) *John is sick* (*thanks to the food here*).

(47) *John got sick* (*from the food*).

(48) *The food made John sick.*

English uses the verb *get* to indicate the inchoative process that brings about the state and a periphrastic causative construction with *make* to indicate the causative event type.

Most causative verb roots that can be used intransitively fit into the *break* pattern, in which the root can function transitively as well, and the stative past participle (the "stative" or "adjectival" passive) indicates the resulting state:

(49) *I broke the vase.*

(50) *The vase broke.*

(51) *The vase is broken.*

However, there are a number of intransitive verbs that are not obviously inchoative, that is, do not obviously lead into a resulting state (they can take the periphrastic causative with *make,* however). These are the "activity" verbs referred to above. Nevertheless, activity verbs can be conceptualized as leading to a resulting state in the right context, using perfectivizing verb particles and adverbs like *all:*

(52) *Torey is all danced out.*

(53) *Torey danced for four hours.*

(54) *We made Torey dance.*

Actually, verbs such as *dance* also fall into the category of "indefinite null object" verbs, verbs that may take an object but may occur intransitively with an understood indefinite object: *dance* (*a waltz*), *sing* (*an aria*), *smoke* (*a cigarette*), *eat* (*a meal*), etc. This alternative construction appears to represent a violation of the event view model: the indefinite object intransitive verb represents an "event view" of just the cause arc. There is another analysis possible, however: there are two sets of event views corresponding to two ways of conceptualizing the event in the cause-become-state structure. The first way, represented by *dance* in (52)–(54), has no object and conceptualizes dancing as an activity involving only the agent:

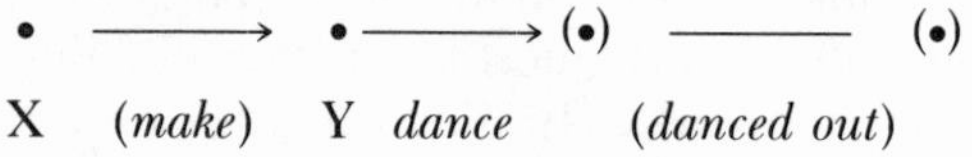

• ——→ •——→ (•) ——— (•)

X (*make*) Y *dance* (*danced out*)

The second way, represented by *dance* in (55)–(57) and *eat* in (58)–(60), has an object and conceptualizes the activity as the creation of a performance:

(55) *Elena danced a Serbian kolo.*

(56) *The Serbian kolo got danced already.*

(57) ??*The kolo is danced.* [stative passive reading]

(58) *I ate the cookies.*

(59) *The cookies got eaten.*

(60) *The cookies are eaten.*

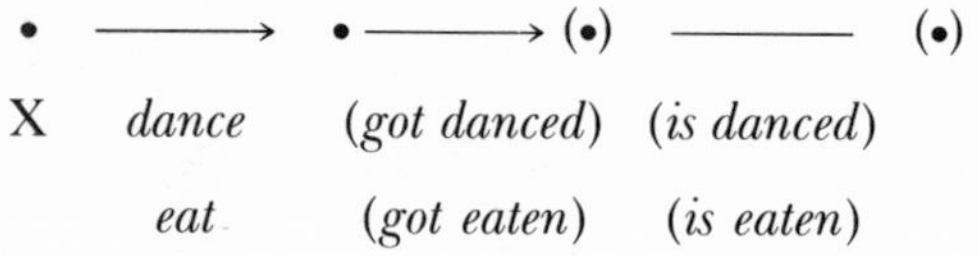

• ——→ •——→ (•) ——— (•)

X *dance* (*got danced*) (*is danced*)

eat (*got eaten*) (*is eaten*)

Thus, we are not dealing with an anomalous verbal pattern of detransitivization; we are dealing with two alternative verbal patterns representing two alternative conceptualizations of the event in terms of the basic event structure.

What all these verbs have in common is that they represent the coming into existence or passing out of existence (usually by ingestion) of the object rather than some alteration of the object. The object is often not a physical thing but a transitory object like the performance of a dance or a song; for that reason, such verbs are also conceptualized as activities of the agent. Either conceptualization—activity or creation event—is possible, although, if the object is not a physical thing, it is difficult to get the stative event view of the creation event conceptualization, and, if the object is a physical thing, it is difficult to get the stative event view of the activity conceptualization:

(61) *They made me eat.*

(62) *I ate.*

(63) ??*I'm all eaten out.*

The reason for these questionable sentences is presumably that it is difficult to conceptualize the activity as a lasting state of the agent (rather than the object created, if the object is itself lasting) and that it is difficult to conceptualize the existence of a transitory thing such as a dance as a lasting state.

The important thing to note here is that conceptualization of the denoted event in all three event views, indeed, alternative conceptualizations of the event, is grammatically possible for any such intransitive verb. The difficulty in processing questionable sentences is conceptual. Can one think of a way in which an activity such as dancing will lead to a state that is the result of that activity? Poor acceptability judgments for sentences such as (52), (57), and (63) are due to implausibility, not ungrammaticality. Activity verbs are intransitive processes that deviate the furthest from the inchoative prototype in that they have a negligible final state, one that is brought out only in certain contexts.

The final case is perhaps the semantically most difficult one. Can an action that requires an external causer, such as building or digging (in which the object is caused to exist), be conceptualized inchoatively or statively? The answer again is yes—or, more precisely, acceptability is a conceptual problem, not a grammatical one:

(64) *The contractors built the cabin in three months.*

(65) *The cabin got built in three months.*

(66) *In three months, the cabin was built.*

(67) *The electric company dug a trench through our backyard.*

(68) *The trench got dug yesterday.*

(69) *The trench is dug.*

The English strategy to get rid of a required external agent is the *get* passive. The *get* passive allows the speaker to represent the event as a process "without an external agent." This does not mean that there is no external agent; it simply means that the external agent is unimportant or is absent for other reasons, as in:

(70) *He got killed (in an accident).*

(71) *I got cut in the arm.*

In these examples, it is possible that the agent is not human or not volitional; the agent may even be the subject of these sentences (i.e., the subject may be responsible for getting killed or cut, or a volitional action by the subject led to his getting killed or cut).

An example from another language in which a nonpassive structure contrasting with a passive one is used for the comparable function will perhaps make the point clearer. In Japanese, the *-rare* passive construction is used for passives by which the subject is affected by the event, even if the subject is not directly involved in the event. However, there are also intransitive forms derived from transitives with nonproductive morphology that are frequently translated as passives in English, such as *makasu* 'defeat'/*makaru* 'be defeated.' These derived intransitives can sometimes be used as alternatives to the passive constructions, but with the implication that an external agent either does not exist or is backgrounded (Jacobsen 1982: 151)

(72) *Saikin* *kanban* *ga* *atti-kotti* *tatu* *yoo ni*
recently signs NOM here.and.there go.up MANNER
natte *-kita*
become -come.PAST
'Recently, signs have been going up here and there.'

(73) *Saikin* *kanban* *ga* *atti-kotti* *taterarete*
recently signs NOM here.and.there put.up.PASS
-kita
-come.PAST
'Recently, signs have been erected here and there.'

As Jacobsen puts it, "What 'happens to' the signs in [72] and [73] is essentially the same, the difference being that the *rare* in [73] makes explicit the fact that the happening finds its source in some (nonspecified) external agent" (Jacobsen 1982: 151). The passivelike intransitive, here translated as an intransitive 'go up' by Jacobsen, corresponds to the agentless *get* (or process *be*) passive of English, there being no morphological difference between the agentive and the agentless (i.e., agent-backgrounding) passive in English.

Another piece of evidence in support of the unity of the ICM event structure is the striking similarity in the expression of inchoatives, whether the root is normally a causative or a stative:

(74) *The house got built in three months.*

(75) *John got well in three months.*

In English, the auxiliary verb *get* is used to express the inchoative of adjectives and the process passive of transitive verbs. In many other languages, the reflexive construction or a "middle voice" construction also combines the functions of the inchoative of statives and the (usually agentless) passive of transitive verbs (see Croft, Shyldkrot, and Kemmer 1988). This combination of functions did not appear to have any obvious explanation. In the analysis of the ICM of events expressed by verbs, however, this combination of functions simply represents the uniform treatment of the inchoative event view regardless of the semantics of the verbal root.

Thus, it is clear that any event can indeed be conceptualized as a causative, an inchoative, or a stative, thereby supporting the hypothesis that the cause-become-state event structure and the three endpoint-oriented event views associated with it represent the idealized cognitive model of events. The idealized cognitive model of a simple event—that is, a possible verb in human languages—can be summarized as follows:

a) simple events are segments of the causal network;
b) simple events involve individuals acting on other individuals (transmission of force);
c) transmission of force is asymmetric, with distinct participants as initiator and endpoint;
d) simple events are nonbranching causal chains;
e) simple event structure consists of the three-segment causal chain: cause-become-state;
f) simple events are endpoint oriented: possible verbs consist of the last segment (stative), the second and last segments (inchoative), or the whole three segments (causative);
g) simple events are independent; that is, they can be isolated from the rest of the causal network.

The cause-become-state structure simply represents the following (idealized) view of events in the world: changes do not occur without something causing them; changes lead to resulting states; and states come into being and pass away—that is, things change.

Moreover, the event classes are associated with the event views in different ways, reflecting yet another level of organization around cognitive prototypes. The English examples illustrate that there are significant markedness relations between event classes and event views, so that, for example, physical state terms such as *sick* (46)–(48) are unmarked states and verbs of creation such as *build* (55)–(57) are unmarked causatives. A four-language study (English, French, Japanese, and Korean) was performed in order to discover the typological pattern of structural markedness underlying the relation between event classes and event views (Croft, in press b). The study reveals that there are typological prototypes—that is, certain event classes that are always unmarked in the event view—for causatives and statives but not for inchoatives, which behave as if they are an intermediate category.[16] This result conforms with the analysis of semantic prototypes for verbs (causatives) and adjectives (statives) but not for any other intermediate prototypes: as I suggested in 5.5.1, intransitive processes are nonprototypical, having among other things highly variable case marking (nominative, absolutive, or two-way or three-way split case-marking systems).

The event classes that are least marked for the stative event view are the categories of color and size—the lexical semantic classes that are "core adjectives" (Dixon 1977; see 2.1–2.3, 3.3.1). Examination of the prototypical and nonprototypical event classes for the stative event view suggests that certain semantic factors account for the prototypicality of the unmarked event classes. If the property in question is inherent in the object, then it is more likely to be conceptualized as an unmarked stative. An inherent property generally does not change over the lifetime of an object and thus is unlikely to be conceptualized as an unmarked inchoative.[17] Moreover, the relatively unchangeable inherent properties that are unmarked statives[18] do not come about—let alone change—owing to an external cause, being part of the object's nature; hence, they are not unmarked causatives. In other words, unmarked statives are relatively persistent and have unary valency, as well as being states—in still other words, they are prototypical adjectives. Noninherent resulting states are more likely to be transitory ones, subject to change, especially change due to an external agent. Hence, they are expressed as unmarked inchoatives or, in particular, unmarked causatives: the universally unmarked causatives are actions that almost always require an external agent, such as verbs of ingestion ('eat,' 'drink'), force ('push,' 'pull'), and creation ('build,' 'write,' 'make'). These correspond to prototypical verbs: transitory, processual, and binary valency (it appears that "superprototypical" [see 3.3.1] verbs are binary valency [transitive] rather than unary valency since no intransitive process prototype manifests itself).

Finally, I return to the problem that was raised at the beginning of this section (and, in fact, motivated the original analysis of verb meaning in chap. 4): the problem of how events are individuated. The prototypical cause-become-state causal structure represents a unit that is easily isolable from the causal network (see Croft, to appear). In order for an event to be easily isolable from the causal network, it must be conceptualized as not having a clear prior cause and not itself causing another event—that is, the event must have a clear starting point and a clear endpoint. These conditions are satisfied by the cause-become-state event sequence. The clear starting point is provided by human causation since human volition is an "ultimate cause" or autonomous source of causation. This explains why subjects are conceptualized as autonomous sources of causation (see 4.2): they are the starting points of the verbal segment and so must clearly delimit its beginning. The clear endpoint is provided by the ending state: since states do not involve change, they also do not involve transmission of force to another individual. This contributes to the explanation as to why the object is conceptualized as more affected (4.2): a completely affected object is not going to change further, and the resulting state is not likely to affect anything else. Objects are the endpoints of the verbal segment and so must clearly delimit its end.

The two possible grammatical extensions to a verb that change subject and object assignment do not destroy the autonomy of the event. Causatives of transitives (see 6.1) are almost always human agents making other human (or animate) agents do something. This is acceptable because the causer, not the causee, is the volitional agent and thus the autonomous cause. Applicative extensions have the effect of making a benefactive/malefactive participant, the possessor or the ground, into the object of the action. The benefactive/malefactive object is a human being whose mental state is affected by the outcome of the event. This is basically the only way in which a physical state can cause something to happen, and the mental state itself is a clear endpoint of the action. The possessor/ground is simply the other participant of a transitive state; the transitive state remains the last arc of the verbal segment and does not affect any other participants.

Thus, exploration of the problem of what is a possible verb, that is, what event structure can be expressed as a verb, ties together the conceptualization of the major syntactic categories (including nouns, which are the nodes in the event structure ICM) and of subject and object—an appropriate conclusion to this study.

7

Conclusion

In chapter 1, I compared two approaches to universal grammar, generally known as the "formalist" and "functionalist" approaches. Among the various differences between formalist and functionalist approaches, I singled out two factors that represent alternative solutions to the problem of establishing a universal basis for grammatical concepts such as "noun," "verb," and "subject" in a highly variable domain, the class of existing human languages. The formalist approach relies on critical definitions for grammatical concepts, that is, concepts with sharp boundaries. In order to accommodate variability in human languages, the formalist then severs (or at least loosens) the link between a universal grammatical concept and particular grammatical constructions that manifest it. For the functionalist, however, the link between a universal grammatical concept and particular grammatical constructions is too important to give up since that is the foundation on which functional explanations—explanations based on the function of grammatical constructions—are built. Instead, the functionalist loosens the definitions of grammatical concepts, allowing for gradience and prototypicality.

In choosing between methodologies, one must ask, How well do they work? How much progress in understanding fundamental grammatical concepts does the method allow? This volume has demonstrated that the functionalist method, in conjunction with typological analysis, brings us a good way toward understanding some of the most fundamental concepts in grammar: noun, verb, and adjective; reference, predication, and modification; subject, object, and oblique. In chapters 2 and 3, I presented a typological analysis that provides a universal basis for the major syntactic categories "noun," "verb," and "adjective." Since the typological patterns are patterns of variation around a prototype and some of the evidence (behavioral markedness) applies to a specific set of grammatical construction types, adherence to a criterial definition of a category and ignoring the relation between constructions and grammatical concepts would not have allowed us to discover the universal pattern.

The same observations apply to the analysis of case marking in chapters 4–6. Focusing on a single construction, the principles underlying the representation of verbal meaning were revealed and significant progress was made in understanding the concepts "subject," "object," and "oblique." Again, a necessary part of the analysis is a prototype approach to verbal semantics and its contribution to subject-object choice, case marking, and voice and valency-changing processes. Analyzing single constructions cross-linguistically and allowing for prototype structures produces significant results.

These chapters provide analyses of a large number of fundamental grammatical concepts. Certain others are still in need of explication, such as the main-subordinate clause distinction and the head-modifier relation. It is hoped that this volume will provide sound foundations for the exploration of more complex grammatical phenomena whose successful analysis relies crucially on the proper explication of the basic grammatical concepts analyzed here.

In presenting the cross-linguistically valid universal analysis of the fundamental grammatical categories, a cognitive approach to functional explanation has been employed. Central to this approach is the notion of *conceptualization:* a human being does not simply absorb an "objective" reality but actively organizes it in a particular fashion for a particular reason, such as communication. More important, the universal linguistic patterns support the cognitive hypothesis that human beings appear to take specific types of experience and structure their conceptualizations around them. This fact underlies the prototypical and gradient character of the universal grammatical categories. The experiences around which human beings structure their conceptualizations are the prototypes (or, as Lakoff calls them, idealized cognitive models). Other experiences that resemble the prototypical experiences are "coerced" to fit the prototype as well as possible; this gives rise to gradience and to the subtle semantic/pragmatic effects described in 3.2, 4.2, 5.5.1, and 6.4. The less prototypical experiences also are well entrenched and give rise to minor or peripheral categories and nonstandard grammatical relations (e.g., the figure-first coercion).

The cognitive approach underlines an important aspect of the functionalist method of analysis, the relation between language and other human activities and cognitive processes. Language studies are uniquely positioned to contribute to our knowledge of human behavior because language is an "externalized" entity that can be studied more concretely than other aspects of mind, culture, and society. Cognitive hypotheses such as the one described in the preceding paragraph gain considerably when support from linguistic analyses can be adduced.

Finally, it must not be forgotten that there are reasons that human beings select certain experiences as the focal ones around which cognitive structures are built. Some of these reasons are certainly buried deep in innate cognitive processes that have evolved over eons. However, some of these reasons can still be unearthed: language is the product of evolution, and the functional adaptive pressures still exist. The adaptive factors are to be found in the dynamics of interpersonal interaction as well as in cognition. This is particularly noticeable in the case of conventionalization. All languages conventionalize grammar to a great extent; it is the conventions rather than the fluid aspects of language that are written into grammatical descriptions. But convention is a matter of degree and can change over time. The analyst must be able to tease apart the conventional and the functionally motivated; they do not occur neatly separated into modules. By recognizing that grammar is dynamic and evolving, one can perceive the consistency of the functional principles that govern language dynamics better than if one treats grammar as a static, abstract structure.

NOTES

Chapter One

1. The aforementioned linguists have focused on discourse function, but other functionalist linguists have also emphasized the role of semantic (symbolic) function and social function in explaining language structure.

2. The term "formal" is actually a bit confusing. The phrase "formal theory" is actually ambiguous: it can refer to either a theory that can be formalized mathematically or a theory that makes primary reference to linguistic form rather than linguistic function. It is the latter meaning that is intended here. It *is* possible for a functionalist linguistic theory to be formalized in the sense of "made mathematically precise," though some functionalists (e.g., George Lakoff) to argue that their theories should not and even cannot be so formalized. This issue will not be discussed here.

3. Other fundamental concepts are "clause" and "sentence"; "head" and "modifier" or "dependent"; "main" and "subordinate" or "complement" clause; and, in phonology, "word," "syllable," "segment," "phoneme," "consonant," and "vowel."

4. The same of course applies to doing phonology: universal criteria for establishing a "word," "syllable," "vowel," etc. are necessary preconditions for studying the universal properties of phonological structures.

5. At the phonological level, it is worse. All we can observe is the sound stream; segmentation into consonants and vowels, syllables and higher phonological units, is extremely difficult.

6. By contrast, the differences between the various theories within each approach are relatively minor.

7. This test makes the additional assumption that we can determine the subject of the passive sentence; we will assume that this can be done or at least that it poses no problems any different from the ones I am about to describe.

8. It should be pointed out that there is some question regarding the data for the criterial test of subjecthood used in Dyirbal, conjunction formation (Heath 1979); for further discussion, see below.

9. Actually, this comparison exaggerates certain differences between the formalist and the functionalist approach. Functionalists must also "parameterize" their analyses, in that they must specify where the boundary or cutoff point is for a particular hierarchical scale or prototype category in a particular language. The difference is that functionalists argue that in their analyses the *same* category, e.g., topic, is being expressed in the equivalent constructions across languages, and in this sense one is dealing with the "same" domain of application cross-linguistically.

10. The term "argument" suffers from analogous boundary problems, as does "passive"; I will not attempt to describe it here.

11. Yet another construction that may or may not be a passive is found in Bambara, where the patient is made the subject, the agent is placed in an oblique phrase, but the predicate does not have a passive marking (affix or auxiliary) associated with it (Christopher Culy, personal communication).

12. There is also a danger of circularity here, of looking until one finds manifestations of the distinctions one had in mind in the first place, which in effect imposes categories that may be of little relevance to the overall organization of the language.

13. Anderson calls the coding rules "morphological." This is not an accurate description of the difference between the two rule types, however. Case marking and verb agreement characterize the relations between a main predicate and its dependent arguments, clearly a syntactic phenomenon. In more recent theories of generative grammar, case assignment and agreement are treated as syntactic rules.

14. In fact, this approach was advocated by Comrie (1978) and Moravcsik (1978) (and also by Perlmutter and Postal in their 1974 Linguistic Society of America lectures—Matthew Dryer, personal communication), with respect to ergativity, as the "rule-based" approach to ergativity. In this approach, one does not try to determine whether a *language* is "ergative" or "accusative" or even "superficially ergative but deeply accusative." Instead, one inquires as to whether a particular *rule* in a natural language is ergative or accusative, i.e., what combination(s) of A, S, and P the rule refers to.

15. This is closely related to the skeptical assertion, occasionally mentioned in the literature, that a purely distributional account of syntactic categories would lead to the postulation of a different syntactic category for every word.

16. It is worth noting at this point that part of the reason that this problem arises in the formalist paradigm is the preference for highly autonomous components, in which interaction of this sort is minimized. Some recent approaches to syntax, particularly Sadock's "autolexical syntax" (Sadock 1985) and some recent work in Lexical-Functional Grammar (Bresnan and Kanerva 1989; Sells, Zaenen, and Zec 1987), question the autonomist view of syntactic components. This development shrinks the gap between formalist and functionalist approaches to analysis. I would still maintain, however, that the logical conclusion of this interacting-components view will be a "component" for every major constructional feature and therefore that explanation will eventually be focused on the function of the construction.

17. This is often identified with the "surface structure" of formalist representations, and for that reason functionalist analyses are sometimes criticized as "superficial" or not "abstract" enough to provide an explanation of the structure. Part of this criticism, of course, has to do with differing concepts of explanation: formal (structural) as opposed to functional (semantic-pragmatic), as was described above. However, it is also worth noting that closer examina-

tion of the surface structure representations of formalist theories, however, reveals that much of the information in the "abstract" representations is actually present in the surface representation. In Lexical-Functional Grammar, the c-structure representations contain equations that will yield the f-structure relations. In Government and Binding Theory, S-structure contains various types of empty categories and nonbranching phrase structure nodes that, when combined with the many principles of the various modules of the theory, will yield the D-structure representation and other types of grammatical relations not "visible" in the surface structure. In Generalized Phrase Structure Grammar, which has only one level of syntactic representation, the phrase structure node features, combined with the general principles governing feature percolation and feature combinations, will provide the kind of information that is captured by the abstract structures of the other two theories. Thus, the surface structure representations of these theories are actually quite rich.

18. It is worth noting that derivational models of syntactic components cannot handle these phenomena without global constraints or output constraints because conspiracies are properties of the surface construction, not the source structure or the derivation.

19. This table of course oversimplifies the situation since the other parameters that affect the ergative/accusative pattern have been excluded. Data is taken from Anderson (1976; Dyirbal, Avar), Bresnan and Simpson (1982; Warlpiri), and Mondloch (1978; Quiché).

20. Although there has been a trend away from derivational rules in formalist theories, most of the formalist theories still have derivational rules of one sort or another. In Government and Binding Theory, relations between structures still play a major role, in particular, in defining relations between traces and their antecedents. In Lexical-Functional Grammar, there are no syntactic derivational rules; however, their role is taken by lexical rules deriving one lexical form from another. In Generalized Phrase Structure Grammar, there are no syntactic derivational rules either, but their role is taken (in some versions at least) by metarules, which relate two phrase-structure expansion rules in an analogous fashion.

21. It should be equally clear that the same ought to be true of a "functional"-typological phonology, in which the interacting extralinguistic factors are articulatory, auditory-acoustic and cognitive-psychological. However, hardly anything has been accomplished in shifting the paradigm in phonology in comparison to what has been achieved in syntax.

22. The following qualifications must be noted here but will not be discussed in the remainder of this book.

23. There is actually a fourth component of utterance structure, the degree of fusion of units (grammatical morphemes and categories). However, this is actually a property of (morpho)phonology, which will not be discussed here. I mention it in order to distinguish MORPHOSYNTAX, the units of gram-

matical systems and their relations and combinations regardless of their degree of fusion, from MORPHOPHONOLOGY, which has to do with the articulatory/acoustic effects of these combinations (the latter is in part what Sadock has called "morphology" in recent work [Sadock 1985]).

24. In certain kinds of serial verb constructions, more than one verb or predicate are found in a single clause (Foley and Olson 1985).

25. There are also "argument phrases" that are not thought of strictly as dependents of the verb, namely, those that are generally called adjuncts; for further discussion, see chap. 4.

26. This definition of the clause does not mention the linear order of these constituents. Although most clauses in most languages make up linearly contiguous units, many others do not, and linearization of the clause constituent appears to be an independent parameter, albeit a very important one. I will henceforth exclude discussion of the linear order of grammatical units except to the extent that it is relevant for determining grammatical dependencies.

Chapter Two

1. This use of "denotes" is equivalent to Mathesius's use of the term "naming" (Mathesius 1975: 23, 38) and Langacker's use of the term "symbolization" (Langacker 1987a: 11–12).

2. Another typological analysis of a syntactic category is that of Steele (1978) and Steele et al. (1981) for auxiliaries. Steele et al. use a similar strategy to Dixon's despite the superficial differences in analysis: they use internal criteria to determine a category membership, and they discovered that certain semantic/pragmatic concepts such as tense and modality are associated with the category, although other concepts could also be found in the category; for further discussion, see 3.3.4.

3. The other major feature of X′ theory is the bar notation, a technique to capture the notion "head" in a phrase structure model of syntactic relations without going to a dependency structure model. The X′ analysis of higher-level (nonlexical) constituents brings up other representational issues, chiefly the issue of using phrase structure as opposed to using dependency structures, that will not be discussed here.

4. The innovations of Generalized Phrase Structure Grammar in the representation of syntactic categories are largely on the level of subclasses of major categories and nondefining properties of the category (e.g., number and gender associated with a noun) and so are marginal to the issue at hand in this chapter, namely, an external definition of the major syntactic categories. Moreover, their feature analysis of syntactic categories and subclasses does not distinguish major syntactic categories for subclasses thereof, a significant failing (see below).

5. Kinkade argues that, since a verb with its "agreement" affixes may stand alone as a sentence, then subject and object noun phrases are in apposi-

tion to the verb and therefore are predications in their own right (Kinkade 1983:33, n. 11). This simply does not follow. It would be analogous to saying that, since Russian verbs may stand without subject nouns since their agreement suffixes suffice for subject reference, and since Russian nouns can be predicated without a copula, then the Russian subject noun is an independent predication.

6. Jacobsen's article also contains a thorough review of the literature on the noun-verb controversy.

7. Anderson (1985:155–58) points out that the ability of almost any Makah form to take the verbal inflections may be due to the likelihood that the verbal inflections are second-position clitics, and so any Makah form that may take initial position appears to be able to be inflected.

8. For further discussion of the relation between conceptualization and discourse function, see 3.2.

9. Hopper and Thompson's evidence also suggests the route to an answer to the problem of distinguishing "main" and "subordinate" clauses cross-linguistically.

10. There are a number of other pieces of evidence that Hopper and Thompson present. They argue that negative and irrealis verbal clauses and pronouns, existential constructions, and copular constructions display lower categoriality. The evidence that they adduce for negative and irrealis clauses is that such clauses display fewer grammatical distinctions than corresponding positive and realis clauses; this is evidence for the markedness of "negative" and "irrealis" relative to "positive" and "realis," respectively (for a discussion of the criteria of markedness, see below and also, Greenberg 1966a and Croft 1990b). The other cases, whose behavior is rather complex, will be discussed in 3.3.1 and 4.

11. This is particularly problematic in the case of predicate nominals since they argue that predicate nominals are low in nominal categoriality but also that copula constructions, which include predicate nominals, are low in verbal categoriality.

12. The work described in this and the following chapters was in fact developed independently of Hopper and Thompson's research (see Croft 1984).

13. This distinction has not been made clear because of the traditional semantic inclination to restrict denotation or "naming" to objects when they are being referred to by the speaker; this inclination has been challenged by Davidson in the representation of events and by Barwise and Perry in general.

14. Unification-based grammars, particularly Lexical Functional Grammar, represent syntactic functions in an abstract dependency structure (f-structure, directed acyclic graph). However, that structure is derived from a surface phrase structure analysis of the usual kind, with annotations (equations) added to the node labels. The syntactic functions do not bear any direct relation to the surface-syntactic lexical category.

15. In many cases, the adjectival form has special connotations and meaning shifts not present in the root. For example, the word *theatrical* now denotes a property associated with being in the theater, roughly "flamboyant, expressive, etc.," as well as the theater itself functioning as a modifier of the head in some way (as in *theatrical supplies*). Terms with such meaning shifts fall under the category of "type-changing" morphosyntax, to be discussed in a later section.

16. All these statements are qualified by "at least as . . ." or a synonym in order to indicate that the possibility of the marked and unmarked values might not differ in the given parameter.

17. It is usually said that in such languages nouns do not have the grammatical category of number. However, in describing markedness patterns, we are interested in the mapping between semantic categories, e.g., one object and more than one object, and the grammatical expression of the semantic category, in this case, zero marking for both categories.

18. These statements are formulated more precisely in P1–P5 and S1–S8 in order to allow one to say that a construction with two morphemes is more marked than a construction with one morpheme or, generally, that a construction with n morphemes ($n \geq 0$) is more marked than a construction with $n - m$ morphemes ($0 \leq m \leq n$); i.e., the marked construction has at least as many morphemes as the unmarked construction.

19. Actually, some stative constructions do lend themselves to the progressive, e.g., *John is being a boor,* but that appears to be a function of their being interpreted as processes in some way (in this case, John's current behavior). A partial explanation of the existence of particular inflectional category behavior associated with each syntactic category in terms of markedness will be made in 2.4.

20. Several of the languages in this survey were taken from a list of languages and language families with nounlike adjectives and languages with verblike adjectives (Thompson 1988: 170–71).

21. One might also argue that the existence of the hitting event also requires the existence of a place and a time at which the hitting occurred—what are generally called the "external" arguments of a predicate. There is a relation between an entity—event, object, or property—and its spatiotemporal embedding environment, but it is a quite different relation, having to do with the way human beings conceptualize individual objects and actions. For further discussion, see Croft in press a.

22. For an alternative analysis of properties and arguments why it still conforms to the hypothesis of the inherent relationality of properties, see 3.3.3, n. 29.

23. The latter do allow the existential bare plural interpretation, so that the second sentence is grammatical with the interpretation 'Some elephants are sick.'

24. It is simply a fact about the world that persistent or relatively per-

manent processes, the type that would most clearly distinguish change and transitoriness, are extremely rare or nonexistent. There are some possible examples: the best case is living. *Live* passes the usual criterion for object-level predicates, ability to occur in generic sentences with bare plural subjects:

(i) *Spotted owls live in old-growth forests.*

On the other hand, *live* may occur with the progressive (a reliable indicator of processuality), in particular, alternating with the simple present with only a subtle difference in meaning:

(ii) *A spotted owl lives/is living in that dead tree over there.*

Another possible case is *glow.* This and related examples, such as *breathe* and *radiate,* however, probably refer to plural puctual events rather than a persisting process.

25. By this criterion, incidentally, living appears to be persistent, but glowing, breathing (perhaps), and emitting radiation are transitory; also, certain stative binary-valency mental concepts such as loving also appear to be persistent.

A more difficult problem is that certain predicates are object level (persistent) or stage level (transitory), depending on the class of the entity of which they are predicated. For example, predicates describing wetness, such as *wet, damp,* and *dry* are stage-level predicates for typical objects but object-level predicates for environments, such as *desert, jungle,* and *forest.* Predicates of lightness, such as *light, bright,* and *dark,* are also stage-level predicates for most objects but object-level predicates for environments or locations such as caves. Also, predicates describing hardness (*hard, soft*) are stage level with respect to bread and pasta but object level with respect to rocks, minerals, and wood. In other words, the persistence/transitoriness of the characteristic depends on both the characteristic itself and the entity with which the characteristic is associated. (I am indebted to Suzanne Kemmer for pointing this out to me.)

26. This means that the distinction between inflectional and derivational categories must be made in some other way than in terms of syntactic category membership of the output (for a proposal, see Croft in press a).

27. In topic constructions in languages such as Mandarin Chinese, this is not always the case; see 3.2.2.

28. Kuno and Wogkhomthong call the classifying construction "characterization" and the equational construction "identification"; the latter is not to be confused with the individualizing *be* described in the following paragraph and in Bolinger (1980b).

29. Kuno and Wogkhomthong (1981) describe several other kinds of semantic relations between NPs conjoined by the copulas *pen* and *khi:* in Thai.

30. Complex nominals can involve the predicational *be* relation; e.g., *woman doctor* and *blockbuster movie* (I am grateful to Tom Wasow for these examples). However, this is simply one of an indefinitely large set of possible complex nominal relations.

It should be pointed out that, if there are any semantic regularities to be found in complex nominal constructions, they will be derivable from the pragmatic function of modification, which is the genuine unifying principle in complex nominals. That is, the semantic relation—and the modifying noun—involved in the complex nominal will be that which the speaker believes will assist the hearer in determining the reference of the head noun. However, a theory of the strategies used for this purpose has not yet been developed.

31. The same argument applies to certain types of derivation. Derived nouns that denote participants in whatever the root denotes require a semantic relation between the participant and whatever the root denotes. Agent nouns (or other participant nouns) derived from verbs or adjectives (rare in English but common in other languages) denote a participant in the event or the possessor of the property, but agent nouns derived from nouns can have virtually any contextually appropriate semantic relation between the agent and what is denoted by the root noun:

(i) *runner, manufacturer, writer, employee*
(ii) *the rich/poor/deprived*
(iii) *machinist, musician, violinist, doorman, contractor*

An agentive noun derived from a verb or an adverb can be paraphrased with a predicative form: a *writer* is 'one who writes' and *the poor* are 'those who are poor.' Once again, nouns cannot be so paraphrased: a *machinist* is not 'one who is a machine.'

Unlike nouns, the subject of a predicated adjective or verb is simply one of the adjective's or verb's arguments. Adjectives and verbs do not stand in any of the relations to the subject that the noun does: *John is sick* does not mean that John is a token of the type 'sickness', or that John is equivalent to a token denoted by 'is sick,' or that John is acting like he is sick (a separate construction, e.g., *seems,* is used for that). Since the noun has zero valency, there is no argument role that the subject can fill, and so the subject takes on some other semantic relation to the predicate noun, namely, predication, identification, or description.

Finally, the kind of action denoted by denominal verbs, and its semantic relation to the root nominal, is also unpredictable whether the denominal verb is zero derived or not (although the irregularities are much more common in the zero-derived forms):

(iv) *The servants were housed in the rear.*
(v) *He wristed the ball over the net.* (Clark and Clark 1979)
(vi) *It was John who orchestrated the piano score.*
(vii) *We vaccinated the whole village.*
(viii) *the youngest child monopolized the attention of his parents.*
(ix) *The industry attempted to standardize communications protocols.*
(x) *The islands were colonized rapidly.*

This may be another instance of the same phenomenon, though there is no comparable verbal or adjectival counterpart.

32. If the adjective follows the noun, it inflects fully (Vogt 1971 : 35); however, the noun-adjective construction is rare in the modern language (I am grateful to an anonymous reviewer for pointing this out).

33. Woleaian requires a reduplicated form for some "verbs": *sar memmasiur* [child RED-sleep] 'sleeping child' (Sohn 1975 : 182). However, the three examples provided are 'sleeping,' 'barking,' and 'white'—the last a core adjective by meaning.

34. The "headed" relative clause may perhaps be better analyzed as an appositive construction: both the head noun and the relative clause (excluding the head) refer to an individual, the same individual.

35. Factive predicates of action nominalizations are not good, as can be better seen with a morphologically distinct nominalization from the *-ing* ending: *Gary's performance of the Liszt sonata was a shock to everyone* is acceptable only if it is the manner and not the fact of Gary's performance that was a shock.

36. This explanation for the relevance of the characteristic inflections of the major syntactic categories to their prototypical members should not be confused with the explanation as to why those members are the prototypical members, i.e., why objects are associated with reference, properties with modification, and actions with predication. This latter account is presented in 3.2.

37. The texts used for this part of the study are "The Adventure of a Man Who Was Eaten by a Fish" (Quiché; Mondloch 1978 : 192–203); "Sokorarua" and "Manulapa" (Nguna; Schütz 1969 : 14–33); "Food" (Soddo; Leslau 1968 : 75–81); and "Hungry Coyote Races Skunk for Prairie Dogs" (Mollie Cloud version; Ute; Givón 1985 : 126–38).

38. Zero pronominals, found in the Ute text, are not included in the tally.

39. "States" are unary, stative, transitory entities, such as "hunger," "health," and "being full" (for discussion of this class, see 3.3.3). "Relations" are binary stative transitory entities, ranging from spatial and possessive relations to mental states ("see," "know," and "want"; see 5.5.1). "Auxiliary" includes aspectual ("begin," "end") and modal ("unable," "try") categories and the auxiliary verb "be" in Ute. Demonstratives, interrogatives, determiners, and adverbs were not counted.

40. The additional texts used for this part of the study are "Why There Was a Famine in Older Times" (Quiché; Mondloch 1978 : 203–22); "Takariki" (Nguna; Schütz 1969 : 34–62); "Drink" and "Butter" (Soddo; Leslau 1968 : 81–90); and "How Sinwav Got His Yellow Eyes" and "Porcupine, Buffalo-Cow and Sinawav" (Ute; Givón 1985 : 75–107).

41. This number includes twelve instances of the word *(xa)sin*, which is glossed as 'diminutive' but is translated with meanings associated with the core property category ('small,' 'dear').

42. I excluded nine "relative clauses" of the form '[the] time that S' since that is one of the ways that 'While S' and 'When S' are expressed.

43. This number includes ten compounds that could be excluded.

44. There were two additional predicate adjectives that had inchoative affixes and interpretations. Since they denote processes, they are excluded from the count.

45. This result differs from that of Thompson (1988); see 3.2.2.

46. As can be seen from tables 2.11 and 2.15, the Soddo text is unusual in having fewer pronouns than nouns. The reason for this is that the text describes Soddo life-styles, not a standard narrative: there are many generic statements, using generic nouns rather than pronouns.

47. Note that removing ordinary pronouns from the counts in tables 2.9–2.12 will not affect the unmarked correlation of roots denoting objects and the referential pragmatic function.

48. This is speculative; text analysis is required to determine if this is true.

49. A more detailed discussion of the semantic classes can be found in Croft (1986, app. A). Numbers indicate that number of roots in that category.

50. Most languages do not include plants in a grammatically-defined "animate" class; it appears that ability to move is an additional necessary condition for "animate."

51. These terms do not appear to be associated with a specific natural or man-made object, instead defining only characteristic shapes, such as a circle, cross, or line.

52. These terms, like shape terms, do not appear to be associated with a particular substance or object but rather with a physical phase: 'dust,' 'steam,' 'flame.'

53. Other than natural units: parts of natural units or collections of natural units other than human groupings (the immediately preceding category, which appears to merit distinct grammatical consideration).

54. Identity and difference in individuals.

55. Dispositions are technically properties of actions—a particular action is cunning, e.g. But a person who habitually performs actions with the property can also be attributed the property directly as a disposition, i.e., a tendency to perform actions in that fashion.

56. For discussion of states, see 3.3.3.

57. Truth and falsehood.

58. Measures are predicates with two arguments: an object and its value on a relevant scale (cost, weight, height, etc.).

59. Inactive actions refer to stative relations such as location and possession that are conceptualized as processes (cf. Langacker 1987b; Croft MSb).

60. This is assuming that the provenance and/or destination, or in general the ground, is not an argument (see 5.4.1).

61. This is the least well-defined category in the classification. The example illustrates one subclass, passing of judgment (another example is *klevet*

'slander, defame'). Other subclasses are authority (*vel/vol* 'will, command, order') and care/protection (*b(e)reg* 'preserve, defend, protect, take care of').

Chapter Three

1. That is to say, COMMONSENSE properties of the scene. Commonsense ontology clearly involves some conceptual processing as well. That type of processing is more obviously applicable to nonlinguistic cognitive activities, but this does not at all imply that the organization of information in discourse described here is relevant only to linguistic processing.

2. Since I will use the term "categorization" with a different meaning in 3.2.2, I will adopt Bolinger's term "classify" here.

3. This is also true in the theory of prototypes as presented by Lakoff (1987). In his view, the gradient effects of category membership popularly associated with prototypes is due to various nongradient factors, the most important of which are a "mismatch" between the idealized cognitive model of the category (e.g., "bachelor") and real-world entities (e.g., homosexual lovers living together, the Pope); the polysemous (in his terms, "radial") nature of a category; and the incompleteness or imperfectness of a metaphoric extension.

4. One cannot say **John is Swede;* but that is because the simple predication of a noun does not imply gradability.

5. I do not know how Langacker analyzes relational nouns (see 3.3.3).

6. Autonomy is distinct from individuation. Autonomy refers to the ability to separate an entity from other entities in its conceptual surroundings (a semantically syntagmatic relation). Individuation refers to the ability to separate an entity from other entities of the same kind (a semantically paradigmatic relation).

7. The verb is put into the habitual form to make it more like the stative predicates; however, a more accurate (and telling) comparison would be made by contrasting the progressive: *Jill is fussing.*

8. In a small number of languages, including English, color terms may also be used to refer to the color: *I like the red in that pattern; The greens are too dark.* However, in English at least, the adjective used nominally denotes the shade or hue of the color and so appears to denote something slightly different than the color itself. I have no explanation as to why the shade or hue is expressed nominally, though.

9. A variant of coercion is the case in which there are two distinct constructions for a given function, such as prenominal vs. postnominal modification or nonverbal predication with and without *a* in English, with distinct conceptualizations associated with each.

10. These are not necessarily mutually exclusive sources of explanation. The factors that shape communication possibly also shaped the evolution of mankind's cognitive makeup, and this is more likely if the communicative functions have more general human cognitive or interpersonal adaptive value.

11. As in most philosophical discussion, "property" is used as a cover term for anything predicated, state or process, and not in the sense used in this and the preceding chapters. Also, Searle restricts his discussion to one-place predicates ('be a student,' 'be red,' 'sleeps').

12. "The tendency to construe predication as a kind of, or analogous to, reference is one of the most persistent mistakes in the history of Western philosophy" (Searle 1969: 122).

13. My choice of the terms "reference" and "predication" was fortuitous, inspired by the general philosophical tradition rather than by Searle's specific analysis of propositional acts.

14. Background dimensions are essentially the same as Langacker's domains (Langacker 1987b: 58–59). Langacker considers domains to be an essential part of the definition of nouns, but predications situate events in time through tense, temporal adverbs, etc. However, Langacker points out that nouns can be situated with respect to any domain, not just space, whereas verbs are situated only in time. Nevertheless, space is the basic domain.

15. In particular, the minor propositional speech acts account for many words that have been assigned to the category "adverb," e.g., *here, now, twice, very, back, again, a lot, yesterday,* etc. This leaves "core" adverbs, manner, and sentential adverbs. These function as modifiers as well, but as modifiers of actions instead of (or as well as) modifiers of objects. Most adverbs are structurally marked in that function: in the twelve-language sample from chap. 2, Swahili, Turkana, Georgian, Chinese, Yagaria, and Lakhota used a nonzero affix to derive adverbs from adjectives, while Turkish (normally), Acehnese, Woleaian, and Diyari did not (no information was available for Quiché). English uses unmarked adverbs for some properties that are more likely to be associated with actions: *He works fast;* and coerces the meaning of other adjectives to one appropriate for describing actions: *He works hard* (cf. Diyari *piṇa* 'big [applied to count nouns], a lot [applied to mass nouns], very much [applied to actions]'; Austin 1981: 108).

16. It is often true that what is accomplished by word order in one language may be accomplished by grammatical structure in another. However, it appears that, in cases of rigid word order languages, grammatical constructions have the effect of rearranging the word order so that the constituents are in the order expected for the discourse function of the construction (cf. Lambrecht's [1987] discussion of various French constructions that have the effect of placing the NP after the verb).

17. In fact, Hopper and Thompson say at one point that prototypical nouns are those that maintain identity in discourse over time (Hopper and Thompson 1984: 711). Before that, however, they state that the prototypical function is *introducing* a "manipulable" (their term for maintained identity) entity into the discourse, not just evoking such an entity: "The extent to which prototypical nounhood is achieved is a function of the degree to which the form in question serves to introduce a participant into the discourse" (708). In

fact, they argue that pronouns are "poor" nouns when in fact they are very good examples of referring expressions (see 3.3.1). I am taking the position here that evoking a "manipulable" entity, not just introducing it, is the core function of reference.

18. Thompson's only example of this type, *There's this one part between this Jewish guy and the girl,* can be easily accounted for: the head noun is semantically empty, and the modifier *Jewish* is used to avoid the connotations associated with *Jew* (Bolinger 1980a: 79, discussed above).

19. However, it may be that some of the predicate adjectives are used to describe a *just*-established referent. That is, owing to the preference to use attributive adjectives with semantically empty head nouns, if a referent is introduced with a semantically fuller head noun, then the descriptive information may be provided in another clause. This is attributable to the "one significant new concept at a time" constraint: do not put two significant concepts too closely together (cf. Givón 1979: 52, n. 25; Chafe 1987: 49, referring to intonation units; Myhill 1988: 282–83, referring mainly to clauses). Functionally, these predicate adjectives may be being applied to basically "new" referents rather than old ones. In this case, the line between the two adjective functions is somewhat hazy.

20. Technically, the "stressed focus *it*-cleft" (Prince 1978). In fact, in many languages (e.g., Quiché), the cleft construction is used for answers to WH-questions.

21. Gender marking, which provides a rudimentary classification system, appears to be a counterexample to this. However, Heath (1975) argues that pronominal gender functions in order to maintain identity of referents across clauses, which is exactly what the cognitive model leads us to expect (see immediately following discussion).

22. This conclusion is the opposite of the one that Hopper and Thompson arrived at (1984: 722–23). However, there is good reason for this conflict in judgment: pronouns are attracted to the verb, whence they become agreement markers. Also, coreference is frequently expressed by zero anaphora. These properties indicate low categoriality. For the hypothesis suggested here to be maintained, alternative explanations are needed for these phenomena. For example, the attraction of pronouns to verbs appears to be associated with the "clustering" phenomenon associated with the high information content of the verb relative to the pronominal argument(s) (Myhill 1988). Zero anaphora may result from high recoverability, the last aspect of given-new described above (cf. Givón 1979, 1983b).

23. A sixth group consists solely of the verb *ngín* 'say, think,' which has a limited distribution as an independent verb (Hutchison 1981: 101).

24. Ladusaw (1985) argues that Kusaal, a Gur (Congo-Kordofanian) language of Burkina Faso, does not have an adjective class. Ladusaw observes, however, that, although Kusaal putative adjectives agree with their head nouns in number, the number morphology of putative adjectives is of the

same type as that of nouns. The most interesting aspect of Kusaal adjectives is that when predicated they may act like nouns *or* verbs: if nounlike, they require the copula and inflect for number; if verblike, they do not use the copula and do not inflect for number. This ambivalent behavior distinguishes the adjectives from both nouns and verbs and represents the intermediate status of adjectives. (Ladusaw states that the verblike predicated adjectives would probably not take the inperfective aspectual suffix for reasons of semantic incompatibility, an example of behavioral defectiveness as predicates.)

25. Prototype analyses speak of objects being members of a category "to a degree," but the scale they are referring to is degree of membership. In a truly gradable concept, the object always has the attribute (e.g., height or speed), and it is only the measurable value that varies.

26. Even in Russian, a language with a morphosyntactically quite distinct, open adjective class, there are a small number of exceptions; the one enumerated in table 2.5 is *dlina* 'length.' There are two more synchronic "exceptions" in Russian that interestingly prove the rule—diachronically. *Vys'* 'height' and *glub'* 'depth' appear to be less marked than their adjectival counterparts *vysok-ij* and *glubok-ij*. Diachronically, the palatalization in the nominal forms goes back to the Proto-Indo-European **-i-* stem (Schmalstieg 1976, 85), which was used to derive nominals from active and stative forms (I am indebted to Joseph Greenberg for pointing this out to me). In the two exceptional cases, one can see that there is a lag from the Church Slavonic period, where the root formed the adjectival stem (Šamskij 1963–82, 1, pt. 3 : 231–32; pt. 4 : 97), and the modern Russian period, where both adjectival forms are marked with *-ok-*. In fact, there also exist unexceptional synonyms *vysota* and *glubina* that are much more common in use, the shorter forms not even showing up in Štejnfeldt's frequency count (Štejnfeldt n.d. : 178), nor in a frequency count of sixteenth- to seventeenth-century Russian (Gruzberg 1974 : 129, 132). The synchronic anomaly is being "corrected" diachronically, in the same way as is the Russian zero genitive plural ending discussed in Greenberg (1969).

27. This appears to hold regardless of the collective/distributive interpretation of the predicate that may be imposed on it; there exist examples of conjunction reduction with a collective and a distributive predicate, e.g., *Three men ate lunch and carried the piano upstairs.*

28. The data are actually somewhat differently presented in the case of the naturally correlated categories. Since the assumption was that the unnatural correlations were *at least as* marked as the natural ones, in cases where there was no difference in structural markedness I gave the natural correlation the benefit of the doubt. Since states are not hypothesized to correlate with any major category, I split the cases in which there was no structural markedness between two categories.

29. Some of the noun roots, such as *thirst* and *health,* appear to be dropping out of the language, leaving the adjectival forms *thirsty* and *healthy* as the synchronically least-marked forms.

30. There is at least one class of exceptions: colloquial evaluative verbs

such as *stink* and *suck: This book stinks/*is stinking.* (I am grateful to Tom Wasow for this example.)

31. A similar analysis is frequently proposed for properties: instead of a property such as 'red' being interpreted as a one-place (i.e., inherently relational) predicate *Red(x),* it has been argued that there is a two-place predicate denoting the attribute, one argument being the value denoted by the adjective: *Color(x,Red).* In this analysis, *Red* is an argument, not an (inherently relational) property. Of course, values are semantically distinct from objects, and they have the property of gradability, which I argued was crucial to the definition of adjectives, so this part of the attribute analysis does not affect my analysis of adjectives. It is not obvious, however, that the valency of values is zero, i.e., that values are not values of SOMETHING. I would be inclined to argue that the commonsense view of the world does not posit abstract autonomous values (including numbers, which as has been seen are very similar to adjectives and otherwise are relational nouns) but treats values as values of something—i.e., values are inherently relational after all.

32. Actually, the inflectional stem ends in a vowel *-i-*, which in most cases acts as a causative type-changing derivation.

33. The derivational suffix *-i-* is from a Latin adjective form derived from the verb, which produced the noun by zero derivation. It should be pointed out also that both English and Lakhota make fairly extensive use of zero derivation for function-indicating as well as type-changing derivations.

34. The categories associated with the auxiliary appear to be a combination of semantic (tense, aspect, possibility) and pragmatic (evidentiality, speech act) properties, perhaps not unlike the definitions I have proposed for the major syntactic categories. However, the pragmatic properties are not elements of discourse structure such as "modifier" or "predication," and individual auxiliaries represent either a semantic property or a pragmatic one rather than an interaction of a semantic and a discourse functional property. Thus, they do not fit the model of syntactic categories used for the major categories "noun," "verb," and "adjective."

35. Quiché has only two, *k-ataxin* [durative] and *raxwašik* [obligation]; this is the smallest number that I know of in a single language.

36. The main reason for the lack of a cline in English auxiliary behavior is that the syntactic constructions used to distinguish auxiliaries from main verbs—use of *do* in negation and question inversion (Jespersen 1940 : 426–38, 504–8) and the use of *to* with infinitives (Jespersen 1927 : 10–11; Jespersen 1940 : 154–55)—were themselves in a state of flux when the "newer" auxiliaries were evolving.

37. It appears that recently developed "auxiliary" verbs have submitted to the requirement for an infinitival *to.*

38. A similar argument can be used to account for subcategorization of complements by auxiliaries: it reflects their former verbal status.

Chapter Four

1. No connotation of "movement," "promotion," or "demotion" should be imputed to this term; it refers solely to the grammatical conditions under which the result of a digging event can be the subject of a clause whose predicate denotes the digging event.

2. This hierarchy was originally christened the "accessibility hierarchy" since it was used to characterize accessibility of an NP to relativization (Keenan and Comrie 1977); but its relevance for predicate-argument relations in general was recognized early (for a summary of typological evidence supporting the grammatical relations hierarchy, see Croft 1990b, 5.3.2).

3. Nevertheless, some of the nonsubject constructions are used to indicate shifts in topics, not continuity of topics, and the more continuous topic NP types are "ordinary" NPs and (especially) pronouns and other anaphoric devices (Givón 1983a: 17).

4. Fillmore (1968) also provides a useful historical survey of case.

5. In an important early cognitive approach to grammar, Lakoff (1977) suggests the same view of sentence generation (in the literal sense of generation as the production of an utterance by a speaker).

6. Fillmore also notes a degree of affectedness effect with the intransitive subject in *Bees are swarming in the garden/The garden is swarming with bees* (1968: 48).

7. The suggestion that there are only a few distinct thematic roles that have to be postulated for a universal characterization of case is originally Fillmore's: "The case notions comprise a set of universal, presumably innate concepts. . . . the cases that appear to be needed include . . . [he describes six cases]. . . . Additional cases will surely be needed" (Fillmore 1968: 24–25). Fillmore has since changed his position (Fillmore 1977: 70–71).

8. A "loose interpretation" of the localist hypothesis would simply argue for a close relation between certain nonlocal roles and certain local roles. Nevertheless, only those three roles are actually proposed by localists such as Anderson (1971).

9. These are only four of several uses of *with* described in Nilsen (1973); "objective" is his term for the last type.

10. I will use this term to describe the synchronic subsumption of different thematic roles (uses, meanings) under a single surface form (case marking), not the diachronic falling together of two forms (though the latter can lead to a synchronic case syncretism).

11. Most of these were taken from Comrie and Smith's (1977) Lingua Descriptive Series questionnaire.

12. I am grateful to Douglas Edwards for providing me with this example from the philosophical literature.

13. The locative can be interpreted as providing a temporal condition on

the event, namely, that the widowing event occured while Mrs. Woodland was in Las Vegas, but then the expression is no longer functioning to delimit spatial location. Also, not all speakers accept *widow* as a verb; the *American Heritage Dictionary New College Edition* states that the verb form is usually found as a past participle.

14. By "cause" is meant "immediate cause," not any one of or the whole of the entire chain of events that caused the event in question to occur.

15. This example is due to Tom Wasow. A possible counterexample was proposed to me by Terry Winograd: *He screeched around the corner.* However, *screech* here describes the manner in which he went around the corner; i.e., it is a property of the motion that causes the change in location. See the discussion of the "manner" thematic role in 4.4.4.

16. This problem could be avoided using predicate operators such as Become(Broken(x)), however. Nevertheless, the use of both predicate operators and propositional arguments puts one beyond first-order logic.

17. For a discussion of evidence suggesting that causal order is relevant to verbal syntax as well, see 5.6.3.

18. It is also worth noting that the aspectual structure of the event—the other major determinant of verbal semantic structure—can change at different levels of granularity. The event described in (25) is a state, while the events described in (26) are all processes or changes of state.

19. I represent a causal arc representing a resulting state without an arrow since no transmission of force is involved (see criterion 3).

20. The semantic transition from speaking of events causing other events to one object acting on another is fraught with difficulties (I am indebted to Richmond Thomason for pointing out this problem to me). The reason for this is that the former representation—something like $P(e_1, x, y)$ & $Q(e_2, y, z)$ & Cause(e_1, e_2)—has less information than the latter, something like $x \rightarrow_p y \rightarrow_q z$. This information is implicitly coded in the ordering of events in the latter representation, but underlying that is a theory of *how* events cause other events or at least how physical events cause other events, namely, the concept of "force" and its transmission, which is discussed below under the fourth criterion. Since I argue here that the additional information expressed in the arc-node representation illustrated in (27) is necessary for defining surface-structure phenomena such as verbal lexical semantics and surface case marking and voice, I will use the richer representation without further comment on this issue for the remainder of the chapter.

21. This is not to say that the speakers of natural language cannot describe situations involving (alleged or fictional) telepathy and telekinesis. However, the way that these atypical or noncommonsensical situations are expressed is either by using an instrumental expression that "invents" an instrument, such as *with mind power,* or by using an expression that explicitly negates the expected instrument, such as *without touching it.* Both expressions imply

that the prototypical causal relation requires a mental-level causation to be mediated by physical entities.

22. Actually, volitionality itself is not a monolithic category. It involves more subtle gradations of subject intention, responsibility, and control (see DeLancey 1984b, 1985). However, I will not discuss the peripheral cases of volitionality here.

23. The example of John running and sweating also illustrates the fact that two causally ordered events may coincide or almost coincide spatiotemporally.

24. As we will see in 6.1, under certain circumstances the causal chain denoted by the verb can be extended by grammatical processes, which allow the assignment of subject and object to participants "outside" the causal chain.

25. In some languages, branching causal chains are indicated by (nonzero) affixes used for distributive and/or plural action readings (a particularly rich system is found in Kwakiutl; Boas 1947 : 246).

26. The problem of symmetrical relations, causal and noncausal, will be discussed in later sections (5.4, 5.5.1, and 6.3).

27. The verb *say* has a number of peculiarities associated with it. Normally, inversion of word order is used instead of passivization to bring the utterance into greater prominence, and this can be done only with direct speech complements (*"Beat it, kid," said the old man; *That he should beat it, said the old man*). However, nouns denoting the utterance usable with *say* can be passivized under appropriate circumstances: *Nothing was said to the launch managers by NASA about technical problems with the O-rings. Tell (to)* does not allow inversion or passivization with indirect speech complents either: **To beat it, told/was told John by the old man.*

28. The thematic role of the "causee" will be discussed in 6.1. I will also restrict experiencer and stimulus to stative affective relations in 5.5.1.

29. Note that one can no longer infer that the boulder broke, without the addition of the parenthesized gerund expression, since the information provided by the main verb does not include that segment of the causal chain.

30. Of course, that segment combines the inceptive and the resulting-state arcs, as discussed in 6.4. Note that, in this sentence, one can no longer infer that a volitional agent caused the boulder to break since that information is not contained in the main verb causal segment, and the commonsense ontology allows for "spontaneous" (perhaps "internally" caused) physical events. Commonsense ontology less surprisingly also allows free will—i.e., spontaneous acts of volitional causation.

Chapter Five

1. The potential for semantic unclearness inherent in this definition is not with the notion of "spread" but with the notion of "domain." In commonsense semantic analysis, many domains are defined in terms of primitive concepts, e.g., space, time, and causality. This forces one to rely on intuitions

about what represents a causal relation as opposed to a spatial or temporal one, and of course intuitions vary, leading to controversy. Future research in commonsense metaphysics may lead to definitions of terms such as "causality" which I take here to be primitive.

2. These roles were named "straight" and "inverse," respectively, in Croft (1986).

3. In the language survey, I include the ergative case as a (marked) antecedent case on the grounds that as "subject" it precedes the direct object, which is found in the unmarked absolutive case, generally the only unmarked case in ergative case systems. As will be seen, this assumption allows one to account for the common ergative-instrumental (and ergative-locative; see 5.3) syncretism found, e.g., in the Australian languages. One also finds an apparently anomalous ergative-dative syncretism, especially in South Asian languages; but, in all these cases, the ergative/dative is also the genitive, and it has been proposed (Benveniste 1971; Anderson 1977) that this is due to the historical development of the ergative from the perfective, with which there is a close association with possession (Allen 1964).

4. Actually, *for* covers many roles, some of which will be discussed in 5.5.2. However, only one of the "major" thematic roles, defined in terms of the core causal situation type, is covered by *for*.

5. Interestingly, I have not yet found a simple system of two case markers, one a perfect subsequent case and the other a perfect antecedent case. The closest system is the Kanuri one (see the appendix).

6. In brief, it may be that subsequent forms can spread to the cause by means of expressions of reason. Expressions of reason, which is a category of intention, not of causation, can represent events that causally follow the verb segment (a goal or purpose) or precede (a source or motivation). The hypothesis is that normal subsequent expressions spread to purpose, thence to reason (which is nondirectional), and thence to true cause. This hypothesis would have to be verified in terms of historical evidence and evidence of intermediate stages (e.g., use of the subsequent form for purpose and reason as well as true cause).

7. Body part terms are a major source of case marking, but these terms generally become case markers via a stage at which they represent a deictic schema of locations based on the body (e.g., 'on' = head, 'inside' = belly, and so on). The only common exception to this is the shift of a term for 'face' or 'head' directly to a mental-level oblique role such as recipient or benefactive.

8. Of course, the metaphor itself was probably licensed diachronically by a natural correlation, namely, the fact that typically a causal relation between initiator and endpoint happens also to involve approach and contact of the initiator with the endpoint. But, once the semantic transfer is made, this correlation loses its significance and no longer plays a major role; the formerly directional forms can occur in causal relations without motion involved.

9. Blake also mentions a locative-ablative syncretism but does not discuss it.

10. It is worth quoting Dixon at this point: "We have not, however, thrown any light on . . . the problem of instrumental—why this function should be shown by ergative case in some languages but by locative in others. This remains an open question—one of the most tantalizing puzzles in comparative Australian studies. It may well be, in fact, that it has a syntactic, rather than a morphological explanation" (Dixon 1980:321). I have demonstrated that this puzzle has in fact a semantic solution.

11. This fact presumably has a processing explanation: since three arguments in a single clause are acceptable, one can avoid unnecessarily complex clause structure.

12. I have simplified the diagrams in the following examples by leaving out the VOL arc. These are actually essential parts of the diagram and will reappear in the analysis of simple motion and location expressions.

13. Generally, selection of the ground as direct object prohibits the figure from taking part in other grammatical phenomena associated with direct objecthood, such as direct object agreement.

14. Actually, it would be more accurate to represent simple motion as allowing a complex ground expression, with both origin (ablative) and destination (allative) represented. Of course, the ground expression could be arbitrarily complex: *John ran from the toolshed, through the garage, over the woodpile to the back of the house.* What matters for the causal structure analysis is that the ground(s) be expressed as oblique phrases.

15. Talmy also observes another type, which he calls figure incorporating, in which the figure or a classifier of the figure is incorporated into the verb. This is an independent parameter from the causal-structure distinction of the first two types, however.

16. Beyond the VOL segment, that is: recall that the means segment must be longer than just the VOL arc. (I did not indicate the VOL arc in the preceding diagrams.)

17. Tom Wasow provides the following counterexample, which does not sound normal to me but certainly sounds better than (35):

(i) *John burst into the room by breaking down the door.*

It may be that the punctual nature of the process makes the means of entering and the act of entering, i.e., the first and second arcs, one and the same, so that semantically (i) resembles (34), not (35).

18. The presence of the verb be_{loc} renders such an analysis implausible in English, but many languages do not require a verb when location of an object is predicated.

19. As expected, object choice involves greater or entire affectedness of the object; hence, (37) is more acceptable when total affectedness is made explicit. *Up* is functioning as an aspectual/affectedness particle. Also, means clauses with *occupy* and *inhabit* are prohibited owing to the lack of a VOL arc; compare *The Germans occupied the Sudentenland by treachery.*

20. Acceptable if *Kansas City* refers to an office or some other entity that can function as a recipient.

21. For an exhaustive list of such verbs, and for discussion of the circumstances under which the "inverse" form may appear, see Salkoff (1983).

22. It is possible that the inversion in *swarm* sentences reflects the historical falling together of the derivational *a-* forms with the unmarked verb root, and the motion and body posture verbs simply did not have that form. But then that historical fact would have to be explained as well. Although I believe that I have isolated the problem correctly and accounted for the presence of the antecedent case form, I still have no explanation for the possibility of the inverse form with this class of constructions and no others.

23. In fact, there is a case for establishing a basic 3-ary noncausal relation, "transfer," involving possessed, former possessor, and new possessor. Consider the differences between *I gave you the book, I got the book from you,* and *I got you the book from Fred.* With *give,* the initiator of the event is the same as the former possessor; with *get* in the absence of a recipient direct object, the initiator of the event is the same as the new possessor; and with *get* in the presence of a recipient direct object, the initiator of the event is a third party.

In some languages, the *former* possessor can be expressed in the same way as the final possessor, so that the directionality of transfer cannot be determined from the morphosyntax. In the following example from Mokilese (Harrison 1976: 133), in which the possessor is realized as a dependent on the direct object, only word order indicates the difference:

(i) *Ngoah dupukla woara -mw pohs -pas*
I bought PCL -2SG boat one.NCL
'I bought a boat for you.'

(ii) *Ngoah dupukla pohs -pas woara -mw*
I bought boat one.NCL PCL -2SG
'I bought a boat from you.'

This may be due to one of two factors. It may be that the directionality of transfer simply has been neutralized. Or it may be that the proper analysis of the thematic role involved is not as a recipient in the possession domain but as a benefactive/malefactive on the causal plane: the new possessor is in the benefactive role by virtue of his coming into possession of the possessed item, and the former possessor is in the malefactive role by virtue of his no longer having the possessed item. A strong confirmation of this hypothesis would be evidence that languages that syncretize benefactive, malefactive, and recipient (new possessor) under a single case marking also allow the former possessor to be expressed with that case marking.

24. Compare Dryer (1986), who suggests a similar explanation for his "primary object" category, which combines direct objects of monotransitives and indirect objects—recipients (*give, send*), perceivers (*show*), and hearers (*tell*)—of ditransitives; see 6.1.

25. Contrast the English verb *give.* Although the possessor precedes the possessed in the double-object construction, it is the possessor that requires a preposition if one of the arguments is absent: *He gives fifty dollars every year; ?Our relatives give *us/to us every Christmas* (imagine a situation in which a poor family receives material support from their wealthier kin). This conflicts with Dryer's (1986) primary object analysis of English (in general, the data here is equivocal).

26. I will discuss the stative verb *have,* in which the *possessor* is subject, in 6.2.

27. The reason for the apparent inversion of the stative and the noncausal possession arcs from the last example to this one can be found in the *uncoerced* representation, in which the initiator as well as the parenthesized endpoint actually consist of the possessed-possessor relation (see 6.2 on reverse verbs). In addition, the temporal/causal extent attributed to the causal arc is misleading, especially for stative arcs: the parenthesized nodes are identical to the nonparenthesized ones. Thus, nothing restricts what "end" of the stative arc the possession is coerced to. The use of the left-hand side of the stative arc for subject, which leads to the "inversion," is just a notational convention.

28. Thus, a *-*ŋu* ablative-cause-material genitive should be added to Dixon's inventory of proto-Australian case forms.

29. The English list was taken from a talk by Paul Kiparsky at Stanford University in 1986.

30. English has two dative experiencer verbs, *seem* and *appear,* and a number of dative experiencer adjectives, e.g., *It is audible/visible/apparent to me . . .*

31. I am grateful to Henry Andery (of Venezuela) for providing the examples and interpretations.

32. The experiencer for many of these stative verbs can also take the dative case marker *ni.*

33. I am grateful to Hung Hsiu-fang for this example and its interpretation.

34. More detailed research will almost certainly reveal still finer-grained patterns. For example, I know of no case in which 'love' has a object experiencer, and this seems true of other verbs denoting strong emotions.

35. One could argue that replacement/substitution involves a slightly different relation than the exchange/commercial situation does. The real question is, Does the semantic difference lead to regular differences in linguistic behavior? This question can be answered only by typological research: if, e.g., one discovered that replacement verbs used a new-first coercion consistently across languages and exchange verbs used an old-first coercion equally consistently. That research remains to be done.

36. The fact that *for* is used only with associated actions is significant since it demonstrates that a genuine causal structure (i.e., an action) underlies the

semantic relation between the noun modifier and the head noun. If one were describing simple spatial configurations, one would use the appropriate path expression, as in the normal object-figure type represented by verbs like *put:*

(i) *the lid on the jar*

37. For example, I find the following differences in acceptability of the possessive *'s* and the partitive *of* in the following examples:

(i) *the ??jar's lid/lid of the jar*
(ii) *the sergeant's dinner/??the dinner of the sergeant*

As mentioned in the last note, there does appear to be a difference between the two possessive types that falls roughly along the predicted lines.

38. These are also called "serial" verb constructions (e.g., Foley and Olson 1985), but the latter term is restricted by some to a different class of complex verb constructions, in which verbs function as case markers.

39. I wish to thank Amy Mathieu for collecting many of these examples. I have also adjusted the orthography used in both sources.

40. The tense-aspect-modality verbs (or auxiliaries) often encroach on aspects of verbal semantics associated with the causal structure, e.g., inchoative markers and markers of external deontic force (equivalent to 'help,' 'let,' or even a regular causative). For example, the Lahu inchoative verb *qai* 'go' patterns with other aspectual verbs and follows the verb rather than preceding it (Matisoff 1969: 102–3).

Chapter Six

1. Also known as "possessor ascension." The possessor of the patient is a subsequent causal relation only indirectly; it causally follows the patient by virtue of its being a benefactive/malefactive participant of the action performed on the patient (see Croft 1985; and 5.4.2, n. 23).

2. In Malay, however, the causative-cum-instrumental affix is also a general applicative affix, except for locatives.

3. In Thargari (Australian; Blake 1977: 50), the instrument applicative suffix (used in a focus form in the text) is the reciprocal form, another antecedent-like function (see 6.3). A number of languages, including Quiché and other Mayan languages (Norman 1978) and Kalkatungu (Blake 1977: 50), have an instrumental voice that can be used only if the instrument is focused (extracted); thus, there are no instrumental direct objects. The Mayan instrument focus voice is parallel to the agent focus voice since both causally precede the object. Finally, it is worth pointing out that comitative applicatives, which sometimes syncretize with the causative, perhaps should not be analyzed as '*X* Verbs-with *Y*' but instead as the causative-like '*X* helps *Y* Verb.'

4. Comrie, however, allows for deviations from his paradigm case of causative formation, on the lines of what would now be called a prototype analysis of causative formation.

5. French also allows the antecedent oblique form (Comrie 1985 : 339).

6. The *-ni* suffix is the only nonlocal case marker, so an alternative approach would be simply to argue that Yokuts is a nondirectional system.

7. The term "mediopassive" is also used; this actually applies to those forms that cover both the middle and the passive.

8. Keenan also lists a "genitive" passive agent, but his examples are ablative in origin, and the possessives found in certain Austronesian languages are from nominalizations with subject possessors and perhaps are not true passives at any rate.

9. There are a number of passive-like constructions in Austronesian languages that appear to have atypical case markings, but they appear not to be passives (Durie 1988).

10. This is true in English at least; in Quiché, however, either passive type can take the passive agentive case marker *umal,* which is also the case marker for cause.

11. Supporting evidence for this would be evidence that means clauses marked by *by* were first used in process passives before spreading to actives.

12. The same is true of the definite markers in Tagalog, which mark "agent" or "patient" regardless of which is "subject" (see Schachter 1976, 1977). They indicate definiteness only, not thematic role, unlike the otherwise fairly normal Tagalog oblique markers.

13. These verbs are used for "adversative" passives in some Southeast Asian languages (Siewierska 1984 : 149–59), not surprisingly.

14. In fact, in those languages in which the NP conjunction is identical to the comitative case marking, there is no difference between the two strategies (a "conjoined" NP is often extraposable, as in Old English, not unlike an oblique phrase).

15. Suppletion is not included in this list of processes because a suppletive alternation represents distinct lexicalized conceptualizations (see 3.2.4; and Croft MS).

16. Although English and French are typologically similar, and so are Korean and Japanese, English and French differ in this aspect of their grammar in that French makes extensive use of a reflexive middle, while English allows a considerable amount of coercion rather than morphosyntactically marked shift. Japanese and Korean are, however, typologically similar in this area.

17. The "exceptions" prove the rule: unmarked inchoatives that refer to colors such as *blush* and *blanch* (almonds, vegetables, people) refer to a transitory, easily altered property, not an inherent, relatively unchangeable one.

18. There are relatively unchangeable properties that do come about through an external cause, e.g., being broken, smashed, etc. These are mostly terms referring to an "unnatural" state of the object, either damaged or destroyed.

REFERENCES

Aissen, Judith. 1983. Indirect object advancement in Tzotzil. In Perlmutter 1983, 272–302.

Akmajian, Adrian, Susan Steele, and Thomas Wasow. 1979. The category AUX in universal grammar. *Linguistic Inquiry* 10:1–64.

Allen, W. Sidney. 1964. Transitivity and possession. *Language* 40:337–43.

Andersen, Henning. 1968. IE *s* after *i, u, r, k* in Baltic and Slavic. *Acta Linguistica Hafniensa* 11:171–90.

Anderson, John M. 1971. *The grammar of case: Towards a localistic theory.* Cambridge: Cambridge University Press.

———. 1979. On being without a subject. Bloomington: Indiana University Linguistics Club.

Anderson, Stephen R. 1970. A little light on the role of deep semantic interpretation. National Science Foundation Report no. 26, II.1–II.13. Cambridge, Mass.: Harvard University.

———. 1976. On the notion of subject in ergative languages. In Li 1976, 1–24.

———. 1977. On mechanisms by which languages become ergative. In *Mechanisms of syntactic change,* ed. Charles Li, 317–64. Austin: University of Texas Press.

———. 1985. Inflectional morphology. In Shopen 1985b, 150–201.

Andrews, J. Richard. 1975. *Introduction to Classical Nahuatl.* Austin: University of Texas Press.

Arnott, D. W. 1970. *The nominal and verbal systems of Fula.* Oxford: Oxford University Press.

Aronson, Howard I. 1982. *Georgian: A reading grammar.* Columbus, Ohio: Slavica.

Ashton, E. O. 1944. *Swahili grammar.* London: Longman.

Austin, J. L. 1962. *How to do things with words.* Cambridge, Mass.: Harvard University Press.

Austin, Peter. 1981. *A grammar of Diyari, South Australia.* Cambridge: Cambridge University Press.

Barber, E. J. W. 1975. Voice: Beyond the passive. In *Proceedings of the first annual meeting of the Berkeley Linguistics Society,* ed. Cathy Cogen et al., 16–23. Berkeley, Calif.: Berkeley Linguistics Society.

Barwise, Jon, and John Perry. 1983. *Situations and attitudes.* Cambridge, Mass.: MIT Press.

Benveniste, Emile. 1971. The passive construction of the transitive perfect. In

Problems in general linguistics, trans. Mary Elizabeth Meck, 153–62. Coral Gables, Fla.: University of Miami Press.

Berlin, Brent, and Paul Kay. 1969. *Basic color terms: Their universality and evolution.* Berkeley: University of California Press.

Blake, Barry J. 1977. *Case marking in Australian languages.* Linguistic Series, no. 23. Canberra: Australian Institute of Aboriginal Studies.

Blansitt, Edward L. 1984. Dechticaetiative and dative. In Plank 1984, 127–50.

Boas, Franz. 1947. *Kwakiutl grammar, with a glossary of the suffixes.* Transactions of the American Philosophical Society, vol. 37, pt. 3. Philadelphia: American Philosophical Society.

Boas, Franz, and Ella Deloria. 1941. *Dakota grammar.* Memoirs of the National Academy of Sciences, vol. 23, no. 2. Washington, D.C.: U.S. Government Printing Office.

Bogoras, Waldemar. 1910. *Chukchee mythology.* Memoirs of the American Museum of Natural History. Leiden: Brill.

Bolinger, Dwight. 1967. Adjectives: Attribution and predication. *Lingua* 18:1–34.

———. 1977. Transitivity and spatiality: The passive of prepositional verbs. In *Linguistics at the crossroads,* ed. Adam Makkai, Valerie Becker Makkai, and Luigi Heilmann, 57–78. Lake Bluff, Ill.: Jupiter.

———. 1979. Pronouns in discourse. In *Discourse and syntax,* Syntax and Semantics, vol. 12, ed. Talmy Givón, 289–310. New York: Academic.

———. 1980a. *Language, the loaded weapon.* London: Longmans.

———. 1980b. Syntactic diffusion and the definite article. Bloomington: Indiana University Linguistics Club.

———. 1987. *Intonation and its parts.* Stanford, Calif.: Stanford University Press.

———. 1989. *Intonation and its uses.* Stanford, Calif.: Stanford University Press.

Borg, A. J., and Bernard Comrie. 1984. Object diffuseness in Maltese. In Plank 1984, 109–26.

Bresnan, Joan, ed. 1982a. *The mental representation of grammatical relations.* Cambridge, Mass.: MIT Press.

———. 1982b. The passive in lexical theory. In Bresnan 1982a, 3–86.

Bresnan, Joan, and Jonni Kanerva. 1989. Locative inversion in Chichewa: A case study of factorization in grammar. *Linguistic Inquiry* 20:1–50.

Bresnan, Joan, and Jane Simpson. 1982. Control and obviation in Warlpiri. In *Proceedings of the first West Coast Conference on Formal Linguistics,* ed. Daniel P. Flickinger et al., 280–91. Stanford, Calif.: Stanford Linguistics Association.

Bricker, Victoria. 1978. Antipassive constructions in Yucatec Maya. In *Papers in Mayan linguistics,* ed. Nora England, 3–24. Columbia: University of Missouri.

Brugman, Claudia Marlea. 1983. Story of *over.* M.A. thesis, University of California, Berkeley.

Buechel, Eugene. 1939. *A grammar of Lakota.* Rosebud, S.D.: St. Francis Mission.

Bybee, Joan L. 1985a. Digrammatic iconicity in stem-inflection relations. In Haiman 1985a, 11–48.

———. 1985b. *Morphology.* Amsterdam: John Benjamins.

Bybee, Joan L., and William Pagliuca. 1988. The evolution of future meaning. In *Papers from the VIIth International Conference on Historical Linguistics,* ed. Anna Giacolone Ramat, Onofrio Carruba, and Giuliano Bernini, 109–22. Amsterdam: John Benjamins.

Carlson, Greg. 1979. Generics and atemporal *when. Linguistics and Philosophy* 3:49–98.

———. 1984. Thematic roles and their role in semantic interpretation. *Linguistics* 22:259–79.

Chafe, Wallace. 1976. Givenness, contrastiveness, definiteness, subjects, topics and points of view. In Li 1976, 25–56.

———. 1979. The flow of thought and the flow of language. In *Discourse and syntax,* Syntax and Semantics, vol. 12, ed. Talmy Givón, 159–82. New York: Academic.

———. 1980. The deployment of consciousness in the production of a narrative. In *The pear stories,* ed. Wallace Chafe, 9–50. New York: Ablex.

———. 1982. Integration and involvement in speaking, writing, and oral literature. In *Spoken and written language: Exploring orality and literacy,* ed. Deborah Tannen, 35–53. Norwood, N.J.: Ablex.

———. 1984. How people use adverbial clauses. In *Proceedings of the tenth annual meeting of the Berkeley Linguistics Society,* ed. Claudia Brugman, et al., 437–49. Berkeley, Calif.: Berkeley Linguistics Society.

———. 1987. Cognitive constraints on information flow. In Tomlin 1987, 21–52.

Chao, Yuen Ren. 1968. *A grammar of spoken Chinese.* Berkeley: University of California Press.

Chierchia, Gennaro. 1984. Anaphoric properties of infinitives and gerunds. In *Proceedings of the third West Coast Conference on Formal Linguistics,* ed. M. Cobler, S. MacKaye, and M. Wescoat, 28–39. Stanford, Calif.: Stanford Linguistics Association.

Chomsky, Noam. 1970. Remarks on nominalization. In *Readings in English transformational grammar,* ed. Roderick Jacobs and Peter S. Rosenbaum, 184–221. Boston: Ginn.

———. 1981. *Lectures on government and binding.* Dordrecht: Foris.

Clark, E. V. 1978. Existentials, locatives and possessives. In *Universals of human language,* vol. 4, *Syntax,* ed. Joseph H. Greenberg, Charles A. Ferguson, and Edith A. Moravcsik, 85–126. Stanford, Calif.: Stanford University Press.

Clark, E. V., and H. H. Clark. 1979. When nouns surface as verbs. *Language* 55:767–811.

Cole, Peter. 1983. The grammatical role of the causee in universal grammar. *International Journal of American Linguistics* 49:115–33.

Cole, Peter, Wayne Harbert, Gabriella Hermon, and S. N. Sridhar. 1980. The acquisition of subjecthood. *Language* 56:719–43.

Cole, Peter, and Jerrold M. Sadock, eds. 1977. *Grammatical relations.* Syntax and Semantics, vol. 8. New York: Academic.

Coleman, Linda, and Paul Kay. 1981. Prototype semantics. *Language* 57:26–44.

Comrie, Bernard. 1976a. The syntax of action nominals: A cross-language study. *Lingua* 40:177–201.

———. 1976b. The syntax of causative constructions: Cross-linguistic similarities and differences. In Shibatani 1976, 261–312.

———. 1977. In defense of spontaneous demotion: The impersonal passive. In Cole and Sadock 1977, 47–58.

———. 1978. Ergativity. In *Syntactic typology,* ed. Winfred P. Lehmann, 329–94. Austin: University of Texas Press.

———. 1981. *Language universals and linguistic typology.* Chicago: University of Chicago Press.

———. 1985. Causative verb formation and other verb-deriving morphology. In Shopen 1985b, 309–48.

Comrie, Bernard, and Norval Smith. 1977. Lingua Descriptive Series: Questionnaire. *Lingua* 42:1–72.

Comrie, Bernard, and Sandra Thompson. 1985. Lexical nominalization. In Shopen 1985b, 349–98.

Cooreman, Ann. 1983. Topic continuity and the voicing system of an ergative language: Chamorro. In Givón 1983a, 425–90.

———. 1988. The antipassive in Chamorro: Variations on the theme of transitivity. In Shibatani 1988, 561–94.

Corbett, Greville. 1978. Numerous squishes and squishy numerals in Slavic. In *Classification of grammatical categories,* Current Inquiry into Language and Linguistics, 21, ed. Bernard Comrie, 43–73. Edmonton: Linguistic Research.

Cowan, J. Ronayne, and Russell G. Schuh. 1976. *Spoken Hausa.* Ithaca, N.Y.: Spoken Language Series.

Craig, Colette, ed. 1986. *Noun classes and categorization.* Amsterdam: John Benjamins.

Croft, William. 1983. Grammatical relations vs. thematic roles as universals.

In *Papers from the nineteenth regional meeting of the Chicago Linguistic Society,* ed. A. Chukerman, M. Marks, and J. Richardson, 76–94. Chicago: Chicago Linguistic Society.

———. 1984. Semantic and pragmatic correlates to syntactic categories. In *Papers from the parasession on lexical semantics, twentieth regional meeting of the Chicago Linguistic Society,* ed. D. Testen, V. Mishra, and J. Drogo, 53–71. Chicago: Chicago Linguistic Society.

———. 1985. Indirect object "lowering." In *Proceedings of the eleventh annual meeting of the Berkeley Linguistics Society,* ed. Mary Niepokuj et al., 39–51. Berkeley, Calif.: Berkeley Linguistics Society.

———. 1986. Categories and relations in syntax: The clause-level organization of information. Ph.D. diss., Stanford University.

———. 1988. Agreement vs. case marking in direct objects. In *Agreement in natural language: Approaches, theories, descriptions,* ed. Michael Barlow and Charles A. Ferguson, 159–80. Stanford, Calif.: Center for the Study of Language and Information.

———. 1990a. Case marking and the semantics of mental verbs. In *Semantics and the lexicon,* ed. James Pustejovsky. Dordrecht: Kluwer Academic.

———. 1990b. *Typology and universals.* Cambridge: Cambridge University Press.

———. In press a. A conceptual framework for grammatical categories. *Journal of Semantics.*

———. In press b. Possible verbs and the structure of events. In *Meanings and prototypes: Studies on linguistic categorization,* ed. S. L. Tsohatzidis. London: Routledge & Kegan Paul.

———. To appear. Voice: Beyond control and affectedness. In *Voice: Form and function,* ed. Paul Hopper and Barbara Fox. Amsterdam: John Benjamins.

———. MS. The relation between grammatical and lexical semantics.

Croft, William, Hava Bat-Zeev Shyldkrot, and Suzanne Kemmer. 1988. Diachronic semantic processes in the middle voice. In *Papers from the VIIth International Conference on Historical Linguistics,* ed. Anna Giacolone Ramat, Onofrio Carruba, and Giuliano Bernini, 179–92. Amsterdam: John Benjamins.

Dahl, Östen. 1979. Case grammar and prototypes. *Prague Bulletin of Mathematical Linguistics* 31:3–24.

Dahlstrom, Amy. 1983. Agent-patient languages and split case marking systems. In *Proceedings of the ninth annual meeting of the Berkeley Linguistics Society,* ed. Amy Dahlstrom et al., 37–46. Berkeley, Calif.: Berkeley Linguistics Society.

Davidson, Donald. 1980a. The individuation of events. In *Essays on actions and events,* 163–80. Oxford-Clarendon (Reprinted from *Essays in honor of Carl G. Hempel,* ed. Nicholas Rescher, 216–34. Dordrecht: Reidel, 1969.)

———. 1980b. The logical form of action sentences: Criticism, comment and defence. In *Essays on actions and events*, 105–48. Oxford: Clarendon (Reprinted from *The logic of decision and action*, ed. Nicholas Rescher. Pittsburgh: University of Pittsburgh Press, 1967.)

Davis, Irvine. 1964. *The language of Santa Ana Pueblo* Bulletin 191, Anthropological Paper 69, Bureau of American Ethnology. Washington, D.C.: U.S. Government Printing Office.

DeLancey, Scott. 1981. An interpretation of split ergativity and related patterns. *Language* 57:626–57.

———. 1982. Aspect, transitivity, and viewpoint. In *Tense-aspect: Between semantics and pragmatics*, ed. Paul Hopper, 167–84. Amsterdam: Benjamins.

———. 1984a. Notes on agentivity and causation. *Studies in Language* 8:181–214.

———. 1984b. Transitivity and ergative case in Lhasa Tibetan. In *Proceedings of the tenth annual meeting of the Berkeley Linguistics Society*, ed. Claudia Brugman and Monica Macaulay, 131–40. Berkeley, Calif.: Berkeley Linguistics Society.

———. 1985. Agentivity and syntax. In *Papers from the parasession on causatives and agentivity, twenty-first regional meeting, Chicago Linguistic Society*, ed. William H. Eilfort, Paul D. Kroeber, and Karen L. Peterson, 1–12. Chicago: Chicago Linguistic Society.

———. 1987. Transitivity in grammar and cognition. In Tomlin 1987, 53–68.

Dik, Simon. 1981. *Functional grammar.* 3d rev. ed. Publications in Language Sciences, 7. Dordrecht: Foris.

Dimmendaal, Gerrit Jan. 1983. *The Turkana language.* Dordrecht: Foris.

Dixon, R. M. W. 1972. *The Dyirbal language of North Queensland.* Cambridge: Cambridge University Press.

———. 1977. Where have all the adjectives gone? *Studies in Language* 1:19–80.

———. 1979. Ergativity. *Language* 55:59–138.

———. 1980. *The languages of Australia.* Cambridge: Cambridge University Press.

Dowty, David. 1979. *Word meaning and Montague grammar.* Dordrecht: Reidel.

Dryer, Matthew. 1986. Primary object, secondary object, and antidative. *Language* 62:808–45.

DuBois, John A. 1987. The discourse basis of ergativity. *Language* 63:805–55.

Durie, Mark. 1985. *A grammar of Acehnese on the basis of a dialect of North Aceh.* Dordrecht: Foris.

———. 1988. The so-called passive of Acehnese. *Language* 64:104–11.

Faltz, Leonard M. 1985. *Reflexivization: A study in universal syntax.* New York: Garland.

Fauconnier, Gilles. 1985. *Mental spaces.* Cambridge, Mass.: MIT Press.

Fillmore, Charles J. 1968. The case for case. In *Universals in linguistic theory*, ed.

Emmon Bach and Robert T. Harms, 1–90. New York: Holt, Rinehart & Winston.

———. 1975. An alternative to checklist theories of meaning. In *Proceedings of the first annual meeting of the Berkeley Linguistics Society,* ed. Cathy Cogen et al., 123–31. Berkeley, Calif.: Berkeley Linguistics Society.

———. 1977. The case for case reopened. In Cole and Sadock 1977, 59–82.

———. 1986. Pragmatically-controlled zero anaphora. In *Proceedings of the twelfth annual meeting of the Berkeley Linguistics Society,* ed. Vassiliki Nikiforidou et al., 95–107. Berkeley, Calif.: Berkeley Linguistics Society.

Fillmore, Charles J., Paul Kay, and Mary Kay O'Connor. 1988. Regularity and idiomaticity in grammatical constructions: The case of *let alone. Language* 64:501–38.

Firbas, Jan. 1966. On defining the theme in functional sentence analysis. *Travaux Linguistique de Prague* 1:267–80.

Foley, William A. 1986. *The Papuan languages of New Guinea.* Cambridge: Cambridge University Press.

Foley, William A., and Mike Olson. 1985. Clausehood and verb serialization. In *Grammar inside and outside the clause,* ed. Johanna Nichols and Anthony Woodbury, 17–60. Cambridge: Cambridge University Press.

Foley, William A., and Robert D. Van Valin, Jr. 1984. *Functional syntax and universal grammar.* Cambridge: Cambridge University Press.

Gawron, Jean Mark. 1983. Lexical representation and the semantics of complementation. Ph.D. diss., University of California, Berkeley.

Gazdar, Gerald, Ewan Klein, Geoffrey Pullum, and Ivan Sag. 1985. *Generalized phrase structure grammar.* Oxford: Blackwell.

Gazdar, Gerald, Geoffrey Pullum, and Ivan Sag. 1982. Auxiliaries and related phenomena in a restrictive theory of grammar. *Language* 58:591–638.

Givón, Talmy. 1976. Topic, pronoun and grammatical agreement. In Li 1976, 149–88.

———. 1979. *On understanding grammar.* New York: Academic.

———. 1980. The binding hierarchy and the typology of complements. *Studies in Language* 4:333–77.

———. 1981. Logic vs. pragmatics, with natural language as the referee. *Journal of Pragmatics* 6:81–133.

———, ed. 1983a. *Topic continuity in discourse: A quantitative cross-language study.* Amsterdam: John Benjamins.

———. 1983b. Topic continuity in discourse: The functional domain of switch-reference. In Haiman and Munro 1983, 51–82.

———. 1984a. Direct object and dative-shifting: Semantic and pragmatic case. In Plank 1984, 151–82.

———. 1984b. *Syntax: A functional-typological introduction.* Amsterdam: John Benjamins.

———. 1985. *Ute traditional narratives.* Ignacio, Colo.: Ute.

Gordon, Lynn. 1986. *Maricopa morphology and syntax.* University of California Publications in Linguistics, 108. Berkeley and Los Angeles: University of California Press.

Green, M. M., and G. E. Igwe. 1963. *A descriptive grammar of Igbo.* London: Oxford University Press.

Greenberg, Joseph H. 1966a. *Language universals.* Janua Linguarum Series Minor, 59. The Hague: Mouton.

———. 1966b. Some universals of grammar with particular reference to the order of meaningful elements. In *Universals of language,* 2d ed., ed. Joseph H. Greenberg, 73–113. Cambridge, Mass.: MIT Press.

———. 1969. Some methods of dynamic comparison in linguistics. In *Substance and structure of language,* ed. Jan Puhvel, 147–203. Berkeley: University of California Press.

———. 1978. Generalizations about numeral systems. In *Universals of human language,* vol. 3, *Word structure,* ed. Joseph H. Greenberg, Charles A. Ferguson, and Edith A. Moravcsik, 249–96. Stanford: Stanford University Press.

Gross, Maurice. 1979. On the failure of generative grammar. *Language* 55: 859–85.

Gruber, Jeffrey S. 1976. *Lexical structures in syntax and semantics.* North-Holland Linguistic Series, 25. Amsterdam: North-Holland.

Gruzberg, A. A. 1974. *Častotnyj slovar' russkogo jazyka vtoroj polovina XVI–načala XVII veka.* Perm': Permskij Gosudarstvennyj Pedagogičeskij Institut.

Haiman, John. 1974. Concessives, conditionals and verbs of volition. *Foundations of Language* 11:341–59.

———. 1978. A study in polysemy. *Studies in Language* 2:1–34.

———. 1980. The iconicity of grammar: Isomorphism and motivation. *Language* 56:515–40.

———. 1983. Iconic and economic motivation. *Language* 59:781–819.

———, ed. 1985a. *Iconicity in syntax.* Amsterdam: John Benjamins.

———. 1985b. *Natural syntax.* Cambridge: Cambridge University Press.

Haiman, John, and Pamela Munro, eds. 1983. *Switch-reference and universal grammar.* Amsterdam: John Benjamins.

Hale, Kenneth. 1973. Person marking in Walbiri. In *A festschrift for Morris Halle,* ed. Stephen R. Anderson and Paul Kiparsky, 308–44. New York: Holt, Rinehart & Winston.

Halliday, M. A. K. 1967. Notes on transitivity and theme, part 2. *Journal of Linguistics* 3:199–244.

———. 1976. *System and function in language.* Edited by G. R. Kress. London: Oxford University Press.

Hancher, Michael. 1979. The classification of co-operative illocutionary acts. *Language in Society* 8:1–14.

Harrison, Sheldon P. 1976. *Mokilese reference grammar.* Honolulu: University Press of Hawaii.

Hawkinson, Annie, and Larry Hyman. 1974. Natural hierarchies of topic in Shona. *Studies in African Linguistics* 5:147–70.

Heath, Jeffrey. 1975. Some functional relationships in grammar. *Language* 51:89–104.

———. 1976. Antipassivization: A functional typology. In *Proceedings of the second annual meeting of the Berkeley Linguistics Society,* ed. Henry Thompson et al., 202–11. Berkeley, Calif.: Berkeley Linguistics Society.

———. 1979. Is Dyirbal ergative? *Linguistics* 17:401–63.

Heim, Irene. 1982. The semantics of definite and indefinite noun phrases. Ph.D. diss., University of Massachusetts, Amherst.

Heine, Bernd, and Mechthild Reh. 1984. *Grammaticalization and reanalysis in African languages.* Hamburg: Helmut Buske.

Herskovits, Annette. 1982. Space and the prepositions in English: Regularities and irregularities in a complex domain. Ph.D. diss., Stanford University, Department of Linguistics.

Hill, Jane. 1969. Volitional and non-volitional verbs in Cupeño. In *Papers from the fifth annual meeting, Chicago Linguistic Society,* ed. Robert Binnick et al., 357–65. Chicago: Chicago Linguistic Society.

Hobbs, Jerry. 1985. Granularity. In *Proceedings of the ninth International Joint Conference on Artificial Intelligence,* 432–35. San Mateo, Calif.: Morgan Kaufman.

Hockett, Charles. 1958. *A course in modern linguistics.* New York: Macmillan.

Hook, Peter Edwin. 1983. The English abstrument and rocking case relations. In *Papers from the nineteenth regional meeting of the Chicago Linguistic Society,* ed. A. Chukerman, M. Marks, and J. Richardson, 183–94. Chicago: Chicago Linguistic Society.

Hopper, Paul. 1986. Some discourse functions of classifiers in Malay. In Craig 1986, 309–26.

Hopper, Paul, and Sandra A. Thompson. 1980. Transitivity and grammar and discourse. *Language* 56:251–99.

———, eds. 1982. *Studies in transitivity.* Syntax and Semantics, vol. 15. New York: Academic.

———. 1984. The discourse basis for lexical categories in universal grammar. *Language* 60:703–52.

Hudson, Richard. 1976. *Arguments for a non-transformational grammar.* Chicago: University of Chicago Press.

Hutchison, John P. 1981. *The Kanuri language.* Madison: University of Wisconsin African Studies Program.

Jackendoff, Ray. 1983. *Semantics and cognition.* Cambridge, Mass.: MIT Press.

Jacobsen, Wesley. 1982. Transitivity in the Japanese verbal system. Ph.D. diss., University of Chicago.

Jacobsen, William H., Jr. 1979. Noun and verb in Nootkan. In *The Victoria Conference on Northwestern Languages,* 83–155. British Columbia Provincial Museum Heritage Record, no. 4. Victoria: British Columbia Provincial Museum.

Jespersen, Otto. 1927. *A modern English grammar on historical principles,* vol. 3. London: Allen & Unwin.

———. 1940. *A modern English grammar on historical principles,* vol. 5. London: Allen & Unwin.

Karttunen, Lauri. 1976. Discourse referents. In *Notes from the linguistic underground.* Syntax and Semantics, vol. 7, ed. James D. McCawley, 363–85. New York: Academic.

Keenan, Edward L. 1976. Towards a universal definition of "subject." In Li 1976, 303–34.

———. 1985. Passive in the world's languages. In Shopen 1985a, 243–81.

Keenan, Edward L., and Bernard Comrie. 1977. Noun phrase accessibility and universal grammar. *Linguistic Inquiry* 8 : 63–99.

Kemmer, Suzanne. 1988. The middle voice: A typological and diachronic study. Ph.D. diss., Stanford University.

Kimenyi, Alexandre. 1980. *A relational grammar of Kinyarwanda.* University of California Publications in Linguistics, vol. 91. Berkeley and Los Angeles: University of California Press.

Kinkade, M. Dale. 1983. Salish evidence against the universality of "noun" and "verb." *Lingua* 60 : 25–40.

Klaiman, Miriam. 1981. Toward a universal semantics of indirect subject constructions. In *Proceedings of the seventh annual meeting of the Berkeley Linguistics Society,* ed. Danny K. Alford et al., 123–35. Berkeley, Calif.: Berkeley Linguistics Society.

———. 1982a. Affectiveness and the voice system of Japanese: Satisfaction guaranteed or your money back. In *Proceedings of the eighth annual meeting of the Berkeley Linguistics Society,* ed. Monica Macaulay et al., 398–413. Berkeley, Calif.: Berkeley Linguistics Society.

———. 1982b. Defining "voice": Evidence from Tamil. In *Papers from the eighteenth regional meeting, Chicago Linguistic Society,* ed. Kevin Tuite, Robinson Schneider, and Robert Chametzky, 267–81. Chicago: Chicago Linguistic Society.

———. 1988. Affectedness and control: A typology of voice systems. In Shibatani 1988, 25–84.

Kraft, C. H., and A. H. M. Kirk-Greene. 1973. *Teach yourself Hausa.* Hertford: English Universities Press.

Kuipers, Aert. 1968. The categories verb-noun and transitive-intransitive in English and Squamish. *Lingua* 21:610–26.

Kuno, Susumu. 1972. Functional sentence perspective. *Linguistic Inquiry* 3:269–320.

———. 1973. *The structure of the Japanese language.* Cambridge, Mass.: MIT Press.

———. 1987. *Functional syntax.* Chicago: University of Chicago Press.

Kuno, Susumu, and Etsuko Kaburaki. 1977. Empathy and syntax. *Linguistic Inquiry* 8:627–72.

Kuno, Susumu, and Preya Wogkhomthong. 1981. Characterizational and identificational sentences in Thai. *Studies in Language* 5:65–109.

Ladusaw, William. 1985. The category structure of Kusaal. In *Proceedings of the eleventh annual meeting of the Berkeley Linguistics Society,* ed. Mary Niepokuj et al., 196–206. Berkeley, Calif.: Berkeley Linguistics Society.

Lakoff, George. 1977. Linguistic Gestalts. In *Papers from the thirteenth regional meeting, Chicago Linguistic Society,* ed. Woodford A. Beach et al., 236–87. Chicago: Chicago Linguistic Society.

———. 1987. *Women, fire and dangerous things: What categories reveal about the mind.* Chicago: University of Chicago Press.

Lakoff, George, and Mark Johnson. 1980. *Metaphors we live by.* Chicago: University of Chicago Press.

Lambrecht, Knud. 1987. On the status of SVO sentences in French discourse. In Tomlin 1987, 217–62.

Langacker, Ronald W. 1974. Movement rules in functional perspective. *Language* 50:630–64.

———. 1987a. *Foundations of cognitive grammar.* Stanford, Calif.: Stanford University Press.

———. 1987b. Nouns and verbs. *Language* 63:53–94.

———. 1988a. The nature of grammatical valence. In Rudzka-Ostyn 1988, 91–125.

———. 1988b. A usage-based model. In Rudzka-Ostyn 1988, 127–61.

———. MS. Foundations of cognitive grammar, vol. 2, Descriptive application, pt. 1, Nominal structure.

Lawler, John. 1977. A agrees with B in Achenese. In Cole and Sadock 1977, 219–48.

———. MS. Time is money: The anatomy of a metaphor. University of Michigan.

Lees, Robert B. 1960. The grammar of English nominalizations. *International Journal of American Linguistics,* suppl. 26.

Lehmann, Christian. 1982. *Thoughts on grammaticalization: A programmatic sketch,* vol. 1 (akup 48). Köln: Institut für Sprachwissenschaft.

———. 1985. Grammaticalization: Synchronic variation and diachronic change. *Lingua e Stile* 20:303–18.

Leslau, Wolf. 1968. *Soddo.* Ethiopians Speak: Studies in Cultural Background, 3. Berkeley: University of California Press.

Levin, Beth C. 1979. Instrumental *with* and the control relation in English. A.I. Memo no. 522. Cambridge, Mass.: MIT Artificial Intelligence Laboratory.

Lewis, G. L. 1967. *Turkish grammar.* Oxford: Oxford University Press.

Li, Charles, ed. 1976. *Subject and topic.* New York: Academic.

Li, Charles, and Sandra Thompson. 1976. Subject and topic: A new typology of language. In Li 1976, 457–90.

———. 1981. *Mandarin Chinese: A functional reference grammar.* Berkeley and Los Angeles: University of California Press.

Lichtenberk, Frantisek. 1985. Multiple uses of reciprocal constructions. *Australian Journal of Linguistics* 5:19–41.

Lindner, Susan. 1981. A lexico-semantic analysis of the English verb particle constructions with *out* and *up.* Ph.D. diss., University of California, San Diego.

Lombard, Sylvia. 1968. *Yao-English dictionary.* Southeast Asia Program Data Paper 69. Ithaca, N.Y.: Cornell University, Department of Asian Studies.

McCawley, James D. 1979. On identifying the remains of deceased clauses. In *Adverbs, vowels, and other objects of wonder,* 84–95. Chicago: University of Chicago Press.

McLendon, Sally. 1978. Ergativity, case, and transitivity in Eastern Pomo. *International Journal of American Linguistics* 44:1–9.

Mathesius, Vilém. 1975. *A functional analysis of present day English on a general linguistic basis.* Janua Linguarum, Series Practica, 208. The Hague: Mouton.

Matisoff, James A. 1969. Verb concatenation in Lahu: The syntax and semantics of "simple" juxtaposition. *Acta Linguistica Hafniensa* 12:69–120.

———. 1973. *A grammar of Lahu.* University of California Publications in Linguistics, vol. 75. Berkeley: University of California Press.

Mel'čuk, Igor. 1979. *Studies in dependency syntax.* Ann Arbor, Mich.: Karoma.

Merlan, Francesca. 1976. Noun incorporation and discourse reference in modern Nahuatl. *International Journal of American Linguistics* 42:177–91.

———. 1985. Split intransitivity: Functional oppositions in intransitive inflection. In *Grammar inside and outside the clause,* ed. Johanna Nichols and Anthony Woodbury, 324–62. Cambridge: Cambridge University Press.

Mithun, Marianne. 1984a. The evolution of noun incorporation. *Language* 60:847–94.

———. 1984b. How to avoid subordination. In *Proceedings of the tenth annual meeting of the Berkeley Linguistics Society,* ed. Claudia Brugman et al., 493–523. Berkeley, Calif.: Berkeley Linguistics Society.

———. 1987. Is basic word order universal? In Tomlin 1987, 281–328.

Mondloch, James L. 1978. *Basic Quiché grammar.* Institute for Mesoamerican Studies, Publication 2. Albany, N.Y.: Institute for Mesoamerican Studies.

Moravcsik, Edith. 1978. On the distribution of ergative and accusative patterns. *Lingua* 45:233–79.

Myhill, John. 1988. Categoriality and clustering. *Studies in Language* 12:261–98.

Nandris, Grigore. 1945. *Colloquial Rumanian.* London: Routledge & Kegan Paul.

Newman, Stanley. 1944. *Yokuts language of California.* Viking Fund Publications in Anthropology, 2. New York: Viking Fund.

Nichols, Johanna. 1984. Direct and indirect objects in Chechen-Ingush and Russian. In Plank 1984, 183–210.

Nilsen, Don L. F. 1972. *Toward a semantic specification of deep case.* Janua Linguarum, Series Minor, 152. The Hague: Mouton.

———. 1973. *The instrumental case in English.* Janua Linguarum, Series Minor, 156. The Hague: Mouton.

Norman, Jerry. 1988. *Chinese.* Cambridge: Cambridge University Press.

Norman, William. 1978. Advancement rules and syntactic change: The loss of instrumental voice in Mayan. In *Proceedings of the fourth annual meeting of the Berkeley Linguistics Society,* ed. Jeri Jaeger et al., 458–76. Berkeley, Calif.: Berkeley Linguistics Society.

Pawley, Andrew. 1987. Encoding events in Kalam and English: Different logics for reporting experience. In Tomlin 1987, 329–360.

Perlmutter, David. 1982. Syntactic representations, syntactic levels and the notion of subject. In *The nature of syntactic representation,* ed. Pauline Jacobsen and Geoffrey K. Pullum, 283–340. Dordrecht: Reidel.

———, ed. 1983. *Studies in relational grammar.* Chicago: University of Chicago Press.

Plank, Frans, ed. 1981. *Ergativity.* New York: Academic.

———, ed. 1984. *Objects.* New York: Academic.

Pollard, Carl, and Ivan Sag. 1987. *Information-based syntax and semantics,* vol. 1. Stanford, Calif.: Center for the Study of Language and Information.

Prince, Ellen F. 1978. A comparison of WH-clefts and *it*-clefts in discourse. *Language* 54:883–906.

———. 1979. On the given/new distinction. In *Papers from the fifteenth regional meeting, Chicago Linguistic Society,* ed. Paul R. Clyne, William F. Hanks, and Carol L. Hofbauer, 267–78. Chicago: Chicago Linguistic Society.

———. 1981a. Topicalization, focus-movement and Yiddish-movement: A pragmatic differentiation. In *Proceedings of the seventh annual meeting of the Berkeley Linguistics Society,* ed. Danny K. Alford et al., 249–64. Berkeley, Calif.: Berkeley Linguistics Society.

———. 1981b. Toward a taxonomy of given-new information. In *Radical pragmatics,* ed. Peter Cole, 223–56. New York: Academic.

Pullum, Geoffrey, and Deirdre Wilson. 1977. Autonomous syntax and the analysis of auxiliaries. *Language* 53 : 741–88.

Ransom, Evelyn. 1986. *Complementation.* Amsterdam: John Benjamins.

Renck, G. L. 1975. *A grammar of Yagaria.* Pacific Linguistics, series B, no. 40. Canberra: Australian National University, Research School of Pacific Studies.

Rice, Sally. 1987. Towards a cognitive model of transitivity. Ph.D. diss., University of California, San Diego.

Rosch, Eleanor. 1978. Principles of categorization. In *Cognition and categorization,* ed. Eleanor Rosch and Barbara Lloyd, 27–48. Hillsdale, N.J.: Erlbaum.

Ross, John R. 1967. Constraints on variables in syntax. Ph.D. diss., Massachusetts Institute of Technology.

Rowlands, E. C. 1969. *Yoruba.* London: Hodder & Stoughton.

Rude, Noel. 1988. Ergative, passive and antipassive in Nez Perce: A discourse perspective. In Shibatani 1988, 547–60.

Rudzka-Ostyn, Brygida, ed. 1988. *Topics in cognitive linguistics.* Amsterdam: John Benjamins.

Sadock, Jerrold M. 1980. Noun incorporation in West Greenlandic. *Language* 56 : 300–319.

———. 1985. Autolexical syntax: A proposal for the treatment of noun incorporation and similar phenomena. *Natural Language and Linguistic Theory* 3 : 379–439.

Salkoff, Morris. 1983. Bees are swarming in the garden. *Language* 59 : 288–346.

Šamskij. N. M. 1963–82. *Etimologičeskij slovar' russkogo jazyka.* Moscow: Izdatel'stvo Moskovskogo Universiteta.

Sapir, Edward. 1921. *Language.* New York: Harcourt, Brace.

Schachter, Paul. 1973. Focus and relativization. *Language* 49 : 19–46.

———. 1976. The subject in Philippine languages: Topic, actor, actor-topic or none of the above. In Li 1976, 491–518.

———. 1977. Reference-related and role-related properties of subjects. In Cole and Sadock 1977, 279–306.

———. 1985. Parts-of-speech systems. In Shopen 1985a, 3–61.

Schank, Roger C. 1972. Conceptual dependency: A theory of natural language understanding. *Cognitive Psychology* 3:552–631.

Schmalstieg, W. R. 1976. *An introduction to Old Church Slavonic.* Columbus, Ohio: Slavica.

Schmerling, Susan. 1983. Two theories of syntactic categories. *Linguistics and Philosophy* 6:393–421.

Schütz, Albert J. 1969. *Nguna texts.* Oceanic Linguistics Special Publication no. 4. Honolulu: University of Hawaii Press.

Schwartz, Linda. 1980. Syntactic markedness and frequency of occurrence. In *Evidence and argumentation in linguistics,* ed. Thomas Perry, 315–33. Berlin: Walter de Gruyter.

Searle, John. 1969. *Speech acts: An essay in the philosophy of language.* Cambridge: Cambridge University Press.

———. 1976. The classification of illocutionary acts. *Language in Society* 5:1–24.

Sells, Peter. 1986. *Lectures on contemporary syntactic theories.* Stanford, Calif.: Center for the Study of Language and Information.

Sells, Peter, Annie Zaenen, and Draga Zec. 1987. Reflexivization variation: Relations between syntax, semantics and lexical structure. In *Working papers in grammatical theory and discourse structure,* ed. Masayo Iida et al., 169–238. Stanford, Calif.: Center for the Study of Language and Information.

Shibatani, Masayoshi, ed. 1976. *The grammar of causative constructions.* Syntax and Semantics, vol. 6. New York: Academic.

———, ed. 1988. *Passive and voice.* Amsterdam: John Benjamins.

Shopen, Timothy, ed. 1985a. *Language typology and syntactic description,* vol. 1, *Clause structure.* Cambridge: Cambridge University Press.

———, ed. 1985b. *Language typology and syntactic description,* vol. 3, *Grammatical categories and the lexicon.* Cambridge: Cambridge University Press.

Siewierska, Anna. 1984. *The passive: A comparative linguistic analysis.* London: Croom Helm.

Silverstein, Michael. 1976. Hierarchies of features and ergativity. In *Grammatical categories of Australian languages,* ed. R. M. W. Dixon. Canberra: Australian Institute of Aboriginal Studies.

Sohn, Ho-min. 1975. *Woleaian reference grammar.* Honolulu: University Press of Hawaii.

Sohn, Ho-min, and Anthony Tawerilmang. 1976. *Woleaian-English dictionary.* Honolulu: University Press of Hawaii.

Steele, Susan. 1978. The category AUX as a language universal. In *Universals of human language,* vol. 3, *Word structure,* ed. Joseph H. Greenberg,

Charles A. Ferguson, and Edith A. Moravcsik, 7–46. Stanford, Calif.: Stanford University Press.

Steele, Susan, with Adrian Akmajian, Richard Demers, Eloise Jelinek, Chisato Kitagawa, Richard Oehrle, and Thomas Wasow. 1981. *An encyclopedia of AUX.* Linguistic Inquiry, Monograph 5. Cambridge, Mass.: MIT Press.

Štejnfeldt, E. n.d. *Russian word count.* Translated by V. Korotky. Moscow: Progress.

Talmy, Leonard. 1972. Semantic structures in English and Atsugewi. Ph.D. diss., University of California, Berkeley.

———. 1976. Semantic causative types. In Shibatani 1976, 43–116.

———. 1977. Rubber sheet cognition in language. In *Papers from the thirteenth regional meeting, Chicago Linguistic Society,* ed. Woodford A. Beach et al., 612–28. Chicago: Chicago Linguistic Society.

———. 1983. How language structures space. In *Spatial orientation: Theory, research and application,* ed. Herbert L. Pick, Jr., and Linda P. Acredolo, 225–82. New York: Plenum.

———. 1985. Lexicalization patterns: Semantic structure in lexical forms. In Shopen 1985b, 57–149.

———. 1988. The relation of grammar to cognition. In Rudzka-Ostyn 1988, 165–205.

Tesnière, Lucien. 1959. *Éléments de syntaxe structurale.* Paris: Klincksieck.

Thompson, Sandra. 1988. A discourse approach to the cross-linguistic category "adjective." In *Explaining language universals,* ed. John A. Hawkins, 167–210. Oxford: Blackwell.

Tiersma, Peter Meijes. 1982. Local and general markedness. *Language* 58: 832–49.

Tomlin, Russell S. 1986. *Basic word order: Functional principles.* London: Croom Helm.

———, ed. 1987. *Coherence and grounding in discourse.* Amsterdam: John Benjamins.

Trithart, Lee. 1979. Topicality: An alternative to the relational view of Bantu passive. *Studies in African Linguistics* 10:1–30.

van Eijk, Jan P., and Thom Hess. 1986. Noun and verb in Salish. *Lingua* 69:319–31.

van Oosten, Jeanne. 1977. Subjects and agenthood in English. In *Papers from the thirteenth regional meeting, Chicago Linguistic Society,* ed. Woodford A. Beach, Samuel E. Fox, and Shulamith Philosoph, 459–71. Chicago: Chicago Linguistic Society.

———. 1986. The nature of subjects, topics and agents: A cognitive explanation. Ph.D. diss., University of California, Berkeley.

Vendler, Zeno. 1967. Verbs and times. In *Linguistics in philosophy,* 97–121. Ithaca, N.Y.: Cornell University Press.

Vogt, Hans. 1971. *Grammaire de la langue géorgienne.* Oslo: Instituttet for Sammenlignende Kulturforskning.

Wasow, Thomas. 1977. Transformations and the lexicon. In *Formal Syntax,* ed. Peter W. Culicover et al., 327–60. New York: Academic.

Wierzbicka, Anna. 1980. *The case for surface case.* Ann Arbor, Mich.: Karoma.

———. 1985. "Oats" and "wheat": the fallacy of arbitrariness. In Haiman 1985a, 311–42.

———. 1986. What's in a noun? (or: how do nouns differ in meaning from adjectives?). *Studies in Language* 10:353–89.

Witkowski, Stanley R., and Cecil H. Brown. 1983. Marking reversals and cultural importance. *Language* 59:569–82.

Wolkonsky, Catherine, and Marianna Poltoratzky. 1961. *Handbook of Russian roots.* New York: Columbia University Press.

Wunderlich, Dieter. 1983. On argument shifting rules in German. Stanford University Linguistics Department Colloquium, November.

Zepeda, Ofelia. 1983. *A Papago grammar.* Tucson: University of Arizona Press.

Zipf, George K. 1935. *The psychobiology of language.* Cambridge, Mass.: MIT Press.

AUTHOR INDEX

LANGUAGE INDEX

SUBJECT INDEX